DEREK LUNDY

Men that God Made Mad

A Journey through Truth, Myth
and Terror in Northern Ireland

VINTAGE BOOKS
London

Published by Vintage 2007

2 4 6 8 10 9 7 5 3 1

Copyright © Beara Inc. 2006

First published in Great Britain in 2006 by
Jonathan Cape
Random House, 20 Vauxhall Bridge Road,
London SW1V 2SA

www.randomhouse.co.uk

Addresses for companies within The Random House Group Limited
can be found at: www.randomhouse.co.uk/offices.htm

The Random House Group Limited Reg. No. 954009

A CIP catalogue record for this book
is available from the British Library

ISBN 9780099469476

Printed and bound in Great Britain by
Cox & Wyman Limited, Reading, Berkshire

For my uncle, William Lundy

Ireland is a little country which raises all the great questions.

GUSTAVE DE BEAUMONT

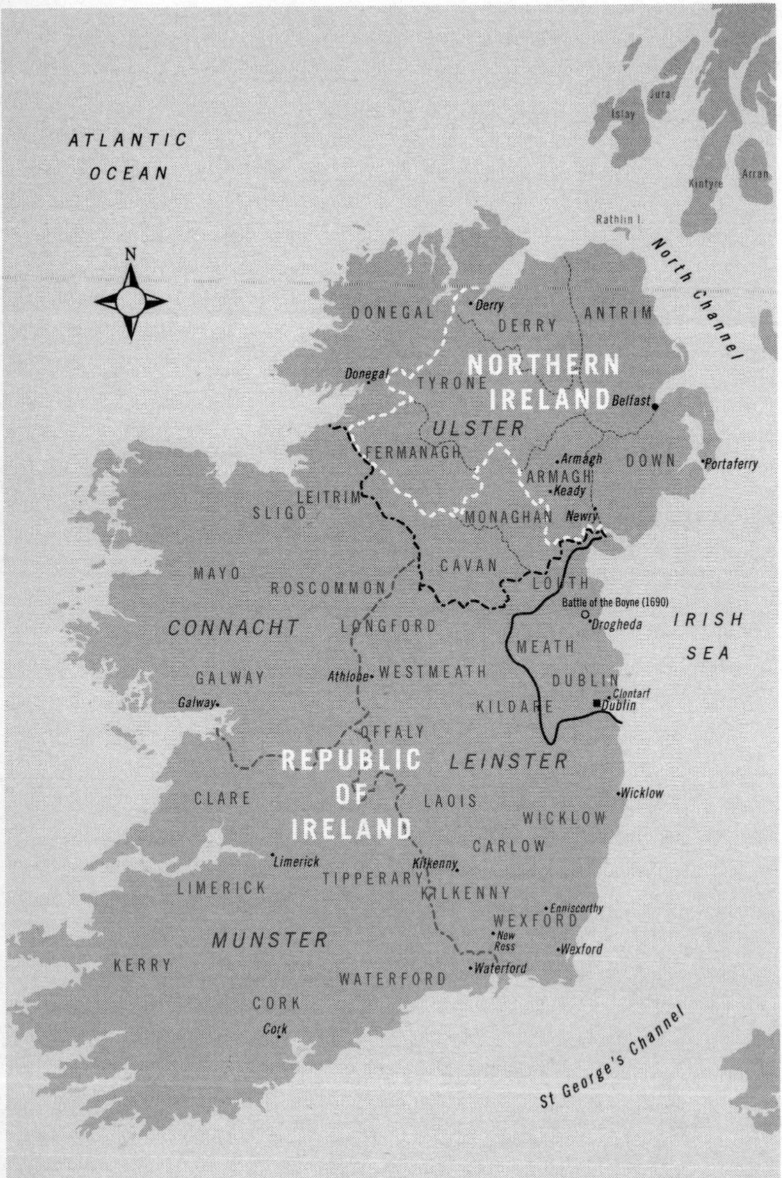
ATLANTIC
OCEAN
N
Jura
Islay
Kintyre
Arran
Rathlin I.
North Channel
DONEGAL
Derry
DERRY
ANTRIM
NORTHERN
IRELAND
Donegal
TYRONE
Belfast
ULSTER
FERMANAGH
Armagh
DOWN
Portaferry
ARMAGH
Keady
LEITRIM
SLIGO
MONAGHAN
Newry
CAVAN
MAYO
ROSCOMMON
LOUTH
Battle of the Boyne (1690)
Drogheda
IRISH
SEA
CONNACHT
LONGFORD
MEATH
GALWAY
Athlone
WESTMEATH
DUBLIN
Galway
Clontarf
Dublin
KILDARE
OFFALY
REPUBLIC
OF
IRELAND
LEINSTER
Wicklow
CLARE
LAOIS
WICKLOW
CARLOW
Limerick
Kilkenny
TIPPERARY
LIMERICK
KILKENNY
Enniscorthy
WEXFORD
MUNSTER
New Ross
Wexford
KERRY
Waterford
WATERFORD
CORK
Cork
St George's Channel

- - - - - Border of Northern Ireland	- - - - - County Borders
- · - · - Provincial Borders	———— The Pale in 1488
- ·· - ·· - Ulster Border	

ATLANTIC

OCEAN

N

Jura

Islay

Arran

Rathlin I.

L. Swilly

Inishowen

L. Foyle

Coleraine

North Channel

Kintyre

• Derry

ANTRIM

DONEGAL

DERRY

NORTHERN
IRELAND

• Larne

• Strabane
Clady

TYRONE

ULSTER

• Carrickfergus

• Bangor

Donegal •

Omagh

Lough
Neagh

Belfast •
Lisburn

Holywood

Donaghadee

• Dromore

Battle of the
Diamond
(1795)

Comber

Ballyhalbert •

• Enniskillen

• Armagh

Strangford
Lough

FERMANAGH

ARMAGH

DOWN

Ballynahinch •

• Portaferry

MONAGHAN

• Keady

Newry •

Battle of
Dolly's Brae (1849)

CAVAN

IRISH

REPUBLIC

SEA

OF

IRELAND

CONTENTS

Men

that

God

Made

Mad

PROLOGUE

THE STORY HAS TWO VERSIONS. In the first, a Viking war party in a lean, dragon-headed longboat closes with the coast of northern Ireland. It is hunting priests' gold and red-haired, smooth-skinned slaves. The leader of the fierce Northmen urges on his warriors: the first man to touch the sweet Gaelic strand with his hand or foot takes possession of it. He gets to keep whatever is there—precious metal, cattle, women, boys. There is a man aboard the longboat called O'Neill. It is an Irish name and, perhaps, in the style of slithery allegiances in Ireland, he is a turncoat. He has abandoned his family and sept and gone over to the Norse raiders, wilder even than the wild Irish. This man desires plunder and the haven of his own piece of land. It seems he craves those things more than reason, certainly more than any Viking aboard. As the longboat approaches the shore, the crew strains for the jump and its prize. Then O'Neill, the man from Ireland, lays his arm along the bulwark. He severs his hand with one swift sword blow and throws it ashore onto the sand before anyone else can make the leap. His Viking chief keeps his word. He gives that part of Ulster to his mutilated mercenary, and O'Neill takes the bloody hand as his crest and symbol.

In the second version of the story, two rival Scottish clans race each other to Ireland across the twelve miles of the wind-whipped North Channel. They have agreed that whichever reaches the Ulster shore first will take the land. The leader of the MacDonnells lusts for it just as O'Neill did—like the intense desire some men

have to keep living when death comes to claim them. He'll do anything for it. But his boat lags behind and he sees beautiful, wild
Ulster, rich in cattle and slaves, sliding away from him. He severs his
hand with one swift sword blow and throws it ashore onto the sand.
He claims the land for himself and takes the red hand as the crest of
the MacDonnells of Antrim.

Ireland has a long and complicated history of conquest, rebellion,
endemic violence, and political tumult. The Irish struggle against
English invasion and occupation now has the aspect of an old story—
of history. The people of the independent, and now prosperous,
Republic of Ireland see it more and more in that way, too. But the severed red hand still seems to be a perfect symbol for the province of the
United Kingdom known officially as Northern Ireland. Its six counties, with their Protestant majority, were partitioned from the rest of
Ireland in 1920 in the course of the Irish war of independence against
Britain. In the North, the malignant motifs of the Irish past hung on:
sectarian hatred, oath-bound private armies, guerrilla war, atrocity
and outrage, riots, bombings, British soldiers on Irish ground, political dysfunction, walls and barbed wire, segregation of Protestants and
Catholics, war drums and triumphalist parades, forced population
movements, propaganda—the whole apparatus of civil war.

   Low-level conflict went on inside Northern Ireland and along its
border from the time of its inception, but chaotic and terrible open
war began in 1969. It went on for thirty years and is known, with
quaint understatement, as "the Troubles."* Now they're probably
over—although perhaps not. To the outsider, their longevity and
intensity are almost incomprehensible. It's as if O'Neill or
MacDonnell never stopped hacking off their own hands. They saw
away at their flesh, driven on by fear of losing the thing they desire
most. Through historical accident during the seventeenth century,
the red hand became the exclusive totem of the Protestants of
Northern Ireland. It fits them well: Celtic in origin but denoting
loyalty to Britain. Yet to the British people it has no meaning. It is,

* The term also refers to the violent period from 1916 to 1923 throughout the
island, but I use it here to describe only the more recent events in Northern
Ireland.

therefore, a near-perfect expression of the strange, ambiguous claim by Ulster Protestants—whose roots in Ireland go back three or four hundred years—that they are "British" and not Irish.

Nevertheless, the bloody red hand is an apt symbol of what both Protestants and Catholics in Northern Ireland have done during the thirty years of the Troubles. Viewed from outside the province, the hard-liners on both sides (who, in Northern Ireland, constitute the majority) seemed to be acting out a part in some bizarre and bloody anachronistic pageant. Could this terrible hysteria really be taking place in Europe in the late twentieth century, among people who look just like us, in a region of Great Britain, supposedly one of the most civil of societies?

The Protestants, in particular, have created an appalling public image for themselves. They look like unreasonable and unreasoning bullies and bigots who refuse to share political power with Catholics, shout "No Surrender!" and "What we have, we hold!" loud and often, and insist on marching through Catholic neighbourhoods in peculiar parades that mix bowler hats and rolled umbrellas with the harsh, primitive rattle of the giant Lambeg battle drum. Many of them follow the preacher Ian Paisley, who isn't kidding when he calls the Pope the Antichrist. During the Troubles, they tortured and killed Catholics and set off bombs in Catholic pubs and sports clubs. On the gable ends of their mean little row houses they painted murals depicting a seventeenth-century Dutch prince called William, whom they idolize. They sprayed graffiti on walls that said "No Taigs on our streets!" ("Taig" is an abusive term for a Roman Catholic and is the insulting equivalent of "Prod" for a Protestant); "Fuck the Pope!" or just "FTP!"; "Remember 1690!" (the long-ago year of a battle on the River Boyne); and "Still Under Siege!" (referring to the Catholic siege of Protestant Derry three hundred years earlier). They formed numerous paramilitary militias—one of which called itself the Red Hand Commandos. They swore loyalty to Britain, a country whose people and government detested them and who thought they were just another bunch of violent paddies. For fifty years, until their sectarian regime went under in 1972, they ran a government that kept Catholics down, using a Protestant police force that looked like an army, with its heavy weaponry, and auxiliaries who were always ready with the truncheon and the gun.

The Catholics have always looked better. They appear to be conducting a version of a political movement—and a guerrilla military campaign—for civil rights and equality, for "liberation," that resembles many such struggles around the world. Their fight also looks like a continuation of the ancient Irish striving for autonomy from British control—or from domination by those British stooges, the Ulster Prods. Catholic ideology and goals appear rational and comprehensible in a way that those of the Protestants do not. However, as we'll discover, that rationality is more apparent than real. And, of course, "there's bad bastards on both sides," as someone once said. No one could outdo the Provisional Irish Republican Army (the IRA) or the Irish National Liberation Army (or more recently, the splinter groups, the Real IRA or the Continuity IRA) for atrocity. The IRA acted at first as a self-defence force to protect Catholics from Protestant pogroms, but it soon branched out into sectarian outrages of its own. It invented the car bomb, the mainstay weapon for all contemporary terrorists. Its hard men, too, killed, tortured, and bombed, often at random. Almost sixty percent of the military, police, and civilian dead of the Troubles were killed by Catholic gunmen whose violence—compared with the sporadic activity of Protestants—was sustained and unrelenting. Their goal was to shoot and bomb the Prods of the North into a united Ireland against their will. The IRA and its offspring, like their Protestant paramilitary equivalents, degenerated into criminal gangs and mafias years ago.

The numbers involved look small (almost 4,000 dead, 40,000 wounded) compared with the casualties in other places—the Balkans, some African countries, the Middle East. But there aren't many Irish (or, if you like, British) in Northern Ireland. If the numbers of casualties during the Troubles were proportionately reckoned in the United States, they would amount to almost 800,000 dead and more than eight million wounded. The effect of such killing was intensified by the small size of Northern Ireland—it's half the area of the state of Maryland. And a majority of the casualties were suffered within a segment of the population: among the farms, villages, and little market towns near the border with the Republic, and especially in the crowded, scummy city precincts of the working class. In the narrow streets of Belfast and Derry, the cramped sectarian territories abut each other in close-by chunks and blocs. The slaying was sometimes intimate—the killer and victim well acquainted, perhaps neighbours. That fit into the ancient Irish pattern; it was a sort of comfortable tradition. But things were worse, went the old saying from some previous insurrection or sectarian outrage, when the hard men began killing people whose names they didn't even know. During the Troubles, both forms of communal murder happened all the time.

In those days, when I travelled from my home in Canada to visit my grandmother in Belfast, I used to buy groceries in a little store over the Ormeau Bridge across the River Lagan, just up the road from her house. Once, I was standing in the aisle down from the single cash register; I had taken a can of stew off the shelf and was reading the label.

I heard a voice say, "Give us the money."

I turned and saw a young man with long dark hair and wearing an old fatigue jacket. He was standing in front of the cash register pointing a small handgun at the owner.

"Bill, you're jokin'," the owner said.

"Laugh this off," said the young man, and he fired his pistol. It made a hollow popping noise. The shot hit the owner in the chest; he collapsed and disappeared from my view behind the counter. The young man reached over, opened the cash register, and scooped out the bills. He stuffed them into one pocket of his jacket while putting his pistol into the other. As he did so, he looked down the aisle and saw me standing, watching him, the can of stew in my hand. We looked at each other for two or three seconds. I noticed that he had bright blue eyes in a wan, pimply face. Then he turned, pushed open the door, stepped out of the store, went left, and disappeared.

I walked to the entrance, opened the door, and looked out. The young man was walking casually down the sidewalk becoming, as I watched, increasingly obscured by the shoppers and by school kids coming home. I turned back and looked behind the counter. The owner was lying on the floor; his eyes were closed and he looked as if he was asleep. There was a small red spot, the size of a large coin, on his shirt front.

I searched for a phone but couldn't see one. I ran out onto the sidewalk and shouted: "A man's been shot in here! He needs an ambulance"—or something like that. I recollect people stopping, staring at me, afraid of me—maybe of my accent, perhaps because I was a bearded young man and might have a weapon myself. I wasn't the only one trying to adjust to an abrupt event. It was one of the worst times of the Troubles and people were edgy. I went into the dry cleaner's next door. That shop had a phone, and the proprietor called the emergency number. Within a minute, an armoured police Land Rover arrived, then an ambulance, then British soldiers. A few minutes later, a Saracen armoured car rumbled up. The soldiers deployed into a ring, watching me, the street, the tree-shadows of the Ormeau Park across the road, the gathered people. They feared an ambush.

I gave my statement to the police, describing what I'd seen. The ambulance took the wounded man away. I heard later that he was all right; it was a small-calibre bullet and had missed vital organs. It was only when the police had finished with me that I realized I was still clutching the can of stew. It was hot and wet from my sweaty hand, and I left it on the store counter.

I most remember two things. The owner called the young man by name; they knew each other. It had been a casual, intimate shooting. Later, I heard that the young man was raising his small contribution of money for one of the Protestant paramilitary groups. I had already assumed that. The store was Catholic, so the logical Northern Irish conclusion was that the shooter was Protestant and that the robbery was political. It hadn't occurred to me that he was a "cowboy," a small-time freelance thug knocking over a grocery store for a few quid—although there were lots of his kind around.

The other thing I remember is the look the young man gave me, after he had taken the cash, had put his pistol away, and was standing with his hands in his jacket pockets. It wasn't the expression of someone who was thinking of shooting me, too; I never had that feeling. But the way he looked at me was so familiar—wary and calculating. Many people had stared in the same way since I'd arrived for a visit. For a long time, I couldn't understand what it meant. Eventually, I knew. They were trying to decide "what foot I kicked with"—what religion I was. There were supposed ways to tell, subtle indicators. Was I someone they should fear? Or was I one of them? That was what the armed robber was doing, too. He had just shot a man who knew him by his first name. But he was looking at me, the stranger, and trying to figure out whether I was a Prod or a Taig.

I've paid particular attention to the Protestants of Northern Ireland all my life because they're my people—at least, in a sense. I was born in Belfast into a Protestant family. I was baptized in the Protestant Church of Ireland (the local equivalent of the Anglicans). My mother brought me home from hospital into a little worker's house on Cadogan Street, on the border of the neighbourhood of the "Holy Land" (not a reference to Christian piety, but so called because its streets have names like Cairo, Jerusalem, Damascus). It was a blue-collar Protestant enclave squeezed between the River Lagan, the Queen's University lands, and the Catholic territories of Hatfield Street and the lower Ormeau Road.

I have relatives who believe that the Taig-hating, Bible-thumping Reverend Ian Paisley is a great man. My mother was born on the Woodvale Road, which is a slightly more genteel extension of the Protestant heartland of the Shankill Road, and she didn't know more than a handful of Catholics personally until she was seventeen and got a job. My father and maternal grandfather, my great-uncles, uncles, and cousins all followed the old Irish tradition of overseas military service and joined the Royal Navy and the merchant marine, or, once in a while, the British Army. One of my great-grandfathers was a policeman in the sectarian Protestant force stationed in County Tyrone, deep in Catholic "bandit country." In 1921, during the war of independence, a Catholic sniper killed my great-uncle Benjamin, who was wearing a British naval uniform and walking near the house I would come home to as a newborn. When the Troubles erupted in 1969, Benjamin's brother, my great-uncle Jack, said to me that the government should turn "the Specials" loose on the Taigs without mercy or restraint. The sectarian Protestant B Specials—the Ulster Special Constabulary—had been set up in 1920 to protect Protestants from IRA attack but also to keep the refractory Catholics in the new state of Northern Ireland under control, to assault or kill them if and when that was necessary. "What else can you do," Jack said, "when they shoot one of your brothers?" Benjamin had been killed forty-eight years before.

I never became a member of the loyal tribe, a true Prod. I left Northern Ireland or, rather, my parents took me away, when I was an infant. We became Irish emigrants, joining the centuries-old diaspora, the Irish nation overseas. First, we went to England and I became a little English boy whose parents confounded my friends with the harsh clack of their Ulster speech. I tried to convince them that I was born in America and that the accents they heard were American, not Irish—anything but Irish. When my father's English workmates came to visit us, I discovered that his nickname, well meant but redolent of history and condescension, was "Paddy." On the walls bordering the train line I sometimes travelled with my mother—before the days of real black and brown immigrants in England—I read "Irish Wogs Go Home" and "Irish Niggers Out." It was an ecumenical advisory: no distinction there between Prods and Taigs.

We visited Belfast often in the summer school holidays and stayed with my grandmother in the little house on the border of the Holy Land. I slept in the bare attic while the cold summer rain hammered down onto the skylight and, during the day, I played war with my grandfather's army helmet. I was disappointed to see that it didn't have any bullet holes in it. I hung about with Bernard Ferguson, a son of the only Catholic family on the street. Years later, he joined the Provisional IRA and was killed. I never found out whether it was the police, the army, or loyalist gunmen who had done it. Ten years after our first move, we emigrated again, to Canada, and stayed there. Soon, I became a Canadian. I visited Northern Ireland from time to time. For my mother and father, it would always be "home." For me, it was a distant point of origin, an unavoidable genetic and cultural inheritance.

Then everything changed utterly, though no "terrible beauty" was born. (William Butler Yeats used the phrase to describe the aftermath of the 1916 Easter Rising in Dublin, the catalyst of eventual Irish independence.) On the contrary, the shocking outburst of bloody sectarian war in 1969 tended to concentrate the mind on sullen evil. All the old and ugly lineaments of Irish history reappeared, strong as ever, potent and murderous.

"We are now approaching Belfast airport," goes the supercilious joke in Dublin in the peaceful Catholic Republic of Ireland (whose own Protestants have declined from ten to three percent of its population since independence). "Please set your watches back three hundred years."

When I stayed in the little house on Cadogan Street, I went to sleep each night—no longer in the rain-troubled attic, but in a damp back bedroom on the ridged mattress my grandfather was laid out on when he died—to the sporadic pop of gunfire and the occasional whump of explosions. The atavistic ferocity of the Troubles was horrifying and frightening, although, of course, it was sometimes exciting, too. Such conflict had happened often in the Irish past (although seldom with this intensity or for as long a time). But most rational, liberal observers of the Northern Irish scene had thought all that was over with in the late twentieth century. I had thought so, too. Everyone was wrong. There were no grounds whatsoever for optimism. History—or the mythology the people had created out of history—reasserted itself. Rage and fear ran so deep on both sides that nothing could control the violence, once it had broken free of restraints that all turned out to have been temporary and fragile.

The Protestants are the key to understanding what has been happening in Northern Ireland. The trick has always been somehow to fit these prickly people into the scheme of Ireland as a whole. If the Ulster Protestants hadn't existed, Ireland would have become a united Free State (with a dominion form of government modelled on Canada's) after the war of independence in 1921, and a united full-fledged republic twenty-five years later. The problem in the North is partly the fact that the minority Catholic population has never accepted the legitimacy of the new political entity. But, because the majority Protestants wanted nothing to do with an independent Catholic Gaelic country, the British government divided the island and hived off six counties into a dysfunctional statelet. The Irish Free State returned the favour, in a way. It coveted the partitioned six counties, but it made no concessions to the Protestants who lived there and, in fact, regarded them with consistent hostility and condescension. It even provided a sanctuary for the IRA gunmen who began attacking across the border after independence, and continued to do so sporadically until the early 1960s, with the goal of recovering the severed part of Ireland. (The southern government made attempts to extirpate the IRA, but they were ineffectual and ambivalent.) The IRA campaign was bound to be futile—as if a few gunmen could scare off the tough Prods who had nowhere to run.

The Protestants don't fit into the standard Irish, or "Oirish" (meaning "stage-" or "professional-Irish"), mould: twinkling-eyed and loquacious; Celtic rhetoric and charm; the Guinness-and-endless-stories crowd of "Faith and Begorra!," "Come here 'till I tell you" storytelling which prizes entertainment above all; the claim that to be Irish is to be a charming, feckless, boozing talker, a virtuous victim of British imperialism to whom the rest of the world owes a hearing. There are two sides to this sort of malarky. It's often harmless fun: Saturday-night shouts of "Up the Republic!"; rebel songs in pubs; praise for "the boys"; movies about the noble republican gunman. The inventions and yarns—the lies—charm and beg indulgence, but they also kill. They have long formed the basis for deadly rationales, and in Northern Ireland they still do.

The Protestant style is more straightforward and unvarnished, and it is seldom entertaining or pleasant. Yeats called the Protestants of the north "a horrid lot," and they can be grim, laconic, constrained by the austerities of Presbyterianism and temperance, thrifty, stereotypically Scottish—as many of them are by ancestry—and not at all stereotypically Irish. Question: "What's the difference between a Ballymena man and a coconut?" Answer: "You can get a drink out of a coconut."

In short, anyone who wants to understand Northern Ireland has to decipher and deconstruct the Protestants—the loyalists, the unionists, the Prods. The secret lies in their collective memory, in how they interpret history, and in the themes that make up their story of themselves: siege, resistance, endurance, sacrifice, loyalty, betrayal, treachery, and, sometimes, although tentative, long in the past and mostly forgotten, enlightened solidarity with Catholics across the old divide.

Protestants and Catholics have contended with each other for four centuries in the constricted territory of Ulster. They have fought elsewhere in Ireland, too, but the north has always been the real battleground. It's where the Protestants are most numerous and where the chaotic and interlocking pattern of sectarian settlement has guaranteed tension, the pull and shove of rival claims to land, power, and the true faith.

The idea of Protestants and Catholics fighting each other seems incomprehensible to most of us, an antique passion long grown out of elsewhere in the Western world. The fact that some form of religious war still seemed to be happening in Northern Ireland (or, at least, enmity between two groups defined and divided by religion) was one of the reasons for thinking the conflict absurd and deplorable, but ultimately incapable of explanation and, therefore, something to be ignored. Anyway, after thirty years of fighting, the old derogatory stereotype might be invoked: the incorrigibly violent Irish still doing it to one another.

However, the behaviour of these fractious people has general significance. All internecine conflicts are unique in some ways and similar in others. The specific circumstances of Irish history established the particular ways in which Protestants and Catholics have defined their dispute and how they have carried it on. But there are many similar contemporary examples: the Serbs, Croats, Kosovars and Macedonians of the Balkans; the Greeks and Turks of Cyprus; the Tamils and Sinhalese of Sri Lanka; the Palestinians and the Israelis—it could be a long list. All of them make contested claims to the same small chunks of land; they have radically different interpretations of the past; they have distinct mythologies of themselves; and they are defined by ethnic nationalism and religious difference. Each has a long memory in which the passage of time is almost irrelevant: last year's battle or massacre calls to mind that of the fourteenth or seventeenth century, the pain and rage of one resonating with and reinforcing the mythic power of the other. The Quebec motto *Je me souviens* ("I remember") might stand as the collective cry of all these small, embittered peoples.

To unriddle the Troubles, therefore, is also to form some understanding of these other conflicts. The facts on the ground and the psychology (and pathology) of the participants are similar enough for that. Northern Ireland might be a rough Rosetta Stone. Perhaps we can use it to interpret the other dark places on the earth. This isn't an idle aim. What happens in Ulster more or less stays there; it won't lead to apocalypse. But that's not the case with the Middle East or the Balkans. And now we also have to contend with a worldwide version of the IRA or the Red Hand Commandos: Islamist terror. Violent Islamist fundamentalism appears to be fighting an unlimited war—of its own political-religious view against that of the entire Western world, and of traditionalism against modernity. But it also has a simple, limited, and comprehensible goal: to effect change in Muslim states. Islamist motivations and psychology would be comprehensible to the hard men of the Ulster paramilitaries. The terrorists of East and West even share a mythology of martyrdom and blood sacrifice. An Islamist suicide bomber or hijacker and an Irish hunger striker fasting to the death or a republican rebel rising in doomed, symbolic insurrection all sacrifice themselves in the name of faith or nation. Each bears witness; each believes he goes to God; each becomes a terrorist for the sake of a kingdom of heaven.

Most directly, terror is terror. Whatever murder and carnage have happened anywhere in the world have also happened in Northern Ireland in the course of the Troubles. Name any category of atrocity. Random bombings of civilians: McGurk's Bar, 15 dead, 24 wounded; Shankill Road fish-and-chip shop, 9 dead, 58 wounded; Enniskillen Remembrance Day service, 11 dead, 63 wounded; 22 IRA bombs on "Bloody Friday" in Belfast, 11 dead, 100 wounded. Random abductions, torture, and shooting: hundreds of killings, one Prod or Taig at a time; but sometimes more than that: 5 Catholics, 4 policemen, 18 British soldiers, 10 Protestants taken off a minibus and massacred. Nothing that Islamist fundamentalists have done to individual hostages comes close to what the "Shankill Butchers" did to a score of Catholic men—except there were no video cameras around to record their torture, mutilation, and murder. The Protestant Ulster Volunteer Force set off bombs in Dublin that killed dozens. The IRA set off bombs in England with the same result. It lobbed mortars at Heathrow airport and would have fired missiles at airplanes if it had had any (it tried to buy them). Any terrorist outrage against humanity you can name is old news in Northern Ireland.

Probe the IRA or the Ulster Volunteer Force, and you learn something about the Basque ETA, the Tamil Tigers, Hamas, or al-Qaeda—and about why people harbour and support their gunmen and bombers. The apparently strange persistence of religious animosities in Ulster is an analogue of the flaring-up of violence between the

West—with its own increasingly fundamentalist Christian tinge in the United States—and Islam all around the borderlands between the two and, through terror and war, in the heartland of each.

"History would be an excellent thing if only it were true," said Leo Tolstoy. There is a familiar problem with both stories of the Red Hand of Ulster: neither is true. Of course, we don't conceive of their veracity in the sense that actual men called O'Neill or MacDonnell once performed their self-amputations as the purchase price of Ulster land. (Although Maud, my grandmother, might have said about those mythic Irish: "I wouldn't put it past yon.") But we do assume their truth as two of the mythical stories from ancient times passed along by word of mouth and eventually written down. These genuine old narratives from the shadowy Celtic heroic age of the great Irish epic the *Táin bó Cuilinge* (the "Cattle Raid of Cooley")—the equivalent of the Greek *Iliad* or the Welsh *Mabinogeon*—are the founding myths of a people.

The red-hand stories aren't like that at all. They are, in fact, late creations that were made up at some time after 1700, long after the English had driven down the old Gaelic society of Ulster, the last stronghold of Irish resistance. The stories of O'Neill and MacDonnell are merely the two most popular of many versions that purport to identify the owner of the red hand.

There are always many different versions of the world and its history. "Reality is not what it is. It consists of the many realities which it can be made into," writes Wallace Stevens. Taking a varied and inventive view of past events is not an exclusively Irish habit, of course. Every people uses the past for its present purposes. We treat history as a kind of existential emporium, and we buy there, or shoplift, what we need to live now. The Northern Irish playwright Brian Friel suggests: "Perhaps the most important thing is not the accurate memory but the successful invention." One of this book's themes is how people in Ireland, and the Protestants of Ulster in particular, have created out of history the myths they have needed to justify their present beliefs and actions. The historian Ian McBride defines "political myth" as "a story about the past told to justify or undermine political institutions and practices; its usefulness depends not on its fidelity to the historical record, but its relevance to the contemporary situation." Governments and their people require historians to be shamans of the nation's orthodox tradition. When the tradition is questioned or second-guessed, that's more than mere historical "revisionism"; it is a kind of heresy. Myth is a narrative of a sanctified history that the nation's people perceive as the absolute truth.

The old cliché about Anglo-Irish relations is that the English never remember, and the Irish never forget. We should insert the words "some things" after "remember" and "forget." Forgetting is as necessary as remembering for a people to create a mythology of itself. And, "Creating a nation involves getting one's history wrong," Ernest Renan observed. Every standard received version of a people's history follows these prescriptions. What have the Protestants of Ulster remembered from the past to forge a collective identity? What have they forgotten or got wrong? The Irish problem—which is now the Northern Irish problem—has not yet passed out of politics into history. Therefore, in Ireland, as in South Africa, Quebec, the Balkans, or the Middle East, historical arguments are still a crucial part of political debate. And we are often forced deep into the Irish past to try to find explanations or to gain a form of understanding. The novelist Dermot Bolger laments: "We must go back three centuries to explain any fight outside a chip shop."

The standard received, and sanctified, version of Irish history is a Catholic and nationalist narrative. It tends to ignore the twenty per-cent of the island's people who now happen to be Protestant. The Protestants have their own standard, received version of the past, but, outside Northern Ireland, it is a pale, hardly known shadow of the stirring and colourful Catholic rendition that came, long ago, to dominate the field. In the Catholic story, virtue eventually triumphs over evil, and the tale ends happily ever after—in a way. It's true in its essentials, but it's a simple story, too—morally and philosophi-cally. So, beware. Life is never simple and, therefore, neither is his-tory; in fact, both are always complex, confused, compromised, ambiguous. "It was all so unimaginably different / And all so long ago"—the historian's caveat—writes Louis MacNeice. But in Ireland, and indeed in any nation when it creates the narrative of itself, it's the story—its mythic force and its self-justification—that's important.

In the beginning, Ireland was a kind of pastoral Eden, pure and egalitarian, in which, wrote G.K. Chesterton, lived the Great Gaels—"All their wars are merry, / And all their songs are sad." They were noble warriors who, to be sure, fought each other over cattle, slaves, and land, but they valued strong drink, talk, and poetry. "I will not wish unto you . . . to be rhymed to death, as is said to be done in Ireland," said Sir Philip Sidney. Every minor king and trifling chief had his pet bard—poets, not the gods, conferred immortality. They all loved the *craic* ("crack")—the Gaelic for good talk, good times. They drew blood from their cattle and mixed it with milk, like the warrior Masai in Africa. The Gaels were tall, handsome, and healthy. The women were feisty and independent. Sexual mores were relaxed and sensible: divorce was easy, and trial marriage, common. One of the greatest Gaelic myths is about Medb ("she who intoxicates"), the warrior queen of Connacht. She could run faster than any horse, and the sight of her was enough to deprive men of two-thirds of their strength. The people spoke a sweet, mellifluous language unadulterated by clattering English and proudly unsuited to commerce or technology. Saints Patrick and Columba made Christians out of the pagan Gaels. Then the Vikings swept down on them, carrying out their usual murder and pillage. The priests had flourished on the island, which was isolated from the barbarian convulsions in Europe, and they preserved precious manuscripts from the raiders and saved civilization.

The Vikings also founded towns—Dublin, Limerick, Waterford, Cork, Wexford, but not Derry or Belfast—and encouraged trade. The Irish high king Brian Bóruma eventually broke the power of the Northmen at the Battle of Clontarf in 1014. (Although, in the Irish way, half the Norse army was made up of Irishmen from Leinster who didn't mind fighting against other Irishmen from Munster.) The Vikings were absorbed into the resilient skein of Gaelic life. But it couldn't last. England lay just across the water. Evil was close by, and Ireland couldn't escape it forever. In the twelfth century, like hostile and powerful aliens from another world, the English landed.

Richard fitz Gilbert, alias Richard de Clare, aka Strongbow, arrived in Ireland with an army and captured Waterford. He was a Norman by his name, one of the Northmen temporarily diverted from Scandinavia to northern France and then, in 1066, to England, arriving in Ireland a few centuries behind the original Vikings, his long-ago countrymen. Strongbow wasn't an invader, although the standard received story of Ireland claims he was. In fact, he was invited. The King of Leinster, Diarmait Mac Murchada, recruited the Englishman—or Norman, or Viking twice removed, whatever he was—to help him fight another Irish king. The bedevilling superiority of the English killing techniques was apparent right away: one hundred English defeated a thousand Norse-Irish soldiers. Strongbow was soon followed by the Tudor king of England Henry II, also with an army. And thus began the 800-year-long occupation of Ireland.

For a while, however, the English faltered; their power waned and contracted, until, by the early 1500s, they controlled the fortified English Pale around Dublin—the "four obedient shires"—and that was it. Beyond the Pale, the wild Irish flourished, and the "Old English" who had settled there became famous, much later, as *Hiberniores Hibernis ipsis,* "more Irish than the Irish themselves"— a phrase not coined until the nineteenth century (an example of a retrospective reach back into history for present purposes).

The English could not avoid the eternal logic of homeland security, or of the security of empires, for that matter: they had to expand into enemy territory to secure what they already held. To defend the Pale, and perhaps to defend England as well against papish adversaries who might use Ireland as a base, they saw that they had to move aggressively. And so they conquered Ireland "once and for all." It took a while—seventy-five years or so—before they could claim success. That was three or four generations of Irish resistance: the Kildare Rebellion; the War of the Geraldine League; the revolt of Shane O'Neill; the Desmond Revolt; the Baltinglass Revolt; the Nine Years War. As one might expect, it was a brutal process, each conflict bloodier than the last. The English burnt crops and killed livestock. There were big massacres at Rathlin, Belfast, Mullaghmast, and Smerwick, and the usual run-of-the-mill massacres almost everywhere else.

The conquest provided all sorts of financial opportunities. At times, resident English administrators deliberately provoked conflict if things had calmed down for a while because land and offices flowed to them whenever their army hammered the Irish. Younger sons, the perennial troublemakers of a system of primogeniture, saw Ireland as a place to come by the land and status denied them in England. In that sense, Ireland was like the New World colony of Virginia, and it was much closer, although not necessarily less dangerous—it seems that the natives were restless everywhere. By the late 1500s, the English had evolved a kind of colonialist approach to Ireland, based on ideas of innate English racial superiority (think Shakespearean chauvinist rhetoric) and—a terrible foreshadowing—Protestant hatred of Catholics. Prods and Taigs already.

To make sectarian matters worse, England planted Ireland not with crops but with people—with Protestants. Plantations were set up in various parts of the island, but the largest was in Ulster. The English drove the Gaels off their land, or the fertile parts of it, and gave it to English and Scottish Protestant settlers. The Ulster Plantation was the biggest because that was where the Gaels stood and fought with the most determination and ferocity. Ulster was the centre of Irish resistance; it churned with rebellion. Its "kerns," the Anglicized Gaelic for the rebel *banditti* of the Irish woods, bogs, and hills ("rough rug-headed Kernes," wrote Shakespeare), gave the English more trouble than all the other Irish put together. The Plantation created the divide between the two Ulster peoples who still contend there. It intimated a future of tribal territories like the Falls and the Shankill roads, the diehard nationalist bombers and gunmen of the IRA, and the obdurate, no-surrender, fundamentalist Prods.

It wasn't a foregone conclusion, but, in the end, the superior technology, organization, and cohesion of the English forces prevailed. "The Gael always went forth to battle and he always fell"—though there's also the fact that the Irish tried to protect women and children and grow food while they were fighting off the invaders. Like the cavalry versus the Indians two hundred years later on a different continent, the conflict ended with the same result. By 1603, most historians agree, the conquest was more or less complete.

Anglo-Irish relations then entered a new phase. For most of Ireland, that phase ended with the conclusion of the war of independence in 1921. In the case of Northern Ireland, the phase has lasted almost exactly four hundred years and isn't finished yet. In the standard received version of Irish history, the English occupied, repressed, punished, discriminated, stole, expelled, and colonized. They killed, too, when they thought it necessary or profitable. The worst was Oliver Cromwell, whose New Model Army slaughtered the Irish—"barbarous wretches," he called them—in massacres that were, even by the standards of the English in Ireland, extravagant and savage.

England passed the penal laws which, at the time, were often called the "popery laws." They kept the Catholic Irish down for a hundred years. The laws said that they couldn't keep weapons, in an age when every man of substance carried one, ostensibly because of their propensity to use them to kill English, and sometimes Scottish, Protestants. Catholics couldn't run schools in Ireland or teach at them or go abroad for education. Priests and bishops had to get out of Ireland, although that law was later eased to limit their number and to register them with the government. The penal laws prohibited Catholics from buying land or inheriting it from Protestants, or from taking out long-term leases. They couldn't practise law, nor could they participate in any form of government. Eventually, they lost the vote. (The standard story ignores the fact that the severity of the penal laws disturbed many Englishmen, and some Protestants in Ireland, and that the provisions were enforced unevenly, sporadically, or, sometimes, not at all.)

And something else happened that was even worse than the penal laws: the Irish gave up their language. Or rather, the story stipulates, England took it from them—cut it out of them. In doing so, it cut out the Irish heart, because so much of the world, how you see and understand it, comes to you through your language. Irish is one of the obsolescent, or already lost, small languages, which, nevertheless, are the unique, irreplaceable vessels of the souls of the people who speak them. Lose that and you lose, not everything, but a great deal of what's most important. Edmund Spenser, the author of *The Faerie Queene,* understood the importance of the form of words: "So that the speache being Irishe the harte must be nedes be Irishe for out of the abundance of the harte the tongue speakethe." The poet, an administrator of the fledgling English imperium in Ireland, advocated draconian martial law against the Irish as the solution to rebellion there. The harsh alien tongue intruded everywhere until the *Gaeltacht*—the Irish-speaking parts of the country—was a mere shadow, a fringe of the Celtic fringe.

As if this wasn't enough, England starved the Irish in the Great Famine of the 1840s or, at least, tried to help along the natural catastrophe of the potato blight by doing nothing or even by exporting grain. Meanwhile, skeletal Irish children perished of hunger or cholera, and a million people died altogether. The causes and progress of the Famine are, in fact, complex and still controversial, but its huge scale and terrible suffering, its losses and silences, are incontrovertible. The Famine and the repression forced emigration upon the Irish, says the standard version. So many left Ireland that there grew up an Irish nation overseas: in Australia, in Canada, in the slums and hovels of England itself, and, most notably, in America. The emigrants created an absence, a sense of Ireland hollowed out and diminished, of men and women, maybe the best and most energetic, lost forever. "Where are our twenty millions?" asked Joyce. If the same proportion of people had been forced to emigrate from India during the same period of time, the number would have amounted to close to 400 million. That would have been some Indian nation overseas.

What the Irish could do, says the standard version of Irish history, they did. They played the English game of politics with panache and considerable success. They formed parties and parliaments, invented the mechanics of mass protest movements—the big public meetings and parades, the infrastructure of local organizations. The "Liberator," Daniel O'Connell, began the process of Catholic emancipation from the penal laws. Like any good mythologizer, he looked back to the golden age of the Christian Gaels before the invaders landed. "They came to a nation famous for its love of learning, its piety, its heroism [and] . . . doomed Ireland to seven centuries of oppression."

Later, the Irish adapted for political purposes the coercive yet bloodless technique of the boycott, an Englishman of that name being the first target of economic ostracism. For a time, the Irish Parliamentary Party held the balance of power at Westminster. It seemed to come very close to solving the Irish problem by peaceful, constitutional means, but the First World War and implacable northern Prods put an end to the home rule movement. Most interesting of all, the leaders of the Irish political drive for independence were, as often as not, Protestants: not of the adamant, dour northern variety, rejectionists in the bone, but Protestants of the Ascendancy, the top rung of social and political life in Dublin and the Big Houses of the countryside. The reserved Protestant squire Charles Stewart Parnell, more English than the English (to reverse a phrase), was, for a time, "the uncrowned king of Ireland." Protestants were even in the forefront of many of the armed uprisings over the years. None was more prominent than the Dublin lawyer Theobald Wolfe Tone. He was one of the leaders of the United Irish Insurrection of 1798, the most serious challenge to English power in Ireland between the conquest and 1916. Tone became known as the father of physical-force nationalism.

Politics was all very well, but the standard story of Ireland favours other means. Parnell's lieutenant, William O'Brien, summed up what even the constitutionalist politicians understood: "Violence is the only way of ensuring a hearing for moderation." Even Parnell used the threat of endemic violence in Ireland—cattle maiming, house burning, and assassination—as his hammer at Westminster. In the last resort, the English responded to force or, at least, to the threat of it.

Irish patriots who advocated physical-force means of kicking the English out had always had that opinion. And so they rebelled. They martyred themselves. They never gave up. In almost every generation, they bore witness in arms and blood-sacrifice to the continuing existence and sanctity of the Irish nation. They rose in 1608, 1641, 1649, 1688, 1798, 1803, 1848, 1867, and, finally, in April 1916. The leader of that Easter Rising, Patrick Pearse, had ended his address at the funeral of the Fenian (a member of the revolutionary Irish Republican Brotherhood) O'Donovan Rossa with these words: "They [the English] think that they have foreseen everything, think that they have provided against everything; but the fools, the fools, the fools!—they have left us our Fenian dead, and, while Ireland holds these graves, Ireland unfree shall never be at peace."

The Rising wasn't exactly a roaring success, the official story has to admit. But what happened afterwards brought everyone to their senses. The English executed the leaders of the Rising over a period of ten days or so with an odd, languorous cruelty (for example, they had to strap the wounded James Connolly to a chair to keep him upright while they shot him). That was what brought the Irish nation round—the exposure once again of England's savagery when it came to Ireland; its inability, even in the twentieth century, to treat the Irish any differently from how Cromwell did, as anything other than barbarous wretches. England's difficulty during the First World War and its aftermath was Ireland's opportunity for the final time. In 1919, the Irish launched their campaign for independence. It soon became a bloody mess: a guerrilla war of atrocity, reprisal, massacre, and murder by both sides. But in the end, after eight hundred years, the English gave up. There was some unfinished business, it's true: a civil war, for example. The Irish fought each other over the question of whether to accept the deal negotiated with England, and more died in that conflict than in the war of independence. One of its most important consequences for history—and its study—was the destruction of many documents of the country's archives when anti-treaty gunmen blew up the Four Courts in Dublin. Henceforth, it would be harder than ever to discover historical fact with which to displace the old myths or to challenge previous interpretations of the Irish past.

Brian Friel asks: "What happens when a small nation that has been manipulated and abused by a huge colonial power for hundreds of years wrests its freedom by blood and anguish?" In the case of Ireland, what happens is more blood and anguish. A serious and intractable problem remained: the small matter of one million Protestants in the north of the island, a fifth of the population, to whom the Gaelic, Catholic Free State was repugnant and unjoinable. The peace treaty partitioned Ireland and created a separate Protestant-dominated province that would remain part of the United Kingdom and outside the new Ireland. The Gaels had envisaged their island as four green fields—the provinces of Leinster, Munster, Connacht, and Ulster. The agreement wrenched away most of the fourth green field from the others and, for the anti-treaty nationalists, it was an unnatural and obscene division of the ancient land. It happened for two reasons: the refusal of the Protestants—the hard, grim Prods of the North whose symbol is the bloody red hand—to accept their place in a united Ireland; and the failure of the English to stand up to them when they threatened to fight to keep Ulster "British" and out of Ireland.

The old story is still being told in Northern Ireland. On its narrow ground, two peoples still jostle and contend. The Catholics have fought their way out of repression into sharing power in the local government. (This victory took place under the 1998 Good Friday Agreement, which consolidated the paramilitary ceasefires and the "peace process" and tried to set out future relationships among Britain, Northern Ireland, and the Republic of Ireland.) Their real goal, however, is to reclaim the fourth green field, to bring it back into one Ireland. The Protestants still resist. The attempt to shoot and bomb them into a united Ireland has failed, it's true, but political and demographic time is on the Catholic nationalist side. Eventually, the Protestants will accept the inevitable and Ireland will be whole—a nation once again. Or so goes the standard received version of Irish history.

Most of the time, I thought the Northern Irish (both Protestants and Catholics) were familiar and comprehensible: they were Caucasian, English-speaking citizens of a First World country. They drove cars on motorways, ate fast food, and flew to the Costa del Sol to drink beer and get sunburned. When I had drinks with them in pubs, they seemed to be more or less like me or my English or North American friends. They drank harder and talked faster and were generally wittier—the *craic* again—but they weren't culturally exotic in the way that Chinese, Russians, or even French or Germans might seem to be.

Yet the comfortable, homey assurance could dissipate in an instant. An amiable pub acquaintance, a Belfast businessman with whom I'd been having a pleasant time, began an abrupt diatribe: the British government had done a proper job of renewing Catholic neighbourhoods destroyed in the Troubles, but not Protestant ones. The rebuilt areas of the Falls Road had as many pubs as before. But on the refurbished Shankill, where there used to be two dozen pubs, he said, now there was one. The fucking Taigs had the upper hand. They'd shot and bombed their way into the government, the murdering bastards, and now they were sticking it to the Protestants. Fuck them all!

"Tiocfaidh ar lá!" my unprejudiced laughing cousin mocked the man— "Our time will come!" It is the ubiquitous Catholic grafitto in Northern Ireland and the motto of republicans. Its meaning is

ambiguous. It promises a new day for a hitherto repressed community, but it is also redolent of payback and reprisal. It may jog Protestant race memories of long-ago risings and massacres, back when they were plantation settlers with a precarious foothold on Irish frontier land, surrounded by armed wood kerns and dispossessed papish Gaels with a grudge. For that matter, it implies that the Troubles, the thirty-years' war, might be over, but that perhaps it is only a truce.

No one in the pub, except me, thought that my cousin was at all funny. I didn't laugh for long. In the room's silent tension, we finished our drinks and left.

The exchange made me think about my family: Northern Irish cousins and uncles and especially my father, Alexander. They are an interesting sample of Protestants in one particular respect: they grew up in Belfast, or even lived there most or all of their lives, but they are not bigots. They escaped both the obvious and the insidious conditioning of the place. Not only are most of them without prejudice by Northern Irish standards—there are various degrees of muffled or genteel sectarian ill-will—but they're enlightened and tolerant by any standard. They would fit immediately into the scheme of things in Canada (to which, in fact, some of them have emigrated, away from the Troubles), England, or the United States. Three of them, exogamously, married Catholics. That's something that very few members of the two distinct, segregated, hostile, endogamous cultures do: cross the divide, marry out of the tribe. (Even now, over eighty-five percent of Catholics and Protestants in Northern Ireland marry inside their own communities.)

My family had lived in Ulster for hundreds of years, throughout the worst of times of rebellion and fear. My father took my mother and me out of Ireland to England, and then to Canada (and out of the working class, too). He made us part of that much larger, and already old, Irish nation overseas, which is as much Ulster Protestant as it is southern Catholic. He was filled forever after with the immigrant's memories of home, with their contradictory mix of nostalgia and aversion. Before his death in the mid-1990s, Alexander was always a path back to Ireland for me. Whatever I think about the place comes through his eyes and mind as much as mine. He transmitted something of the essence of life there, with its odd mix of confrontations and evasions. How strange it is that in Belfast, I feel the pull of home even though I know that, for me, home never was in Ireland. But sometimes it takes more than one generation to complete an immigration.

The Protestants' mythology of themselves was hard formed by the time Alexander was born, and he spent his time in Northern Ireland within the ambit of the harsh and static myth. But he saw the situation there from all sides; it was a tragic whole for him. He was a humane and unbiased Protestant (in his case, the term being merely a label), a nationalist in favour of a united country, if he had to be anything in relation to the Irish conflict. Perhaps his impeccable freedom from prejudice is a reason for optimism, a locus for understanding inherited hatred and the occasional mystery of its avoidance. Or perhaps it's just chance and means nothing.

A living family's genial and generous ecumenism brought ancestors to mind, two of whom, I knew, had done notable things in the Irish past. One of them, Robert Lundy, may have been related, although it's impossible to trace a sure connection. However, the surname is an uncommon one in Ireland, and Robert certainly left descendants in the country. My family's standard version of its story has always claimed Robert as an ancestor, and there are good reasons to treat him as one. For a writer looking for a human synecdoche—an individual to represent a whole mythology—he's simply too useful a person to discard.

Lieutenant-Colonel Robert Lundy was a Scot, not an Irishman. He was appointed governor of the Protestant city of Derry (a creature of the Ulster Plantation) in 1688, just before it came under siege by the Catholic Irish army of James II. Robert prepared the city for siege as best he could, but, when the Irish approached, he ordered Derry's surrender on the generous terms offered by King James. Like many professional soldiers, he was more inclined than the warlike civilians he governed to compromise or to fight limited war. However, the Protestant hard men of Derry would have none of it. They staged a *coup de ville,* refused to surrender, and denounced the governor as a traitor. Robert was expelled from the city in disgrace before the siege began in earnest. With notable bravery and endurance, the Protestants survived 105 days, losing thousands to battle, starvation, and disease, before being relieved by Protestant ships that broke the siege boom on the River Foyle.

Robert is one of those enigmatic, mute men in history, and it is his enemies' version of events that has descended to us: he was an incompetent or a coward, or both, and certainly treacherous. As a result, in Northern Ireland, "Lundy" has some of the same connotation as Benedict Arnold in the United States or Guy Fawkes in England, although it also bears a great deal more contemporary symbolic weight—perhaps like that of Vidkun Quisling, the Nazi puppet and collaborator in Norway, whose name has also become a common noun. *The Oxford Companion to Irish History* says that "'Lundy' survives in unionist rhetoric as a synonym for 'traitor', his effigy being burned annually by the Apprentice Boys of the city [of Derry]." In 1974, I watched on television a group of Protestants burn the photographs of their moderate co-religionists who had signed the Sunningdale power-sharing agreement with the British government and Catholic politicians. The general strike of the Protestant Ulster Workers' Council and the threat of full-scale rebellion killed the agreement before it began. As the photos burned, I heard one man say, "There go your Lundys."

I think my family chooses to claim Robert as one of its own because, like many of them, he was detached from the hard-line Protestant cause. Whatever his reasons, he behaved like a peace-seeking moderate. We claim Robert as an ancestor in spite of the discomfort, ridicule—and outright physical danger—that possessing the name "Lundy" has sometimes caused. We've taken pride in the supposed connection because it says that we, at least, may not be mindless ideologues or killers.

Robert's story is one of the seminal myths of the Ulster Protestant tribe: a traitor expelled, a siege endured, no surrender for ever and ever.

The other man from long ago is the Reverend William Steel Dickson. He was a Presbyterian minister in the late eighteenth and early nineteenth centuries, and he was my great-great-great-great grandfather. With eloquence that grew famous, he preached in favour of Catholic emancipation from the penal laws, and of violence if it was necessary to resist tyranny. English repression and arrogance (and Anglican establishment prejudice) in Ireland made him a revolutionary, a prominent member of the Society of United Irishmen, a general in its armed militia (which fought the Insurrection of 1798), a political prisoner held without charge or trial for almost four years, a Protestant willing to take up arms with Catholics for the independence of a united Ireland.

The nomenclature of violence is relative, of course. It's hard to tell the difference between a "terrorist" and a "freedom fighter," goes the old English comedy routine (from less parlous times), particularly when you're being disembowelled by one. Irish nationalists think of William as a freedom fighter. To the English, and to many other Irishmen, even if he was a distinguished man of God, he was never more than a mere terrorist.

William suffered during imprisonment but was never broken by it, nor by the destruction of his life and livelihood. His poverty persisted because, stiff-necked and principled as he was, for the rest of his long life he refused to explain, or apologize for, his role in the United Irishmen and the planning of the rebellion. On the contrary, he argued, with his characteristic passion: Why should he be the one to apologize for something for which he was never charged, let alone tried? The government and his church (which also condemned him) should damned well apologize to him.

My father's father was William Lundy. His friends and family called him Billy and so will I, to avoid confusion with William Steel Dickson. All these "Williams"—it's also my middle name and my uncle's first name—are the Ulster Protestant analogue to "Muhammad" for a Muslim. The pious homage to the seventeenth-century William of Orange is similar in nature, if fuzzier in memory. English reporter to Orangeman: "Just who *was* King Billy?" Orangeman: "Och away, man, and read your Bible!"

I have the Orange sash Billy first wore when he joined the Orange Order as a teenager. He was a Protestant bigot who did not like Catholics at all. He signed Ulster's Solemn League and Covenant in 1912, pledging to fight against the British Crown to keep Ulster British (not the first manifestation of the confusing and apparently contradictory ideology of loyalism). I recognize his handwriting on the Covenant website: William Lundy, Irish Quarter South, Carrickfergus. He joined the 100,000-strong Ulster Volunteer Force (the UVF) formed to back up the Covenant's rejection of home rule (which, to Protestants, was really "Rome rule"). When the First World War began, UVF members seized the moment to prove themselves as loyalists distinct from the sly Fenians, with their "opportunities" when England had "difficulties" (ignoring the fact that many thousands of Catholic constitutional nationalists joined up, too). The Protestant illegal army offered itself to the empire and its King-Emperor and formed the British Army's 36th (Ulster) Division. It was almost destroyed in a few hours on the Western Front during the first day's slaughter of the Battle of the Somme. Later, Billy joined the B Specials, apparently comfortable with their reputation for harsh policing and sectarian violence. He died before the Troubles began of kidney disease that might have been a result of swallowing too much sour gas as a gasworks labourer. It was a toxic job, at a time when workmen were still merely cheap bodies in motion.

Billy's life straddles the ambiguous end-time of the standard Irish story's 800-year occupation of Ireland. When he was born in 1890, the country was tied to Britain through the *Act of Union* of 1801; peaceful nationalists were agitating for home rule, and Fenian gunmen were plotting for independence. He lived through revolution, civil war, sectarian hate, and butchery. By the time of his death, Ireland was divided into the independent republic and the still-British province in the north. That province itself was divided, the usual mundane Ulster violence going on, but the mad eruption of terror and killing rumbling below, rising closer to the surface.

Billy represents the antithesis of the tolerant, ecumenical William Steel Dickson, and he was a living summation of what the Ulster Protestants had become by the beginning of the First World War: a tribe united in their hostility to Catholics and to the project of an independent Ireland. By then, the Prods had done their historical spadework, turning up what they needed for their armoured, self-justifying story—siege, unity, exclusivity, and endurance—and burying what they didn't need: the memory of an open, generous moment in the past. Martyrdom isn't a motif restricted to Catholic nationalists—the hopeless Easter Rising of 1916, hunger strikers fasting to the death. The Protestants would make their own blood-sacrifice for their beliefs at the Battle of the Somme. The killing field before Thiepval Wood was a field of fire that would anneal the political mythology of the Ulster Protestants into a still-harder, yet-undissolved form.

The historian T.W. Moody wrote: "It is not Irish history but Irish mythology that has been ruinous to us and may prove even more lethal." I will try to substitute some necessary complexities for the distorting simplicities of myth, for the good old Irish story, for the standard received version—Protestant as well as Catholic. I'll attempt to unravel more of the "truth" of things in Ulster history and to see what memory and the selective, myth-making plundering of history has made of the truth.

The lives of Robert Lundy, William Steel Dickson, and Billy Lundy encapsulate many themes in the northern Irish past. Robert and William played roles that can be described as pivotal. In telling their stories, and Billy's more modest one, perhaps I can lay bare the harsh and sometimes murderous mythologies of the Protestants of Northern Ireland. The lives of my ancestors resonate in the very core of Ulster history.

PART ONE

ROBERT

A DECISION

HE KNEW IT WAS OVER when he saw his men break and run. From his position on the hill overlooking the Clady ford, he watched them stream back towards the city, twelve miles to the north. The Irish cavalry jostled at their rear, the horsemen swooping and circling around the running infantry, driving them as if they were a panicky herd of cattle, swords hacking them down like scythes topping tall grass. He could see the weak sun's flash and glint off the blades as they twirled and gyred, and then the reflections' quick suppression as his men's blood coated and dulled the metal.

He'd seen it before: an abrupt dissolution of the courage and resolve of inexperienced troops. And most of these men were mere civilians wielding unfamiliar weapons—pikes, muskets, staves. They had started out before first light, marching through the Bishop's Gate, half fearful, half exuberant, four hours to Cladyford and, making up their lines well enough, standing firm when the Irish loosed off some shots from the other side of the Finn. But then the cavalry crossed the river and came down on them.

Even experienced soldiers found it difficult to set up their "hedges" of pikes and stand firm against cavalry. He had stood in lines of pikemen himself, outside Tangier when the French charged. Five hundred horsemen pounded down on them in an indescribable rush and thunder. It was the sound and sight of hell, or the Apocalypse, coming at you, coming for you, full tilt. He had been too terrified to run, even if he had been able to find a way out of the silent, dense formation. The cavalry hit the pike wall in an explosion of gore. He couldn't tell if it was the men or the horses who screamed the louder. He got a wound that day that nearly did him in. The line held, but only just. And they had been veteran soldiers, long adapted to the mortal vagaries of battle. No wonder these Londonderry men had buckled—city merchants and tradesmen, farmers from both sides of the Foyle who had run for safety behind the city's walls. Memories of the slaughter of the Great Rising and Cahir O'Doherty's massacres were still fresh enough in every Protestant's mind.

He had always thought, when you came right down to it, that Londonderry was indefensible. True, it had the river on one side, the bog on the other. But its fundamental flaw to his soldier's eye was that it didn't have the high ground. It was on a hill, but all around it, higher hills loomed. That was where the Irish would set their siege pieces and mortars and pound away at them. Still, he was the city's governor, and he'd done what he could to get it ready: cleared the dunghills away from the walls, demolished the nearby houses so that attackers would have no cover, strengthened the battlements, set up a gallows on the southwest bastion to give would-be mutineers something to think about, and ordered a ravelin to be built by the Bishop's Gate, the most vulnerable part of their perimeter. At least it gave the defenders a clear field of fire to turn back sappers trying to lay a mine, or fusiliers rushing in with ladders to scale the wall. And he'd constructed an outer line of defence in that direction—earthworks from the Windmill down to the river—which would give the men on the walls some breathing space when the assaults came. But he'd put his reliance on defusing the attack before it got close to the city's inadequate fortifications: a sally in force to stop the Irish as they tried to cross the rivers. Soldiering was his profession, and he knew all about this classic military tactic. Forward defence in the form of daring offence was always better than defending close in, which meant your enemy already had his hands halfway round your throat. Boldness might carry the day, even though most of his troops were raw as pulled turnips.

And so he'd led his companies, seven or eight thousand men, south to the fords on this arse-freezing April morning in time to set them up on good ground. From what he could see, they out-

numbered the Irish force, but it was made up of regular soldiers
and fierce kerns. It had good French generals, too, whose expert-
ise he'd suffered from before. The Irish cavalry was among the
best in Europe, and it was his real worry. He had good reason.
They swam their horses fast across the Finn. When they made
their textbook charge, no more than six hundred of them, yelling
in Irish, their three-line battle formation holding all the way, the
massed thousands of the English and Scots settlers of Londonderry
wasted no time. They cut and ran.

And that decided it for him. He had been balancing on the edge
of a knife anyway—in fact, on more edges than one. He was an officer in James's Catholic army; then, as things got confused, he found
himself with a commission from the Protestant king, the Dutchman,
William, to govern and defend the city against James. Two kings on
one side and the damned reformed-church zealots of Londonderry
on the other, with their long memories of bloody 1641, their hatred
and fear of the Catholic mere Irish. Protestants had been planted on
this wild-wooded frontier that swarmed with armed Irish kerns—
bandits and rakehells—tending their own long memories of dispossession by the Plantation. The settlers were out on the very edge of
things, far beyond any pale. He had had no peace from these hard
men, who questioned his every decision. They saw betrayal and traitors everywhere. The city was not yet surrounded, but its people
were already under siege—they had been, in fact, from the day they
laid its walls' first stones.

He had no choice but to make for Londonderry himself. He
would send back the English relief regiments, which were not far
away now. There was no sense in bringing them, too, into this trap.
He would sue for terms and surrender, and march his own men back
east to the Protestant heartland across the River Bann with their
arms and colours and honour intact. Only fanatics fought on when
there was no chance. He was a professional, and he knew a hopeless
cause when he saw it. He was finished with this damned place.

2

THE TRAITOR

THAT'S ONE WAY of looking at it. That might have been the way it was at the battle of the fords. It could have been Robert Lundy's version of things, part of his narrative of himself, his story.

History says otherwise. In this case, "history" means Robert's contemporaries inside Derry. They portray Robert as a traitor who conspired with the advancing Catholics, and a fifth column of fellow travellers within the walls, in a cunning and elaborate plot to betray his fellow Protestants and hand the frontier city over to the Catholic Irish army and its king. In the context of seventeenth-century religious politics and the brute fact of Protestant settlers planted on Catholic Irish land, this decision might be no mere political treachery, with one faction gaining power at the expense of another. It might trigger wholesale butchery of the Protestants, soldiers and civilians alike; that had happened before, even in living memory, in the Great Rising of 1641. In those days, surrendered cities might be well treated; but, more often, rampaging undisciplined troops and bands of kerns turned them into abattoirs. The English—above all, the death-angel, Cromwell—were the master practitioners of that approach. Protestants and their reformed church hung on by a thin thread in the remote and hostile west, far away from their safer redoubt of Antrim and Down. From the woods, the hills, and bogs, the Gaels watched, as they awaited their next chance.

Some modern revisionist historians are kinder to Robert: he was a pessimist and a defeatist, maybe an incompetent. The most generous analysis of his actions—at Clady ford, and throughout the events leading up to the siege of Derry—is that he was a skilled and honest soldier whose preparations before the siege made the difference in the city's endurance of it. But his nerve broke after the debacle at the fords, when his thousands of amateur pikemen and musketeers buckled in terror under the charge of a few hundred wet Irish cavalry.

We don't know which of these versions of Robert is accurate. The evidence was in long ago, but perhaps it isn't complete. Maybe its interpretation has been defective for reasons of politics or religion or personal animosity. The events around Derry's walls are more than three hundred years in the past. Over such a long time, things shift and slip. The memories of those who were there were always unreliable. Some of the men who libelled Robert in their written accounts had reasons to shift attention away from themselves. They had their own ambiguous actions to account for, which might well have called into question their own steadfastness and loyalty to the Protestant Dutch king, William. But if Lundy was a traitor—*the* traitor—then that would explain all the ambiguous goings-on behind the walls, as the people died of siege-shot, starvation, and the bloody flux. There would be one straightforward reason for all that went wrong or that didn't look right in retrospect: a scapegoat. The complex, unsettling, real course of things could be reduced to one clear, satisfying, and, above all, simple story.

There are other complicating ingredients in this stew of a narrative. The siege happened when the various peoples contending for land and a place in Ireland had already co-opted history (or the attempt it represents to get at some kind of truth) for propaganda. The Gaelic Irish—who for all intents and purposes now included the descendants of the "Old English" Anglo-Norman invaders and settlers of the twelfth to fifteenth centuries (more Irish than the Irish, and Catholic, too)—had their agenda; and so did the Anglo-Scots settlers of the Plantation. The siege of Derry was yet another epochal chapter in the book each side was composing to justify its existence in Ireland, although the Protestant version of the siege is set out in half-a-dozen accounts, and the Catholics produced only a scanty record of it.

There's no doubt that the outcome was momentous for each people. For the Catholic Irish, Derry was, in part, one more lost battle among many. But if the ill-equipped, hungry, wet, diseased, and inexperienced besiegers had been able to breach the walls and overrun the stubborn, even more debilitated defenders, perhaps that would have been the miraculous thing that changed everything: the beginning of ruin for the Protestant people of Ulster and the restoration of the Gaelic ascendancy. Probably not, though. As they always had, the English would keep coming, their greater cohesion and stronger purpose giving them the upper hand in the end. They were aggressive and warlike, imperialists to the core, with a fast-developing sense of racial superiority and manifest destiny. And they had an overriding need to secure Ireland, the slippery, alien, papish entity on their western sea-border which was an open door for their French or Spanish enemies to walk through. Even the fall of Derry wouldn't have altered that.

It was different for the city's Protestants. Although they, in turn, were rancorously divided into Anglicans and Presbyterian Dissenters, most of them thought the same thing: lose Derry and they lost their land, maybe their lives. They had their backs to the wall there. Across Ulster, they had their backs to the sea. By all means, No Surrender! Surrender meant destruction. The survival of Derry was, they believed, a simple necessity, and the alternative, unthinkable. If they could survive that siege, they could withstand the longer, perhaps endless, siege to come. Small wonder they considered anyone who betrayed that profound cause to be a great traitor indeed.

There are surviving likenesses of almost all the prominent men of the siege of Derry. The kings, of course: James and William, looking much alike in their ringlet wigs and lacy ruffles, with their long noses and pickle-sour gazes. James is often shown in full armour with jewelled sword, cradling a battle-axe with awkward unfamiliarity. He looks as though he can't wait to get back to the warm, comfortable embrace of women and courtiers, the bountiful table of meat and wine. William wears royal robes and a golden chain in one painting and looks intelligent (kings seldom do), more scholarly than kinglike. It's difficult to imagine him splashing across the River Boyne on horseback and standing his ground among his Protestant mercenaries throughout the thickest of the fighting in 1690. Nevertheless, he did so. But not James, at the head of the Catholic army, who fled the ground and earned the contempt of his own men as well as the enemy's. The intense irritations and provocations of the modern Twelfth of July parade celebrations by Protestants in Northern Ireland commemorate the Battle of the Boyne. It wasn't the most decisive clash in the war between William and James, but the Protestants remember 1690 mostly because it was their king who stood and fought with courage, and it was the papish bastard who ran.

There are also paintings of the kings' commanders. The Duke of Tyrconnell, made Lord Deputy of Ireland by James, purged the Irish army of Protestants, turning it into a Catholic force that the hardline men of Derry could never trust. Tyrconnell was a duellist and a rake; in one portrait, he wears his robes of state, stares with cold hauteur, and looks more like a king than the kings do.

His deputy, the Protestant Lord Mountjoy, in working doublet and high ruffle collar, resembles the honest broker he tried to be. Tyrconnell sent him to Derry to persuade the city to surrender. Distrust and suspicion soon did in the agreement they made. One of the lieutenant-colonels of Mountjoy's regiment was a former member of the Royal Scots of the Earl of Dumbarton, a veteran of the siege of Tangier, a Scottish Protestant professional soldier called Robert Lundy.

We know what many of the prominent men of Derry looked like, too: the fleshy-faced Anglican clergyman George Walker, whose amplitude was no doubt reduced by his siege diet of boiled cowhide and sewer rats. There are the austere soldiers Henry Baker and John Michelburne. Baker became governor of the city after Robert, with Walker as either joint-governor or a glorified storeskeeper depending on who's writing the account. Michelburne succeeded to the governorship when Baker died of disease. Portraits of the Scottish settler Adam Murray, a farmer (although he may have been a soldier earlier in his life), seem to convey the man's intransigence and his energy. The city's war chief during the siege, he turned out to be a naturally bold and sound tactician whose specialty was fast, audacious sallies out of the walls. These raids, in which he deployed cavalry and foot soldiers in intuitive classic harmony, helped keep the hungry, wet (it was a particularly bad Irish summer), and demoralized besiegers off balance. Murray foreshadows the hard Protestant men of twentieth-century Northern Ireland. His position was consistent throughout the siege: "unwavering resistance"; no negotiations; no surrender.

All the main actors in the drama have faces, but the man who became the symbolic centre of it all has none. There's no record of Robert's appearance or demeanour: no etchings, paintings, or portraits, no representations of him in the great panoramic paintings of scenes of battle during the siege. He is faceless, a visual mystery. We'll never be able to examine his features in search of signs of trustworthiness or instability. How ever to judge a man never seen? The face always tells a story—although it's as likely to lead astray or even to fool completely as to show a limpid window into the soul. We can fix Robert with any aspect we desire.

In a painting, dated around 1830, celebrating the siege of Derry, the unknown (and mediocre) artist shows Robert as an effigy carried in a tumbril and about to be burned. Superimposed over half of his body is the form of the Devil, naked and with horns sprouting from his forehead. Both Robert and Lucifer sport the same grotesque, grimacing face.

It is similar to the face on Robert's effigy, which is burnt each year as the climax of the Lundy Day parade in Derry. This event marks the pivotal moment in the city's apotheosis: the closing of the gates against the enemy outside and the expulsion of the traitor. Robert's effigy has a crude cartoon face: black button eyes with huge, arching black eyebrows; a black, rictal grinning mouth; and all set off by two bright-red rouged cheeks. The great traitor of the Protestant tribe has been stuck with the absurd, garish features of an oversized doll. This grotesque figure would give the parade a complete air of folkish carnival if not for the celebration's deadly history and the accompanying paraphernalia, even as it takes place today: five-hundred armed police; fifty armoured Land Rovers; barricades along the route; the army outpost nearby; the helicopter and spotter plane overhead; the Lambeg drums' loud rattle; the angry, derisive Catholic crowd; hatred and disgust clogging the air; the sense of violence immanent.

———

The Reverend George Walker was the man who got his "quick-and-dirty" version of history out there first. Within months of Derry's relief in 1689, he published his diary, entitled *A True Account of the Siege of Londonderry*. In it, he condemns Robert Lundy as a coward and a betrayer, but he displays at times an odd, and tantalizing, ambivalence about him. After the siege, Walker would intervene in the official investigation of Robert's actions to keep him away from Derry as a venue for a trial. Perhaps the supposed traitor was a man who knew a little too much for comfort about the Reverend's own actions. Walker also attributes a great deal of Derry's survival to his own exertions and stiff backbone. The supposed hero of the siege became, for a while, a lion of English "society." But his book caused a clamour of outraged scoffing from other siege survivors. There were so many objections that, later in the same year, Walker had to publish an aggrieved supplement: *A Vindication of the True Account of the Siege of Derry*.

However, the next year, in 1690, the Reverend John Mackenzie, a Presbyterian who had been a chaplain to one of the city's regiments, published his version of the story: *A Narrative of the Siege of Londonderry*. Its express purpose, he writes, is to set the record straight in the face of Walker's egregious errors and omissions. The disputed view of history held by Mackenzie, the nonconformist, and Walker of the established church reflects their intense intra-Protestant sectarian animosity. Mackenzie, for example, points out that Walker lists all the Anglican ministers who endured the siege and those who died, but is somehow unable to remember the names of the more numerous Presbyterian ministers who fought and fell, even after six months of close cohabitation with them. He misspells several of the names he does manage to recall. In one odd and childish example, the Reverend Gilchrist becomes "Kil-Christ." Walker may claim to have done great and glorious things during the siege, writes Mackenzie, but, in fact, "Governor Baker had been pilfered of several of his merited plumes, and Mr. Walker adorned with them." And it was Adam Murray, the dashing—and Presbyterian—cavalry leader, who really saved the city: he was the one who confronted Lundy and his council of appeasers, telling his fellow-Scot that he was either a fool or a knave. Murray stopped the surrender and set Derry on its course of resistance—and its eventual symbolic fame.

Mackenzie also alludes to Walker's somewhat diffident treatment of Robert Lundy. In fact, says Mackenzie, Walker "speaks very guardedly" (that is, protectively) of Lundy's behaviour. And did not Walker try to persuade Lundy to stay on as governor after his attempted betrayal and then help him to flee the city when he declined? Mackenzie insinuates that the traitor might, indeed, have some stories of his own to tell about the self-advertised heroism of the unreformed minister. As for Lundy himself, Mackenzie proposes a choice: the governor's "ill conduct" was due either to negligence or to design. "The reader must be left to judge." Mackenzie himself opts for treachery.

Robert has no face, but he has left some words—not many, and not anything like an account of his part in the affair. He was not one of those military commanders who lead action-filled lives along the imperial borders, putting down the uppity natives, building up the body-counts, and then retire to some tranquil country house to recall, and to justify with huffy querulousness, their bloody lives. On the contrary, Robert is taciturn and utilitarian to the end. A few of his letters remain, ones he wrote to other commanders in the days leading up to the siege, when he was scrambling to get the city in some way prepared for it and trying to interdict the approaching Irish army. These messages contain the concise, soldierly directions of the colonel to his subordinates and fellow-officers. They are literate in the style of the times, full of politesse and elegant compound sentences. There are also Robert's paraphrased statements to the Parliamentary Committee of Inquiry set up after the war to find out what happened in Derry, why the besieging army was allowed to get close to the city, and why the siege went on for so long without relief when relief was available. He wrote several letters to influential peers (Lords Melvill, Shrewsbury, Dorset, and Monmouth), asking for their help in getting him out of the Tower of London on a writ of habeas corpus. He was being held there pending the inquiry's outcome. Finally, Robert may have had some part in composing the resolutions put out by the Council of War, of which, as governor of the city, he was the head. More likely, however, they are the compilations by the council's secretary of its discussions.

Nothing else remains on the historical record of Robert's own words, except for those few scattered exclamations or paraphrases cited by Walker and Mackenzie. "You are all cut off! Shift for yourselves!" they have Robert shout in a panic at the Battle of the Fords. "Gentlemen, I see you will not fight," he reportedly cries during his last sally to confront the Irish army as it closes with the walls—even though, Robert's detractors assure the reader, the men of Derry were most willing and, indeed, eager to fight.

Robert never replied to George Walker or John Mackenzie or the other self-interested narrators of the siege who vilified his character. Perhaps the soldier knew another hopeless cause when he saw it. The only defence he mounted was contained in his testimony to the Parliamentary Inquiry and in his letter of supplication to Lord Melvill (to whom he seems to have been related). He restricts it to a single reasonable argument: if he had had the least intention of betraying Londonderry to the Irish, would he have fled from the city to Scotland at his life's hazard? Surely if he were a traitor, he would have gone over to the Irish in expectation of his just rewards and promotion. All men of honour knew that the charges against him had to be false. He concluded by asking the peer to request some ready money from the King; the Tower was a very expensive place to put up in, and the cost would ruin him and his family in short order without some help.

We know only a few things about Robert before and after his time of fame and infamy at Derry. It seems impossible that a man who became a malign symbol to a whole people can be almost anonymous (although, on second thought, perhaps that's a helpful precondition). It's as if he fell out of dim-lit shadow into the glare and clamour of sectarian war in Ireland, and when he'd served his mythic purpose, he slipped back into the same obscurity. And another odd thing: his military career before and after Derry was filled with honour, commendations, and acts of courage. It was only during the city's siege that anything uncomplimentary was said about him. And there, the apparently good and competent soldier was suddenly and unaccountably a bungling coward and a traitor. Or so the respectable Protestants of Derry had it. In any event, only a few scattered details bracket the very public, examined two years or so of Robert's life.

He came from Fife, the peninsula of flat lands and low hills on the east coast of Scotland between two estuaries: the Firth of Tay and the Firth of Forth. It juts out into the North Sea, which Robert's ancestors certainly crossed from Norway or Denmark. The Norse longboats made their direct passage to this coast with its obvious, inviting river mouths long before they found Ulster, although no bloody-handed legends attest to it. The name "Lundy" comes from the Norwegian "Lundin," which is still a name there. Its root, "Lund," is common throughout Scandinavia. "Lundy" is a word in modern Danish and means "puffin." Lundy Island in the Bristol Channel used to be a puffin rookery, before the birds died off from various toxins. Like many of the people of Ireland, Robert comes from the Vikings, although, in his case, he's seven or eight centuries removed from them.

He came from a well-connected, landed family. They had estates, a coat-of-arms (its motto was *Iusticia*—Justice), and a castle at Balgonie, although the family had lost it by Robert's time. His grandfather, Andrew Lundy (or Lundin—both versions of the name appear), was a younger son of a previous Robert, and he had friends in high places. One account says that Andrew "was much with James VI and in a good degree of favour." He accompanied the King to England when the Scottish monarch succeeded Elizabeth in 1603 and became James I of England. But Andrew spent too much time living it up in the palmy south and had to mortgage a good chunk of his estate, even though he also had a generous royal bounty. It seems that the Catholic king liked the company of his boozy, good-time Protestant countryman.

Andrew's eldest son, David, was a different matter. He began a family tradition and joined the army. He was the inheriting son, but his father must have left him little to live on. It was the time of civil war. There were casualties and, therefore, openings, and he rose fast to be a captain. He was also, says the chronicle, "a gentleman of courage, prudence and industry," and frugal, too—that supposed Scottish trait his father had conspicuously lacked. No king sought out David's reserved, perhaps dour, company. In any event, David's frugality got back his father's estranged estate and then more, through purchase and marriage, both canny. He had two sons (daughters are never mentioned in this genealogical record). George was the elder, and he inherited the beefed-up Lundy holdings. Robert was the second son, and here his fragmentary story begins.

We presume he had the perennial problem of all non-inheriting sons—how to make a living—and solved it by joining the army, as his father had done. He became a captain in the Earl of Dumbarton's regiment (also known as the Royal Scots), which had been raised in and around the town of that name in the west, on the Clyde, not far across the water from Ulster.

Robert makes a momentary break from obscurity when his regiment is recorded as fighting the French when they besieged Tangier, in Morocco. Robert was wounded in action there and saw up close the skills of the French army siege engineers. It must have influenced his later opinion of Derry's vulnerability; he knew that many of the Irish army's generals were French, and he must have assumed they would use the same techniques on Derry as at Tangier. On his return from North Africa, he transferred to the regiment of Lord Mountjoy in Ireland, probably to get a better chance at promotion. Indeed, soon afterwards, he was made a lieutenant-colonel, and his acquaintance with Ireland began.

He was part of an old tradition: Scottish soldiers doing dirty work in Ireland. The Irish kings and chiefs of the eleventh and twelfth centuries recruited soldiers called gallowglasses (from the Gaelic for "foreign warriors") from Argyll and the Hebrides to fight the English invaders. The Scots' specialty was to stand fast with only sword, spear, and battle-axe—no "hedges" of pikes—in the face of cavalry charges and, somehow, break them. Later, in the sixteenth century, the Highlander redshanks (they went bare-legged in kilts in all weather) in the pay of the O'Neills and the O'Donnells of Ulster slaughtered English soldiers and settlers. They became so troublesome that the English maintained a small fleet in the North Channel to intercept their boats and finally paid some of them off to stay home.

Things had changed in the late seventeenth century. The conquest of Ireland had been complete for eighty years, and the refractory Ulster Gaelic lords were dead, or dispossessed and in exile, or running war parties of wood kerns. Some were trying to make the best of things under the new regime. Robert was a Scottish officer in an Irish regiment and part of England's occupying army. Mountjoy gave his new lieutenant-colonel command of a company stationed in the far north of Donegal at Castledoe on Sheep Haven Bay. The remote castle had withstood twenty sieges over the years, and any garrison there was buried deep among the wild Irish. The following year, in September, 1685, Robert and his men were brought in from the cold and moved to Derry. He remained in Ulster until the events of 1688 and 1689.

At some time during these years, he married. He was the younger son of landed Scottish gentry, a grandson of a man who had boozed for years with the King of England and Scotland, a travelled man of the world, a wounded soldier, and a commander of men. Maybe he was handsome, too, or talked a good game. Anyway, he did well. His wife was Martha Davies, a daughter of the Anglican dean of Cork. Perhaps Robert proverbially swept the clergyman's cosseted daughter off her feet. There are no details of how they met or where—Cork is at the other end of Ireland from grim Derry. They had at least two children, a son and a daughter. The son is nameless, but he, too, eventually joined the army. He became a captain, and maybe reached a higher rank—that's all that's recorded about him. Perhaps he remained in Ireland and founded a line there. The daughter has a name (finally a named daughter) and one entry in the Lundy file. Robert must have died in or just before July 1717, because on the twentieth of that month, his daughter, Araminta Somers, who had been baptized in Derry cathedral on May 17, 1686 (which gives a clue to when Robert and Martha were married), petitioned that a £200-a-year pension be transferred to her.

The military tradition, and its consequences, continued in Robert's collateral family. Two of his three nephews joined the army. John, who had attended the university of St. Andrews, got a commission in his uncle's old unit, Lord Dumbarton's Regiment. He was killed at the age of twenty-five at the battle of Sedgemoor in Somerset in 1685, a Protestant soldier fighting for the Catholic King James II against the Protestant Duke of Monmouth—a nonsectarian death, at least. Robert's youngest nephew, David, was "a captain in the war in Ireland and died with the character of a very brave man." The chronicle doesn't specify when. It was a long war.

3

RÍ *SEAMUS* AND RÍ *LIAM*

IN TIME, the Protestants came to see Derry's endurance as the glorious symbol of their resistance to Catholic domination in Ireland. The siege is a living inspiration to the hard-line Protestants of Northern Ireland today. God was on their side in 1689, and He's on their side now. At Derry, they believe, the chosen people of Ulster began the heroic story of their defiance of evil and the preservation of what they still refer to as their "way of life." In his *History of England,* Thomas Macaulay, one of the main creators of the symbol the siege became, wrote: "The wall of Londonderry is to the Protestants of Ulster what the Trophy of Marathon was to the Greeks . . . the whole city is to this day [1855] a monument of the great deliverance."

In fact, there was no need whatsoever for a siege of Derry—no good, or even sufficient, military or strategic reason to attack it. The siege happened only because of a king's stubborn stupidity, and its prosecution by both sides was a shambles. If Robert was, in fact, incompetent, he was far from being alone. (And, of course, incompetence is much the rule rather than the exception in warfare, because soldiers are sometimes stupid, and because waging war is so difficult and unpredictable an enterprise that few men are up to its demands.)

The Irish-Catholic besiegers were a levy of green and unblooded Irish recruits, barely trained, with hardly a musket among twenty men. They were supposed to conduct a siege but didn't have nearly sufficient cannon with which to carry it out. They needed heavy guns to batter down the walls of Derry, low and exposed but eighteen feet thick, designed to deter disgruntled, lightly armed kerns, not an up-to-date army. And the weapons the Irish did have weren't much use because no one knew how to use them properly. Some of the Irish army's generals were French—provided by the Sun King, Louis XIV, to his brother Catholic King James II. These professionals may have shone when they were wheeling orderly veteran formations around the Continent's tidy ground, but Ireland baffled them. The country was wild and rough. Their Irish troops were undisciplined and often could speak only Gaelic—an incomprehensible gabble to French ears. In a dispatch, the French ambassador complained that "never have troops marched like this lot; they came like bandits and plunder all that they find in their path." The Irish officers were strange: often uncooperative with orders and resistant to advice. The weather was awful. Summer was only a word. The siege took place during that alleged season, but it was cold and it rained. Even by Ulster standards, it was a very wet summer. The troops had to live in leaky mud hovels and in tents that streamed water. Supply lines were unreliable and food scarce—at times, the Irish were as hungry as the Prods inside the walls. Ammunition was scarce, too, even though there weren't many guns to supply. To the French generals, the country and its people seemed alien and remote in a way that no European country was. Of course, camp fever (mostly typhus, but cholera and scurvy appeared, too) got in among them right away. As always, a few men died in battle and many by disease—that happened no matter where a campaign was conducted. The Irish army's commanders had to bring fresh troops up to Derry all the time. Even though about 25,000 men spent time around Derry at one time or another during the siege, there were seldom more than 10,000 to 12,000 men there at any one time—not many more than the defenders could muster.

The only exception to this gloomy catalogue was the Irish cavalry. They had carried the day with ease at the Battle of the Fords when the massed Derry infantry broke and ran. But with a city under siege, you needed big guns to pound the walls, sappers to dig the trenches under fire and set the mines, and, as always, infantrymen—the gruntish boots on the ground—to rush forward and do the close-combat dirty work. Cavalry was a flashy ornament in a siege force.

In fact, this was one siege in which the defenders inside the walls were, for part of its duration, in better shape than the besiegers outside. The Protestants were better armed, had real shelter, and, even for some time after the close investment of the city got under way in April, 1689, were better fed. The real question is why the 7,000 or 8,000 amateur and professional soldiers of Derry (there may have been as many as 10,000 fighting men at the beginning of the siege) didn't stream out from their walls one day through the Bishop's and the Butcher gates, sweep the Irish off the surrounding hills, and send them packing.

The answer is simple: the Protestant leaders in command were mostly as inept, befuddled, and indecisive as the Catholic ones (perhaps not excepting Robert). They did have some grounds for caution and pessimism: they always overestimated the strength of the Irish army (even Robert, an experienced soldier, did that), and they believed it to be a well-trained professional force under veteran French officers. That judgment was formed in part by their direct, devastating experience of the Irish cavalry at the Fords. And perhaps the men of Derry weren't worth much themselves as fighting men, as Robert claimed at the time and later. Or maybe they were, and there's something to the judgment against Robert that, in spite of his reputation before and after Ireland—at Tangier, Gibraltar, and in Portugal—he was incompetent and defeatist at Derry. Perhaps, at the very least, he did lose his nerve after his men ran at Cladyford. Some of the Derry forces did very well under Adam Murray, the talented, no-surrender Scottish amateur cavalryman. When he made his sallies out to the battles north at Pennyburn Mill and south at the Windmill to try to take pressure off the city's walls, his men fought with determination and skill. Probably, as in any battle, some men fought with bravery; others broke. It's impossible to know much for certain because the events of the siege were fraught with ideology and politics and lies from the moment they occurred.

The defenders of Derry had another debility. They were far from the united community of Protestants that the siege-myth proposes: 30,000 (the number is almost certainly exaggerated) resolute refugees and fighting men within the walls bound together for the common purpose of resisting the Catholic "tyrant," James, and his Catholic "slaves." In fact, in Derry, there were many discordant factions. The split between Presbyterians and the established Anglican Church of Ireland had the bitter whiff of schism and heresy. These were post-Reformation Christians who regarded each other as little better than devil worshippers. The two churches did manage to agree to a schedule for each of their services in Saint Columb's Cathedral—one in the morning, one in the afternoon—and that is cited as proof of their unity. In fact, they disagreed on almost everything else.

There were secular divisions, too. Robert's detractors make it clear that he didn't act alone. He was the *über*-traitor, but he had the help of others within the city: clever, devious conspirators, or gullible marks, or cowards and defeatists, depending on which version of Robert's motivation is believed. George Walker is circumspect in describing his own dealings with Robert. John Mackenzie, the Presbyterian, all but accuses Walker, as well as Robert, of trying to deal with the enemy (and Walker of hoarding stores for himself towards the end of the siege when the city was starving). Many of the defenders did come together with courage and defiance, but the city was never united in its purpose. It was riven with religious differences, fear, defeatism, and by a genuine sense of loyalty to the legitimate king—the succession had passed to James according to law. No wonder the Protestants had a hard time getting together to engage the debilitated Catholic army roosting in misery on the cold, wet surrounding hills. For many reasons, neither side was able to fully engage the other.

None of this would have mattered, or happened at all, if the Catholic army hadn't been perched on the hills in the first place. It didn't need to be, but the dithering, supercilious, and vainglorious King James II had decided that he had to overcome Derry. To be fair, James had had his good moments: he had a reputation for courage as a soldier in the 1650s and as a naval commander in the 1660s. Perhaps age had made him timid and skittish, or his recent experience of having been driven off the English throne—that might change a man. But his decision made no sense. He should have made for Scotland with as many Irish soldiers as he could find.

His French, and most of his Irish, generals advised him to do just that. He was James VII there, and he could have got an army together that might have had a chance of getting back the English throne before William could get established. He might find enough Scottish soldiers like the Lundys to make a fight of it. If he got England back, Derry and its stiff-necked Prods wouldn't matter a jot.

The Catholic James succeeded to the thrones of England, Scotland, and Ireland in 1685, four years before the siege of Derry began, when his Protestant brother, Charles II, died. In England, James's policy of favouring fellow Catholics aroused Protestant opposition. The most serious reaction came in the same year as James's accession, when the Protestant Duke of Monmouth staged an armed rebellion. James's loyal commanders defeated Monmouth at Sedgemoor, the battle in which Robert's nephew, John Lundy, was killed, fighting in the Earl of Dumbarton's regiment.

The reaction of Irish Protestants to James's policy was a complicated one. There was almost no support among them for Monmouth. In fact, Arthur Rawdon, who, a few years later, became a prominent officer in the army of William of Orange, offered James a regiment to fight against the insurgent Protestant Duke. These were other signs of general ambivalence about the Catholic king. In the atmosphere of sectarian animosity of the time, any religion would feel apprehension, sometimes outright fear, at the ascendancy of another. As the minority in Ireland, Protestants were always aware of their vulnerability among the Catholic majority, which viewed them as usurpers of native Irish land and power. However, the Protestants were far from being a monolithic mass more or less of one mind in opposition to James—which is how the standard received story usually treats them. The Protestants in Ireland in the late 1680s were confused about who they were and where their loyalties lay—not unlike Ulster Protestants three hundred years later.

Any ambivalence in England about James evaporated when he fathered a son, thus making the beginnings of a Catholic dynasty. The powerful faction in England that wanted to secure the Protestant succession had had enough. In 1688, seven Protestant notables invited James's son-in-law, the Dutch prince, William of

Orange (in the complicated religious affiliations of the day, he was married to the Catholic James's Protestant daughter, Mary), to invade and take the kingdom as joint monarch with Mary. William was already a very busy prince, but England was an offer he couldn't refuse. The country and, later, Ireland as well became parts of William's grand international strategy to stymie the ambitions of Louis XIV. It was a *realpolitik* chess board: Louis had designs on the Spanish Netherlands, which in turn threatened William's homeland, the United Provinces (the independent Netherlands); William had helped form a coalition with Catholic Spain and Austria, which was supported by the Pope (favouring a Protestant prince over a Catholic king); Louis had managed to buy English neutrality in all these manoeuvrings; but William saw the invitation to assume the English throne as a chance to complete Louis's encirclement and deprive him of a potential ally—England or Ireland. Keeping all this in mind, the war between William and James in Ireland (in Irish, it's the war of the two kings: *Rí Seamus* and *Rí Liam*) was important far beyond the outcome there. And it sets the stage for the Irish Protestant view (and also Macaulay's) that the siege of small Derry was a monumental event and that, in enduring it, the Protestants of the city made world history. It was no backwater or sideshow.

When William landed in England on Guy Fawkes' Day, November 5, 1688, James panicked and ran to France. Once in Versailles, he was unable to accept the consequences of his precipitous getaway; he decided that he wanted his throne after all. If he had used as much energy and determination to fight William in England, he might have held his kingdom and never needed to plot his return from France. His path back led straight and clear through rebellious, Catholic Ireland.

There, his viceroy—the cold, regal, ruthless Duke of Tyrconnell—was loyal, but not that loyal. He tried to play all sides. It may have been true, as reports said later, that he sent a secret message to Louis: if James did not agree to lead the Irish, then Tyrconnell would hand over Ireland to become a province of France. (No wonder England thought of Ireland as a security risk.) At the same time, Tyrconnell dropped hints in London that he could be persuaded to bring the country over to William.

He soon had to abandon that line of inquiry. Even the all-powerful viceroy couldn't resist the surge of passion throughout the country. The Catholic Irish thought that their time had truly come: *Tiocfaidh ar lá,* indeed. England was in difficulty—it was the time to strike at the Prods: drive them out once and for all; kill them if they wouldn't go. Four-fifths of the country was Catholic, but four-fifths of its property belonged to Protestants. In 1688, there was the sense among the Catholics in Ireland that this was their chance to reclaim their fields and herds, to take over the Protestant towns and cities. They made banners with the words "Now or Never! Now and for Ever!" (in English—it was already the coming language, even for Irish revolution). Perhaps even the heart of Tyrconnell, the crafty survivor, was stirred by their call. In any event, he had no choice, with the people rising around him. They forced him to decide to hold Ireland for James.

In fact, Tyrconnell had made a swift transformation of the country since his appointment as Lord Lieutenant in 1687. He was from an Old English family and, therefore, a Catholic long identified with the Irish cause. He had fought against Cromwell and had just escaped death at Drogheda in 1649, when the Englishman massacred 3,000 people there, including 1,000 civilians, after the city had been promised quarter and had surrendered. That was something a man tended to remember. Tyrconnell (Richard Talbot before his peerage) was in reality a leader of the Catholic Irish, and he used his old intimacy with James as a means of bringing Ireland back to the Irish. James made him head of the army in Ireland, and Tyrconnell purged it of Protestants. He appointed Catholic judges and put Catholics into key posts in the civil administration. He subsidized Catholic bishops and ignored the Protestant church's growing number of vacancies. He revoked town charters and replaced them with Catholic administrations. He planned a parliament in Ireland which would finish off his plan to transfer land and power from the Protestant Plantation settlers and restore it to the Gaelic Irish and their Catholic Old English allies. Tyrconnell's steady progress was a revolution by any other name. It would reverse the conquest.

Even these radical initiatives throughout 1687 and 1688 didn't tip the Protestants in Ireland into unambiguous unity. Protestant landowners, including many in Ulster, supported James. Like all landowners and landlords, they were conservative and valued stability, but they also regarded him as the rightful king, even though the king's deputy, Tyrconnell, was energetically eroding their positions. There were many signs of support: an Ulster Presbyterian minister who preached that the accession of a Catholic king obviated loyalty and invited rebellion was shut up right away by his presbytery; when a group of Protestants tried, unsuccessfully, to seize Belfast in March 1689, twenty-three prominent Protestants sent a letter to Tyrconnell which said: "We will declare ourselves as becomes loyal and obedient subjects"; in Fermanagh, a good percentage of the Protestant gentry held out against declaring for William until they were forced into it by fiercer Prods; in Clare in the south, the Church of Ireland bishop and dean of Killaloe urged the Protestant Sir Donat O'Brien (his name a marker of a past conversion) to accept James as his king and take his appointment as sherriff of the county. The Protestants of Ulster (and of all Ireland, too) were a loose and conflicted coalition of interests and allegiances, far from being the united people of contemporary Northern Irish mythology. With time, however, that would change.

Protestants in 1688 also had a lot more to worry about than Catholic town councils, or even a Catholic parliament. For example, there were the usual intra-Protestant sectarian fears: some Anglican Protestants in Ulster, members of the official Church of Ireland, supported James—and Tyrconnell—because they feared that William's accession to the throne could give the vigorous, fast-growing Presbyterians a leg up and perhaps lead to the disestablishment of the Anglican Church. These were bad years economically. The French imposed duties on wool and butter, the main Irish exports. The weather was poor—the cold, wet Derry siege-year summer of 1689 was one of many in a row. Some Protestants immigrated to England (or, from the Catholic perspective, returned to England), although probably only five percent of a Protestant population of around 300,000 got out. Even fewer Ulster Protestants left. But the ones who did go were the important people with money and something to lose. Their absence was felt, and it created the sense of a large-scale exodus.

Hard times threw more people than usual out onto the streets and fields. Violence, endemic and ubiquitous in Ireland, especially in rural areas, got even worse. For Protestants, it seemed to fit the old pattern: native Irish thievery and assaults, shading here and there into low-scale guerrilla warfare—and always directed against them. The wood kerns—part bandits, part rebels—were always prowling, awaiting their opportunity. More Catholic violence tended to reinforce the old Protestant fears of a general rising. As the year of 1688 went on, rumours bubbled everywhere. Perhaps the Taigs were planning another massacre like 1641. Maybe they were already gathering the pikes and *skeans* (daggers) to gut Prods with at the rising of the moon. Tension tightened into fear, and it grew.

4

PLANTATION

FEAR IS THE DRIVING FORCE of Ulster Protestant ideology—and has remained so for three centuries. Today, the fear in Northern Ireland is mostly a pervasive and inchoate apprehension of change—the sudden descent into minority status in a united Ireland. But for some Protestants, it's also the dread of payback in one form or another for the fifty years of their repressive sectarian government after the island's partition in 1920.

In 1688, things were more straightforward: the Protestants feared that the native Catholic Irish would rise up in a general insurrection and slaughter them. The farther away they lived from the Old English or new settler concentrations—the Pale around Dublin or eastern Ulster, for example—the more they felt their isolation. Derry was one of the faraway places. It is on the border of wild Donegal and lies across the River Bann and over the Sperrin Mountains from safer ground. (Even today, a drive from Belfast to Derry seems to take a surprisingly long time, part of it on narrow, winding roads through unkempt country and isolated towns and villages.) Protestants in that wild west felt exposed and vulnerable. Some of them—especially Scots, who had been sailing across the 20-kilometre-wide North Channel from Argyll to Ulster, seeking living space for generations—lived on plots they had bought from Irish landowners. But, of course, many Protestants were the Plantation settlers sitting on land confiscated from the Catholic Gaels.

We might suppose that the settlers felt guilt as well as fear. But that's certainly an anachronism. The Irish had used the land as pastoralists, grazing their cattle in the old way, or as haphazard agriculturalists. The settlers did a proper job (in their view) of clearing trees and planting the fertile fields. They built neat cottages and tidy, orderly towns. Their countryside looked like England or lowland Scotland, not like the rough fields, or the unameliorated forest, bog, and hills of the Irish. The settlers saw this transformation as an improvement, the land used as it should be, as God intended. The Irish treated the land much as animals did: it was there and they passed over it, but often left little sign of human husbanding. And to the Prods, in any event, the Irish were barbarous, savage. Homesteaders busting sod on the North American prairie in the nineteenth century felt no guilt at having driven off the Indians, in effect ending their civilization. Indians were savages and they were beneath the necessity, the compliment, of feeling guilty about. The Protestants in Ireland felt the same way about the native Irish. Yet in both cases, contempt did not eliminate fear. A despised barbarian was still a barbarian who would creep back, or sweep down, from his wood or mountain and do what these men always did: kill and destroy. The fear of that was always there.

The conquest of Ireland was accomplished by 1603 (through a negotiated settlement, not punishment of the rebels—the Irish had fought well). Large-scale, organized resistance to English forces ceased, if only for the time being, and the Irish kings and chiefs—most significantly in Ulster, the epicentre of resistance—submitted to English power. They remained in their positions at the pleasure of the English, and they became landlords charging their people rent, instead of independent leaders of their people, with land and cattle and splendid little wars and poets to sing about them. The conquest also meant that the old Gaelic warrior society—its language, its legal system, its unique social arrangements—began its long withering. Cultures take longer to die than stars, a poet wrote. But they do die, and Gaelic Ireland began to do just that after the conquest. "The high poets are gone / and I mourn for the world's waning," wrote Dáibhí Ó Bruadair. This is all part of the standard received version of Irish history, but it's true, too.

The conquest also began the Irish tradition of exile, which is really the aristocratic version of emigration. Irish peasants would become immigrants; Irish kings and chiefs went into exile. The difference is that the peasants would be gone for good—their lives lay in London, or Boston, or busting sod on Indian land, for that matter—whereas kings might come back when England's difficulty became Ireland's opportunity.

Four years after the conquest was complete, the last Gaelic leaders—Hugh O'Neill, Red Hugh O'Donnell, and ninety others—sailed for Europe from Lough Swilly (not far from Derry). They had to make a living and they knew how to fight, and not much else. The fledgling tradition of Irish soldiers serving in the armies of Spain and France was firmly established when many of the O'Neills and the O'Donnells and their followers became part of Spain's Irish Regiment. By the mid-seventeenth century, Spain had formed five more Irish regiments, and France an entire Irish Brigade, out of the exiled soldiers of Ireland. Later, they became known as the "Wild Geese." These mercenaries fought foreign wars for their employers for centuries—one of Napoleon III's marshals was called Patrice MacMahon. Sometimes they came home again, skills honed, to fight the English.

The "Flight of the Earls"—O'Neill, O'Donnell, and the others—in 1607 was pivotal enough to earn capital letters in Irish history. And the conquest was finished only when Ulster had been subdued; the province was the heart of the Irish problem then, as it is now. The conquest was not complete, however, in the sense that it made the bewildering complexity of interests and factions in Ireland any simpler, or that it allowed a solution to the problems of governing the country. On the contrary, the conquest arguably made things even more complicated. Worse, it led, through the iron logic of domination and control, to the single most disruptive event in northern Irish history: the Plantation of Ulster.

Plantation had long been the presumed obvious path to security in the country, especially in the north: fill it up with English Prods who would have no interest in risings and who would be eager to join a militia when the Taigs got their second wind. Not least, it would be much more difficult for England's papish enemies—France and Spain—to use Ireland as its backdoor proxy in their imperial power struggles. But the government could do nothing as long as Hugh O'Neill and Red Hugh O'Donnell were still there, resentful, watching their chance, weapons buried somewhere and far from "beyond use." The two Hughs were from, or connected with, the two clans in Ulster that claimed the bloody red hand as their sign and token, and they had lived up to it. As long as they remained in Ireland, the English government would never have dared to put in place the assumed cure for perpetual rebellion in Ulster. The Flight of the Earls was an abdication that made it easy for the English. With their leaders gone, the Gaels would be unable to resist the final solution.

Originally, the Plantation created three distinct populations: the native Gaels, the English Planters, and the Scots, the latter two mainly Protestant but divided into Anglicans and Presbyterians. (The Scots and English would coalesce into one Protestant bloc, for political if not confessional purposes, only in the late nineteenth century.) The three peoples confronted each other over what the historian Ernest Gellner calls the classic questions of an agrarian society: Who has the land? Who holds power? How should God be worshipped? Or, more succinctly, "plough, sword, and book."

The Ulster Plantation was successful in a sense. It wasn't destroyed by war parties of O'Neills and MacDonnells, as piecemeal attempts in the previous century had been. In the longer term, the Ulster settlers were not eventually absorbed by the exotic seductive aspects of Gaelic Irish culture. They didn't become drinking, fighting, cattle-hoarding, storytelling, poetry-spouting warriors. In other words, they weren't like the Vikings, the Normans, and the Old English, who had come as raiders and invaders and, after not much time at all, had gone native.

Nor did the Ulster Plantation become watered down, with the settlers and natives subsiding into a surprisingly relaxed accommodation, as had happened earlier in the southwestern province of Munster. "Lord, how quickly doth that country alter men's natures," wrote the poet Edmund Spenser, who was a Munster Planter himself. His advocacy of harsh measures, and even extermination, to keep the Gaels under control was an attempt to resist his own fear of sliding down into Irishness. It didn't do him much good: there was the usual intermarriage and, within forty years, even Spenser's descendants were Catholic and called themselves Irish. But the settlers of the Ulster Plantation, Protestants and not Catholics like earlier arrivals in the province, drew lines between themselves and the Irish (and among themselves) that remain as clear and unambiguous—and as grotesque—as the steel and wire wall that now separates the sectarian territories of the Falls and the Shankill roads. It seems that Protestantism was able to inoculate new arrivals in Ulster against contracting Irishness.

And that's the reason the Plantation was an obvious and colossal failure. Its rationale was to stabilize Ulster, the most refractory part of Ireland before, and after, the conquest. But, in fact, it had the opposite effect, ensuring that Ulster would never be stabilized. The 1603 conquest hadn't even been "complete" militarily. The Plantation merely began the payments of blood and treasure in the north. England had to make two more conquests of Ulster (and of the rest of Ireland, for that matter) in the seventeenth century—through Oliver Cromwell and William of Orange.

More important, the Plantation turned Ulster, or that part of it that now constitutes Northern Ireland (six of the nine counties), into an "ethnic frontier" between Great Britain and Ireland. The province became the part of the British archipelago whose ethnic and religious mixture, and its resulting violent strains, was (and is) unique. Ulster is still the sore that won't heal. And it won't heal because of the pattern of settlement and religious division that the Plantation created.

Large-scale government schemes involving the movement of hostile populations and land redistribution over a large area rarely work as planned. There was a theory and a practice of plantation, but they were far from the same thing. The theory was simple: kick the natives out; move the settlers in.

The plan for the Plantation belonged to the King, James I, and Sir Francis Bacon, who was a corrupt, later impeached, Lord Chancellor before he became a philosopher: divide the land into three sizes of "proportions" of 1,000, 1,500, and 2,000 acres to be granted to English and lowland Scottish chief planters called "undertakers." These men, in turn, were responsible for bringing settlers over and for building settlements and fortifications to protect them from the encircling Irish. Twenty-eight baronies or precincts were established, of which eight would each go to English and Scottish undertakers, and the remainder, jointly, to important English officials or war veterans and native Irish.

The Plantation did not include three of the nine counties of the traditional province of Ulster. Counties Antrim and Down in the northeast had been partly planted through private schemes. And, thanks to the constant traffic across the North Channel, there were also a great many long-arrived Scots settlers there. Geologically and topographically, the north of Ireland is a continuation of Scotland separated by a few kilometres of salt water. The sea wasn't a barrier, but an easy path between two parts of the same cultural unit. In calm weather, merchants crossed from Scotland to County Down for the day to trade with their kin there. Later, when Ulster Presbyterian ministers were suppressed by the government, their congregations would row across to Scotland on Sundays to attend services, and row back before dark. They had to be devout to do that, but it was possible.

The beautiful, isolated coastal glens of Antrim had, in fact, been formally acquired through a strategic marriage in 1399 by the Macdonnells of Islay, an island just off the Scottish mainland (a less dramatic but much saner method of acquiring land than hacking off your hand and flinging it ashore). In the 1400s, large numbers of Scots from the Mull of Kintyre and the Western Isles settled throughout northeastern Ulster. They weren't Irish, but, unfortunately for the English, too many of these Highland Scots and their descendants were the same unreliable, Gaelic-speaking Catholics they were trying to exclude from the Plantation. (Today, the coast and the glens remain a Catholic, Gaelic, if Scots-like, enclave in the Protestant fiefdom of Antrim.)

In County Monaghan, a separate scheme had already been set up—its Gaelic lord Hugh Roe MacMahon executed, the county garrisoned, and the land parcelled out to government cronies.

The other exception in the Plantation scheme was its treatment of the region between the Bann and the Foyle rivers (mostly present-day County Londonderry). At this area's western edge, on the west bank of the River Foyle, ten kilometres south, upstream from the sea-lough of Foyle, lay Derry (from the Irish *Doire:* "place

of the oaks"). It had long been the site of a monastery, founded by
Saint Colum Cille (Saint Columba in English, yet another Northern
O'Neill by birth) in the sixth century. It became an ecclesiastical centre with a small, dependent settlement. For nine hundred years, it
attempted the role of a tranquil place of Christian works and medi-
tation, but that was impossible in those unquiet centuries. Derry suffered the inevitable raids up the wide-open Foyle by fierce, long-
boated Vikings, and they burned it down several times. The
developing town was an obvious strategic site dominating access to
the interior up the River Foyle from the lough, and it inevitably
attracted the attention of soldiers: the Normans, for example, and
Shane O'Neill, when he rose against the English in the 1560s.

In 1600, the English established a new fortification at Derry (a
previous garrison had abandoned the town after a catastrophic
explosion of the powder magazine), one of a chain of forts set up
across Ulster during the Nine Years War with the O'Neills and the
O'Donnells. English troops marched out to burn crops and slaughter animals—the classic tactic of "civilized" occupying armies
fighting "savage" indigenous guerrillas—to force Irish rebels into
submission by starving their women and children. The tactic
worked, as it usually does.

The King and his Lord Chancellor had a different plantation
plan for Derry and the surrounding country. They offered it to the
City of London and invited the City Guilds to act as a "collective
undertaker." The City had often helped bail out the Crown with
money for its wars, and it had contributed to the costs of the Nine
Years War. The plantation arrangement was, in part, a payback and,
in part, an attempt to use the City's prestige to attract other investors
in the scheme to anglicize, or civilize—it was considered the same
thing—the rebellious north. Both the town of Derry and its county
of Coleraine were renamed Londonderry in 1613 in honour of the
City's participation, a change the native Irish never accepted. One of
the City's obligations was to rebuild the town of Derry.

Rebuilding had become necessary because the Plantation hit a
few snags right away: the native Irish, for example. Their earls had
run out on them, but they were not quiescent. The Plantation's cav-
alier expropriation and division was a clear effort to obliterate their
ownership and entitlement to the land of Ireland, and they knew it.

"There is not a more discontented people in Christendom," wrote an English official to Arthur Chichester, the Lord Deputy.

In 1607, while plans for the Plantation of Derry were in the making, Sir Cahir O'Doherty, the last Gaelic lord of Inishowen (the peninsula west of Derry, formed by Loughs Foyle and Swilly), became a good example of the essential fragility of Anglo-Gaelic relations. He had formally submitted to Elizabeth and had been proclaimed "the Queen's O'Doherty." He had been knighted for his bravery fighting for the English against O'Neill at Augher during the Nine Years War, and he was foreman of the jury that found the earls O'Neill and O'Donnell guilty after their flight. But the English could alienate even this tame Gaelic lord. In the paranoid style of the conqueror, fearing rebellion, they created it. They suspected conspiracy and tried to arrest him for treason. Worst insult of all, an Englishman, Derry's governor Sir George Paulet, struck O'Doherty.

It was just too much. Like any Gaul, Lakota, Zulu, or Maori pushed beyond endurance by the invaders, O'Doherty reacted as a man would in a warrior culture. Perhaps, too, he was full of guilt at his collaboration, and sought redemption in the simplicity of violence. He rose in rebellion, attacked Derry, slaughtered the garrison, killed Paulet, and burned the town to the ground. The English had to hunt him down through the beautiful, rough hills and woods of Donegal. They found O'Doherty the following summer and killed him.

English forces had continually to hunt the kerns who were harassing the Plantation, the operations often taking on the character of a template for later punitive campaigns against uppity aboriginals: like Newfoundland Beothuks, Tasmanians, Tierra del Fuego Indians, or almost any indigenous people you can name, the Irish were often pursued for sport as much as security. Fighting them frequently took on that same air of brutal, reductionist entertainment. Thomas Blenerhasset of Norfolk, who wrote *A Direction for the Plantation in Ulster* in 1610 for the edification of Prince Henry, the son of James I, advocated hunting the Irish wood kerns and Irish wolves alike, together with the former's sympathizers, "and no doubt it will be a pleasant hunt." Blenerhasset's manual was notorious and considered politically incorrect even in its time, but it nevertheless represented a vigorous school of English thought on how to deal with the recalcitrant Taigs.

The practice of the Plantation unexpectedly deviated from its theory in other ways as well. For one thing, the Plantation suffered the same problem as all frontiers: it may have attracted many good, industrious, and enterprising people, but it was also a bolt-hole for wastrels, debtors, felons-on-the-run, con men, younger sons with nothing to lose, loose women, and fancy boys. The Reverend Andrew Stewart of Donaghadee said in 1610: "From Scotland came many and from England not a few, yet all of them generally the scum of both nations. . . . Going for Ireland was looked upon as the miserable mark of a deplorable person, yea it was turned to a proverb, and one of the worst expressions of disdain that could be invented to tell a man that Ireland would be his hinder end."

More seriously for the plan, not enough English colonizers were willing to settle on the frontier. They weren't up to the harsh and dangerous life. It was a problem England would face during its early days in North America as well and, in this respect, as in many others, trying to colonize Ireland was a dry run for America. In both cases, the land was hard and strange, and the barbarous natives were a formidable obstacle. The country and the weather were "found unwholesome to English bodies, more tenderly bred and in a better air," wrote Thomas MacNevin. The Earl of Essex, who had tried a plantation in the 1570s—the Enterprise of Ulster—had grown disgusted with his "adventurers," most of whom, "having not forgotten the delicacies of England and wanting resolute minds to endure the travail of a year or two in this waste country, have forsaken me, feigning excuses to repair home." It's hard to blame them. It wasn't the farming so much as the fighting or, rather, the dying— in frequent attacks by the Irish raiders of Brian MacPhelim O'Neill and Sorley Boy MacDonnell.

English reluctance opened the door for the Scots. The official government policy of settling Protestants in Ulster encouraged more Scots to cross the North Channel. And the policy made it easier for those already there to move farther inland. They spread throughout the north, and this pattern of internal migration became the norm. They soon dominated trade and commerce in Derry, for example, a short coasting sail along the north shore of Ulster to the sea-lough of Foyle.

The Scots settlers were simply hardier than the English. It wasn't that much different trying to coax some crops out of the ground in

Antrim, Down, or farther inland than it had been on stony Islay or the Mull or anywhere in the barren Highlands. In fact, Irish ground was often a damn sight easier to work, and the Scots flourished. For Englishmen coming from the green, rolling West Country of Gloucestershire, Somerset, or Devon, Ireland could be hard and unforgiving. And more of the Scots than the English had been farmers at home and knew what they were doing. During the Earl of Essex's Enterprise of Ulster, the English had been unwilling to plough and plant, and the Irish didn't do much of it anyway. If it had not been for the Scots, who did both, the country would have starved. It was the same in many regions of the Plantation.

The Scots were good for the Plantation in some ways, but they rattled the English, too. There were just too many of them; they began to outnumber the English settlers. The Lord Deputy, Arthur Chichester—when he wasn't hanging wood kerns—disliked and distrusted the Scots. He feared they might overrun Ulster. And worse, they showed a distressing willingness to fraternize with the Irish, who were, after all, fellow Celts. The fraternization may have been mainly for economic reasons, but it threatened to undermine the Plantation's whole rationale, which was based on displacement and segregation. The settlers were supposed to kick the native Irish off the land altogether, or at least make sure they got coastal or exposed land where they could be watched. It wasn't necessarily poorer land—that wasn't part of the Plantation theory—but it worked out that way in practice.

However, a shortage of settlers and the need for labour encouraged the undertakers and their tenants to keep the Gaels around as rent-paying subtenants and labourers. The sons of Gaelic chiefs worked the land their clans had owned—originating the later folk claim that every Irish peasant thought himself the son of a king. The Scots became notorious for making these arrangements with the Irish. The resulting pattern of settlement was not the one envisaged by the theory of the Plantation: neat ethnic blocs that could be defended and that would stabilize, perhaps even civilize, the surrounding marginal Irish. Instead, it was a complete muddle, a hodge-podge of settlers and natives jumbled together. The Prod Plantation was riddled with bitter, debased, disinherited Taigs.

5

THE GREAT RISING

THE PEOPLE OF DERRY had lots to think about in 1688 as the Irish army of James II marched towards them. They may have recalled Sir Cahir O'Doherty's sudden, devastating attack on their city in 1607. Even if it had been carried out because of an arrogant Englishman's blow rather than through a considered plan of rebellion, the result was the same. O'Doherty's former, and still hostile, territory began right outside the Butcher Gate on the west side of the city, where the Catholics, barred from living inside, had settled on the marshy ground of the Bogside. But that had been another generation; there was no one alive who had experienced O'Doherty's shocking attack. In any case, it had been a small local event compared to what had happened in more recent, real, and living memory. If the Derry Protestants were inclined to nervousness in 1688, with another Catholic-Irish army at their throats, it was because of something worse that had befallen their city and, indeed, all of Ulster and parts of the South: the Rising of 1641 and the years of killing and chaos that followed.

The opportunity for the rising came about, as all Irish risings have, with England's difficulty. This time, the problem lay not with some papish European competitor for empire but with a constitutional crisis among the Scots, a pigheaded king (a common condition for kings, it seems), and a militant and intolerant Protestant Parliament. Charles I had long been stumbling down the path to civil war and his own eventual execution. Parliament's demands for power-sharing became so bothersome that he sent the parliamentarians home and ruled without them for eleven years (from 1629 to 1640). But disagreements between himself and the Presbyterian Scots erupted into war in 1640, and Charles was forced to go back to the resentful and vengeful elected men of England to ask for money. He got it, but Parliament extracted the concession of much of his power in return. The Irish and the Old English in Ireland feared that the sudden emasculation of the King might put them in grievous jeopardy: the Catholic worship that Charles had permitted might be in danger from a rejuvenated anti-Catholic Parliament or the anti-Catholic Scots or both; and English secular ambition and the sectarian zeal of Parliament or the Scots could lead to an expanded Plantation.

One or the other of these possibilities might not have been enough to convince the Irish that armed rebellion was a good idea, but both together certainly were. Two of the great questions of seventeenth-century society had been raised yet again: how to worship God, and who held the land. The Irish in Ulster had still not reconciled themselves to the Plantation or to having Englishmen run their lives. With the fight between Charles and Parliament reaching a crisis, the Ulster Irish came to believe that armed resistance was a necessity.

The Rising began, as rebellions and revolutions so often do, with a set of moderate and not unreasonable demands by a relatively privileged class of men—in this case, the native Gaelic families that had, if anything, benefited from the Plantation. They may have been in debt and psychologically toppled by the Plantation and its destruction of the Gaelic-Irish society of Ulster, but they were beneficiaries of the new system as much as its victims. They were loyal to King Charles, they said. In fact, in an attempt to win over more support, they forged a commission from the King approving their rebellion. They wanted guarantees of religious freedom and confirmation of their existing property rights. That they couldn't get such assurance "doth more discontent them than that plantation rule," said one of the Farrells of Longford. The pre-eminent leader of the Rising was, inevitably, another red-hand man—Sir Phelim O'Neill. His title indicates again, as with Sir Cahir O'Doherty's, the irony that rebellions are made by men whom the conquerors have raised up and brought close to their hearts.

The Rising of 1641 was, in other words, at first a rising of the Gaelic gentry. But it continued to follow the usual path of rebellions: other men who were poor, more desperate, filled with rage, with nothing to lose, with old scores to settle, with bloody revenge on their minds, took over. Risings begin, like the French Revolution, with peaceful, if emotional, Tennis Court oaths by lawyers and journalists and end with the Terror and peasant butcheries. Or the moderate liberal reformers who began the Russian Revolution are soon thrust aside by the Bolshevik absolutists who get a quick start on the killing. Soon after the Rising of 1641 had got under way, the gentry lost control of events, and then they themselves were swept along by the spontaneous violence of their undisciplined soldiers.

The native Irish massacred the Plantation settlers, who retaliated with massacres of their own. The upper-class rebels at first spared Scots settlers; even if they were Protestants, they were also not English, which meant a great deal. All the Scots had to do was put a mark above their doors, and they would be spared. The Scots, perhaps out of dislike of the English, but also in the spirit of self-preservation, went along with this discrimination. But that reserve—which cost the rebels tactically—broke down, and the Irish began attacking their fellow-Celts, too. The common Irish had never drawn that much distinction between English and Scots anyway; they were all damned Prod land thieves. The killing took place mostly outside the walls of the fortified Plantation towns and strongpoints, which had been built, after all, with just this disaster in mind.

The violence made radicals of everyone. The Old English, who weren't involved at first (there were few of them in Ulster anyway), soon joined their fellow-Catholics as the campaign spread out of Ulster to the south. There was supposed to have been a coordinated attack on Dublin at the same time as the Ulster assault began, but it was betrayed by a drunken conspirator, Owen O'Connolly. It was not the last time that alcohol would confound an Irish rebellion. Four months into the Rising, the Gaelic gentry were asking for far more than clear legal title to the land they held. By then, they wanted back all the land that had been alienated since the time of Elizabeth's reign—the whole Plantation.

The Rising of 1641 expanded into what variously became known as the Confederate War, the Irish Civil War (not the last of the

name), or the Eleven Years War. Less than forty years after the conquest of Ireland was "complete," the English had to conquer it all
over again. The war became a fight to the finish. It attracted home
some of the Wild Geese. They included, above all, Owen Roe
O'Neill. He was an experienced professional soldier of high reputation who had been fighting for the Spanish in Flanders, and he was
a nephew of Hugh O'Neill, one of the flown earls of 1607. The war
laid waste the country; there was famine and disease. When he came
back to Ireland, Owen Roe was appalled by the state of his ancestral
ground. He said: "It not only looks like a desert, but like hell if there
could be a hell upon earth."

O'Neill won victories by ingenious and brilliant tactics, but there
was that curious self-destructive fragility to the Gaelic effort; they
could never land the final blow. Their disunity was almost a tradition: O'Neill himself ended up isolated from the other Catholic
Royalist confederates and negotiated separately with the English
Parliamentarians. The Confederate War developed into a complicated
and confusing mélange of forces and personalities. The categories
were endless: English, Irish, Scot, royalist, republican, parliamentarian, Presbyterian, Catholic, and Protestant, all mingling in battles,
alliances, argument, and double-cross. O'Neill even helped relieve
the five-month-long siege of the English garrison of Derry by royalist
Catholics in 1649. This was another siege of Derry, but one forgotten and never commemorated because it didn't have the stuff
Protestants needed later to legitimize their position in Ulster; Robert
Lundy's reviled actions in 1689 wouldn't have raised an eyebrow if
he had carried them out forty years earlier.

The war ended when Cromwell crossed to Ireland in 1649 with
his disciplined, shiny New Model Army, relying on supply lines that
actually worked, a naval blockade, and very big guns that could
batter down any fortified wall in Ireland. His campaign was one of
methodical conquest, but of revenge, too. He slaughtered the people
of Drogheda and Wexford because of what he believed the Irish had
done to the Protestants in 1641.

From the moment it began, the Rising was one of those turning
points in Irish history—like the siege of Derry itself—that are rife
with exaggeration, propaganda, and gross, destructive inaccuracy.

It's an event that has stirred up the Irish ever since. But it resonated with Ulster Protestants in particular because it seemed to prove that their deepest fear was justified: that one day, the Irish would turn on them and kill them. And there were the natural corollaries: that on some later day, the Irish would do it again; that the day would never come when Protestants could be sure the Irish would never do it again.

By twentieth-century standards, the numbers are small: at least 2,000 Protestants killed, maybe as many as 4,000. An undetermined number of Catholics killed in revenge. Some events were notorious: four hundred Scots soldiers were massacred near Augher in County Armagh after having been given quarter. A Protestant refugee convoy was forced into drowning near Portadown. Hundreds of Protestants were evicted by force and stripped naked in the brutal winter of 1641—it was one of the so-called Little Ice Age winters. The Irish killed men, women, and children. They destroyed everything that was English: burnt the wooden buildings and tore down the stone ones, slit the cattle's throats, hamstrung the horses, killed dogs if they'd sniffed around English hearths, wrung the necks of chickens if they'd laid eggs for English tables. Later, they killed Scots in much the same way. When the Protestants recovered from the first onslaught, they retaliated in kind: for example, they massacred most of the Catholics living in Islandmagee in County Antrim.

The suddenness of the Rising and the rage of the Irish was harrowing enough, even with "only" a few thousand dead. The exaggerated reports of atrocity during the first months intensified the panic and hysteria. It seemed as though scores of thousands were dying. Estimates at the time ran as high as 100,000 Protestant dead, a ludicrous overstatement, but many of the English and Scots settlers believed it. Later, the Protestant survivors' accounts of the Irish atrocities, the *Depositions* (in thirty-three volumes), became the main—and questionable—source of information about the events of 1641. There's no comparable Catholic account.

A modern historian describes the *Depositions* as resembling "a pornography of violence." They are first-hand stories of eviction, torture, sexual assault, and murder. If the numbers they propose are hyperbolic, the terrible things they recount did happen. And the problem was that, thanks to the Plantation's defective reality, the enemy was inextricably among them. The Irish servant washing his Protestant master's clothes one day was stripping them off the next. The able, if sometimes sullen, field hand (the son of a Gaelic king?) became the stone-cold killer.

The real and ingrained fear formed by the events of that year—what one historian calls its "occult power"—persisted and reverberated in the Protestant subconscious with the same intensity as the penal laws or the Great Famine among Catholics. During the Troubles, when Protestants read the Catholic grafitto on a Belfast wall, *Tiocfaidh ar lá*—"Our time will come"—they inferred its threat, its whiff of violence, in part because of the state of mind that the Rising created and the tradition of remembering that dire winter. Maybe, in Protestant minds, there was even a veiled, if irrational, intimation of massacre, a residue of anxious sweat at three in the morning in the narrow, shoddy, Proddy streets of Belfast or Derry or in the isolated, Union-Jacked, red-handed farmhouses of Fermanagh, Tyrone, and Londonderry. Who knows what might happen where the old hatred runs so deep?

6

SHUTTING THE GATES

As THE YEAR 1688 wound down, the Protestant people of Derry sat uneasy and isolated behind their low walls. Refugees came straggling in every day from smaller indefensible towns and villages and from outlying farms on both sides of the Foyle, people who didn't trust Irish assurances they'd be left alone. There were many women and children, but also able-bodied men who had military experience or who were tough and capable settlers on this English frontier and knew something about using weapons. Word had spread about the mighty Tyrconnell and James II purging their forces of Protestants, making it a Catholic army, gathering their strength. William of Orange landed on the south coast of England in November, and the arrival of a Protestant prince heartened and encouraged the people of Derry, especially when James himself legged it for France without a fight. But that was England, a long way from any Irish shore, and farthest of all from cold, wet, misty Derry. Anything might happen before William could make his way through England to Ireland and then fight his way across the country to secure the city. In Ireland in the meantime, the writ of Tyrconnell and, through him, James, the lawful king, still ran.

Besides that, the Great Rising of 1641 was recent enough to live in vivid, Protestant memory. It would certainly have been in the mind of the Reverend George Walker, the first "historian" of the siege, its self-described hero, co-governor (or stores-keeper) after Robert, and Robert's first libeller. Walker's father had been a refugee from the Rising, making a desperate escape to England in 1641. George was born there during his father's exile and didn't return to Ulster until he was fourteen. Memories of the sudden eruption of violence, fear, and forced flight were like a memento mori in the Walker family. Perhaps no one whose parents had lived through the "Massacre of the Protestants" could react with anything other than suspicion and resistance when another collection of Catholic Irish levies came down on Derry from its surrounding hills. No Ulster Protestant could ignore those corollaries of the Rising: that it could happen again; that they could never be sure it would not. By the winter of 1688, Derry was full of such people.

All they had to do was to look around them, to lend an ear to the susurrations of disaffection throughout Ulster. There was no need for Catholics to scrawl an anachronistic grafitto on the city walls rearing over the Bogside. If the Protestants listened carefully, they could almost hear the hum of the coming time—the background noise of a resurgent Gaelic energy.

There were rumours: at masses in the market places, the priests were hinting at something imminent that would change the whole nation; a few sympathetic ones warned Protestants they knew to get out while they could; lay Catholics talked openly about the plans; Irish blacksmiths were working day and night on half-pikes and *skeans*—they were arming men all the way down to the young boys, and the women as well. All of it within the context that the times, too, were different from 1641. Now there was a Catholic king with a Catholic viceroy in Ireland who had made a Catholic army and a Catholic judiciary and civil administration. It seemed as though everything was tilting against the Protestants.

Then, a letter tipped the balance. Someone left an anonymous note to the Protestant Earl of Mount-Alexander lying in the street in Comber, County Down, on December 3, 1688. It began: "Good my Lord, I have written to let you know, that all our Irish men through Ireland is sworn, that on the ninth day of this month, they are to fall on and kill and murder man, wife and child." Look out for yourself, the writer advised, and for other noblemen too, because a man who kills any of you will be made a captain. "Let no Irish man come near you, whatsoever he be."

The "Comber Letter" was unsigned and ill written and one of
many anonymous messages in circulation during those weeks. But it
was ominous that they all mentioned December 9 as the date the
massacre would begin. Historians have reached a consensus that the
letters were hoaxes—based on the fact that nothing happened on
December 9, 1688. It's theoretically possible that nothing happened
because the Irish conspirators realized that the various letters had
blown the scheme. But no one has ever found any evidence of a
planned rising, let alone a massacre. Such a radical and far-reaching
plot would have left a trace; there's always evidence of real conspir-
acies—as distinct from the far more numerous imagined ones for
which the absence of evidence is just more proof, for credulous
believers, of their ingenious existence. It's possible that the documents, including the Comber Letter, were written by Protestant
extremists who were trying to alienate moderates from their endearing allegiance to James, a Catholic, but the true king nevertheless.
People took loyalty to kings seriously in those days. Native Irishmen
may have written the letters as an inexpensive method of scaring
Prods out of the country: remind them of 1641 and make them
sweat. And the missives of 1688 were part of a long line of warnings
and rumours of popish plots in Ireland. A message from the Lords
to the House of Commons in January, eight years earlier, states that
the Lords are fully satisfied that there is now, and has been for
"divers years last past," a "Horrid and Treasonable Plot and
Conspiracy contrived and carried on by those of the *Popish* Religion
in *Ireland,* for Massacring the *English,* and Subverting the *Protestant*
Religion, and the ancient establish'd Government of that Kingdom."
The Comber Letter followed an old and dishonourable tradition.

Nevertheless, there was no doubt in the minds of most Irish
Protestants that the letter was genuine. It was one of those artifacts
that fit with perfection the tenor of their time. With everything else
in Ireland in 1688 that was rumoured, or in the air, or in the mutter-
ings of the marketplace, or in the hostile faces of the intermingled
Irish, the letter was only confirmation of the obvious. "For several
Sundays," writes one chronicler, "the Protestants carried weapons of
all sorts with them into their churches, and even their officiating
Ministers were armed with sword and pistols in their pulpits."

Protestants in Comber made copies of the letter and circulated it.

One copy caused such an uproar in Dublin that even the magisterial and powerful Tyrconnell had to react. He called the city's prominent Protestants to the Castle and tried to tell them it just wasn't so. If there was going to be a rising and a massacre, he'd damn well know about it, and he didn't. He called the wrath of God upon his head if the letter was not "a cursed, a blasted, a confounded lie." When the Protestants reacted with silent scepticism, Tyrconnell flung his wig into the fire in frustration and rage.

A copy of the Comber Letter got to Derry, too. If the timing of its appearance was perfect for boosting Protestant paranoia in Ireland as a whole and Plantation Ulster in particular, the note hit Derry like a bomb from one of Cromwell's giant siege mortars. It precipitated the city's defiance and its historical moment of suffering and fame.

First of all, there was a certain amount of urgency. If the prediction was right, the massacre was only three days away—the letter probably reached Derry on December 6. On the 9th, the Irish would rise up out of the Bogside and stream across the Foyle and in from Donegal and up from the south. It would be 1641 all over again. William, the Protestant prince, was still two countries distant. And in this new Catholic Ireland, who would now ride to the rescue of the Plantation Prods?

The Comber Letter also shoved Derry into desperate action because of a coincidence: Tyrconnell had ordered its garrison to Dublin and another one to replace it. The regiment already marching away was one of the very few units in Ireland that had somehow escaped Tyrconnell's purge of Protestants in the army; only a few of its officers and men were Catholic. It was, in fact, the regiment of Lord Mountjoy, and it included the Scottish lieutenant-colonel, Robert Lundy.

The one reassuring thing that Derry had had among all the rumours and night-sweat fears was the presence of Protestant soldiers on the city's walls. Their departure was ominous enough. But their replacement was a Catholic regiment. On December 6, messengers reaching Derry reported that it was only a day or so away, marching down on the city. Bad enough that it was a Catholic regiment—with officers called O'Reilly, McManus, O'Callaghan, and, inevitably, O'Neill. To have men with names like these inside the walls was terrifying. Worse, there were also twelve officers called MacDonnell, and these included the commander: Alexander MacDonnell, 3rd Earl of Antrim, head of the Ulster MacDonnells, whose emblem was the bloody red hand.

Even worse than a MacDonnell of Antrim for the Protestants of Derry was the composition of his regiment. It included Irish, of course, but also many redshanks—the wild Catholic Highlanders from Kintyre and Argyll—the legendary mercenaries who had fought for O'Neill and O'Donnell in the Nine Years War, the last, bloody phase of resistance to the conquest. They had fought for different factions, except the English and Cromwell, killing everyone, but mostly Protestants, during the Confederate War that followed the Rising of 1641. Now here they were swinging down to Derry, the tall, long-haired, Highland warriors, kilted as always, even in this frigid winter—savage men—half of the 1,200-strong regiment (the citizens of Derry had expected only four hundred). If you could call it marching, said the messages reaching the city. They were striding in their casual, loping way, and behind them was a mob of women and boys. Did not the *Ultoghs* always bring their women with them when they expected spoils?

It was difficult even for sane, reasonable Protestants in Derry to believe that all of this was a coincidence—in the midst of the rumours of a new 1641 and the ferment of Tyrconnell's undoing of the conquest, the Protestant regiment ordered out, the Catholic regiment ordered in, the Comber Letter with its warning of massacre. Were the redshanks the means by which the Irish would get inside the walls and kill the people of Derry root and branch? Surely they had no choice but to shut the city's gates and keep out Antrim's men.

But the modern claim of absolute Protestant solidarity throughout the crisis at Derry showed itself as myth from the beginning. The city's aldermen dithered. They asked church leaders for their advice. James Gordon, a minister in the prickly, dissenting Presbyterian Church, said, "Close the gates; keep out the redshanks." (Gordon, who was already known for "swearing, drinking, and lying," would later be excommunicated for "fornication" with his domestic servant.) The Anglican bishop, Ezekiel Hopkins, said, "A subject must obey his king; to refuse the Earl of Antrim was rebellion."

And indeed, that was the nub of Derry's dilemma. Maybe the redshanks were there to carry out the Comber Letter's chilling prediction. But they had been ordered to Derry by Tyrconnell. An order from the King's Lord Deputy was an order from the King himself. William may have landed in England, but he was as yet merely a foreign prince invited in by seditious English aristocrats. And a more practical consideration was the determination and ferocity with which James had put down Monmouth's rebellion three years earlier. There had been enough hanging, disembowelling, and quartering after that to give pause to would-be rebels.

On December 7, 1688, during the very hours that the citizens of Derry were reading the Comber Letter and debating their life-and-death decision, they saw the first soldiers of Antrim's regiment appear on the Waterside, the east bank across the River Foyle from the city. An advance company rowed over, and two tall, kilted redshanks officers walked through the Ferry Gate facing the river and presented to the city's sherriff their warrant from Tyrconnell demanding—not asking—that their men be quartered and their horses fed. The officers were not notably polite. The sherriff noticed a technical defect in the warrant and delayed giving his permission. The Catholic officers cooled their heels while the Protestants carried on their increasingly frantic discussions.

It was the young men of the tribe who made the decision. They were probably egged on by some older men "who were not openly seen in it, that they might act the more securely under the umbrage of the mob." Thirteen apprentice boys from the guilds drew swords, took the city's keys from the guards, rushed to the Ferry Gate and closed it, then shut the other gates and posted guards on all of them. Antrim's redshanks were only sixty yards away. Derry's defiance had begun.

The Catholic soldiers had no intention of massacring anyone. All they wanted was some warm quarters and a bite to eat after their long, cold march. They milled around in confusion. When the gates didn't reopen, they crossed the river back to the Waterside and did what soldiers do when they're frustrated: stole food and booze from civilians, slapped the men around, bothered the women. Antrim decided he didn't want to start a civil war then and there; he marched his regiment back northeast to the town of Coleraine and waited for orders.

————

Tyrconnell had had bigger things on his mind when he ordered the change of garrisons in Derry. It was a simple matter of moving around his military assets in response to William's landing in England. Tyrconnell sent three of his Irish regiments from Dublin to reinforce James's army in England. He then ordered the Derry garrison—Mountjoy's regiment—south to Dublin and told the seventy-six-year-old Earl of Antrim to raise a force to replace it. In line with his policy of Catholicization of the army, Tyrconnell stipulated that the new regiment be Catholic, and if it included the fierce redshanks, so much the better. Antrim was eccentric and wanted his men to be a good-looking unit, and that meant tall men—what was the point of being called out of retirement to lead soldiers again and have them look like *gossoons,* or stunted yokels from the bogs? It took time to find them. When he didn't get to Derry to relieve its mainly Protestant troops on November 20, they followed their orders and marched south anyway. That left Derry without a garrison until Antrim's men crossed the Foyle on December 7. The old earl's vanity lost the city. If he'd got there on time—with shorter men—the garrison changeover would probably have gone without a hitch. The Protestant Lord Mountjoy's prestige among the citizens would have carried the day, and the city would have been in Catholic hands, just like that, without a fight. Derry, and the Protestant people of Ulster, might not have needed the traitor Robert. They could have blamed their fall on trivia: Antrim's efficiency and Mountjoy's reputation.

When word reached Tyrconnell in Dublin Castle that Derry had closed its gates to Antrim's men, he reacted as usual: flung his wig into the fire in rage and frustration. Then he ordered Mountjoy, whose men had arrived in Dublin only three days earlier, to take six companies and march back to Derry. Mountjoy rounded up his grumbling men—they were getting damn tired of slogging back and forth across the bloody width of Ireland—and headed northwest again.

December 9 came. The Protestants of Derry manned the walls. Across Ireland, the Protestants kept watch through a long winter night. According to Macaulay: "There was scarcely one Protestant mansion from the Giant's Causeway to Bantry Bay in which armed men were not watching and lights burning from the early sunset to the late sunrise." Nothing happened. There was no rising; there were no massacres: "Not even in the most secluded glen in Ulster had a single cabin been invaded by the presence of an enemy."

In Derry, the people were relieved, but now some of them thought they had even more to worry about. They had defied the King and Tyrconnell; maybe they had made very big trouble for themselves. The divisions in Derry hadn't been bridged. Many of its people were appalled by what the apprentice boys had done. Maybe the cautious Bishop Hopkins had been right and the reprobate Dissenter, Gordon, talking through his hat. They decided they'd better start backtracking, and fast. Some of the aldermen and their allies wrote a letter to Mountjoy asking the patient Protestant lord to intercede on their behalf with the irascible Tyrconnell. It was the "rabble" who had done it, they wrote. No one could restrain them. But, in their defence, there had been so much talk of massacre. Priests and friars had been buying weapons and horses. "Very odd sermons" had been preached in the neighbourhood. The citizens hoped that the King would view their actions as "a great and very acceptable service." They bore to him only "true faith and allegiance."

However, it was too late for the moderate Protestants. The extremists had already taken control of the city, and they wanted nothing to do with James. They purported to speak for all of Derry when they swore their allegiance to William and Mary, who had, after all, been proclaimed king and queen by the English Parliament. The former Protestant civic administration, which Tyrconnell had replaced with a Catholic corporation, reassembled. It expelled the few remaining Catholics within the walls and packed off a "convent of Dominican friars."

The city was in a perilous position. It had, perhaps, three hundred men with experience under arms. Antrim's redshanks could have simply walked in if they'd felt like it, and if the old earl hadn't marched them back fifty-five kilometres to squat in Coleraine. But news of the dramatic action in Derry spread fast, and Protestant volunteers rushed to the city: three hundred horsemen from Donegal (their commander had ignored Tyrconnell's order to disarm his men and, indeed, had run guns and powder for them from the Netherlands), an infantry company from up the Foyle, and small units of armed militia, families, and groups of settlers and restless young men. A loose civic democracy, they organized themselves into six companies and stood constant watch on the mile-long enclosure of Derry's walls.

Just before Christmas, Mountjoy arrived in Omagh, about sixty-five kilometres south of Derry. The new Derry junta sent a delegation to parley with him. They were loyal to James, they said over and over again, but they would permit no Catholic soldiers inside their walls. Eventually, the weary Mountjoy agreed to placate these strange men, both aggressive and fearful, with their mixed message of loyalty and defiance. Two of his companies, every man a Protestant, would enter Derry under the command of his lieutenant-colonel, Robert Lundy.

Mountjoy must have well and truly trusted his Scottish officer, to leave him to deal with this delicate situation: the volatile, suspicious, armed Prods in the city; Antrim and his redshanks waiting nearby. Mountjoy left them to it and turned to march, for the third time in a month, the road from Ulster to Dublin. He had bigger things to think about than this scruffy little frontier town. Mountjoy feared that events were about to get very confused, and very dangerous, for a Protestant officer in Tyrconnell's Irish-Catholic army. Before starting out for Dublin, Mountjoy did one more thing: he appointed Robert Lundy military governor of Londonderry.

Things happened thick and fast. Tyrconnell raised a citizen army. By February 1689, about 100,000 men (equal to the entire Protestant population of Ulster) were under arms, although only half could be called soldiers; the rest were amateurs or kerns of one sort or another. All were ill trained and short of weapons. Nevertheless, the army grew from eight to forty-eight regiments. Across the south of Ireland, the Irish disarmed the Protestants, drove them out of their farms and country houses before burning them down, and slaughtered their cattle and sheep. The people were usually allowed to live if they agreed to leave Ireland. Some packed up, burnt their own houses before the Irish had a chance to do it, and ran for safety. Those who resisted were "tried" and executed. The French ambassador to Ireland told Louis that it would take ten years to make good the damage done in Ireland in six weeks in early 1689.

None of that happened in Ulster. There, the Protestants were numerous enough to deter attacks; the Plantation had made a critical mass of them. They were already a people, sufficient and concentrated enough to run athwart the plans of the Catholic Irish (as they still are in the statelet of Northern Ireland). The gentry enlisted their tenants into militias and formed a Council of the North. Their first act was to "supplicate" William for men and arms so they could hold Ireland for him.

On March 7, 1689, Tyrconnell issued a proclamation to the Ulster Protestants: submit, and he would pardon them; fight, and his army would "fall upon them wherever they meet them and treat them as Rebels and Traitors to His Majesty." He added that "the country Irish" were armed—the rumours in the previous year of pikes and *skeans* in the hands of all Catholics were true. If the Protestants resisted, the men, women, and boys of Cavan, Monaghan, Tyrone, and Londonderry will "immediately enter upon a massacre of the British." Tyrconnell said that he would be unable to restrain "the force and violence of the rabble." He may have denied the previous year that a slaughter of Protestants was in the making, but now he threatened one.

The Irish army moved north. In their first battle, the Protestant militia (under the command of Arthur Rawdon, who, four years earlier, had offered James a regiment to put down the rebellious Monmouth) broke and ran and lost Dromore. The catastrophic defeat began the flood of Ulster Protestant refugees—to England and Scotland, but to the other fortified towns of Ulster, too. After "The Break of Dromore," they believed that the Irish, as Tyrconnell had said they would, "were coming down, sparing neither age nor sex, putting all to the sword without mercy." It got worse: the Protestants lost, or abandoned, Omagh, Lisburn, Antrim, Massereene Castle, Strabane, Coleraine (not Belfast; it was a muddy village of a few hundred cottages). They fell back on the town of Enniskillen and, especially, on the fortified city of Derry—a mass of women and children, a beaten and demoralized militia.

Their morale was further broken down by the return of the King. On March 12, 1689, James landed at Kinsale on the south coast, the first time he'd set foot in his Irish kingdom. The French had been glad to see the last of him. He had soon bored them with his never-ending story of how the throne had been taken away from him, and that it certainly hadn't been his fault. They had grown to dislike him and his habits: "He eats, that King, as if there were never a Prince of Orange in the world," said Madame de Sévigny. In southern Ireland, the Catholics welcomed him with joy, the Protestants with warmth—for many of them, too, he was the king by Divine Right. And, perhaps—a more practical consideration—he was their best protection against the armed and vengeful Irish rabble. James heard that three of the four green fields were his already and that his army was campaigning to win the fourth, the ever-refractory Ulster.

In Derry, refugees filled up the small space inside the walls. They were already short of food, arms, and powder. The Irish army, soon to be beefed up with experienced French officers, was closing in on the city. Derry was isolated, beyond all help for weeks or months. There were only two sources of hope and encouragement. With the influx of men from other towns, the city's garrison had expanded to at least 7,000 fighting men, and perhaps as many as 10,000. Like the Irish, many of them weren't trained or well armed, but they were determined. All had heard the lurid stories of destruction, murder, torture, and sexual assault by the Irish. Whether they were true was irrelevant; the Protestants believed them; it was 1641 again. They thought they had their backs to the wall in Derry, with nowhere else to run; they would have to stand and fight, or die there. It's easy to see how the battle cry of "No Surrender!" would suggest itself.

The second piece of good fortune for the city was its "new and noble" governor. Lieutenant-Colonel Robert Lundy, an anonymous witness told a House of Lords committee, was "very much esteemed not only for his forwardness in their Majesties' service but for his military knowledge and courage and his extraordinary care and vigilance." With such a man in charge, their lordships responded, "we are in hopes" that Derry "may hold out some time."

7

ROBERT *AGONISTES*

NOW WE ARE BACK to Robert, to "the uneasy camber" of his "night-mare way" in Derry, the disaster about to envelop him, the coming of his apotheosis as arch-traitor of the Ulster Protestant people.

His new command was a heavy freight to bear. He had never officered more than a few companies of men; now he had a threatened city and its hinterland to govern, a ghastly mixture of soldiers and amateurs to control, a mass of fearful, squabbling Anglicans and Presbyterians. Robert must have felt even more abandoned when he heard about his commander. Mountjoy had been right to fear his future. Tyrconnell sent him to France with a message for James, but also with a secret message denouncing his loyal Protestant as a traitor. For one reason or another, none good, Tyrconnell had become suspicious of Mountjoy—perhaps only because he was, after all, a Protestant. James would have let Mountjoy return to England, but Louis, a French king and, therefore, without sentiment, imprisoned the Irishman in the Bastille. (He was released three years later, in time to die fighting for William.)

We will assume that Robert's own wife and three-year-old daughter, Araminta, lived in Derry; he was a young father and had to think about their safety, too. Who was more of a danger to them: Antrim's redshanks or the hard Prods of this rebellious garrison town? James was his king twice over—of England and the army he served, and of Scotland, his country, which had its own ambivalent feelings about the *sassenachs* to the south. But James had abandoned his throne and run to France. William's Dutch troops had entered London, and the revolution in England seemed complete: bloodless and "Glorious."

Where was Ireland in this mélange? Or Derry? Where was Robert?

Once again, all we can say about him is speculation. The "evidence," such as it is, will support any one of several interpretations of his character—or more than one at the same time, for that matter. There are many possibilities. One: he was an earnest man but a lousy soldier who was just not up to the complicated demands of his new job, an incompetent who had no idea how to command thousands of men in the complex and dangerous game of battle and siege. Two: he was steadfast and loyal to James, his Scottish king, no matter what had happened in England; in that time and place, such loyalty, admirable and constant, would have made him a traitor, indeed, to the Protestant Williamites of Ulster. Three: Robert was intelligent, a good soldier, prepared to do his job for whichever king seemed to have the best claim, but he suffered from an individual weakness—pessimism, defeatism; he had a depressive personality and couldn't see any way out of the impending debacle at Derry; he tried, but just didn't have the psychological stamina to lead the city through its travail. Four: he was a solid professional soldier who believed that the city couldn't be defended and that surrender on the generous (surprisingly so) terms offered by the Irish was better than watching thousands of women and children dying, as they surely would, of disease, hunger, siege shot; his own wife and little daughter were at risk, and he had the power to prevent that. Five: he and the few other knowledgeable military men in Derry were surrounded by a passle of rabid Prods who knew damn all about soldiering and, in any event, were terrified of a massacre if they surrendered (although it was hard to blame them for that); Robert had learnt at Tangier that a siege was a terrible thing to go through. He held no special brief, religious or political; like any professional soldier, he knew that battle was something to be avoided if there was any reasonable alternative.

One thing was certain: he was military governor of a walled city, most of whose inhabitants believed they were in mortal danger from

Catholics outside and from the Irish army, which was as close as Antrim's redshanks. If Robert did believe the city was indefensible—at least in the face of attack by a good, regular army, he wouldn't have been the first. In 1628, as the Plantation was under way, an English Commissioners' Report on Derry reached the same conclusion. The city was so situated that its walls, houses, and streets were open to the raking fire of any ship that could make it upriver to its harbour. The Commissioners said the same thing about the danger from the surrounding hills. Derry was not much better than a free-fire zone. "In our judgment," they wrote, "it is not a place of defence nor tenable if any foreign enemy should come before it." The commissioners must have meant the word "foreign" to include an Irish enemy. The walls had been built with great effort and expense, but now they were decrepit, overgrown with weeds, good enough to keep out the marauding kerns but not much else. Besides, there was no ditch or moat, and the drawbridge chains were so rusty that the gates could hardly be moved.

Nevertheless, Robert did what he could. In less than a month, he repaired the walls, oiled the chains, mounted new guns on new carriages, built gun platforms, had new stocks made for five hundred musket barrels found in a storeroom, bought other muskets and powder, and appealed to various lords and the King himself (William, not James) for more resources. He also got rid of the dunghills and houses immediately outside the city and began to build the ravelin at the Bishop's Gate, the most vulnerable point in the vulnerable walls.

So far, so good. Not even a fanatical, Taig-hating Prod could object to any of these preparations. But then Robert made a number of military decisions that the amateur soldiers of Derry, and even some of his fellow-professionals, thought problematic. Whispers and suspicions about him began to circulate. That's all they were at first. He had a lot of capital in his good reputation, and it took a while to run out. Furthermore, he was more than the mere governor of Derry. He had become King William's de facto commander-in-chief for the entire northwest theatre of war in Ireland. No one at first was inclined to question the decisions of such a man. But perhaps there were already intimations about his ambivalence in this matter of *Rí Seamus* versus *Rí Liam*. If there was a conflict in his heart, maybe it showed in those small things—the messages his body could not avoid sending, a shadow of doubt or dissent flashing across his face—that raised questions in the mind of the watchful, mistrustful observer. In that time of chaos, fear, and shifting allegiance, men would search hard for the small signs of unreliability.

Robert ordered the outlying Protestant garrisons to fall back on Derry: "Draw down immediately . . . and join the Derry men." So, the Protestants abandoned Dungannon and all the valuable stores there to the Irish. They withdrew from Sligo, even though holding it would prevent an Irish invasion of Ulster from the west. The Sligo commander did what he was told, but was so disturbed by his orders that he sailed for England to report Robert's actions. The garrisons from Cavan and Monaghan marched in to Derry. The town of Enniskillen in Fermanagh fortified itself; it would hold out but would remain only a nuisance behind the Irish army's front lines. Robert may have been following the laudable military principle of concentration of forces when he withdrew the garrisons, but suspicion grew in Derry that he was concentrating them so he could hand them over to James in one easy go.

Then people thought they recalled that Robert had promised reinforcements before the disastrous Break of Dromore but had not sent them. Maybe if he had, the Protestants would not have lost the desperate battle and the hundreds of good men. Some said they had heard the governor say he would heartily fight Tyrconnell (who had, after all, double-crossed his beloved commander Mountjoy) but would never bear arms against James. Someone else maintained that Robert had promoted a captain who had sworn openly he would not serve William.

While all this questioning was going on, the Reverend George Walker arrived in Derry from his rectory in Donaghmore, County Tyrone. The militant Anglican, with his ancestral memories of 1641, his family once again refugees from an Irish rising, cast an immediately wary eye on both the city's heretic Presbyterians and its shifty governor. Then there was the matter of the oath.

William's concern about the possibility of Louis XIV's France becoming the dominant power in Ireland—a radical redistribution of the balance of European power—made him take very seriously Derry's appeals for help. The small, remote seaport had become one of the linchpins of his continental strategy. He was reluctant to fight in Ireland, but James, by refusing to do the sensible thing and head directly for Scotland, was forcing him to do so. William ordered two regiments, which happened to be based near the port of Liverpool, to get ready to head for Derry, "wind and weather permitting"—it was unruly winter in the Irish Sea and the North Channel. William also sent more immediate assistance: a supply ship, the *Deliverance,* and a naval frigate, the *Jersey,* with arms, ammunition, and stores. The King's message referred to "our trusty and well-beloved Lieutenant-Colonel Lundy," and it instructed his governor to take various steps for the city's defence.

William ended his commission by ordering Robert and all his officers to swear an oath of loyalty. It was a matter of tidying up possible loose ends in Ireland. William's messenger aboard the *Deliverance,* Captain James Hamilton, had secret instructions to return to England with all the supplies and commissions if Robert refused to take the oath of fidelity. An oath was then a very serious undertaking, probably even more important in Ireland's society than in England's. Ireland was full of men who had sworn allegiance to James, but not yet to William. The King needed this profound assurance that his liege-men in far-off Derry—whom he expected to die for him if necessary—were truly loyal.

Hamilton and his ships arrived in Derry on March 21, 1689. Robert went aboard the *Deliverance* with his officers to swear the oath. They couldn't do it ashore in front of the city's mayor—as William had instructed—because his name was Cormac O'Neill, and he was on active service with the Irish army that was on its way to attack them. In the city's paranoid state, even the mayor's deputy, the Protestant John Buchanan, was for some reason under suspicion as a papist sympathizer. When it was Robert's turn to swear the oath, he directed most of the men present to go on deck and wait in the cold rain while he did so, thus eliminating them as witnesses.

There can be no doubt that Robert took the required oath. The Parliamentary Committee that investigated him later in 1689 (while he was making the best of things in the Tower of London) decided categorically that he had done so—in the presence of James Hamilton and at least three other officers. Two of them signed certificates to that effect. And the committee was, if anything, hostile to Derry's former governor and disparaging of his actions; it had no reason to give him the benefit of any doubt. Nevertheless, Robert's insistence on a private oath stoked the rumour that he had refused to take it.

The next day, Robert made matters worse. Other leading citizens and officers were lined up in front of him taking the oath. Someone suggested that he should do it again in public, to put to rest any doubts on the matter. It was reported that Robert became angry and refused. That was the end of any trust between the citizens of Derry (or the hard-line faction among them) and their governor. "Stupid obstinacy," says one modern historian. All part of his plan to "profess to fight for William while still acting as a traitor," writes another. Robert's refusal "does not at all answer the character most people give him," said the soldier and, later, governor, John Michelburne. John Mackenzie, the Presbyterian chronicler, said that Robert's refusal "was a very suspicious sign of his ill intentions and therefore justly taken notice of."

Indeed, Robert's behaviour during the oath-swearing doesn't look good. It appears as if he was hedging his bets, keeping his options open, creating the cynical opportunity for "deniability" later—if it came to pass that James won back his kingdom or, at least, kept Ireland. But of course, we don't know. It's just as possible that Robert was a serious man in agony, that William's requirement of fidelity had thrown Derry's governor into a terrible conflict of loyalties. Robert had taken his oath to James years before. Did that mean nothing now? Just because a Dutch usurper had been approved by English Protestants didn't mean that Scotland and Ireland, James's other two kingdoms, had been thrown into the bargain. Maybe the only way out, for a loyal man, was to swear the oath in private and hope for the best—short of damning them all, of course, getting on his horse, and riding out the gate to join the Irish not many miles over the horizon. But he didn't do that, either. James had landed in Ireland, but Tyrconnell ran the Irish army. Perhaps after what Tyrconnell had done to Mountjoy, Robert thought he didn't have an exit that way. Even an honest Protestant might find himself in the Irish equivalent of the Bastille. Anyway—the clinching factor—his wife and young daughter were in Derry. He might not have liked their chances if he left them in the city without his protection. And it was certain he couldn't take them out onto roads and through hills alive, as he may well have thought, with kerns and armed Irish peasants happy enough to come upon a party of Plantation settlers and their spawn.

After the incident of the oath, it all went downhill fast for Robert. The libellous accounts of Walker and Mackenzie, his hostile chroniclers, go on, seeding the ground for the simple, stirring myth of the gathering siege, the gallant city, its true-believer defenders, the exposure and expulsion of the traitor within, the tribe's purity and honour restored, its very existence maintained as it endures the siege for Protestant king and religion. The two accounts also emphasize the sectarian rift between Anglicans and Presbyterians which would persist for generations in a form almost as poisonous as the divide between Protestants and Catholics. Walker and Mackenzie, and the many subsequent historians and polemicists who have relied on their accounts, created the standard received version of Derry's siege in Protestant Irish history. As always in this story, however, there is the complex possibility of an alternative narrative—one that is kinder, for example, to the actions and motivations of Robert (perhaps the conscience-stricken soldier) and more critical of Derry and its riven people: courageous, fanatical, panicky, resigned, compromising, all at the same time.

Robert began to hand out passes to any officer, soldier, or citizen who wanted to leave the city; as military governor in time of war, he had to give his permission. One outraged Protestant defender wrote that the governor had actually urged people to go "and spoke so despondingly to many of them concerning the indefensibleness of the place that they could see little hope and were unwilling to stay." Or perhaps—the alternative "history"—Robert was just giving people the freedom to decide for themselves where their best chances lay; in good conscience he could not demand they decide for William, and not for James, and force them to go on with resistance that went against their allegiance. In the past, it had always been Irish rebels against the legitimate (by whatever means the legitimacy was first established) king and government in Dublin or London. This time, the city's Protestants were the rebels against the true king and his will—or so one could argue. And if the city could not be defended against the quality of an army he believed to be nearby, then who could ask men to die for nothing?

In mid-April, the main force of the Irish army converged at the fords of the Finn and the Mourne rivers, which they had to cross to reach Derry. Robert led the troops and irregulars of the city out to the Battle of the Fords and the debacle that followed, when the Irish cavalry made its audacious assault on the massed lines of Protestant infantry. According to Walker and Mackenzie, Robert had to be pried out of his house in Derry to go to a battle for which he was ill prepared and which he prosecuted with negligence: his men had almost no ammunition; he panicked before they did and ran for the city, where he closed the gates and refused entry to thousands of late arrivals from the battle who had to huddle outside the walls overnight in constant fear of slaughter by the Irish. Walker claims that when the Irish cavalry commander advanced to the river's bank, Robert "gave him the sign to come over and ran away." In a dramatization of the siege written some years later (probably by the city's eventual governor, John Michelburne), Robert never made it to the fords but stayed hunkered down in Derry drinking himself stupid. One of the play's characters says: "He is safe and we are not. . . . We have enemies both before and behind us. We are betrayed, sold." This is dramatic licence; Robert was certainly present at the battle.

However, it doesn't look good for him. Testifying before the Parliamentary Inquiry, Robert admitted he ran with the rest: "As to the fight at the Pass, the men would not stand but run away, so he fled away among the rest; but denies he bid them shift for themselves." He also had to admit that he had shut the gates against many of his own men—between 4,000 and 8,000 of them. "If the enemy had pursued, all these poor souls might have been lost." Robert's only, and lame, explanation was that he had "shut the gates against the rabble, knowing it would quickly make a great scarcity of provisions." One of the men kept outside that cold, terrifying night was George Walker. He got back in the next day only by forcing his way past a sentry. His account of Robert's conduct had the colour of payback for that, too.

The relief regiments that William had sent from Liverpool finally made it through winter's cold, narrow waters and into Lough Foyle. By coincidence, they anchored just as the Battle of the Fords was getting under way. It seemed as though they had arrived in the proverbial nick of time. But in a display of incompetence, or of

Jamesian loyalty cum Williamite treachery, or of defeatism, Robert prevailed on the English commander, Colonel John Cunningham, not to march his regiments to Derry's relief but to return to England without firing a shot or even bringing his men to land. Cunningham and his aide, Colonel Solomon Richards, themselves travelled over-land to Derry, took a look at the situation, and agreed with the gov-ernor, their fellow professional soldier, that trying to defend the city was a waste of time and of men's lives. Cunningham was later cashiered for his inaction—an odd contrast to Robert's eventual rehabilitation—although perhaps the Englishman didn't have the Scot's noble connections, those ancestral boozers with the king.

Robert tried to surrender the city. Meeting with his Council of War, he reported that Derry had provisions for ten days at most, that the Irish army of 25,000 men was a few miles away, and that the city would surely fall. But, as we know, the Irish had nowhere near that many troops, and their army was unprepared and unequipped to lay siege to anything bigger than a fortified Protestant country house. Later, the Parliamentary Committee found that the city had plenty of provisions (demonstrated by its endurance of 105 days, once the unnecessary and botched siege began). It seems at this point that Robert just wanted out. Whatever his reasons, he was prepared to fudge anything necessary to get the terrible load—of responsibility, of antithetical claims on his loyalty, of the fear of dying—off his back. Or maybe this moment really was the opportunity to achieve his long-standing intention to hand the city over to James, his true liege-lord.

However, as with everything that happened in Derry during the two years of 1688 and 1689, the surrender attempt became a sham-bles of ineptitude and confusion, although one that would soon be resolved by the warlike Presbyterian hard man, the Scottish settler Adam Murray, the Protestant paramilitary prototype.

Robert and his council feared what the city's radicals would do if they heard about the surrender negotiations, so they tried to keep them secret. Of course, the people found out anyway. "This discov-ery occasioned great uneasiness and disorder in the Town which had like to have had very ill effects upon the governor and some of the council." Indeed, the governor's very life came into jeopardy from some men who concluded that it might be a damn good idea to drag him out into the street and hang him. The no-surrender faction in Derry must have thought: When you got right down to it, what did Lundy know about the true state of affairs in Ulster? His family hadn't been around in 1641 when the Irish rose and slaughtered the Plantation English and Scots, or when the "Queen's O'Doherty" reverted to his natural nature as a kern and destroyed the city. While all that had been going on, Robert's family had been lolling comfortably on their pleasant, safe, ancestral land in Fife. No one there contested their right to have it, their right to live. It was all very well for the Scottish governor to blithely consider surrendering the city to the Irish. He didn't know what they were really like. They might offer good terms, and then turn and do what they had always wanted to do in Ulster: destroy the Protestant people—beginning with Derry. Why, indeed, would they not take the opportunity to do so? If the shoe were on the other foot, they—the hard-line Prods—wouldn't hesitate to do the same to the Taigs. Even if the Irish didn't go that far, the days of the Protestant ascendancy in Ulster would be over. Lose Derry, said one dissenter (probably the only one) in Robert's council meeting, and you lose the kingdom.

Still, there were people in Derry besides the council who agreed with Robert's desire to surrender. The moderates were encouraged by another coincidence: the arrival before the city's walls of James himself, just as the negotiations were going on. Surrendering to Tyrconnell or to the ferocious French cocommander of the Irish army, the Lithuanian mercenary warrior Conrad de Rosen, was one thing. They could never be sure these men would honour any agreement. (Rosen had led the Irish cavalry in person in their headlong swim across the icy Finn and their charge down on the Derry men—at the age of sixty-two. Later, during the siege proper, James was forced to intervene to reverse Rosen's brutal tactics.) But submitting to the King was a much better proposition. He would guarantee their protection. Perhaps they had heard that Protestants in the south and in Dublin had received James with warmth and that he had reciprocated. His aim was London and the three thrones. Massacre was not his style, nor in his practical interest.

As usual, however, James did more harm than good. The tentative surrender terms assured the city's garrison that they would be allowed to live on in peace if they gave up all serviceable arms and horses (the Irish army desperately needed both). The agreement also stipulated that the Irish would keep a certain distance away from the walls while the factions in Derry haggled with each other, so the war party wouldn't get alarmed by the sight of papish soldiers on their doorstep. James either didn't know or didn't care about the latter provision. With his colours flying, every inch the victor, he drew up close to the shaky Bishop's Gate. Some of the hotheads on the walls fired on the King with cannon and musket, killing some of his personal bodyguards and coming close to hitting James himself. If they had succeeded, it would have been a quick and unexpected end to the war of the two kings. With admirable forbearance, James got himself out of range fast and waited around the rest of the day in the cold, steady spring rain for Derry to make up its mind.

It was a hard mind to make up. Some of the "quality" in the city were appalled that the "rabble" had fired on the King, just as they had been when the apprentice boys closed the gates against the Earl of Antrim's redshanks. Even George Walker and Henry Baker, the soon-to-be co-governors, joined in the grovelling and mendacious apology sent to James: the shooters had been drunk and had seized cannon and fired "without order from any people of authority in the town." The message added "that the better sort were generally resolved to surrender and did all they could to persuade the common people to the same." Some of the men within the walls made personal decisions: they laid down their weapons and went out to James and surrendered. Others continued to make use of Robert's passes and got out of the city. There are no reports that the Irish army, the kerns, or the peasants with the now-legendary pikes and *skeans* harmed any of these Protestants.

The city was leaning towards capitulation. But any worthwhile myth of endurance and redemption needs a saviour as well as a traitor. The man appeared who would head off the surrender, expel the traitor, and save the Protestant soul. Based on the Anglican George Walker's account of the siege, readers would barely know that the Presbyterian Adam Murray existed. That was one of the grievous omissions that fellow Presbyterian John Mackenzie sought to rectify with *his* account. In fact, Murray seems to have been the decisive actor of the moment. He was with his horsemen north of Derry where there was fodder; he heard about the negotiations and rode down to the city with a body of cavalry. He had some trouble getting inside the walls. None other than George Walker, still for giving in (although his account of the siege is silent on his pacifism), had ordered him kept out, and they had a tense conversation over the parapet. Murray got in when a no-surrender officer opened the gate. He began to organize the citizens who were in favour of fighting on, and several thousand tied on the white armband Murray suggested as a sign of their solidarity. Those who were for surrender made themselves scarce in the face of these fierce armed gangs. Murray bulled his way into the council chamber with some of his troopers and, in effect, staged a coup. He confronted Robert. He was "either a fool or a knave," said Murray. He had cocked up the battle at the Fords—where a good number of Murray's cavalry had gone down fighting to cover the unnecessary rout. The council, an apparently supine group, had easily acquiesced in Robert's surrender plan. Now it accepted Murray's hard line just as readily, although the presence of his armed men and his white-armbanded gangs in the streets must have been persuasive. The council dissolved. Robert went home, guarded by a platoon of redcoats in case the mob tried to drag him out. His governorship was over.

There's one more piece of evidence to consider. It was revealed long after the creation of the siege myth and its necessary Judas. The "Dopping Correspondence," dating from 1694 but not discovered until the 1940s, contains information from Captain Charles Kinaston. He was one of the three men Walker and Baker sent to James to apologize for the hotheads who blasted away at him from the city's walls. Kinaston reports that Robert had sent a request to meet with him before he left on his mission. Robert asked him to keep a great secret: to tell James (whom he called "the King") that he, Robert, had been a very faithful servant to him. In proof, he had managed things at the Battle of the Fords as much in the King's favour as he could. He had also falsified Derry's situation to Cunningham to induce him to go back to England, and he had forged a letter from Cunningham to the council advising it to surrender. Kinaston finished by writing that he delivered Robert's message to James, who replied "Alas, poor man!" and saying he was satisfied that Lundy had done all the service that lay in his power.

If Kinaston was telling the truth, then Robert was always James's man. He was a Protestant loyal to the Catholic king—admirably oblivious of sectarian imperatives—but a traitor, indeed, to William. He was also neither stupid nor incompetent. How simple if that were the end of the matter. But inevitable questions arise: Was Kinaston telling the truth? There's a distinct absence of that basic requirement for witness credibility: a second corroborating source. If he was telling the truth, why didn't he come forward to inform the Parliamentary Inquiry into Robert's actions? Why didn't he tell anyone at all? To protect Robert? But he barely knew the man when Robert told him his great secret. Almost everyone else who wrote about the siege was mistaken or told the usual human self-serving version of events or lied outright. Why should we think Kinaston was any different?

There are other questions: If Robert was loyal to James, why did he not go over to the Irish? Surely the King—Robert's King—would have given him a great reward for such long and perilous service in the heart of the enemy's camp. When George Walker interceded on Robert's behalf and persuaded the government not to send him back to Derry for trial, he gave as his reason that it was not fit "to send Lundy into Ireland as yet (and much less to Londonderry where he had a faction for him)." Was this faction for Robert because they shared his loyalty to James? Or because Robert's urge to surrender, whatever his motive, suited men with no stomach for war and siege? The committee concluded that they would not even bother bringing Robert's case before William because they found "such difficulty in the matter, both in law and prudence." Finally, if Robert was a thoroughgoing traitor, how did he get rehabilitated and back in the Crown's service so soon—becoming one of England's trusted men on the ground with the army of its ally, Portugal? The government thought that getting Robert back after he was taken prisoner at the Battle of Almanza was worth twenty men in exchange.

Kinaston's report settles nothing for certain. Robert's motives remain enigmatic.

———

After Robert was deposed, the war faction in Derry asked Adam Murray to become governor. He was the natural choice, but he declined in favour of keeping his position as a field commander. True to his type, Murray preferred the simplicity of vigorous exercise in battle to the complications and necessary compromises of running the fractious, divided city. He'd stiffened their backbones; now someone else could govern——replete with the energizing knowledge that Adam Murray (backed by his cavalrymen) had intervened once to keep the Protestants honest, and he'd certainly do it again. Henry Baker was asked to be governor, and George Walker his co-governor——or an assistant to the governor, if you believe John Mackenzie's version of events.

One of the strangest things of all in this story is that the first thing Baker and Walker did was ask Robert to resume his position. "But he positively refused to concern himself any further." They even sent a message to Colonel Cunningham asking him if *he* would take command of the city——anyone but themselves, it seemed. But Cunningham was already preparing to up-anchor and head back to England and his comeuppance there. Finally, the two Derry men agreed to accept the governorship. Even then, they treated Lundy the Traitor with surprising solicitude. As long as he stayed in Derry, his life was in danger, and they arranged for his escape from the city. Walker said they did so because "the Commission he bore, as well as their respect for his Person, made it a duty in them to contribute all they could to his safety." More likely, they wanted to help a fellow Anglican gentleman escape from the Presbyterian rabble. Robert disguised himself as a common soldier with a load of match (material used to ignite the powder in a musket) on his back. One of the versions of the legend says that he didn't go out through one of the gates but climbed down the wall by way of a pear tree growing there (it would have been a handy way up for attacking Irish infantrymen). The tree is supposed to have remained growing until 1840, when it blew down in a storm.

There is no indication that Robert took Martha and Araminta with him; it was too dangerous an exit for that. In fact, there's evidence that "Mrs. Lundy" wrote a letter from Derry to one of James's commanders perhaps as late as the beginning of May, two weeks after her husband's escape. There's no evidence of what she said, although the fact that she was writing to the Catholics has been used as further evidence of Robert's treachery. It's also unlikely that she stayed in the city during the siege but rather travelled to London after Robert had been transported there.

We don't know whether Robert had time to make it back to the familiar green fields of Fife and his kinsmen. King William's men arrested him somewhere in Scotland and deposited him, like so many other traitorous subjects before him, into the Tower of London. Robert's self-defence was that he had fled, in innocence, to Scotland and not to James in Ireland. But perhaps, after everything he'd been through, he was tired, at the end of his tether, heartsore at having abandoned his wife and child. Maybe the only thing he wanted was to go home.

8

GLORIOUS, PIOUS, AND IMMORTAL MEMORY

ROBERT IS THE ODIOUS and necessary traitor of the epochal siege of Derry and the prototype of all Protestant compromisers, but the actual siege began only after he escaped to Scotland. It lasted for 105 days. In conventional military terms, it may be an exaggeration to call it a siege, although that's always its designation in the Protestant mythos. Perhaps "blockade" is a more accurate description of the porous and fitful nature of the Irish war effort around Derry. Most of the time, those of the city's inhabitants who had simply had enough were able to leave unhindered. By the standards of continental Europe, Derry was a sorry excuse for a siege. There were no big guns and nothing for troops to use to get over the walls. Perhaps six-hundred mortar bombs were fired into the city, instead of the tens of thousands that would have been launched in the real thing in Europe.

Nevertheless, it must have felt like a siege to the defenders. They could see the Irish troops on the hills all around them. They were short of food to begin with, and thousands eventually died of starvation and the diseases that accompany short rations and crowded living conditions (although casualties from these causes were comparable among the besieging Irish). Before the city was relieved, George Walker recorded the going rates for scarce protein (we assume he's reliable enough for these nonpolitical, nonsectarian details): horseflesh sold for 1shilling and 8pence a pound; a quarter of a dog ("fatned by eating the Bodies of the slain *Irish*")—a kind of indirect cannibalism—5shillings and 6pence a pound; a cat, 4shillings and 6pence; a rat, 1shilling; and a mouse, 6pence. This sounds worse now than it was then; people were more used to eating anything that moved on four legs, however small and scuttly. Nevertheless, Derry went very hungry towards the end.

Even a mere six hundred mortar rounds could do a lot of damage to the buildings and people crammed within the walls, quite apart from the terror an indiscriminate bombardment must have induced among civilians. Underlying it all was the memory of past massacre and the blank, unreasoning fear of its repetition. Inside were Protestants; outside were Catholics. That fact alone induced dread—among these Protestants, although not, apparently, among the thousands still living more or less unmolested in the countryside round about. And while the besiegers could at least withdraw for some rest and relaxation or call up fresh troops to the front, the defenders had a finite supply of fighting men which dwindled. Walker's numbers may not be accurate, but his record of the steady attrition is chilling enough. In his diary, he notes: "July 8. The Garrison is now reduced to 5520 men. July 13. The Garrison is reduced to 5313 men." By July 22, Walker reports 4,973 men remaining; in the next five days, 517 men died—although the city was then *in extremis* and was, in fact, relieved just over a week later.

The numbers are of live soldiers, but many of them were debilitated and incapable of fighting. Women and children were dying, too, of course, the latter with their usual higher mortality in hard conditions. And that was a very big difference for the men on the walls compared with the army outside. The Derry defenders were fighting for their families, who were beside them. That must have encouraged them to fight on, but it must also have augmented their agony when they had to watch wives and children die of typhus or cholera, or of mortar fire. It was a problem finding places to put the dead. The survivors buried them or dumped them where they could; there was very little ground not built upon within the walls—an area of about 500 by 300 metres. For centuries afterwards, new building in the city would uncover skeletons of that spring and summer's dead.

On July 28, 1689, three ships broke the siege boom under heavy fire. The myth says that the first to reach Derry was one of its own vessels, the *Mountjoy,* with its Derry-born captain, Micaiah Browning, lying dead on deck. That's a nice image but probably not true. The *Mountjoy* broke the boom, but the Coleraine ship, the *Phoenix,* sailed up the river first and anchored off the city around 10 p.m. It must still have been light on that high-latitude, long summer day. A little while later, boats towed the *Mountjoy* up to Derry in the dying evening wind. The ships unloaded bushels of meal, cheeses, bacon, peas, sides of beef, kegs of butter, casks of brandy. All this for fighting men whose ration a few hours earlier had been half a pound of tallow and three-quarters of a pound of cowhide. "The bonfires shone bright along the whole circle of the ramparts," writes Macaulay. "The Irish guns continued to roar all night; and all night the bells of the rescued city made answer to the Irish guns with a peal of joyous defiance."

Sieges are the stuff of national myth-making. Think of Troy, Masada, Quebec, the Alamo, Leningrad, the Battle of Britain: everyone's finest hour. The siege of Derry became such an event, although not right away. It would be almost two centuries before the divided Presbyterian and Anglican Ulster Protestants were able to create the siege as the pre-eminent foundation myth of a united people.

At first, the siege-as-metaphor had a halting and decrepit existence. The main characters faded away. Governor Baker died during the siege. George Walker was killed at the Battle of the Boyne the following year, still the Reverend-in-arms. Adam Murray, who was severely wounded in one of his last brave sallies out of the Butcher Gate, recovered very slowly and then disappeared from history. Micaiah Browning, the Derry captain of the *Mountjoy* who was killed in that final battle, may well have been the proverbial last man to die in the war. John Michelburne, Baker's successor as governor, lost his entire family to disease. He was the only major participant who lived on and kept in close contact with the city and its people. Robert Lundy flashed in and out of view a few times over the next two decades and died in anonymity.

When the centenary celebrations of the siege took place in 1788 (reckoned from the shutting of the gates in December 1688), the people of Derry included what had become, by then, all the long-standing elements of commemoration: drums, cannon (the same ones used for real 100 years earlier), free beer, the blood-crimson flag that Michelburne had first ordered flown. They made martial parades to the cathedral and around the walls, had dinner in the town hall, and, ceremoniously, closed the gates again. The Dean of Derry preached a sermon in the cathedral, and the Reverend Robert Black did the same in the Presbyterian meeting house. On this special anniversary, the citizens also staged a robust mock re-enactment of the siege. It got out of hand, wrote one observer; the "gallant lads" attacked the defenders with such ardour "that it was with the utmost difficulty that they were restrained from returning real shot, and many now bear the honourable wounds of that glorious day."

Two other new things happened during the centenary celebrations. The first was that the great traitor was reborn. Someone (whose identity is lost to us) had the idea of bringing Robert Lundy into the liturgy of the siege. It was also a kind of homage to the bold revolutionary, and plebeian, actions of the thirteen apprentice boys who had defied the authorities and the respectable citizens and shut the gates in the faces of the Earl of Antrim's redshanks. After the organized, official parade in December 1788, a second, guerrilla procession formed up. "Some of the lower class of citizens," says one condescending account, "had provided an effigy representing the well-known Lundy, executed in a very humorous stile, and not without ingenuity." The lads hefted Robert's caricature around the streets for a while, where it was duly insulted by the crowds and then "they burned it in the market place with every circumstance of ignominy." This was entertaining, says the chronicler, but Derry's hoi polloi had also made an instructive point. Their demonstration "marked out, in striking character, the unavoidable destiny of Traitors."

One hundred years after his brief moment in history, Robert returned in myth. His first public disgrace and immolation struck such a chord with the people of Derry that they never gave it up. "Lundy the Traitor" lives on; perhaps he will never die. He is the most famous of all the men of Derry and the only one still necessary to the scheme of inspiration and vindication the city embodies for the Prods of Ulster. He was no longer a mere man but had become the treasonous Everyman, a representative of all compromisers.

One historian writes that if Robert Lundy had not existed, it would have been necessary for the Protestants to invent him. The traitor is a necessary part of the siege myth because he reflects with precision the real and fearful state of things on the ground in Ulster. And that takes us right back to the Plantation, with its failed plan and the reality of the jumble of Catholic Irish tenants and sub-tenants living among their Protestant landlords and the run-of-the-mill Protestant settlers. There were no physical barriers between them, no defensible positions. It was as if the settlers of the American West had not exterminated the Indians or bundled them into small, separate reservations but had, instead, allowed the natives to continue to live among them. There could be no security in such an arrangement: an unstable mélange of violent appropriators and the bitter dispossessed.

However, the second new thing in the centennial commemoration of the siege provided a brief, fragile, and now mostly forgotten moment of enlightenment and moderation. The two sets of Protestants behaved amicably towards each other and, most remarkably, Catholics—both priests and lay people—took part as well. In the context of Northern Ireland today, it was an enviable display of getting along. "Religious dissension," said one observer, "seemed to be buried in oblivion, and Roman Catholics vied with Protestants in expressing, by every possible mark, their sense of the blessings secured to them by our happy Constitution."

That constitution was the crux of the amity. The story of the siege of Derry had evolved from a symbol of Anglican-Presbyterian contention—embodied in the conflicting accounts of George Walker and John Mackenzie—into its second mythical form: Derry had made possible the Glorious Revolution with all its legal and political benefits. The city's resistance had brought down James the despot and ensured the throne for William the enlightened constitutional monarch. This was the emphasis that made it possible for Presbyterian dissenters and especially the Catholic Irish—or, at least, the moderate, urban, better-off Catholic Irish—to believe that there was something in the festivities for everyone to celebrate.

However, this sectarian camaraderie was only an interlude. It couldn't possibly survive the huge, pivotal, radical events of the next few decades: the formation of the revolutionary United Irishmen, culminating in the great, and failed, rebellion of 1798; the 1801 Act of Union, which joined England and Ireland into one constitutional and political unit; and the drive for Catholic emancipation—the first genuine political, as opposed to insurrectionary, native Irish campaign—led by the "Liberator," the lawyer Daniel O'Connell. All that would change the meaning of the siege of Derry once again.

There's an equation that expresses the Protestants' view of the zero-sum game in which they were involved in all of Ireland and that still applies in Northern Ireland: any Catholic gain represents an inevitable and simultaneous Protestant loss. To almost all Protestants, both Anglicans and Presbyterians, the sectarian slaughters that took place during the 1798 rebellion demonstrated yet again the ineradicable savagery of Irish Catholics. But the radical political movement—the original Catholic civil rights campaign—begun and carried on by Daniel O'Connell was something new to worry about. It meant that the enemy was becoming sophisticated; it was turning into a problem whose solution was no longer strictly a matter of military force, land expropriation, penal laws, and eternal armed vigilance. Catholic resurgence in the early nineteenth century reminded Protestants of what had been muffled or submerged for a while: that they were a small, vulnerable minority in Ireland.

In 1814, two events occurred that were no coincidence: the English House of Commons passed O'Connell's first Catholic emancipation motion; and the Apprentice Boys society was formed. Protestant radicalism and sectarian sensibility, and a lessening of the tensions within the Protestant camp between Presbyterians and Anglicans, rose in proportion to the level, and effectiveness, of Catholic political agitation. The Apprentice Boys were the self-appointed keepers of the Derry siege myth, and they had the sole and limited purpose of commemorating the great anniversaries: the shutting of the gates and the relief of the city. (The radical Orange Order, in existence for almost twenty years, had assigned itself the more general responsibility of defender of Protestantism.) The club members were neither apprentices nor boys but, in fact, included many of the Protestant elite. The clubs became a long-standing component of the Protestant power structure—the ideal route to getting anywhere in Ulster was to be an Orange, Freemason, Apprentice Boy. Until recently in Northern Ireland, it still was.

Protestant fears had already changed the nature of the Derry siege celebrations. O'Connell's first large-scale demonstration in the city had taken place three years earlier in 1811. Some Derry Catholics, including a priest, were tied into violence carried out by the Ribbonmen, the oath-bound, underground guerrillas who were mostly the Catholic rump of the revolutionary United Irishmen of 1798, any vague nonsectarian ideals long forgotten. Orangemen and Ribbonmen fought each other with regularity in the countryside throughout most of the northern counties of Ireland. The parades in Derry became more military in character and less carnivalesque.

The Apprentice Boys seemed to come into existence as an unconscious avatar of sectarian animosity. Their very formation embodied the renewed Protestant sense of unease and apprehension. And with everything they did to forge the mythology of the siege, the clubs consolidated the divide between the two peoples and ensured that the long slide into episodic and endemic violence—shading from time to time into local civil war—would go on. The Apprentice Boys also stated: "We are not actuated by factious or sectarian feeling, which we consider would be at variance with the cause of Civil and Religious Liberty." Nice words and, perhaps, believed in, but they did not contain a shred of truth.

Between 1826 and 1828, the Apprentice Boys built a monument that was the most dramatic demonstration of the mutating meaning of the siege myth. It was a three-metre figure on top of a twenty-seven-metre column, built on the Royal Bastion on the highest section of Derry's walls overlooking the Bogside. The statue was of none other than George Walker. History had made its choice or, rather, the Protestants of Derry had chosen the history they wanted and thought they needed: Walker was the siege hero most worth memorializing. The pompous, self-aggrandizing, surrender-prone, quasi-"Lundy" had made the big time. He would loom fifty metres over the hovels of the Catholic Irish squeezed into the boggy lowland below the walls—until 1973, when the IRA blew him up.

The Protestants could make no greater show of their attitudes and intentions. The fine, stone houses and the citadel, with the power and glory of its high walls, belonged to them, but the foul little ground of the adjacent bog was where the Catholics would have to lump it. The Protestants would hold their high ground, at whatever cost, as they had in 1689. They would never surrender; the Catholics would never break them. "POPERY . . ." went one speech during the 1826 ceremonies, "*ever was, now is,* and *ever will be* INCORRIGIBLY THE SAME.*" To drive home the lesson, the man who led the resistance to the siege (or who had now been chosen for that part) would always stand over the Irish with his overbearing height. Walker held a Bible in his left hand and a sword in his right. The sword was blown down, according to local legend, in a storm that swept over Derry on the day that Catholic emancipation passed in Parliament. Myths can work both ways: the sword isn't everything; God may not be on your side.

Soon, the Walker monument served another, utilitarian, purpose. The Apprentice Boys flew the crimson flag beside it and fired off cannon over the Bogside. And instead of burning the effigy of Lundy the Traitor in the Diamond (the city's centre), they attached it to the base of the monument and burned it there instead. Every year (except when the action was proscribed in especially violent years), Robert went up in flames at the feet of his ambivalent libeller. Seeing his immolation from that high vantage point, the Catholics could be edified by seeing how Prods treated one of their own who went against the tribe, let alone a rebellious Taig.

This rampant clubbing together into a tighter solidarity was part of the Protestant reaction to the Catholics' movement for political reform, but also to their physical relocation into the hitherto Protestant city. The Irish couldn't breach the walls in 1689, but they walked in through the gates, and stayed there, in the nineteenth century. Derry's new textile industries needed workers. Catholics responded, moving in from the countryside, especially from Donegal; by 1851, more than half of Derry's people were Catholic. To these internal immigrants, the siege meant nothing more than defeat, Protestant Ascendancy, and the penal laws. The Protestants of Derry more and more felt the chill wind of demographic inevitability, the brute fact of Catholic numerousness, the weight of the Irish on their own ancient ground.

It is theoretically possible for people whose cultural rituals and traditions are threatened and devalued to react by loosening up, letting go, modifying their behaviour to accommodate the new and different people among them. But even modern immigrant countries like the United States and Canada have had difficulty with such open-minded ecumenism. For nineteenth-century Ulster Protestants, it was unimaginable. Their fear and distrust were already far too strong and ingrained. The pattern of sectarian life in the city of Derry became more and more like the intermingled and jumbled population of the Ulster Plantation as a whole.

The mid-century consolidation of the Apprentice Boys clubs and the Protestant community in general—less and less of the old Presbyterian-Anglican animosity—also coincided with, and was encouraged by, two quite different and apparently unrelated events. A book was published, and the train came to town.

The book was Thomas Babington Macaulay's *History of England*. His history was a hymn to the Glorious Revolution of 1688. The victory of *Rí Liam* over *Rí Seamus* had ensured progress and constitutional government for Britain forevermore. Macaulay's dictum that the siege of Derry was to Ulster Protestants what the Battle of Marathon had been to the Greeks meant that it was a victory for the rule of law over tyranny. More important than Macaulay's thesis, however, was his sheer literary power. His account of the siege was a thundering good story (it would make a terrific movie)—and historical accuracy or serious analysis be damned:

> Thirty thousand Protestants, of both sexes and of every age, were crowded behind the bulwarks of the City of Refuge. There, at length, on the verge of the ocean, hunted to the last asylum, and baited into a mood in which men may be destroyed, but will not easily be subjugated, the imperial race turned desperately to bay.

This was the stuff of myth-making all right, and it was the apotheosis of the Derry siege myth. Macaulay gave Ulster Protestants a vocabulary ("City of Refuge," "the imperial race") to validate their sacrifice on the city's bloody walls. And he created a sense of destiny because the resistance had literally changed the world. Macaulay's book was one of the most important creators of the simple (and simple-minded), reductionist interpretation of the siege as Protestant solidarity in opposition to Catholic despotism. "Mythology is much better stuff than history," one novelist writes; "it has form, logic, a message." But things never really happen like that; if it's neat and gratifying, it can't be history. The myth of the siege, like all such fabrications, had to eliminate complexity and ambiguity. It had to deny bleak, uncomforting history so that it could become reassuring and cosy myth. Macaulay fashioned the transformation.

However, even the great polemicist had reservations when it came to the Irish. Writing about Ireland, he said, was like treading on a volcano whose lava was still glowing. Ireland was "cursed by the domination of race over race, and of religion over religion." Macaulay was English, and by the middle of the nineteenth century his country had long reached the point where orderly, gradual political reform had replaced religious enthusiasm. But the damned, unstable, unruly Irish, including the Protestants of Ulster, had not changed at all. For them, it was still life and death. The great issues represented by the three words *plough, sword,* and *book* still meant everything to them. Macaulay had advocated celebrating the past, but the Irish took his rhetoric as a blueprint for the future. He had to write an introduction to his *History.* It was all very well to celebrate deliverance from the siege; doing so "belongs to the higher and purer part of human nature." But Protestant triumphalism was the unpleasant side of all such "dominant castes and dominant sects." The "expressions of pious gratitude which have resounded from [Derry's] pulpits have too often been mingled [with] words of wrath and defiance." Having lit the fire, or at least having added a great deal of fuel to it, Macaulay made a half-hearted and useless effort to contain it.

The other event, which by its coincidence enabled the Derry Protestants, especially the Apprentice Boys, to celebrate the siege more aggressively, was the invention of the railway and its arrival in Derry. The new form of mass transportation meant that a hitherto local event could be amplified by hundreds, or even thousands, of Protestants shuttled in for a day or two. This support changed the nature of the occasion. It was one thing for a thousand Protestants from Derry and the Waterside to march along the walls and fire off cannon over the Bogside. They would see their Catholic neighbours the next day at work or in the market. There would be the opportunity to ameliorate the triumphalist tenor of the event through conversation, the camaraderie of male insult, the simple fact of dealing with each other. It was a completely different thing to have the place fill up with many more unknown Prods from Coleraine or Strabane, and later, as the rail system developed, from much farther away—East Belfast or Larne on the Antrim coast, or even Scotland. That amplified the aggressive aspects of the marching, the way it marked territories: "This is ours; that's yours" or "We can march through yours because we're really in charge of everywhere here." In reality, the marching meant: "We fear that we will lose what is ours and this is a defiant attempt to defend it." Nevertheless, the abrupt influx of strangers felt to the Catholics like an invasion, or like a brutal didactic demonstration that the Protestant overlords still ruled them. Fear was the motivation on one side; resentment, the consequence on the other.

By the 1860s, the mould of the siege myth's modern meaning was not yet set, but it was hardening. Demographics got worse for the Protestants. In 1868, there were 8,800 of them in Derry, compared with more than 12,000 Catholics. The increasing threat of Catholic political power was bad enough, but, then, the physical-force side of Irish resistance reappeared.

It had done so twice since the Insurrection of 1798: in 1803 and again in 1848, in the Irish version of the Europe-wide revolutions of that year for democracy and the rights of man. These were extensive and serious events in Europe, but, in Ireland, it was a "cabbage-patch" rebellion (as 1803 had been), confused, ill run, and soon put down. Like any battle, however short, it produced its embittered veterans. Ten years later, some of them, led by James Stephens, set up a new type of Irish organization in Dublin: a secret, oath-bound, cell-structured revolutionary group whose goal was the establishment, by any means, of an independent Irish republic. (Its secrecy and cell-like "need-to-know" characteristics turned out to be mostly theoretical.) It had no defining name but, Cosa Nostra–like, was variously known as "The Society," "The Organization," or "The Brotherhood." Later, it would consolidate itself as the Irish Republican Brotherhood (the IRB).

This latest band of kerns had two important aspects: it was international in character and, many years later, its members would form the heart of the Easter Rising of 1916. Its formation had been inspired, and was financed, by members of a new Catholic-Irish nation overseas. These Irish in America were there because they had been forced into emigration by the holocaust of the Famine; their hatred of England was bright and hot. It was fuelled by isolation from Ireland and by nostalgia for it. They formed their own analogous organization in the United States and called themselves Fenians, after the *fianna,* the warriors of ancient Ireland. The Irish home base of the American branch of these new republicans soon became Fenians, too. The transatlantic link between the two groups—from one perspective, they could be called terrorist organizations—was prophetic and would have profound consequences in Ireland. The Irish in America would buy guns and bombs and provide money for radical nationalists in Ireland throughout the coming wars. An unknown number, but certainly hundreds, of Protestant civilians, policemen, and British soldiers would be killed by the IRA in Northern Ireland's Troubles, using weapons and explosives bought with American money.

The Fenians in Ireland staged an armed rising in 1867. It was yet another archetypal blood sacrifice in the name of Mother Ireland and so was revered by the standard received version of Irish history. The rising itself was ineffectual, but the aftermath, in the perpetually clumsy hands of the English, had great and lasting effect. Three of the Fenians, the so-called Manchester Martyrs, were executed. The resulting outrage in Ireland mobilized nationalist support far in excess of what living Fenians could have managed, and it launched the constitutional Irish Home Rule movement. The Fenian martyrs also provided a prototype for the leaders of the 1916 Easter Rising, men who would become the quintessential self-sacrificers for the *Shan Van Vocht* (the anglicized spelling of the Gaelic *Sean-bhean Bhocht*)—the "Poor Old Woman" who stood for Ireland.

In Protestant Ulster, the Fenians provoked the same disgust and fear as the IRA does today (or as Islamist terrorist groups do). It was bad enough that the Fenians had rebelled, but worse that the ordinary Catholic Irish were so ready to stand behind them and to grieve at their executions—which had, after all, been carried out according to law in retribution for an armed rising. Protestants believed that Catholics had disclosed yet again their disturbing love of violent revolution and of the Fenian-kerns who perpetrated it.

Derry, the city out on the Protestants' frontier, was the most sensitive register of their jitters, becoming the tripwire for political and religious explosions in the north of Ireland. (It would remain so: events in Derry in 1968 and 1969 tipped the endemic fear and loathing on both sides of the sectarian line into open civil war and the deployment, yet again, of British soldiers on Irish land.) In 1868 and 1869, the years after the Fenian revolt, fierce riots took place in the city. Protestant and Catholic gunmen fired on each other. The template of urban mobs, stones, guns, and territories was already set. A combatant in Derry in 1869 would have felt right at home rioting in the city a hundred years later.

Commemoration has long been a lively industry in Ireland; in a kind of time-warped dialectic, it continually reshapes present views of past events and, in the process, reinforces the effect of the past on the present. The Derry siege commemoration parades developed early on into the prototype for the thousands of parades that still take place in Northern Ireland—at least 3,500 of them each year, mostly Protestant. They are *sui generis,* Ulster to the core, alien to England—and to the Republic of Ireland for that matter. That's because their purpose is to reiterate the sectarian boundaries and to affirm symbolically the settlement territories established during the period of the Plantation in the seventeenth century, patterns almost unchanged since then. Neither of these purposes has any bearing outside Ulster. The combination of elements in the parades is a northern Irish invention, too: the bands, flags, banners, antique (and culturally confused) regalia—the bowler hats and rolled brollies of the Orange Lodges and the Apprentice Boys clubs, the accoutrements of English gentlemen worn by Irish roughnecks. It's theatre, religious display, and political demonstration in one provocative, aggressive package. In today's celebrations of the siege of Derry in 1689 or the Battle of the Boyne in 1690, the Protestants recall what the Great Rising of 1641 taught them: be on guard forever; seek out and destroy the Lundys; never trust the Catholics, whose vengeance is unrelenting.

9

LUNDY BURNS

WHEN I VISIT Derry, people often respond to my name and always with the same wry start; there are no Lundys in the city these days. Once, while attending a lecture at McGee College, a friend and I ran into Nobel Peace Prize–winner John Hume. He is a moderate Catholic politician who has pursued peaceful political solutions in Northern Ireland for thirty-five years and has survived assassination attempts and many death threats for his trouble. My friend knew Hume and introduced me. The tousled, unassuming, un-colour-coordinated, friendly Nobel laureate laughed and said: "I never thought I'd be shaking the hand of someone called 'Lundy' in Derry."

Earlier, the general secretary of the Apprentice Boys of Derry had invited me to their hall for a few drinks on the evening before the 2003 Lundy Day parade, on December 6. He had been surprised and amused that someone called Lundy had contacted him a few days before his boys were to burn the great traitor's effigy. He asked if we were related. I said I didn't know, but it was possible.

The Apprentice Boys Memorial Hall is situated just inside Derry's walls where they are at their highest, overtopping the low land of the Bogside. About seventy metres of the ramparts had been reinforced with a ten-metre-high wire-mesh fence to deter Prods from throwing anything over it onto the heads of Taigs below. Looking down into the old Catholic-Irish ghetto, I could see the H-Block Prisoners' and Bloody Sunday memorials, the murals of republican gunmen-heroes, the famous "You Are Now Entering

Free Derry" house-end. The Apprentice Boys Hall, from a distance, is not a handsome building, but it's an interesting one in the ornate style of its time, part neo-Gothic, part Scottish Baronial. Close up, I saw the splatters of paint bombs, the heavy wire mesh over the windows, the thick steel doors. Even in these days of ceasefires and the Good Friday Agreement, it's fortified like a biker-gang's clubhouse. The base of the George Walker memorial—minus its gelignited subject and his column—is nearby.

At first, I couldn't get inside. The doors were locked and the building showed no lights, disclosed no sound. Three policemen with assault rifles and body armour watched me impassively from the other side of the narrow lane. I wandered around trying to find another way in, but the hall's back and sides were protected by high iron fences, razor-wired across the top. After a few minutes, a couple of the boys came along with keys and let me in. There were two sets of steel doors, which they locked carefully behind us. To my surprise, there were scores of people in the noisy second-floor bar and the lounge. My overwhelming first impression was of shaved heads, beer bellies, tattoos, fat men and some women, a few fat kids eating chips topped with melted cheese, blowsiness, yob-dom, a sense of jazzed-up menace. With my careless haircut and beard, I had more hair than any dozen of these men put together. They looked at me with curiosity, without friendliness. I was aware again of my "Catholic" appearance—a beard, especially, signifying Taig, not Prod. There was no doubt about it: I felt a shaky, gut-stirring apprehension. I consoled myself with the thought that I was Protestant and that they wouldn't hurt a fellow-member of the tribe.

However, things got better right away. I asked for Billy, the general secretary. He wasn't there yet, but one of the club's lesser officials could help me. Like Billy, he was surprised and tickled that a Lundy had arrived on their doorstep. It was the first time he'd ever heard of that happening. Was I related? he asked. Maybe, I said. He took me down to the basement room where they had constructed the Lundy effigy. It lay on its side like a giant, painted doll. The boys would hang it up the next morning, no longer provocatively in the Diamond or on the stump of the Walker memorial, but on a street corner near the hall. Around it the police would set up a defensive cordon to keep beyond stone-throwing distance the ninety-six

percent of the city's inhabitants who are now Catholic. I made com-
plimentary remarks on my possible ancestor's seven-metre-high,
dark-coated, epauletted, cock-hatted form, his bizarre rouged
cheeks and malevolent idiot grin. I meant what I said; as effigies
went, this was indeed a humdinger. Robert already had his signs
attached: the accusatory "Lundy the Traitor" on his front; the min-
atory "The End of All Traitors" on his back.

Billy still hadn't arrived. My guide was a sandy-eyebrowed,
buzz-haired, pot-bellied, quiet-spoken, seemingly gentle man
whom I was beginning to like. He took me into the museum room.
It was lined with glass-fronted wooden cabinets, all of them stuffed
with an eclectic jumble of every artifact and gewgaw imaginable:
cups and saucers bearing likenesses of monarchs, a statuette of King
Billy, a portrait of George Walker, coats-of-arms, old and contemporary books, a model of the boom-busting ship *Mountjoy,* old
swords and clocks, parchments and proclamations, medals, a piece
of the pear tree that Robert may have climbed down to escape, an
old milk jug, cannonballs supposedly dating from the siege, a large
bowl of plastic flowers.

Several new members were getting inducted that day, and other
Apprentice Boys were showing the museum room to them, too. At
the time, I was still nervous of these hard-case men; I suspected
them of prejudice and malevolence. Now when I examine the
photographs I took of them, they look like ordinary, nice, though
tough, blokes who are proud and pleased with their new sashes on
one of the most important days of their lives. They pose like chuffed
college graduates.

My guide told me that, one day, the club would set up a proper
museum, with an interpretive centre, videos, and books where they
could celebrate their great legacy and properly display their history
to the Protestant people of Ulster. Fat chance, I said to myself at
the time. But, later, I thought what a fine thing that would be. If the
Apprentice Boys could set up a real museum as if they were
Shriners or an old regiment or a social club with a violent past that
was truly in the past, without having it paint-splattered or fire-
bombed or shot at, then that would mean the mythology had
shifted once again: the immediate and murderous meaning had,
finally, been leached out of the old siege. The Apprentice Boys

would become a tourist attraction, part of northern "Oirishness"—the memory of the United Irish Insurrection of 1798 was already beginning to move in that direction. Some day, I thought, but not yet, not by a long shot.

Upstairs in the bar, still waiting for Billy, I met Jim, a man in his seventies who was drinking Irish whiskeys neat, one after the other, without apparent effect. He lived in the last Protestant West Bank pocket, the Fountain district. It was petrol-bombed every day, he claimed (which must have been true in the past, but not now), or the Taigs threw stones over the security fence at the Prod houses. I had seen the wall, topped by a high wire-mesh fence, separating the Fountain from the surrounding Catholic area; you'd have to have the arm of an Olympic javelin-thrower to get a stone over it, but I supposed it was possible. Jim said he was bothered in the streets every time he left the Fountain; he couldn't walk down Bishop Street without getting stoned by kids. He was contemptuous of his fellow-Prods—"heroes," he called them—who had given up and left the Fountain for the safety of the Waterside over the Foyle or even farther away to the east. He hated Catholics, of course, and avoided them unless he could "use them"—for example, if they were selling something cheaper than a Protestant was. When I referred to the city as "Derry" by mistake, Jim angrily corrected me. All evening, I had tried to say "Londonderry," not just "Derry." I had slipped up twice with some of the other men, but they had just laughed at a stranger's error. Jim said he had been a B Special. So had my grandfather, I said. I told him my name was Lundy. He took the news sourly, without the interested amusement of the younger men. Are you related? he asked, belligerently. It's extremely unlikely, I said.

Nearby, three particularly big-bellied, bald, tattooed, loud men drank fast and talked in an incomprehensible dialect I recognized as Scottish. A local man at the bar told me they were from Glasgow. He couldn't understand what the hell they were saying either, he said. He just smiled at them and nodded. Leave them alone, later on, he warned me, when they've a wee bit too much drink taken. My gentlemanly guide had soothed my queasiness. But he had disappeared, and it surged up again as I listened to Jim tell me how much he hated fuckin' Taigs; as the Glaswegians worked themselves up like incomprehensible, savage kerns; and as the drinking all around the room turned ugly as men started to lurch to the loo, shout and sing the old songs—"The Sash," "Dolly's Brae" (the site of a massacre of Catholics by Orangemen in 1849)—and stare at me with alcoholic belligerence. I noticed some prison and paramilitary tattoos. The men seemed more and more like the Proddy shock troops I had believed them to be. In a Catholic bar, I thought, the drinkers would be singing the old rebel songs, or songs that had nothing to do with Ireland, loose and easy, having a good time, revelling in the *craic,* confident of the future. Here, the atmosphere was tight, defensive, combative, because these men feared the uncertain future.

I was thinking seriously of getting the hell out of there when Billy arrived. He's a big man, sliding into corpulence and with the regulation shaved head, but obviously intelligent. He was courteous, friendly, and wore a businessman's suit. He had been a member of the club since 1973, when he was fifteen, and had been its general secretary for nine years. The Troubles had gone on for almost his whole life. As we spoke, attitudes around me changed: I caught glimpses of deference and respect. Billy was obviously the club's liked and esteemed Big Man. If he was talking intimately to me, I must be okay. I felt as though I had come under his protection.

At first, Billy said that Robert Lundy was English, but then he agreed with me that he was Scottish. I had noticed this historical casualness all evening. My museum-room guide had told me that Robert was in the city when the apprentice boys closed the gates against his orders—whereas, in reality, Robert was still slogging around Ulster with Mountjoy's regiment, not yet even the city's governor. Other men I had talked to were equally confused about the sequence of events. It was the mark of myth; the precision of history (such as it is) is unimportant so long as the good old story—the standard received version of Protestant history—serves its purpose.

Billy said that, in his opinion, Lundy had, in fact, been a military genius who had looked around Derry, decided it couldn't be defended, and got the hell out. He took great pains to tell me that they didn't burn Lundy in effigy because they enjoyed burning people; they weren't bloodthirsty. They burn him because the flames, the fire, purge the Protestants symbolically, cleanse them of traitors. Lundy is merely the symbol. Only in a place whose people have recently spent a great deal of time committing atrocities would someone think it necessary to emphasize this obvious point.

Another man who had joined our conversation suggested to Billy that he introduce me to the room as a Lundy. It'd be a quare laugh, he said. Billy smiled, considered the proposal for a while, and then said no, he didn't think that would be a good idea. Maybe earlier on, but not now that the boys had had a bit of drink.

After a while, Billy had to leave to take care of business. The Lundy Day parade was the next day and he had much to do. He had spent a lot of time with me; I liked the man and was grateful for that. The drinking was going on more than ever, the shouting and singing intensifying, the Glasgow men looking for a fight. If these men marched through my neighbourhood tomorrow, I thought, they would certainly piss me off. It was late and I decided to leave. I had to find someone to let me out and lock the steel doors behind me.

It was near midnight, and things had changed outside. There were two armoured Land Rovers and a dozen or so policemen. A crowd of about forty young men were clustered on the city walls behind police barricades. They shouted and jeered at me as I came outside. A couple of them made throwing motions, although I couldn't see whether they were actually lobbing anything my way. One of the coppers said, smiling, "Up that way, mate, you'll be okay," and directed me up the secured lane towards the Diamond, away from the Catholic youths. The Apprentice Boys were like captives in their fortified hall, besieged in their shrunken territory inside Derry's walls. As I walked away, I felt intense relief, as if I had just managed to get myself out of a weird and dangerous place.

There were only a few police about as I walked along the deserted streets to the Diamond, under the old walls through the arch of the Butcher Gate, where Prods and Irish had fought the bloodiest, most desperate battles of the siege. I went down along the edge of the Bogside to Waterloo Place and Strand Road. The now-Catholic, nationalist city council has not felt the need to change the *sassenagh* names or to put up signs in Irish. They have nothing to prove; the city is theirs. Here the pubs were jammed and the streets full of drinking and tipsy people, mostly kids, gangs of them everywhere. It was just a regular Friday night in Derry. But down among the Catholics, I felt set free, at ease, not threatened at all by the sorts of loud, happy carousers you would see in any city at midnight. I felt that I fit in here with my beard and Fenian look. It was a rough, tough place, Derry, but it all seemed normal compared with the harsh, belligerent tension in the Boys' Memorial Hall, where the feel of violence was barely contained. As I walked up Great James Street to my rented room, two heavy armoured Land Rovers passed me, having just driven out of the fortress-like Strand Road police station. A few minutes later, I heard five or six loud bangs from the downtown area I'd just left. I couldn't tell if they were explosions, stun grenades, or something innocent. Next day, there was nothing in the news to explain them, and no one I asked about them had noticed.

All the newspaper, radio, and television commentators agreed that the Lundy Day parade the next day was a success. There was no rioting or stone-throwing, no gunshots. No one was killed or even hurt. The police deployed hundreds of men and dozens of armoured Land Rovers. They lined the sensitive part of the route with stout steel and Plexiglas barriers and formed up in front of them, rolling their forces along with the parade's progress in a disciplined manoeuvre at which they had obviously had a lot of practice. Heavily armed riot police and other "robocop" units stood by in side streets. The army helicopter and spotter plane flew overhead.

The Prods marched and played the old songs. As I watched, Billy swung by, splendid in his dark suit, sash, bowler hat, and tight-rolled brolly, and gave me a big smile. A few other men recognized me from the evening before. "Hey, Lundy," they shouted out. I noticed some of the other spectators round about looking at me hard. I didn't know if it was my name or the fact that I knew someone in the parade. Still, it was friendly and festive, and I wondered if I might have been too suspicious of the boys, too ready to stereotype them.

The marchers prayed in Saint Columb's Cathedral—from which, during the siege, the bloody crimson flag had flown and cannons had fired—their colours and banners piled against the ancient wall outside as if the men were soldiers praying before battle. They stopped for lunch and drinks in and outside The Talk of the Town, the only Prod pub left in the city. As they drank, the surrounding police riot squads observed them with the weary, thoughtful wariness of veteran coppers. The Catholics ignored the parade, or watched with gloomy contempt, irritated by the disruption of traffic and the difficulty of getting to the stores to do some Christmas shopping. From behind the barriers, their young men yelled and jeered.

As darkness fell, three thousand or so people gathered around the traitor Lundy, who had been hung from a portable scaffold. The Lambeg drums began their staccato clatter, the sound loud and harsh. They had been the battle drums of William of Orange, their rhythmic orders designed to be heard above the tumult of combat, and their sound rose easily over the noise of a jubilant crowd. Robert's effigy caught fire quickly—it was impregnated with pitch—and flamed up, first the legs, then the torso, and last the head. The heat was apparent fifty metres away. In the dark, from a distance, the scale of things became unclear and the burning dummy looked as if it could have been a real man. The fire, the drums, the singing and cheering people were a savage, atavistic spectacle that shivered my skin. The burning was over in twenty minutes, and the satisfied crowd dispersed. A police line contained a few score of shouting young Catholic men. Soon, only the giant drums remained near the traitor's smoldering remnants. Shifts of men beat them, the sound rolling out over the city walls and the Bogside and the rest of the West Bank, and across the Foyle to the Waterside, as it had on that day every year for a hundred years.

For many Ulster Protestants today, Derry is a terrible portent of emasculation and decline, a symbol of the falling away of their power and demographic heft in Northern Ireland. The population trend begun in the nineteenth century has reached its inevitable conclusion. The remnants of the Protestants of Derry are clustered in their seedy little district beside the river. The most visible end-house grafitto says: "Londonderry West Bank Loyalists. Still Under Siege. No Surrender." Derry was always "The Maiden City, wooed but never won," the true loyal stronghold, which resisted penetration by the brutish Irish and retained its purity, a Protestant analogue of the Catholic Mother Ireland, the *Shan Van Vocht*. It doesn't matter now. The Protestants have finally lost what they expended so much to keep more than three hundred years ago.

Even the east bank of the Foyle, the Waterside, has far fewer Protestants these days. Indeed, over the course of the Troubles, there has been a silent and mostly unremarked exodus of Protestants away from the west of Ulster, from counties Londonderry, Fermanagh, and Tyrone, to the east across the ancient dividing line of the River Bann and back into their old redoubt of Down and Antrim—or out of the country altogether in the traditional escape of emigration. They have gone for various reasons: some left voluntarily because they no longer felt comfortable or at home in the west; others were intimidated away or burned out. A historian, a Catholic, who lives in Derry told me that during the Troubles along the border, the IRA carried out a long campaign of assassination, killing the sons of Protestant farmers. The shocked, bereaved fathers sold out cheap, and the buyers were always Catholic. This was just the old pattern playing out yet again—of vicious local campaigns to try to reverse the conquest and the Plantation. The emigration east or away has been a trickle of people, but a steady one. It's another sign of the coming times for Protestants: the greater siege for which no relief will ever arrive.

As for the man Lundy himself, we can say what's known about the last twenty-seven years of Robert's life in a few sentences. The Scottish records and accounts of his family have only one laconic comment on his culpability in the little *contretemps* at Derry: "After this episode he was initially accused of Treason, being held briefly at the Tower of London, but he later had his conduct approved by the English Parliament."

After that, he remained the professional soldier, fighting everywhere for the emerging British Empire. He spent a brief time as a military adviser to Prince George of Hesse in Darmstadt. He applied to the Lord High Treasurer in 1704 for money so he could carry out his commission as adjutant-general of the King of Portugal's forces in the Queen of England's pay. He got £108 out of secret service money. He fought against the French and Spaniards during their siege of Gibraltar and, according to one historian at least, "achieve[d] glory" there. Once more we're aware of the anomaly of his valour before and after Derry and his supposed cowardice while he was its governor. He was taken prisoner in April 1707 at the Battle of Almanza. Once again he was in jail, perhaps because, for the second time, the men he led had let him down—the

Portuguese army behaved as badly as the men of Derry may have at the Battle of the Fords. After two years, Robert was released in exchange for twenty French captives. Two months later, he petitioned the government for pay for the time he had been imprisoned, to be allowed out of the Portuguese King's English subsidy. There's no record of the outcome. Indeed, there's no record of anything else in Robert's life until Araminta's pension petition in 1717 and her father's presumed death. Perhaps he was finally happy to stay home and quiet. He never knew that the Protestants of Ulster would never forget him.

PART TWO

WILLIAM

10

A SUSPICIOUS PERSONAGE

THEY WERE GENTLE ENOUGH when they arrested him, but that soon changed. He had been riding here and there for days on his old and fading mount. That was one of the things they used against him: his peripatetics during those warm spring days of late May and early June 1798 while bloody murder was going on in Leinster. But he had had good and sufficient—and innocent—reasons, he said. He had ridden to Newtownards and to Ballee to conduct services. After all, he was in demand as a visiting preacher and he could never refuse to bring the New Light and his vigorous adumbration of scripture politics to whoever was interested in them. Besides, May was the month for administering the sacrament of the Lord's Supper, and he was obliged to assist in the various congregations near his own in Portaferry. All that had required travel.

He had also been obliged to go to Saintfield Fair to look for a new horse. There had been none suitable there—it was surprising how difficult it could be to find a good horse in Ireland, which was supposed to be full of the beasts. His bilious complaints, which had been ameliorated by the change of air in Scotland, and perhaps by sea-sickness, too, had soon come back on his return to Ulster. A medical friend had told him to change his sedentary habits and to take some exercise by riding every day. His sacramental duties provided ample opportunity for that, but he needed a stronger horse. His friend had also advised him to take the waters at Ballynahinch, and that was where he really wanted to end up, to try to relieve, as soon as he could, his intestinal uproar.

He knew they were trying to implicate him in the rebellion, and that belief had been confirmed by their behaviour on his return from Scotland the previous month. He had travelled there to visit one of his wife's uncles who was dangerously ill. Indeed, the uncle had soon died, and it had taken weeks to sort out the man's affairs, which were in an unsettled state. When he had arrived home again, his servant, who had brought his luggage from Donaghadee, was stopped in the street in Portaferry and taken to the guardhouse. The soldiers had scrutinized everything with a minuteness which, to their credit, they had ridiculed even as they performed the task. Any object that might have contained a dangerous concealment had been tossed, shaken, and turned inside out, to no purpose. They had treated a large tobacco box as if it hid more evils than Pandora's box. It had belonged to a sea captain, and William had brought it from Scotland as a curiosity. It couldn't be opened; the soldiers thought it had some kind of concealed spring. They were about to demolish it when their captain, noticing it was just rusty, stopped them and let it go. They had suspected that his visit to Scotland to comfort a dying friend was a pretext and that his real reason had been to promote United Irish societies there and to carry messages to those of Ireland. Naturally, like any cunning conspirator plotting revolution, he would have carried sensitive documents in the underwear in his luggage or inside an old rusty tobacco box that stood out like a priest in Larne.

They had carried out this search of his belongings in April, even before any violence had broken out in the south. Small wonder they were sniffing along his trail now, in late May, as he rode between Newtownards, Ballee, and home in Portaferry performing his liturgical duties—and to Saintfield for a horse. He had ridden into Belfast a couple of times because someone had told him about an animal for sale there, and that must have added to their suspicion.

As he was pursuing these peaceful and lawful pursuits, the southern United Irishmen rose in rebellion. It was bloody insurrection from the beginning. The government's troops killed three hundred rebels at Tara—where the old Gaelic high kings had held their courts and where pagan gods like Lug and Medb had squabbled and contrived. Two hundred rebels died at the Curragh; the troops slaughtered them as they tried to surrender. A few days later, the United Irish rebels attacked the town of Carlow, but the government garrison repulsed them, killing many. Three days after that, the uncoordinated and chaotic rising began in County Wexford, and this time the Catholic elements within the United Irishmen—the secret society of the Defenders—were more prominent. The insurgents massacred government militia and yeomanry—mostly Protestants—at Oulart. Then they captured Enniscorthy and Wexford Town, and set up the headquarters there for a provisional revolutionary government. Small wonder that the authorities in Ulster, the heart of the United Irish societies, were on tenterhooks. If there was going to be a revolution, it should have started in Ulster; Irish rebellions always broke out there first and worst.

As he rode about the roads of County Down and as the risings in the south erupted, William could feel the hot and avid breath of suspicion and mistrust on his neck. They were waiting for him to inculpate himself, to let a word slip out that would show his guilt. A friendly officer (in fact, the one who had saved his tobacco box from destruction) met William at Downpatrick on his way to Ballee and told him he had just been to Portaferry to look for him there with a message from Colonel Stapleton, the commander of the surrounding military zone. On what authority, the colonel wanted to know, had William said that "a party of the Black Horse had gone over to the insurgents?" William had made the remark two days earlier in Belfast, and apparently the walls had ears and the mobile ability to report to the government. He wrote a note to the colonel in reply, saying he had only been repeating common reports around the city that day about the Black Horse cavalry and some of its apparent defectors. There were many similar rumours in circulation. He didn't write that such conjecture was to be expected, given that the people had been under severe suppression for many months and that general and fierce war had burst forth in Leinster. This episode was but one of William's many experiences with shadowy and corrupt informers. Their whispers and sly probing had dogged him for years.

On his second day in Ballee, he baptized a child and, afterwards, dined with John M'Neown, a respectable farmer, and some other men of the neighbourhood. After dinner, the talk turned to the various punishments the government had been carrying out around the country for some time as a means of heading off Irish unrest, yet, in the usual English ham-handed way, creating more of it: floggings, shavings with red-hot iron, half-hangings. How this harsh response was supposed to reduce the likelihood of insurrection in a country that had seen and felt little but the necessity of it was beyond most of the attendees at the dinner. One of the company was sanguine, however. "Very well," he said, "if they do not proceed to whole-hanging." William replied: "Well, indeed; for my part, from what I am experiencing, and the manner in which I am hunted, I am sure they will hang me if they can find any plausible pretext." There must have been a government spy at that otherwise convivial and confidential table. William's words would haunt him later.

He finally got to Ballynahinch, where he stayed and ate alone in the inn. The next day, he rode out to the well at seven in the morning and drank the water. He hoped for a quick result, but feared that his chronic biliousness would need a good many gallons of Ballynahinch's best. He visited and drank again at one in the afternoon and at five in the evening.

As it happened, this was on June 5, the very day of the rebel attack on the town of New Ross. It might have been the crucial battle of the revolt in Leinster. If the United Irish insurgents had succeeded there, the rebellion would have spread into Munster and certainly Ulster, and become very difficult to contain. Perhaps the French allies would have made their long-promised and planned landing, their veteran troops, no longer *sans culottes* but the best in Europe, stiffening the amateur Irish rebels, sweeping north and east to Limerick and Dublin, maybe to Derry, too, and no need for a siege this time—the corrupt landlord's government brought down; the English driven out; and the Irish, no longer divided into Taigs, Prods, and Dissenters but united as Irishmen, creating their government, like the Americans and the French, on the principles of liberty and equality. Ireland, that most distressful country, a nation once again.

But New Ross was a terrible failure. During the very hours that William was riding to and from the well and taking his cure, fifteen hundred rebels and townspeople were dying in the narrow streets and alleys, the former cut down in the fighting, the latter slaughtered by rampaging troops in the aftermath of the battle.

William returned to the inn after his third ride to the well. He had just sat down when a servant informed him there was a gentleman in the street who wanted to speak with him. He went out and found Captain Magenis and a lieutenant of the Castlewellan yeomanry waiting for him. William knew the captain and, in fact, had met him on the road and travelled a mile or so with him into Ballynahinch the previous day. Magenis was hesitant and embarrassed but finally revealed that a number of yeomanry officers had met that day in Clough, and that he had received a letter from Colonel Lord Annesley ordering him to detain William as a prisoner until he got further instructions. It was all very civilized. William reassured the agitated officer: "I was perfectly easy, as I could bid defiance to malice itself, if unsupported by villainy, in respect to every part of my conduct." William asked for his warrant of arrest. He had none, replied the captain, but only his lordship's letter. Not a shred of due process of law; it was all suspicion and pretext and the caprice of arbitrary authority. There was no surprise there, however. The government's cruel repression had long been extra-judicial—to put it mildly.

Then the two yeomanry officers did something extraordinary, a mark of the esteem in which many in the north of Ireland held this radical minister. William had a horse, they observed; perhaps he might like to take a ride—alone. It was nothing less than the offer of a chance to escape: he could ride to the coast, to Donaghadee, and get a boat for Scotland; or he could go south to the safety (albeit temporary) of the rebel forces in arms.

Perhaps he was too sick, too weary, or maybe he thought he'd take his chances because he believed there was no good, if any, evidence against him to support his arrest and detention. And there was his family in Portaferry—Isabella and the children. The government had never shrunk from making women and children hurt for the sins, actual or suspected, of their men. In any event, he declined the offer.

At noon the next day, a Colonel Bainbridge arrived and, without interviewing William, ordered him taken to Lisburn. William sent a message to the colonel requesting a ride or a chaise; the weather was intensely hot, and he was in delicate health. He received this response: "A chaise, and be damned! Let him walk, or take a seat on the car, which goes to town with the old guns." There was the real face of authority, exposed to him at last. Now they were treating him like the rebel they had long suspected him to be. No more courtesies and, for certain, no more chances to head for the sea or the hills. William Steel Dickson, son of a poor tenant farmer in Ballycraigy, County Antrim, and risen to become a Doctor of Divinity from Glasgow University, a distinguished preacher and scholar, dedicated minister to his congregations of Ballyhalbert and Portaferry, ex-moderator of the Presbyterian Synod of Ulster, eloquent advocate of Catholic emancipation, in his fifty-fourth year, bilious and saddle-sore, would be held in hard confinement without charge or trial for the next three years, seven months, and seven days.

We should be on firmer ground with William than with Robert. And we are, although there are still uncertainties, hedges, and evasions. The governor of Derry acquired immortality as a mighty and long-lived symbol, but that was an accidental result of the intense myth-building need of Ulster Protestants. Robert was a faceless, ambiguous man who left almost no written imprint of his life. We know only a little about him and must speculate about the rest.

William was different. He left behind him whole books of sermons and a detailed, although oddly selective, autobiographical account: *A Narrative of the Confinement and Exile of William Steel Dickson, D.D.,* which provides the basis for the account of his arrest. He was famous for his witty, ironic speeches, and the newspapers of his time delighted in the ready-made quotes he was always good for. He had been an eminent and emphatic critic of the British war on the American colonists in 1775 and a supporter of the French Revolution for the rights of man, even through its degeneration into regicide and terror. He was a public man in the life of his country, which wasn't really a country, but rather a misshapen, ill-wrought bastard of a place, part colony, part subject kingdom. It was distressed, hate-filled, and violent, and he proposed to redeem it through liberal, inclusive politics and the good graces of his benevolent God. Was he also a member of the Society of United Irishmen? Was he a rebel waiting for the word to rise under arms and strike for his country?

With all this writing and information, we should have no trouble placing William with precision in the scheme of things in the turmoil of the 1790s and the Insurrection of 1798. But it was Ireland after all, and it's also history. Neither one is conducive to sure knowledge, only to more or less safe bets. And William himself is not straightforward. In his *Narrative,* which was published fourteen years after the event, in 1812 (he must have been sixty-seven years old), he seems to equivocate and temporize.

The country was roused and animated by the spirit of reform, he writes. The people realized they must unite into a great body which could petition the Throne and Parliament for the attainment of freedom and equality—the very principles that underlay the great revolution of the French people against arbitrary government and tyranny. So the Irish formed themselves into societies, first in Ulster, and then throughout the kingdom. So much was at stake that they drew up a test for initiation into these societies, and admission became regular and solemn. He records that he himself took the test "in presence of the first society of United Irishmen in Belfast" in December 1791. He hadn't wasted any time: he must have been among the very first to do so. Yet, he says, "I do not know that my name was ever enrolled, as a member." And he's positive that, as far as he can recollect, he was never present at any society meeting, in Belfast or elsewhere, where any member was admitted or other United Irish business transacted.

This account seems evasive. But then William elaborates, and we begin to understand his style of thought and writing: its careful, precise, and, one might say, lawyerly, rigour combined with a fluent, contained passion. He may not have been a card-carrying rebel, but he doesn't hesitate to put himself at the centre of agitation—within the law. It was well known, from as early as 1778, that parliamentary reform and Catholic emancipation—and Catholics had to be emancipated for reform to mean anything—were "objects near and dear to my heart." He had always been in the thick of elucidating these principles and of proving their necessity. He did so fully convinced that reform would secure both His Majesty's throne and the independence of Ireland. Besides that, he added, his activism was the discharge of a most important moral and religious duty.

There's no doubt that William was a serious man, principled and energetic, an opponent of which any government would take very close notice. He was without sectarian prejudice, one of only a few Protestant reformers who advocated immediate and complete emancipation of Catholics through the removal of the hateful, leftover penal laws. He was also a dissenting Protestant, a Presbyterian, and a descendant of Scottish settlers, yet an Irishman, nevertheless, whose cause was Irish independence. The question was how far he would go to get it. Clearly he was prepared to campaign for reform as a member of the United Irishmen when they were just troublesome, if radical, political debating clubs. The authorities kept a worried eye on them in those years of revolution in France, penetrated them with informers and spies, but allowed them to operate.

Up to a point, that is. When the jittery and fearful government clamped down on the United Irishmen and forced them into becoming a revolutionary brotherhood geared for armed rebellion, that was a different matter. Where did William stand then? Perhaps, along with most of the society's members, he did travel the well-worn Irish path to insurrection—the pikes were always ready at the rising of the moon. But his *Narrative* is vague about whether he was a rebel commander. He makes a breezy and offhand dismissal of the matter: "Yet I may have been a General, for aught that appears to the contrary; and I may not have been a General, though people said I was." If he had been free on June 7, when Ulster rose, we would have had a sure answer. But, by then, the yeomanry had held him in its harsh custody for two days.

In fact, historians are mostly unequivocal: William was a rebel leader, a man of the cloth turned wood kern. He did join the Society of United Irishmen soon after its formation in Belfast and Dublin in 1791. At some point after its transformation into a revolutionary organization, William became adjutant-general of its County Down forces. When he and the Down colonels were arrested on June 5, 1798, the Ulster phase of the insurrection was just two days away. In spite of the arrest of many of its leaders, the rebellion broke out anyway, and eleven thousand men fought at Randalstown, Ballymena, Antrim Town—and Ballynahinch, to which William had ridden to drink the soothing waters and where the yeomanry officers had so respectfully arrested him.

All the contemporary sources refer to him as adjutant-general, although some say he was appointed in 1796, others not until 1798. He is variously described as one of the "more notorious" of the Presbyterian "clerical conspirators," as the "first in command" in Down and "the centre of unity" there, and as the replacement for the ex-soldier and librarian Thomas Russell, the undoubted United Irish revolutionary who was seized by the government in 1796 and held without trial for five years.

William's close friends and brother ministers, Ledlie Birch and Sinclaire Kelburn, and five or six members of his own congregation were arrested for United Irish activities during the winter of 1796 and the spring of 1797. William was, unaccountably, untouched. The authorities did, however, note his travel to Dublin in December 1796, ostensibly to try to get free some of his congregation who were imprisoned in Kilmainham Jail. The government couldn't help but notice that the visit corresponded with the appearance of a French fleet off the south coast of Ireland. Although it did not try to land, William was an important enough troublemaker that the government saw no disproportion between his solo visit to Dublin and an abortive invasion by the French— once again, England's enemy and, therefore, Ireland's friend. In an official dispatch, Lord Londonderry describes William as "one of the more violent and seditious characters in the country" and suggests that he "should be hunted out in Dublin, and if possible taken up and detained as a suspicious personage; which the suspension of the *Habeas Corpus* Act enables Government to do." If William wasn't a United Irish military leader, the government certainly feared him as much as if he were.

In his *Narrative,* William neglects to include certain details of his movements between Newtownards, Ballee, Portaferry, and Belfast during the week or so before his arrest: he stayed on May 29 with the Reverend William Sinclair, who was later transported for his role in the insurrection; he spent the day with John Crawford, a government magistrate but known to be a United Irish supporter; he stayed the night of May 30 with Robert Rollo Reid, a United Irishman (Reid later swore an affidavit that William had told him he was adjutant-general); the next day, he visited David Shaw, a United Irishman; on June 1, he spent the night in Belfast with John Coulter, a United Irishman. A man who was in charge of a secret revolutionary force and who wanted to coordinate with his comrades a plan to rise in arms within a few days would have had an itinerary much like William's in late May and early June 1798. He would even have much use for a new mount: generals led their men into battle on horseback.

Later, other evidence emerged. William's appointment is expressly mentioned in a report of the Committee of Secrecy to the House of Lords. There is confirmation in the examinations of several United Irishmen who were definitely not government informers, one of whom, the lawyer Thomas Addis Emmet, was arrested in March 1798 and held for four years without trial. In the correspondence, now in the British Library, between the Reverend Robert Black, who would oppose William's rehabilitation for a decade (and who, we may recall, gave the celebratory sermon at the Presbyterian meeting house in Derry during the 1788 centenary siege celebrations), and Viscount Castlereagh, William is never referred to otherwise than as "The Adjutant General." And, of course, there were rumours: that just before riding to Ballynahinch, William told a man that he would never see him again; that he told someone else that the town was a good place from which to issue orders to his officers and that he intended to establish his headquarters there; that the County Down colonels had sent him a message urging him to put his United Irishmen in motion without delay.

The battle at Ballynahinch began a week after William's arrest. It was the decisive engagement of the Ulster rising. Henry Munro, a linen draper from Lisburn, outside Belfast, led seven thousand men, only some of whom had arms. The arrest of their colonels (and of William, their presumed general) had thrown the rebels off balance, and they mobilized in haste. The disciplined government troops cut them down in desperate street-to-street fighting. At least four hundred United Irishmen died in the town or were killed by pursuing cavalry after they broke and ran. The government court-martialled Munro and hanged him in front of his own house. William's arrest and detention, unpleasant as they were, probably saved him from the same gory public death.

However, the most ominous thing about Ballynahinch was that splits had appeared in the United Irish ranks, both before and during the battle, between the Protestants and the Catholics, who were drawn from the secret society of the Defenders. The Catholics accused Munro of trying to put them up front as sacrificial shock troops, and seven hundred Defenders deserted before the battle. Afterwards, in the misery of defeat and in the wake of the rebellion's sectarian massacres, little remained of even the pretense of United Irish religious unity.

William's evasiveness in his *Narrative* about whether he was a United Irish general makes sense for reasons of practicality and principle. When he finished his book in 1812, ten years after his release as a state prisoner, he was still engaged in a bitter fight with his church over his status and livelihood. Many Presbyterian clergymen joined the United Irishmen, and a surprising number of them took up arms. William shared his imprisonment with several other dissenting ministers, and a few more were so much involved in the rebellion that the government thought it worthwhile to pay their way to a new and permanent life in Australia or America, or, in the extravagant style of execution of the time, to hang and quarter them.

But the church, like Protestants generally, was split on this matter of reform and revolution. When the "Year of Liberty" ended and the thirty thousand dead had been counted, reaction set in across the country, and among the Presbyterian clergy in particular. The dismal after-effects of the rebellion gave the "I told you so" faction all it needed to predominate at Synod meetings. Seventeen months after William's arrest, the Synod declared his Portaferry congregation vacant and cut off his stipend. When he was released and returned to Ireland in 1802, he, like most ex-prisoners, was stone broke with no prospects. Apart from his regular pay, he had lost the income from the boys' boarding school he had run to help make ends meet. His son, a surgeon in the navy who had helped the family with part of his pay, had died in 1798. His wife, Isabella, was an invalid, from unknown causes. Even after he found another congregation, the Synod continued to deny him the traditional full remuneration, and he and his family lived like paupers. In the protracted and rancorous campaign to restore his living, he was not likely to crow about, or even admit to, his part in the insurrection. On the contrary, the *Narrative* was one of his weapons in the fight, part apologia, part catharsis, part argumentation for his personal cause. William was one man representing himself who did not have a fool for a client.

Of course, he had another motive to dissemble in the *Narrative*. For a man like William, this incentive was probably even stronger than the fair pay denied him by the ascendant conservatives within the church. Everything we know about him is consistent with a stiff-necked, uncompromising addiction to principle. And that applied above all to his part in the rising. Perhaps his arrest as a rebel general had pre-empted by two days his orders to his colonels: Gather the United Irishmen, bring out the pikes and muskets, strike for liberty! What the Irish stitched onto their banners in 1688 when they saw their opportunity against England—"Now or Never! Now and For Ever!"—they could have shouted a hundred years later when they went for broke in furious rebellion. William may have been a few hours away from all that.

But for him the point was clear: Where was the proof? They arrested him without a warrant, only on the say-so of a corrupt, toady aristocrat. They held him in hard conditions in the notorious "Black Hole," on a noisome prison ship in Belfast Lough, and then in a Scottish prison. They destroyed his livelihood; they forced his beloved wife and children to flee their home and live in fear and want for almost four years, a traitor's kin. They arrested his second son, who was only fifteen, and subjected him to two weeks of hard detention and rough interrogation; the boy refused to answer questions about his father's movements even when they told him they had hanged William and the son no longer had cause to protect him. Yeomanry and marines seized the cattle, horses, and sheep on William's farm at Portaferry, the remaining source of support for him and his family.

Most important, the government never charged him with any crime. It never brought him to trial. At one point, eager to be rid of this troublesome minister, it offered him freedom if he would agree to emigrate. It wanted to shuck itself of another potential Irish martyr. William refused. When he petitioned the government from his cell, he didn't ask his accusers to let him go; he asked them to bring charges, to let him see the case against him, to go to trial and let the judgment fall where it may. That was what he wanted. Why, therefore, should he say more than he did in his *Narrative?* Why should he admit anything, when nothing had been charged and nothing proven? For certain, he had no need to apologize and recant—even if that would make it easier to get his just recompense from his church. It was the government that should be doing the apologizing, not him. And so he ducked and dodged. William wrote his *Narrative* to tread the delicate wisp of a line between defiance and justification. That is what accounts for its odd elusiveness, its fierce defensiveness, its lawyerly detachment, its vagaries and elisions.

The government held William in judicial limbo, neither prisoner-of-war nor felonious citizen. As Lord Londonderry had noted when he advocated William's arrest in 1796, habeas corpus had been suspended in Ireland. It is the foundation of the rule of law which says that the state must bring a person before a judge to justify its detention of him. Not that it had ever had a vigorous existence in Ireland. By their fierce and savage recalcitrance (or, from another perspective, their simple unwillingness to be conquered or repressed), the Irish were often considered to have exempted themselves from the protection of the ancient writ.

When the government finally released him from Fort George in the Scottish Highlands, the destitute William needed to get back to work. The congregation of the village of Donegore near Templepatrick in County Antrim asked him to take over from their aged pastor, but the appointment never happened. In his *Narrative,* William blames his old enemy within the Synod of Ulster, Robert Black, and others, who insinuated to the Donegore congregation that if they took William, they and their old pastor would lose the *regium donum,* the state grant towards the payment of Presbyterian ministers. William had to look elsewhere for a job. In the autumn of 1802, a new congregation in the little market town of Keady in County Armagh braved the Synod's bullying and took on William as its first minister. The congregation wanted the old United Irish general enough that, on its own, it raised his starvation pay of £50 a year.

———

I drove to Keady from Belfast one mild, rainy Sunday morning in December. Off the motorway, I navigated the narrow, meandering country roads with their sectarian signatures. The old settlement pattern of the Plantation was as intact here as anywhere in the north. It was marked by the alternating tribal signs: Gaelic-language names and Celtic crosses in the graveyards, *Tiocfaidh ar lá!* on the walls; a hundred yards farther, red-white-and-blue curbstones, "Taigs Beware!"; Union Jacks and Red Hand of Ulster flags; and then the unseen line again and the Gaelic once more.

At first, I couldn't find the Second Keady Presbyterian Church, where William had been minister for thirteen years. In the manner of small towns on Sunday, the streets were empty. I found the Catholic Cathedral by its tall spire, and it was near my random parking space. I walked by the large, elegant building and heard a hymn in mid-verse. The Church of Ireland was easy to locate; it had taken the high ground—the hill that overlooked the town—and could be seen from anywhere below. It was the old symbolism: the Prods above, the Taigs and Dissenters below. The Established Church on the hill looked like any English country church: solid, modest, a battlemented tower, yew trees clustered close to the building, a tall clipped hedge along the road, the feel of easy entitlement and prosperity—although the people who worshipped there now would be more likely to feel the noose of unwelcome change, of unsettling Protestant vulnerability drawing tighter around their necks. But where was the dissenting Protestant church? I asked a man inside the Church of Ireland, an official of some sort there. In the manner of the Irish of whom one asks directions, he took me by the arm and walked me almost all the way down the hill and around several corners. "You can't miss it," he said reassuringly when he let go. Indeed, William's last church was already in sight.

The building looked as plain and severe as I had expected it to: a whitewashed rectangle with a shallow-peaked slate roof. Its only ornaments were a pattern of stone blocks at each corner and five arched windows on the long sides, each with a simple stained-glass pattern of a stylized cross. It is a place for the unadorned and direct conversation with God which is every Presbyterian's expectation, and as much meeting house as church. In the tidy graveyard, the names are those of the Planters: Robinson, Coulter, Rule.

I had arrived just before the main morning service. The minister was at the door greeting his parishioners as they came in. They were, literally, in their Sunday best, and I looked shabby in my casual travelling clothes. I told the minister who I was: a Canadian, born in Belfast, and a descendant of the Reverend William Steel Dickson. The news stopped everything. The pastor announced that the service could be delayed "for just a wee minute." Their revered founder's great-great-great-great-grandson was visiting, and God would wait a little longer for their devotion. An assistant took me upstairs to the display the church had set up to mark the bicentenary of its official formation in 1803. There were photographs, paintings, or etchings of its twelve ministers since. And one of them was a likeness of William himself.

Robert Lundy was a faceless mystery; but here was William in the flesh, or at least a reproduction of it. Here was a face to read, a character to infer, my forebear, about whom I had read and thought so much, brought to abrupt life. William's portrait is a conventional and unsurprising representation in the style of its time. But I study its small (it measures seven-and-a-half by six inches) oval for the subtle signs and intimations of temperament and intellect it might disclose—although these readings of a person from one captured, frozen-in-time image may mean nothing: the handsome, open-faced murderer; the mousy, furtive humanitarian.

Nevertheless, I can't help trying to interpret William from this single tenuous link. He is a balding, fleshy-faced, double-chinned man—we can't see his body, but he must tend to corpulence—probably around sixty years old, with fluffy white-haired sideburns, a prominent nose, delicate, shapely lips, the eyes of a man who makes a serious matter of life and has suffered for it. He glances off to his left with a wary, watchful expression. He looks as if he's waiting for the next hard word or blow, which he will withstand, though it will take a little more out of him. His face has an aspect of intelligent vulnerability. He is unsmiling and probably does not smile often or with ease. He appears proud, almost haughty, although perhaps this is a pose to ward off fools or to protect his own foolish heart. He looks like a man who has enemies.

But would I make this induction if I didn't know he had been driven to armed rebellion and had almost been executed? Many men in Ireland had hated and feared him and wanted him dead. Indeed, I don't know how much I truly see in his face, and how much I read into it from his biography. But I can't stop trying to look through the opaque reproduction of the flesh and into the mind and soul of my long-ago ancestor. From all I've read about him and by him, I like him very much. I've gathered that a conversation with him would always have been something to remember: intense, yet full of intelligence and humour (in spite of his severe expression here—another unreliability of the image). I imagine his views on the Troubles in my time: his weary acceptance of their ferocity, his disappointment that the encouraging alliance between Presbyterians and Catholics, whose destruction had begun as soon as the Insurrection of 1798 broke out, had never been revived; his surprise, perhaps, and certainly his grief that, at least in northern Ireland, not much had changed in two hundred years. There were still secret guerrilla armies, the sectarian divide, a shaky peace, dysfunctional politics, British soldiers, un-united Irishmen.

There was something else about William's portrait, too. It was a balding, sideburned version of my grandmother Maud Dickson. Or, if my grandmother Maud had dressed up in early nineteenth-century, high-collared, ruffled drag, she would have looked just like William. I had seen this strange genetic continuity before: my great-great-uncle Benjamin Lundy (I wrote a book about his first passage as a square-rigger seaman) resembled my father, Alexander, his great-nephew, with eerie similitude. Here it was again, this persistence of living form through time, although a much longer interval in the case of William and Maud, and therefore more surprising.

As it had with Benjamin and my father, the resemblance of long-dead William to Maud, whom I had known and loved, seemed to bring him very close. I felt the pull of those lines that join generations. They had uncoiled and slithered through time, surviving William's death and all the deaths after him, and had found their way to me. Perhaps they would feel their way on, death-defying tentacles, through my daughter and her children, keeping the sense of me alive in their future. There would certainly be portraits of me for them to see. But in William's case, his writing disclosed the man. I also write, to make a living in the present, but to leave that small connecting trace in the future, too.

This sorting of the portrait's entrails was taking time. The present minister of William's church in Keady joined us. We talked for a while about William. The minister told me he would leave Keady soon, and the severe little church would have another successor to the great United Irishman. I had an appointment in Belfast, and I was feeling guilty about the delay for the waiting worshippers. I said I had to go. The minister took William's portrait down from the wall—it was a photographic reproduction of the original—and gave it to me. I protested, of course, but he insisted: I had to have it. Who had a better right to this clear proof and celebration of the fact of my ancestor's existence? We shook hands and I left. I drove back in the rain, through the marked territories of the Planters and the Gaels, to grim Belfast and the apartment I had rented there. It was snug within the safe, nonsectarian precinct of Queen's University, just a kilometre from where I was born in the little house on the border of the Holy Land and separate, but not far from the seedy, scary streets of the contending Prods and Taigs.

11

WILD COLONIAL BOYS

WILLIAM WAS BORN on Christmas Day, 1744, at Ballycraigy in the parish of Carnmoney, now a suburb of Belfast. His middle name, Steel, came from his mother, Jane. His birth took place fifty-five years after the siege of Derry, and twenty-seven years after Robert Lundy's death. The Insurrection of 1798 was more than fifty years away. It had been 141 years since the putative end of England's conquest of Ireland in 1603, and Irish independence, or at least its freedom to win freedom, in 1921 was 177 years in the future. William came into existence near the middle of the centuries between conquest and Free State. In 1744, all the familiar themes of that long swath of Irish history and politics were in full swing. And the three "peoples" of Ireland—Anglicans, Dissenters, and Catholics—lived their distinct yet interlocking lives.

If the Protestants of Ireland had anything like a golden age or a time before the fall, it was the eighteenth century. The war of William and James, in which the siege of Derry had played so large a part, had ended with a great defeat for the Irish-Catholic cause. William's victory established the principle that only Protestants would be permitted to sit on the throne of the three kingdoms of England, Scotland, and Ireland. From that top-down ascendancy, the Irish Protestants grasped their entitlement and power, and, in the eighteenth, nineteenth, and early twentieth centuries, they dominated the political and intellectual life of Ireland. It became known as the

Protestant Ascendancy. Later, when the Catholic Irish Free State had drained away what was left of the Protestants' power, when both their existence and their state of mind had become ghettoized, they would look back on the high old times with the luminous nostalgia of adults for their childhood. Elizabeth Bowen wrote: "Life still kept a touch of colonial vigour; at the same time, because of the glory of everything, it was bound up in the quality of a dream."

Bowen's use of the word "colonial" applies well to the Ascendancy Prods. They were a governing caste that controlled politics and defined "society" in Ireland but was always subservient to England. The Irish Parliament passed bills that the English Parliament could add to, delete from, or amend wholesale without further reference to the Irish legislators; in 1720, Westminster gave itself the right to legislate for Ireland directly (although, in practice, it seldom exercised any of these powers). There was a fundamental anomaly in the constitutional position of Ireland. The executive—headed by the Lord Lieutenant and his secretary, who were always Englishmen— and the officials of the administration were accountable not to the Irish Parliament but to the English ministry that appointed them. They were, therefore, susceptible to English government policy and party politics, just as they were not subject to the electors of the Irish Parliament. This Parliament could pass laws until Doomsday, but their effect might be completely theoretical if the executive didn't feel like paying attention to them.

Irish Protestants could never forget that their ascendancy was limited and subaltern. It existed at the pleasure of England and ended at the shore of the Irish Sea. Ireland's position was ambiguous: it wasn't really a colony, but it wasn't part of the metropolitan centre either. The Ascendancy was, in its way, grand and shining, but it wasn't a real colonial elite: there were none of the normal racial distinctions between the settlers and the natives. The Protestants knew that only England and its military power kept them safe from invasion by France or Spain and, far more ominous, from another Catholic rising. The Ascendancy was a minority among the Catholics, who fell into one of two species: those already hostile or those potentially so.

On paper, the Protestants should have felt more secure; in the mid-1700s, they made up twenty-five percent of the Irish population.

But this number is deceptive because it includes the Presbyterians, and "Protestant" then meant only Anglican. There was not yet such a thing as an Irish Protestant in the modern sense, but Irish Protestants divided into two distinct and violently opposed churches. (Remember the animosities during the siege of Derry.) Anglican propagandists often described the Dissenter as just another version of a papist: each was a member of a kind of slave-congregation, run by Rome or the Synod of Ulster with fanatical absolutism and dedicated to the destruction of rival creeds. The distaste was mutual; to the Presbyterians, Anglicanism was just popery without the Pope. The exclusion of Dissenters put a limit on the Protestant elite's numbers. The Presbyterians were numerous in Ulster, especially in Counties Antrim and Down. Belfast was a Presbyterian town. There were probably half a million Presbyterians in Ulster by 1775, despite the fact they had also been emigrating to America for fifty years—enough of them to call it an exodus. Many of the penal laws that made constitutional serfs of Catholics had analogues for Presbyterians and kept them firmly outside the Ascendancy.

The Ascendancy saw itself as a fluid and open elite in the sense that it didn't care where its members came from or how they had acquired their land or made their money. They didn't have to be a landed aristocrat to join up. Dissenters, or even Catholics, who converted to Anglicanism were accepted, if not wholeheartedly welcomed. Protestants in the professions and poor Protestants who made good became paid-up members of the top class right away, as long as they were Anglican. However, membership in the club did not necessarily translate into political power. In Ireland, as elsewhere, that was based on owning land, which was the only way to get into Parliament or to vote for its members—a feature of all *anciens régimes.*

In any event, the Anglican Protestants believed that there was no need to cater to Dissenters; when things got bad, Presbyterians would have no choice but to bind with the Anglicans against any Catholic rebellion. The Scots Presbyterian settlers in Ulster had been protected during the first days of the 1641 Rising, but it wasn't long before the Irish, one Prod much like another in their eyes, began to slaughter them as well as the English. In the meantime, however, the Presbyterian businessmen, lawyers, and churchmen of the north had no reason to feel part of the Anglican elite. And as the Insurrection of 1798 took shape, many of the northern Dissenters, like William, not only declined to take up their associate membership in the Ascendancy but instead became the backbone of the United Irishmen. They joined with Catholics—although most of them with half-hearted trepidation—to try by force of arms to bring down the whole structure of the corrupt Ascendancy.

The standard received version of Irish history treats the penal laws (or the popery laws) as part of England's repression of Ireland, as one more facet of the 800-year-long occupation. In fact, the laws were enacted by the Irish Parliament's Ascendancy Protestants to address their enduring fear of massacre in another rebellion by vengeful Catholics. The first two laws, passed in 1695, four years after the end of the war between William and James, reflected immediate Protestant concerns. They forbade Catholics from keeping weapons (for obvious reasons) and from travelling overseas for education. The latter was an attempt to break the links between rebellious Catholics in Ireland and the Wild Geese, the mercenary brigades and regiments of European armies, and especially those of France—the armed, trained Gaels dispossessed and alienated from home, yet with their long memories of it. This Irish army overseas might be the spearhead of invasion, and the less connection ordinary Irish Catholics had with it the better.

The English government was complicit in the scheme of penal-law repression in the sense that it did not stop it. But England's strategic interests dictated being kind to Irish Catholics; it made sense to convince them that England's difficulty was not Ireland's (meaning Catholic Ireland's) opportunity. For this reason, England always sought to ameliorate the effects of the penal laws through pressure on the Ascendancy Parliament in Dublin. The Ascendancy's already complex relationship with England was exacerbated by the unsettling fear that the English would let it down by liberalizing the laws against Catholics, and against Dissenters, too. The Ascendancy was fearful, insecure, ambivalent. Its state of mind became bitter, resentful—and sometimes ferocious.

In 1745, the year after William was born on the little tenant farm near Belfast, Jonathan Swift died. By then, "the Dean" had been isolated by deafness and dementia for almost ten years. Swift symbolizes the Ascendancy sensibility of dependence and indignation. Above all, he craved grand success in the imperial centre: a bishopric would do. But he got St. Patrick's Cathedral in Dublin on the imperial periphery. He saw himself in exile there, doomed to die "in a rage, like a poisoned rat in a hole."

In fact, he had not done badly for the son of obscure "colonial" parents. He had begun his religious career in a far worse spot: the tiny parish of Kilroot, near Belfast, close to William's birthplace. There, he had been surrounded by Dissenters, "all Presbyterian and Scotch, not one natural Irish in the parish, or a papist." Swift always thought that the Dissenters were more of an enemy to his Established Church than the Catholics were. The Catholics' indolence and fecklessness, as well as the penal laws, had made them "as inconsiderable as women and children." (Swift was not short on misogyny, either.) Catholicism would crumble away. Dissenters were different: cunning, hard, resourceful men, northerners and Scots, with their harsh, fast speech; they were the real threat. The Ascendancy could never tolerate or include them.

England was enough of an imperial power, staffing a colony, to give the best administrative and religious jobs in Ireland to Englishmen. Not only was someone like Swift unlucky in England, but he was cut off from advancement in Ireland, too, and by a pack of incompetent mediocrities—the toffee-nosed twits of the time—or by crooks. He sardonically speculated that the English actually appointed good men to Ireland, but, for some reason, they were always set upon and murdered by bandits, probably near Chester, who stole their letters of appointment, crossed to Ireland, and took over their jobs.

Swift was enraged by his rejection, which was one instance of the peculiar insecurity of the Ascendancy's political and social position. It made an Irish patriot out of him. In a series of vitriolic pamphlets, he proposed a boycott of English goods (long before that became an eponymous tactic); he attacked English misgovernment and absentee landlords. He abhorred the Catholics' misery, which was partly caused by the popish laws but mostly by English economic policies. The standard received story of Irish history is on firm ground here. Like any good colonial power, England took what it could get out of

Ireland but would not tolerate even the hint of competition from Irish industries or resources. In 1699, for example, it passed legislation intended to destroy the Irish woollen industry, along with butter, the most important industry in the country. The *Woollen Act* may not have succeeded in doing that—although it was very damaging—but the perception in Ireland was that this destruction was England's aim. Such mercantilist hostility began to bring the Ascendancy Protestants round to a new idea of themselves: perhaps they were no longer displaced Englishmen in temporary exile but Irishmen with an Irish agenda, which might be inimical to England's desires.

We associate Irish poverty and hunger more with the nineteenth century. But things weren't much different in Swift's (and William's) time. In 1728–29 and in 1740–41, the Irish went very hungry indeed. The early forties were, in fact, the first potato famine. Its mortality rate as a percentage of population may have been higher than that of the Great Famine of 1845–49, which got its sobriquet because it was the last and best remembered of all the famines over the centuries.

Swift had a solution; it made him famous as a ferocious satirist and an outraged Irishman. In 1729, he wrote *A Modest Proposal for Preventing the Children of Poor People from Being a Burthen to Their Parents or Country and for Making Them Beneficial to the Publick*. He affects the earnest and hesitant tone of a conscientious, banal bureaucrat proposing a final solution, or of an amateur scientist submitting to a scholarly journal what he hopes will be a worthy idea for social betterment. He calculates children's rate of birth, the difficulty of feeding and clothing them—as evidenced by the large numbers everywhere of hungry children in rags—and the age when they can start to make a living by stealing. But he has a scheme for one year olds. A child of that age is "a most delicious, nourishing and wholesome food, whether stewed, roasted, baked or broiled. . . . A child will make two dishes" if one is entertaining, and, if a family dines alone, "the fore and hind quarter will make a reasonable dish." In grotesque prophecy of the twentieth century, he writes that the skin can be used too. Flay the little carcasses to make gloves for ladies and summer boots for gentlemen. No need to worry about the huge numbers of adult poor Irish who are old or diseased: "They are every day dying, and rotting, by cold, and famine, and filth, and vermin, as fast as can be reasonably expected." *A Modest Proposal* was satire, but also mere exaggeration. In the recurrent cycle of famine in Ireland, cannibalism was unusual but far from unknown; death from hunger and disease a commonplace.

Swift was part of what the Irish historian Roy Foster calls the "great intellectual triumvirate of the Ascendancy." Its other members were George Berkeley and Edmund Burke. Berkeley wrote the philosophical work *A Treatise Concerning the Principles of Human Knowledge,* but he was also Bishop of Cloyne in Cork. He believed it was his duty to try to convert the Catholics of his poor diocese, but he treated them with tolerance and generosity. He wrote *The Querist* in the 1730s, in which he posed hundreds of questions about the distress of Ireland and its people; for example, "Whether there be any country in Christendom more capable of improvement than Ireland?" (an early example of Irish "exceptionalism") and "Whether my countrymen are not readier at finding excuses than remedies?" Berkeley was an Ascendancy Prod who, Foster points out, began his writing career referring to the Irish as "the natives" but soon shifted to the inclusive plural: "We Irish. . . ." In this, he encapsulated the Ascendancy's overall shift towards a new self-awareness. In the 1690s, they called themselves "the Protestants of Ireland," or "the English of this kingdom." By the 1720s, they were "Irish gentlemen," although the English might quibble with the second word and the Catholic Irish might reject the first. It was, in a way, the old story: the conquerors, the new men, going native, certainly not more Irish than the Irish but Irish nevertheless, a different kind of hibernicization.

Edmund Burke, like Swift, was denied the high political office he deserved and to which he aspired. The English thought the gifted Dubliner a mere "Irish adventurer." He was, in any event, a torn man: a Protestant father (who may have been a convert), a Catholic mother, and a wife whose family was caught up in the rigged trials of prominent Cork Catholics triggered by the Whiteboys, a violent agrarian protest movement. Burke came to abhor the excesses of the French Revolution and thought that Catholic relief and emancipation were the only things that would prevent revolution in Ireland. He died in 1797 and was spared the experience of the partly French-inspired revolution of the United Irishmen the following year.

The scientist and political writer William Molyneux was a Dublin contemporary of Swift's, and we should add his 1698 book, *The Case of Ireland's Being Bound by Acts of Parliament in England Stated,* to the list of theorists of Ascendancy rights. In response to the proposed *Woollen Act,* Molyneux submitted a series of sophisticated arguments. Strongbow and Henry II had not conquered the Gaelic kings and chiefs in the twelfth century. The Gaels had submitted voluntarily. (Indeed, Mac Murchada did invite Strongbow over from England.) In any event, conquest did not confer unlimited rights on the conqueror. In the alternative (as lawyers like to argue), Molyneux wrote, everyone had a natural right to live only under laws to which they had given their consent—reflecting once again the seminal influence of the philosopher John Locke.

Molyneux, Swift, Berkeley, and Burke were concerned with the other Ireland of the Catholics, a world far more various and complex than the standard version of Irish history allows. It was certainly composed of the "hidden world" of ragged, starving, Irish-speaking peasants prescribed by the standard version, but also of prosperous Catholic businessmen, traders, and professionals, some of whom renounced their Catholicism and went over to the Established Church as a means of participating in the political and legal, as well as the economic, life of the dependent colonial kingdom. (They had been excluded from Parliament since 1691, and the last penal law, passed in 1728, took away their right to vote.)

The Ascendancy—concerned as many of its members were with horses and bonhomie—often abdicated trade and commerce to the men of the urban Catholic middle class, who may even have been predominant in Irish business, though Protestants always held the "commanding heights" of the economy. The Ascendancy was often a debtor class, and the Catholics, like the Presbyterians of the north, its creditors. However, Catholic landowners were the real losers in the eighteenth century. They didn't own much of their old country anyway after the conquest, the plantations, and the confiscations following William's victory over James. In 1688, Catholics still hung on to twenty-two percent of Ireland. By 1778, however, they owned only five percent of the country. Many of the popery laws may not have worked well, if at all, but the law restricting Catholic land ownership and leasing was effective. And many Catholic rural landlords, like

their urban counterparts, went over to Protestantism. These oppor-
tunists kept their land but were no longer counted as Catholic owners.

There was a layer of Catholic well-being during the Ascendancy's
heyday, making do, and often doing very well, in the interstices of
the mostly ineffectual penal laws and the offhand disdain of many
Ascendancy Protestants of working for a living. But the mass of the
Catholic Irish were not in that category at all. Apart from their
general poverty, they were continuing to live through the long,
unsettling death of their culture. Its laws and social structures were
almost all long gone, and the language, their last great cultural possession, was moribund. The standard received story of Ireland
blames the loss of Gaelic entirely on repressive English policies, but
its disappearance—as is the case with all aboriginal languages—is
far more complicated than that. The eighteenth-century Irish were
giving up Gaelic because they associated it with deprivation and isolation. The public discourse of law, leases, and politics was in
English, and English was also the language of opportunity—for the
Irish, a way out of their hovels and bogs. Fewer and fewer people
could read Gaelic, although it was still alive for everyday country
speech. And oral Irish poetry had kept its hold on them; that old
affinity between the Gaels and the astringencies of the poetic word
was still there and vigorous. Even near the end of the century in
1790, the Frenchman Coquebert de Montbret, travelling in Kerry,
thought the people saturated in poetry and with "a strange preoccupation with things of the mind."

There was also the Irish preoccupation with violence. That was
certainly not strange but was, in fact, entirely comprehensible in a
conquered, subject nation with a touchy ruling caste and a sullen,
repressed majority. It was a country with a subterranean warrior
culture, full of complex grievance, hard men, and men on the make,
a frontier that allowed for all the usual ruthless opportunism and
"self-help" remedies of the fringes of "civilization." The roots of
violence in present-day Ulster are deep and tenacious, and they form
a recognizable line to the present.

The Ascendancy was an elite, but a boozy, turbulent one.
"Drunkenness is the Touch Stone by which they try every man; and
he that cannot or will not drink, has a mark set upon Him," wrote

Lord Orrery in 1736. Claret was known as "Irish wine," its alcoholic fortification speeding up the process of becoming paralytic. Drunk or sober, the Ascendancy Prods tended towards extreme resolutions. They became famous for their duels and abductions, although litigation was always popular, too. They were, according to one historian, "willful men who put their individual reputations above their lives, their families, their religion, and the law." We're struck by a sense of continuity: these Protestants sound almost like the old Gaelic chieftains and petty kings with their affairs of honour and ingrained, joyful, alcoholic unruliness. The vehement exertions were all part of the *craic*. For the Ascendancy men, there may have been some overcompensation involved: to show the effete English that if they weren't quite top-drawer, they at least still had the balls to fight it out when integrity so required. Perhaps the frustration of thwarted ambition—of a Burke or a Swift denied advancement because he was a sort of paddy—produced a necessary reaction of coiled, irrepressible, and self-lacerating force. "A civilized state of war is the safest and most agreeable that any gentleman . . . can suppose himself in," wrote Lord Clonmell in his diary.

War at the top and at the bottom, too. Of course the native Catholic Irish were violent. They had always had that reputation in England. How could they not, these unshakable papists, with their intractable unwillingness to be "civilized," their risings and rebellions, and, above all, their massacres? In the sixteenth and seventeenth centuries, they were "the moste salvage Irishe." The west of Ireland was "a wild, mountainous country in which the old barbarities of the Irish are so many and so common." During the Ascendancy, in 1753, it was common knowledge that the Irish were "violent in all their passions . . . inconstant, cruell, bloody, thievish, perfidious, seditious [and] revengeful." In 1766, Ireland was "noted above all nations in Europe" for its "many riots, violences and murder." Not much had changed a hundred years later, when Benjamin Disraeli described the Irish as "this wild, reckless, indolent, uncertain and superstitious race. . . . Their history describes an unbroken circle of bigotry and blood." He was generalizing wildly in the manner of the imperial overlord, as if a Ballymena Scots Presbyterian, a boozy Dublin Ascendancy almost-blue-blood, and a bogside peasant were all one and the same.

Some historians have questioned whether the level of violence in Ireland was unique. This query is part of the general scheme of revisionist history which, among other things, questions the entire shibboleth of Irish exceptionalism: Was it really the *most* distressful country (as the old revolutionary song claims)? Did it experience the *worst* famines and the *most* terrible oppression? In other words, just how much truth is there in the standard received version of Irish history, which emphasizes with so much force and simplicity (or simple-mindedness) the country's uniquely bloody and nasty experience?

Taking the question of violence as an example, we can draw two conclusions from the historical studies: in the eighteenth century (and in later centuries, too), Ireland was, indeed, a brutal and violent society compared with England; but its levels of violence were not unique and were probably similar to those in other peasant societies within weak or underdeveloped states that did not have the means to suppress private action. Much more significant, the amount of violence in Ireland was similar to that in colonial America (which, of course, contained many Irish immigrants, mostly from Ulster). Nevertheless, the lacerated and intimate connections between Ireland and England meant that the comparison of those two nations was the one that counted. It was the English view of things from "on top" which set the agenda for the image of Ireland "on the bottom": if the Irish were seen as "savage," it was because the English, who lived in an unusually peaceful state for the time, thought they were. Many other countries were at least as violent and troubled—and as cruelly repressed—as Ireland. And because the Irish tended to bring up the perennial question of their subjugation whenever England was in one kind of crisis or another, the English impression of Ireland as a country of disorder and rebellion was reinforced.

Accepting that context, however, crime rates in Ireland were high indeed, and, the more serious (in the English view) the crime, the greater the disparity between the two kingdoms. For example, in the 1730s, the murder rate in County Armagh was almost four times that in any English county. The differences were probably much greater in reality because murder was both under-reported and under-prosecuted in Ireland. Once again, we come across the curious Irish indifference to death, which was certainly a character-

istic of the native culture—the Gaels were notoriously reckless
with their own lives and those of others who offended them. A
seventeenth-century observer wrote that they were "impatient of
abuse and injury, in enmity implacable, and in all affections most
vehement and passionate." That attitude was reflected in their
greater concern with crimes other than murder. One English judge
wrote that the Irish "will carry on a prosecution with more spent for
the theft of a cow or a sheep than they will for the murder of a near
relative." Irish juries were reluctant to convict a man of murder
"unless 'tis attended by a robbery." And there was in any event "a
mistaken tenderness to the lives of criminals." John Wesley wrote in
1756 that "murder is a venial sin in Ireland." Later, in 1825, Sir
Walter Scott said that the Irish "will murther you on slight suspicion
and find out the next day that it was all a mistake and that it was not
yourself they meant to kill at all."

Individual murders or other violent acts committed so casually—
and Irish insouciance about them—were one thing; they appalled
the English and confirmed them in their racist view of the Irish as
irredeemable ruffians, but that was all. However, the same activities
carried out in an organized and purposeful manner in the plural by
"the boys" was something else. (The historian A.T.Q. Stewart points
out that, in Ireland, the word "boy" has kept some of its Elizabethan
connotation: a swaggerer, a warrior, an armed man.) That smacked
of rebellion and a degree of disorder that might not be containable.
It reminded the English, and the Irish Protestants, of 1641 and 1688,
of the risings and the killings. It was a characteristic of the
eighteenth-century Irish countryside that the sectarian tensions
resulting from plantation settlement patterns (for example, in Ulster
or Wexford) or arising where the old Gaelic sensibilities and affiliations persisted (in the west) were expressed from time to time in concentrated and purposeful campaigns of violence carried out by
agrarian secret societies and brotherhoods.

It's remarkable that, from 1691 until 1798, the Catholics staged no
insurrection against the Protestant Ascendancy and, indirectly,
against England: no risings, no massacres, no blood sacrifices for
Mother Ireland, the *Shan Van Vocht,* or even a decent conspiracy.
There is no comparable period in Irish history. By definition, the

Taigs were refractory and rebellious; yet for more than a hundred years, they kept quiet. The Prods should have been reassured and, indeed, they did relax; for the first time in their residence in Ireland, they began to act as if they might not have to jump for their swords and muskets at any moment and fight off the barbaric natives. It was partly their new ease in Ireland that encouraged their progress towards thinking of themselves as Irishmen. It fostered their romantic interest in exotic Gaelic antiquities and culture, and in the Irish landscape, with its strange abrupt transitions from gentle fields and farmland to misty bogs, jagged mountains, lost valleys, the rough, blank seawall of the ocean to the west. But the Ascendancy could only unwind so far. In the background of the Prods' privileged lives, the secret societies carried on their protests—part theatre and ritual; part real, if low-level, guerrilla war.

However, for most of the century, the boys were not the proto-revolutionaries the Ascendancy feared. In fact, they were mostly conservatives who were concerned with local issues and were similar to many popular movements elsewhere in Europe. Their violence was local, occasional, and restrained. And they weren't just disgruntled Taigs; Dissenters and, occasionally, even poor Anglicans joined in, both, it seemed, sufficiently hibernicized to relish uncouth remedies.

The Houghers maimed cattle in the west to protest cattle rearing, which hurt small tillage farmers. They set the tone for most of the later groups: the use of disguise, night forays, the issuing of formal letters and proclamations under the name of a mythical leader—in their case, "Ever Joyce," but later also "Slasher," "Cropper," "Starlight," "Dreadnought," and so on. The Whiteboy movement developed in the southern counties of Tipperary, Limerick, Waterford, Cork, and Kilkenny. These lads wore white shirts over their everyday clothes and added mass demonstrations to the usual tactics; their grievances were enclosure of common land, rents, evictions, and tithes on potatoes—many of the main concerns of a downtrodden rural society. The law required Dissenters and Catholics to pay tithes on crops to the Established Anglican Church, a requirement that was an enduring source of resentment and often outrage. It was a good issue on which to base a nonsectarian agitation and, indeed, another group—the Rightboys—included

Protestants as well as Catholics in Cork and Kerry. Their protests became so widespread that they drew in local gentry, some of whom even became active leaders. All the secret societies came to be known as part of "Whiteboyism," and the legislation to proscribe them, the "Whiteboy Acts." There were some trials (including the ones that caught up members of Edmund Burke's family) and executions, but the government had trouble with sympathetic juries.

The violent demonstrations, cattle-maiming, and night raids carried out by the societies over most of the eighteenth century may have been local and limited in their aims, but they were, nevertheless, an unnerving backdrop for the Ascendancy. Any Catholic violence was a Protestant memento mori.

These groups formed in the south of the country and represented the poor and the Gaelic native Irish (who were usually, though not exclusively, the same people). But there was another world beyond the pale and outside the Ascendancy: Ulster. As it had been since the Plantation and as it would remain, the fourth green field was different and distinct. The French traveller Michel de Crèvecoeur was surprised by Ireland's complexity: "The Irish themselves, from different parts of the kingdom, are very different. It is difficult to account for this localization. One would think, on so small an island, an Irishman would be an Irishman: yet it is not so."

What was alien in Ireland, of course, might be familiar and reassuring to Englishmen. "No sooner did we enter Ulster than we observed the difference," wrote John Wesley, with relief, during his first Irish tour in 1756. "The ground was cultivated just as it was in England, and the cottages not only neat, but with doors, chimneys and windows" (the latter detail gives an idea of the state of things in the rest of Ireland). Some travellers thought that eastern Ulster resembled the Scottish Lowlands. Many remarked that Belfast had "an English look"—and an English feel, too: a French visitor said that whenever you began a conversation in Belfast about politics, the people would immediately relate it to the price of linen or sugar. The Plantation had established unique patterns of settlement in Ulster, but economic development—and above all, the linen industry—had accelerated and accentuated the differences. Industrialization was under way in the late eighteenth century, and it took place disproportionately in the north (although historians have underestimated its extent in the south). In fact, an economic analysis might describe industrialization and its demographic consequences as the crucial precondition for later political developments in Ulster: Protestants were more likely to emigrate than Catholics; industrial towns were an alternative to emigration and encouraged Protestants to stay and to multipy; this stability ensured that there were enough of them—a million instead of, say, half a million—to stop home rule in the nineteenth and early twentieth centuries. The beginning of this process in the mid-1700s would seal Ulster's status as a separate culture within Ireland, more tied economically—through the Industrial Revolution—as well as politically to Britain than to the rest of its island.

Differences between north and south also showed up in the development of the secret societies in Ulster. There, the brotherhoods first resembled their southern counterparts, with their limited rural issues. Later, however, they became something else more familiar and ominous. And they were one of the elements of late-eighteenth-century Ireland that make comprehensible, perhaps inevitable, the formation of the Ulster-born Society of United Irishmen—which eventually became another kind of secret society.

The Oakboys of Armagh, Tyrone, and Monaghan included all three religions, but they were the last ecumenical group. The Steelboys, or Hearts of Steel, were south Antrim, Down, Londonderry, and Armagh Presbyterians whose raids forced the landlords to fortify their houses. They proclaimed the egalitarian and loyalist principles of their church. Sometimes they congregated in large and menacing numbers. In December 1770, more than five hundred Steelboys invaded Belfast and rescued one of their members who was being held a prisoner. There was more than a whiff of political activism among these boys, which prefigured the later, overtly political groups. They were self-consciously Protestants and did not necessarily make the distinction between Anglicans and Dissenters. They were concerned to maintain the Protestants' privileged position in the north, and loyalism was already part of their platform: "We are all Protestants and Protestant Dissenters and bear unfeigned loyalty to his present majesty," they said in one of their proclamations.

The oath-bound, underground societies had two ominous characteristics. They acted as systems of law and enforcement outside, and alternative to, the formal law, in pursuit of their own popular ideas of fairness and justice. And they used violence and intimidation to further their aims and impose internal discipline to keep the bumptious lads in line. The societies became a rural tradition, a feature of the countryside, not so endearing to the Ascendancy gentry but tolerated, admired, and connived at by Catholics, Presbyterians, and occasionally poor Anglicans.

These were dangerous traditions with baleful possibilities, underground resistance networks in embryo. It would be crucial for the success of both the United Irishmen of the 1790s and the Irish Republican Brotherhood of the nineteenth century to form among a people long used to conspiracy, oath-taking, and bearing and using arms. If legal means failed to achieve the satisfaction you wanted, then there would never be a reason to stand down the boys; there would never be a good time to put your weapons beyond use.

Towards the end of the eighteenth century, the Ascendancy's inchoate fear of all this extra-judicial self-help became ever more focused and justified. In retrospect, it seems inevitable that the secret societies would evolve into more political organizations. How could they not, in a country with such a tumultuous history and a fractured, inequitable, harrowed present? And, of course, the societies coalesced in Ulster. Irish political culture was infected by the viruses of violence and exclusion, and Ulster was the breeder of the most virulent strains. New societies formed, with more on their minds than tithes and rents—the fairness and justice issues of the so-called moral economy. Their concerns spiralled out to those old, and unresolved, questions in Ireland of plough, sword, and book.

In the mid-1780s, vicious sectarian warfare broke out in County Armagh. Soon, the county looked like the "bandit country" it would become during the Troubles of the late twentieth century. Two gangs formed: the Catholic Defenders and the Protestant (probably mostly Presbyterian) Peep o' Day Boys. They seem very familiar to us, much like the Northern Irish paramilitaries we know today: they were completely sectarian, they fought each other, and the conflict had the bitter savagery of civil war. The Peep o' Day Boys attacked Catholic homes at dawn (hence their name). The Defenders defended. The Prods were reacting to Catholic intrusions into their hitherto exclusive bailiwick of linen weaving and to Catholic competition for land in the densely populated county.

Behind this economic anxiety lay the old Protestant fear: the government was beginning to repeal the penal laws, and this relaxation reminded the Protestants that they hadn't exactly been enforced in any event. The Peep o' Day Boys found weapons, which weren't supposed to be there, in some Catholic homes. Worse, the government began arming some Catholics as members of the Volunteers, the defence militia set up to replace the English regulars sent to put down the American rebellion. The fear and rumours were like old times. As one account says: "One day they tell the credulous peasant, that the Scotch are to rise on a certain night, and massacre all the Papists. . . . The Papists are next to rise on a certain night, and destroy the Scotch." These same shivers have troubled the people of the north of Ireland ever since.

Near the end of the eighteenth century, the Peep o' Day Boys produced an offshoot called the Orange Boys, who fought a pitched battle with a large force of Defenders in September 1795 at the Diamond, a crossroads in County Armagh. The victorious Protestants, celebrating afterwards at a nearby inn, formed the Orange Order, which was dedicated to preserving the "glorious and immortal memory" of King William and his victory at the Boyne. The first item on the order's agenda was the "Armagh outrages": a series of attacks against Catholics, seven thousand of whom became refugees. Later, the order became the twin sectarian organization to the Apprentice Boys, who had a more limited mission to celebrate the siege of Derry and to give its great traitor his just deserts each year. The Orange Order was the Prod secret society with staying power; it became the enduring brutal, rejectionist face of Ulster Protestant loyalism.

The Defenders grew from their self-defence origins in Armagh into an Ulster-wide, and then a national, organization. At first, they wanted only to protect Catholics and their economic interests. However, events elsewhere intruded. France, with its Wild Geese brigades, was the long-standing symbol of help against England. Soon, the Defenders were discussing the French Revolution and the possibility of a similar social and political transformation in Ireland. When the middle-class Presbyterians who formed the Society of United Irishmen looked around for a bridge to the Catholics, they found the like-minded Defenders. Sporadic contact soon after 1791 became a formal alliance, probably by 1796 or so—it's difficult to be exact because, by then, both had been driven underground. And as we have seen, when the Insurrection of 1798 broke out, Protestant United Irishmen and Catholic Defenders fought side by side against the government. It was, at best, an uneasy and querulous coopera- tion that soon collapsed under the habitual dead weight of sectarian suspicion. It had been only a few years since the Defenders and the Orange Boys had fought at the Diamond. Small wonder that the ini- tial amity of 1798 broke down and that the Defenders began killing Prods again, and the Orangemen, Taigs.

The lines from past to present seem so clear: the Defenders to the Provisional IRA, the Peep o' Day Boys to the Ulster Volunteer Force and the Red Hand Commandos. They're all kerns by other names. During one of my visits to Dublin, in 1982, while the killing in the North continued unabated, I watched a republican parade forming in front of the General Post Office on O'Connell Street. Its purpose was to support the H-Block prisoners—IRA and Irish National Liberation Army men held in the Maze Prison outside Belfast.

The previous year, republican prisoners had gone on hunger strikes to support their claim to be accorded political-prisoner sta- tus—they had all been convicted of serious crimes—and ten of them had fasted until death. The most famous was Bobby Sands, who, as he lay dying, was elected a member of parliament to Westminster. The hunger strike is an old Irish weapon, part of the mythology of martyrdom and sacrifice that permeates the Catholic nationalist tradition. In Dublin that year, emotions were so intense and explosive that a march to the British Embassy had ended in a ferocious riot. It took the biggest police operation in Dublin's history (and that's saying something) to contain the almost uncontrollable rage of the mob.

A year later, the parade was much smaller, but in the same cause, and things were tense, with many heavily armed *gardaí* (the Irish police) everywhere. About five thousand people assembled in wide

O'Connell Street in front of the the General Post Office, from the steps of which in 1916 Patrick Pearse had read out the Proclamation of the Republic to start the Easter Rising. As I stood and watched, a tall, gaunt *garda* officer in black uniform stalked through the crowd. I saw him methodically catch the eye of every man he could. He maintained contact for five or six seconds with a fierce glare. He was like a warrior moving among the enemy counting coup in a single-handed foray. I assumed he was also looking for people he might recognize, hard men on the run or provocateurs who might turn the parade into a riot. Maybe he was just playing a personal game. It was a long time to be under the gaze of a large, armed, and obviously angry copper. He did it to me, too. He didn't know that I was a harmless visitor; I must have seemed like any other sympathizer for the boys.

The parade moved off with its banners and slogans. I didn't follow them but, like a good Canadian, went into the post office to buy stamps. Inside, I saw the statue of Cúchulainn ("Coo-*hull*-in"), the great mythological warrior-hero, the Irish Achilles. He is out of place in Dublin, because it was Ulster he defended single-handed against the southern Irish army of Queen Medb of Connacht— Ulster loyalist paramilitaries today also claim him as their hero for that reason. Everything seemed as it always had in Ireland: the police, the imprisoned gunmen in the North, the parade before the post office with the ghosts of the martyrs of the Easter Rising hanging in the air, the old Irish warrior inside with his meaning intact.

Dublin changed over the following twenty years and, when I visited in 2003, it had become a city under construction, a boom town fuelled by European Union money and a new economy. It seemed to me like any modern European city, filled with prosperous young people—Irish and, for the first time (if you don't count the English), foreigners, too, drawn there by jobs. In 2003, the population of the Republic of Ireland passed four million for the first time since 1871, and it had increased by more than a million since 1971. (The Great Famine of 1845–49 began the process—completed by disease, emigration, and cultural trauma—of cutting Irish numbers by half from over eight million.) Now, the Irish were returning from the diaspora in a kind of *aliya,* an in-gathering of the exiles. Dublin was still an Irish city, where some people smiled at you and said hello in

the middle of a busy street; but, above all, it had the air of a contemporary place in which business and consumption were the main
concerns. The H-Block, mob outrages, Cúchulainn, Patrick Pearse,
the "terrible beauty"—all the mementoes of the violent and mythic
past seemed distant and irrelevant. Surely that must be a good thing,
I thought.

After a while, I took the bus from Dublin back to Belfast. The
hilly border between the Republic and County Armagh in Northern
Ireland was open in these days of the Good Friday peace treaty and
was marked only by a sign. During the Troubles, the police or the
army would have stopped and searched the bus and examined documents. Armagh was the "bandit country" where the eighteenth-
century boys had fought it out and where the IRA and the British
Army, and rural Prods and Taigs, had ambushed and assassinated
each other for thirty years—following the long-held conventions of
sectarian warfare in Ulster. Now, we crossed the border as if we
were driving from Massachusetts into New York or from Ontario
into Quebec, and I thought: This is all a good sign of peace and the
end of the bad old days.

I looked up at the small, grim British army fort, one of a series
strung along the border hill tops, dominating the high ground. It
looked like a Roman tower on some old frontier wall built to guard
against the barbarians. From a distance, it appeared decrepit and
unused. I thought: That's another sign that things are better. First,
the open border; now, these abandoned forts. Then, as I watched, an
army helicopter rose up out of the tower. It hovered for a few seconds and swung away to the north, flying low over the green hills
and scattered woods. As we drove closer, I could see a camouflaged
vehicle trundling away from the small base, the glint of razor wire
on its perimeter, the high communications array of cameras, listeners,
satellite devices. I was back in the North, and the army was still
here, still watchful. Things were better, but my gloomy sense on that
cloudy, mild day in the borderlands of Northern Ireland was of a
hiatus, a mere pause in the ancient hostilities. They went back so far;
the patterns of conflict were set and unremitting. It seemed too
much to hope that they were over for good.

The tower I saw in 2003 could have been one of several south
Armagh army observation posts and forts dismantled two years

later in response to the IRA's announcement of the end of its "armed campaign." If I had taken the same bus across the border in the autumn of 2005, I may have been more optimistic. After all the violent centuries, maybe the venerable and bloody continuities will finally be broken. If Armagh can become open and tranquil, there's hope for the whole place.

SCRIPTURE POLITICS

WILLIAM, the poor country boy, got nothing out of what he later called the "almost useless routine" of the little "hedge-school" in Ballycraigy. But he must have had that air of possibility about him that made adults take notice. Perhaps he was unusually articulate or literate, the quality of his brain obvious in its quick and agile absorption. We know nothing of his parents. His father, the small farmer, and his mother were probably literate (Presbyterians usually were). Perhaps John Dickson was a clever man, too. Raw intelligence is inherited from the female side, however, and Jane Steel must have been the real source of William's intellectual power. We imagine that she was the one who read to her brainy little eldest son and talked to him about God and the world. Perhaps his parents looked at their promising son with awe, or even with trepidation, seeing already in those rough, open-air surroundings the future strange, pudgy, devout intellectual. At least things must have seemed secure and steady there in Carnmoney, near Belfast. It was the Protestant heartland, as much Scotland as Ireland, populated by fellow Dissenters and mostly separate from the troublesome Irish—memories of war and massacre very distant by then.

It was clear from the beginning that William was one of those low-born children who would cross the lines of class and sensibility through his intelligence, talent, and energy. He also had the apparent good luck to find a mentor. He came to the attention of the Reverend Robert White, the Presbyterian minister of the nearby town of Templepatrick, who saw the potential in the farmer's son. His parents must have given up at least some of their jurisdiction over him, and turned him over to the pastor for education. White provided him with "paternal attention and valuable instruction," William wrote later in the sparse early autobiographical paragraphs of his *Narrative*. The minister taught him Latin and Greek, logic, metaphysics, morals, and natural theology. More than that, and more valuable, "he first taught me, not only to reason, but to think."

William followed those old and strong connections of culture and affiliation between northeast Ulster and Scotland when he went to Glasgow University at the age of seventeen. (Even the archetypal Ulster hero, Cúchulainn, had gone to Scotland to be schooled—though under compulsion from his future father-in-law as a precondition for marrying his daughter.) He had no thought of going to England, and certainly not to Dublin. Presbyterians were treated almost as badly as papists, and no Irish university would have admitted him. In any event, the intellectual action was in Glasgow. The Scottish Enlightenment unfolded there and in Edinburgh in the last half of the eighteenth century. Adam Smith and the philosopher-historian David Hume (who would describe the Irish as "buried in the most profound barbarism and ignorance"—he presumably didn't mean to include the Dissenters of Ulster) were its pre-eminent scholars. The *Encyclopaedia Britannica* began as a dictionary of arts and sciences issued by a "Society of gentlemen in Scotland." William took classes with Smith and recorded that he owed "very much indeed" to him.

William also singles out as a formative influence John Millar, a professor of law at Glasgow. Millar made his young friend interested in law and jurisprudence: "the principles of government, and the respective advantages and disadvantages of the different forms under which it may be constructed and administered." William read Locke, Montesquieu, and Samuel Pufendorf (whose great work was entitled: *On the Law of Nature and Nations*) and he came to some definite conclusions:

> [That] absolute monarchy is not the best possible government, except in the hands of absolute perfection—that aristocracy is, and ever must be, a bad government—that despotism,

under the *masque* of limited monarchy, a mixed government, or a free state, is worse still—and, that a government,
of whatever description, the administration of which is
entirely submitted to a faction or sect—and particularly, to
upstarts and underlings of such faction—subject to the
influence, and liable to the control, of spies, informers, and
mercenary clerks in office, is worst of all.

He was talking about Ireland, of course, and of the Ascendancy
government in Dublin and, indirectly, of its English backers. He was
also writing in retrospect in 1812 what he purported to have concluded
in 1763; but, in fact, he never did alter his convictions. He wasn't one
of those radicals at twenty who becomes a crusty, harrumphing reactionary at forty or fifty. William kept his youthful principles intact
through outrage, insurrection, prison, ostracism, and poverty. He
believed about "rational republicanism" what people often say about
Christianity—that "it has never had a fair trial." His practical political
philosophy was uncomplicated: since the executive power under every
form of government must, it seems, be entrusted to an individual, and
because "the right of legislation is inherent in, and inseparable from,
the people," then the chief magistrate (the leader) must be elected and
"amenable to the laws, under which he derives his authority."

William's early interest in law and politics set the tone of his
writing. His arguments in his own defence are devastating in their
restrained logic and clarity, and in their irony, too. In his *Narrative,*
he also tries to explain and justify why a peaceful resistance to a
corrupt, yet determined (or perhaps merely desperate) sectarian
government must, on occasion, resort to physical force. Sometimes,
those on top are so despicable that rebellion is justified to bring
them down. William always writes as a Presbyterian looking at the
Anglican government and administration, from which he was
excluded. Behind that government lay the perennial heft of the
English ministries that condoned its discriminatory practices.

How not to like William? He believes in the rule of law. He is
against cant and faction and grubby patronage. He believes that people are capable of good government and of good action. He may
sometimes be idealistic to the point of unrealism, but he would be
good and wise company anywhere in any time.

———

When William finished university, he came home to the little farm at Ballycraigy. He provides few details of his life then. He seems to have been at loose ends—perhaps like any college boy finished with his studies. He may have done some teaching. He thought he would go into law. But his "early and venerated friend Mr. White" intervened. With "flattering solicitations," Robert White prevailed upon the young scholar "to become a candidate for the office of a preacher of the gospel." William could not resist his old teacher's desire. White was the man who had, literally, lifted William out of his social class, changed his destiny, and made him ready to insert himself into history. Perhaps White also confirmed in William what his mother and father had already taught him: the kinship of "Scotch" Dissenters and Irish Catholics, both trodden down by the arrogant and corrupt Ascendancy men of Dublin and the rural Big Houses, who were, in turn, only the front-men for English domination of Ireland.

William was licensed in 1767, but for four years no congregations were available. He travelled around, filling in at various churches, a substitute minister in Carrickfergus, Islandmagee, Dunmurry, Bangor, and Killead. It was a nuisance, but it created for him a network of well-to-do families in Counties Antrim and Down. In particular, he became associated with Alexander Stewart, one of the better landlords in the country, a public-spirited man, liberal in politics and religion.

In those early, happy times of his ministry, William found and influenced many friends. Subsequent accounts of his personality always mention his humour and charm, his wit and irony. These qualities appear hardly at all in his sermons and, except for the irony, rarely in the *Narrative*. They're not character traits evident in his portrait, either. But newspaper reports of his speeches during the days of public United Irishmen agitation, before the society was forced into underground conspiracy, always describe how he carries his audiences with his extemporaneous, overwhelming, logical wit—a kind of political, rhetorical *craic*. He would have done well even among the savagely funny and coruscating orators of Dublin. In the north, among the dour Scots Presbyterians, he must have stood out with—to risk a stereotype—his Irish flow of words. Perhaps his fluidity of expression and his easeful public manner were things that drew suspicion to him later. The austere northerners often valued the laconic. Volubility was unsound; it was too much like the feckless Taigs.

In 1771, a congregation finally became available, and William was ordained minister of Ballyhalbert, a small village strung out along the seafront of the gently rolling, fertile land of the Ards Peninsula in County Down. The Mull of Galloway on the coast of Scotland is visible on clear days. He might have got his congregation thanks to the influence of Alexander Stewart, who was as much a patron to him as his grandson, Viscount Castlereagh, became a persecutor—during the days of "the Ninety-Eight," when everything had changed. One Presbyterian Church historian says it took William a long time to get a church because he wasn't a good preacher and was unpopular with his temporary congregations. Perhaps his predilection for the law was a factor here, too, if his published sermons are good examples of what he was telling these parishioners on Sundays. Each begins with a precise general statement of his thesis; he develops his points methodically, if with eloquence; at the end, he sums up. He follows the golden rule of persuasive delivery: tell them what you're going to say; say it; tell them what you said. Maybe this didn't impress the farmers, businessmen, and landlords of Carrick or Bangor, who might have been used to warmer, more homely homilies.

More likely, the delay in William's getting a ministry was a combination of bad luck and the fact that it often took several years for a church to pay off an old minister and go through the long, democratic process of hiring a new one. The procedure was as different as you could get from the top-down Catholic or Anglican system of clerical appointments. It's easy to see the connections between Presbyterianism and ideas of political egalitarianism—the Dissenters were already practising democracy in their church. They were, in a way, natural democrats and republicans. They elected their moderator; they decided among themselves whom they wanted as ministers; and the individual churches voluntarily associated themselves into the Synod of Ulster—in about 1690. It was the first dissenting synod in the British Isles. In a very real sense, the Presbyterian community organized itself on its own principles and regulated its own affairs. According to one historian, it was "a free assembly accountable only to God, that is, to its own interpretation of God's will." This independence and separateness was what disturbed

Anglicans the most: "the government's toleration of such a state of affairs was barely credible." Presbyterians were contrarian and fractious by nature; they were, after all, Dissenters. Congregations were always splitting up and forming anew.

When William began preaching at Ballyhalbert, it seems that, for whatever reason, he was immediately popular. Its people may have been happy to get anyone to minister to them, and especially in their remote little village. William often delivered special sermons against specific sins—one against cockfighting apparently ended the brutal sport in the neighbourhood (or at least drove it underground).

As was customary, William had to become a farmer on the side to provide extra money and food, presumably easy enough for the former farmboy. In that same year—he was twenty-seven—he became a husband. He married Isabella McMinn (or Isabella Gamble—there's historical disagreement about her birth name, and William never mentions it): she was from a "genteel family, brought up in affluence and liberally educated." Like the soldier Robert Lundy, William married well. For Robert, a younger son of landed gentry, that was natural. In William's case, his marriage was part of his upwardly mobile transformation from tenant-farmer's son to middle-class respectability. William's portrait doesn't imply that he was a handsome man in his youth. Perhaps his charm and conversational skills made up for it—when you looked like him, you had to talk fast. There's no record of Isabella's appearance; indeed, there's virtually no history of her at all. She comes down to us as anonymous as the wife of a strict Muslim. For the next four years, William writes in his *Narrative,* "I devoted myself, almost entirely, to my parochial and domestic duties, or the studies connected with them." It was the last quiet time for William. Because he lived in Ireland, it was his destiny to live in unquiet times.

Certain kinds of events outside Ireland have always reverberated within the country in a particular way. The Irish (however they're defined) have always judged the nature and importance of affairs overseas through a particular prism: To what extent and in what way will those events enable Ireland to become more independent from England? In the standard received version of Irish history, as we've seen, England's difficulties create Ireland's opportunities. In the last quarter of the eighteenth century, England had many difficulties, and the results in Ireland were predictable. Many Irish Protestants didn't want independence, but, like the Catholic nationalists who did, they had to pay attention to what was going on in France or Spain. Or in America—that was where the Insurrection of 1798 began its long gestation.

In 1775, American colonists fought skirmishes with British regulars at Concord and Lexington and a battle at Bunker Hill, Massachusetts. In 1776, the colonists precipitated all-out war with England by issuing a declaration of independence. When France allied itself with the American rebels, the war became international and dragged on for six years.

The rebels were the armed radical minority who had decided to resist British imperial tax impositions by force. They had agitated against the stamp tax and the tea tax and had tossed 340 tea chests into Boston harbour two years earlier. Their slogan was: "No taxation without representation." The coercive English response didn't calm anyone down.

Remember how many Ulster Presbyterians there were in the Thirteen Colonies. Perhaps 250,000 emigrants left Ulster ports directly for America during the first seventy-five years of the eighteenth century, and large numbers of emigrants to Canada "re-emigrated" by crossing the border into the American colonies. Most of them were Presbyterians, and they constituted between a third and a half of the entire Presbyterian population of Ulster during that period. It was the first great wave of Irish emigration to the New World, the real beginning of the Irish diaspora. The famine exodus of the following century merely added to it.* So many people left that the ones who stayed in Ulster feared for the security of

---

* Today, the majority of Irish Americans are of Ulster Protestant origin, not southern Catholic. Protestants have been mostly eliminated from histories of the Irish in the United States. This strategic forgetting or denial is deeply embedded. In a *New Yorker* magazine article in November 2004, even the scholarly critic Louis Menand refers to John F. Kennedy as "the first Irish-American President." In fact, by Kennedy's time, almost a third of American presidents were the sons, or the descendants, of Ulster Protestant immigrants. Menand—as well as the publication's notoriously picky editors and fact-checkers—somehow forgets or doesn't know this point, or, perhaps more tellingly, he doesn't consider the Ulster Prods to have been "Irish."

Protestantism in the north—fewer of them to keep the Irish at bay—and for the economy as well, as skilled artisans, traders, and farmers were lost. Sometimes whole congregations went at once. In 1764, for example, the Reverend Thomas Clark led three hundred families from his Ballybay congregation to America. William said in one of his sermons that they left "in Quest of that Liberty and Peace which their Country denied them." There was scarcely a Protestant family "of the middle and lower Classes among us, who does not reckon Kindred with the Inhabitants of that extensive Continent."

As with all immigrants, the Ulster Dissenters in America kept in touch with the people back home. They continued to inhabit the same world of ideas and politics. The Presbyterians of Massachusetts were unlikely to submit there to what they considered the same sorts of arbitrary measures that they, or their parents or grand-parents, had left Down or Antrim to escape. Because Ulster Presbyterians suffered from almost as much discrimination as Irish Catholics, they got the increasingly strong idea that the American colonists were fighting for their rights, too. Yet the colonists were, literally, up in arms, while the Ulster Presbyterians continued to acquiesce in their oppression.

A Belfast town meeting drank a toast to "the American Colonies and may the Descendants of those who fled from Tyranny in one Country never be forced to submit to its galling Yoke in another." An Armagh minister wrote later of how proud Ulster Presbyterians were that their friends and relatives made up "the flower of Washington's army . . . still, as their fathers had been, the deter-mined enemies of tyranny and arbitrary power, which ever pursued them, and by a strange fatality from the same quarter, *England.*" Talk like this might convince an imperial government that its own people (particularly second-class Irish Dissenters) weren't much less dangerous than the American rebel faction.

The rebellion in America jolted William out of his mundane, rural routines. He became the political man he had always been by inclina-tion and education. On December 13, 1776, he preached a sermon to his Ballyhalbert congregation which he entitled "On the Advantages of National Repentance." A little over a year later, he gave a second one called "On the Ruinous Effects of Civil War." In them, he excoriated the English government's "mad crusade" against its American colonists: "While I regretted its folly, I execrated its wickedness." The war was "unnatural, impolitic, and unprincipled." However, William's objections are, somehow, just what we would expect from a practical, hardheaded northern Prod. He has neither taste nor inclination, he says, to get into a discussion of political theory (although we may doubt that): American rights, the omnipotence of Parliament, whether the Americans were forced into resistance or were a collection of mere rebels without a cause. Who gives a damn about all that cant, he implies, when the war is making people suffer and die—even more terribly and indiscriminately than ever because of the new, improved firearms and the use of guerrilla tactics? It is the real consequences of the war that are so damaging: taxes going up; trade restricted and ships captured (all big blows for the sophisticated trading and industrial culture of northern Presbyterians); the danger that France or Spain would attack and invade England and Ireland greatly increased with the British forces fighting a dirty war of occupation with a 3,000-mile-long, saltwater supply line. William may not be enamoured of the state of freedom for Dissenters in Ireland, but he has no illusions about what an invasion by one of the absolutist continental powers would involve: "With all our Murmurs and Complaints, do we imagine, our Liberties would be extended, our Taxes diminished, or our Properties better secured?" Not a chance, he assures his little Sunday congregation.

On top of all that, this war in America is an apocalyptic civil war for the Protestants of Ireland and especially Ulster. The colonists had so recently stood with British troops to fight the French in North America. All those ties of immigrant kinship meant that the war had turned brother against brother, and Protestant against Protestant.

William's two sermons were published in Belfast sometime in 1778. It doesn't seem like much to us—a couple of Sunday addresses in a tiny church miles from anywhere; a pamphlet circulated months later. But that's ahistorical hindsight. Together with the new medium of newspapers, the sermon in the church meeting house was one of the most important ways political opinion and information got circulated among the tight-knit and politicized northern Presbyterian community. William's Ballyhalbert sermons could easily reverberate in Belfast and elsewhere among the Ulster

Dissenters. His words in that small country church could even outrage and anger a government and an Ascendancy. And they did.

In his *Narrative,* William recalls the "great offence" his sermons
gave to "all the dependents of government" and "the landed interest
of the country." "A general outcry was raised against me, in which
those, who never heard me preach, were very loud; and those, who
had never seen me, were louder still." They called him "Traitor!"
"Rebel!" "Trumpeter of sedition!" When the government's cronies
and hangers-on got together and into their cups, he said, they all
agreed that "I ought to be d——d, as hanging was too good for me."
But he got his revenge on these atrocious hacks. William writes,
with one of his occasional gloats: "I published the sermons, as they
were preached, without the retraction, alteration, or addition, of a
single word." And in the end, he points out, his words proved to
have been fully justified.

Once again, his *Narrative* provides few details of his conversion
from country preacher to political agitator. He says only that he had
read Locke and Montesquieu and studied jurisprudence in
Scotland, and his "mind instantly revolted" against the war.
"Feeling as I did, and detesting the meanness, as much as the
immorality, of dissimulation, I never concealed either my ideas, or
sentiments, on the subject." He was a man who always came
through loud and clear: you couldn't change his mind; you couldn't
shut him up without putting him in prison or killing him; you
couldn't calculate the uprush of rebellious emotion he could inspire
in a country full of sore, cranky Taigs and dissenting Prods.

In fact, William was too hard on the Parliament in Dublin. Like
many Presbyterians in the north, he was understandably angry at his
exclusion from full citizenship. Any Dissenter living close to Belfast
must have been incensed by the form of local government there: the
earls of Donegall ran the city through a closed Anglican corporation, like a private fief, which completely excluded Belfast's
Presbyterian lawyers, merchants, traders, and doctors. They were
middle class and political in the bone. Yet not only were they cut out
of their country's government but they had no say in their city's
affairs. From Antrim and Down, the Presbyterians cast a cold and
furious eye south to the Anglican Ascendancy Irish Parliament
and its English executive.

Nevertheless, some members of that Parliament had continued to conduct their own campaign for rights and freedoms. The Ascendancy's intellectuals, Swift, Berkeley, and Molyneux, had prepared the ground. The transformation of the Ascendancy's image of itself into a form of Irishness developed it. The Protestants saw their goal more and more as *Irish* rights and freedoms. England, not Ireland, was now the "other" for the Protestant reformers of Dublin, the so-called Patriots. They wanted only what was due to Ireland— its rightful status as an independent nation—although they accepted the reality that it would remain affiliated with Britain through their common monarch and the close similarity of their laws and political conventions.

The American rebellion reverberated in Dublin as much as in Belfast, if, perhaps, without the immediacy created by Ulster's strong immigrant connection. No Irishman could fail to see the analogue between the Thirteen Colonies and his own situation. They all had their representative assemblies and, in Ireland's case, a form of parliament, but England still ran the show. It had the power to pass laws for the Americans or the Irish whenever it felt like it, and local assemblies or parliaments be damned. No wonder that the Patriots in Dublin couldn't help but conclude, as had the Dissenters in Belfast and William in his little village on the Ards coast, that the Americans were fighting for Irishmen, too.

The American war had another crucial consequence in Ireland. Like any overextended imperial power, England had to strip forces from one colony, which in this case was only fractious and potentially rebellious, to fight the open revolution that had broken out in another. It pulled its regulars out of Ireland. French fleets were always sniffing around the island—which they correctly perceived as the weak section of England's security perimeter. Only eighteen years earlier, a French squadron had landed and captured Carrickfergus Castle on Belfast Lough (the castle is a few hundred metres away from my grandfather Billy's birthplace in the Irish Quarter). The army hadn't been available then either, and a force of local volunteers had had to form up and throw out the French sailors and marines. That was a memorable precedent of French aggression, army unreliability, and the necessity of self-help. When France and Spain entered the war in support of the rebellious colonists in 1778, an invasion of Ireland, denuded of its British garrison, became an immediate danger. The English government declared that Ireland must look to its own defence. There were the Catholic Irish to worry about, too. They had been quiescent for almost ninety years, but one could never tell what they might do when the army departed. Irish Protestants responded right away and with enthusiasm. With England's acquiescence, they began to form themselves into an armed force, the Volunteers.

William was in the thick of things. He had had a taste of political action and notoriety, and it seems to have suited him. Writing his *Narrative* twenty-four years later, his exhilaration is still obvious. "In a few weeks, a generous patriotic ardor, as if excited by a spark from Heaven, pervaded, animated, and actuated the great body of the Irish people." By the spring of 1789, 12,000 enthusiastic men were under arms; by September of that year, 40,000, a little later, 60,000. What comes through most of all in William's and other accounts of the Volunteers is that it was great fun. Like all military service, signing up had a universal attraction for men: the chance to ameliorate or abandon boring routine, to wear fancy uniforms, to march and carouse together, to carry and handle weapons—all the profound and frivolous bonding activities of males in armed groups.

William's description of the formation of the Volunteers reveals two interesting side effects, which would have worried any imperial power and did, indeed, cause England great anxiety. Military service levels social class and rank and creates a sense of solidarity. Among the Volunteers, William writes, "the idea of profession seemed to be obliterated. Physician, surgeon and apothecary; lawyer and attorney—all were soldiers." Farmers, weavers, tradesmen joined, too. Even Presbyterian ministers exchanged one uniform, "the rusty black," for "the glowing scarlet" of another, as William put it. Sometimes a preacher would enter the pulpit in full uniform, put his sword to one side, take up his Bible, and give a sermon. The Volunteers in his congregation would applaud by pounding their musket butts on the floor. Coming together for mutual defence against the papist states of Europe (and to overawe the papists within) encouraged Protestant men to think of themselves as Irish Volunteers rather than Ascendancy Anglicans or Presbyterian

Dissenters. Their pride and self-confidence grew. The "lower ranks of the community" acquired "an independence and a republicanism of spirit," wrote one observer. Within the armed collective of the Volunteers, an Irish Protestant Nation began to unite.

The second consequence of the countrywide organization was that the Protestant men of Ireland got a political education. For most of them, they had a taste of citizenship for the first time. They elected their officers (almost all Ascendancy aristocrats), held meetings, discussed resolutions and petitions, and made their collective views known to members of parliament. The Volunteer units easily became de facto political clubs and debating societies. Their members got a clear sense of what it meant to be part of "the people," and an armed one at that. There's nothing like a weapon—a sleek musket or a shiny sword, even a plebeian pike—to empower a man. It adds a jaunty confidence to his political aspirations.

The Volunteers were another baleful legacy for England of its stupid policies and disastrous war in America. The government had lost its traditional monopoly of force to a politically charged people-in-arms who were, in the Irish pattern, turning out not to be the envisioned docile and loyal regiments. It was a force that focused the minds of English administrators and the English Parliament when the Irish Protestants demanded legislative independence. It was far from the last time that Irish constitutional agitation—both Protestant and Catholic—joined in uneasy, reluctant, ambiguous yet symbiotic alliance with the implied threat of physical force. But, William writes: "Amidst the pleasing circumstances, which surrounded this institution, one equally shameful and impolitic, occurred." Catholics, "in great numbers, and with great zeal, offered themselves as volunteers, in common with their Protestant and Presbyterian countrymen. Through the greatest part of Ulster, if not the whole, their offers were rejected, and, in some places, not without insult. In my own neighbourhood, this was universally the case."

It may seem strange that many Catholics (although not as many as William implies) wanted to join Protestants in a people's militia, but they were willing to do so for a number of reasons. Most important, they saw the chance of achieving a de facto right to bear arms, in spite of the penal law prohibiting their doing so. Volunteering gave legitimacy, and added energy, to the sporadic campaign of Catholics, mostly Dublin businessmen, for political redress. Catholics, as well as Protestants, had got caught up in the general elation of the American rebellion and its implications for Ireland. Many middle-class Catholic merchants and traders had done well under the Ascendancy and had as much to lose as any Protestant if the French invaded. Catholic politics were invigorated because, in 1778, the government finally passed a *Catholic Relief Act*—the first formal roll-back of a penal law—and the English, eager to tap into the large pool of Catholic manpower for military purposes, were clearly interested in pressuring Dublin to pass more legislation. After a century of peace, or what passed for it in a country of kerns, violent secret societies, and paramilitaries—and a casual attitude to capital crimes—sectarian tensions had eased. Remember the siege of Derry centennial celebrations in 1788, in which Catholics joined Protestants in praising the constitutional Glorious Revolution they believed the siege had made possible.

It's an important point that Irish Catholics, like the Protestants—like any group of people—were not a single bloc of believers in one thing. That's what the standard received version of Irish history dictates, with its categories of "Catholics" and "Protestants," "Planters" and "Gaels." But, as usual, complexity keeps intervening. A well-off Dublin Catholic merchant—perhaps a member of the Catholic Committee working for penal-law relief—might well be very interested in the Volunteers. But a hungry, Gaelic-speaking peasant farmer looking for work and living in the Bogside beneath George Walker's overbearing statue on Derry's walls might sign up with the secret society of the guerrilla Whiteboys, never the Volunteers.

William was one of the minority of Protestants in favour of allowing Catholics to join the Volunteers. It was always a small radical minority concentrated in the middle class and geographically confined to Belfast and Dublin and their surrounding areas. In the countryside—in Armagh, for example, or in Derry's hinterland, where Prods and Taigs still lived in their complicated proximity—the usual fears and prejudices remained dominant. Few Protestants there favoured giving an inch to their Catholic neighbours, let alone letting them bear arms. They thought they still had good reason to take seriously the penal law prohibiting Catholics from owning weapons.

William did what he could: he preached another sermon. He entitled it "On the Propriety and Advantages of Acquiring the Knowledge and Use of Arms, in Times of Public Danger" and gave it to the assembled Volunteers of Echlinville in March 1779. Most of the sermon was a vigorous defence of the right and, in parlous times, the obligation of the citizen to bear arms and to learn how to use them. William's text was grounded, as usual, in the scripture-politics of biblical allusions and examples, but it was, nevertheless, a barn-burner: a standing army has its uses, but only an armed people can truly safeguard its liberties and defend the nation against foreign enemies and internal tyranny. This part of his sermon might well have been a defence of the second amendment to the United States Constitution, guaranteeing the right of the people to bear arms— although as part of a "well-regulated militia."

In the spirit of that giddy year of Protestant empowerment, most of William's address was radical, but not revolutionary. However, he had taken note of the hostile Protestant reaction to Catholic partici-pation in the Volunteers. He writes that he was "impressed with a sense of the impolicy and danger of such conduct, and equally so with its injustice." Catholics must be admitted without reservation, he said. Once again, the country preacher had crossed the line. His opinions, he observed, offended "all the Protestant and Presbyterian bigots in the country." He was accused of advocating rebellion. Some called him "a Papist in [his] heart," not least, he adds sarcasti-cally, for the "very substantial reason" that the birth name of the local parish priest's mother was Dickson (those confused confes-sional pedigrees again).

Patriots and radical Dissenters wanted him to publish the ser-mon, but so incendiary was the suggestion of arming Catholics that he had to excise that portion of his speech. This time, William allowed himself to be censored "in the public cause," though what remained in print was, he said, "so much in shadow of what I expressed, in substance, from the pulpit." Still, even his written words could be a model plea for tolerance in any age:

> As our enemies are generally of the Popish religion, those
> of that denomination, among us, are apt to construe meas-
> ures of public safety into private design, and attribute every

174 Men that God Made Mad

armament to enmity against them. To remove such injurious suspicion is an object well deserving your attention, and your conduct ought to shew, that ye have not taken up arms, for this or the other denomination, but for your country . . . that it is only against the enemies of your country, liberty, and peace, be their religion what it may, that your arms are pointed—and, that whoever is a friend of these, is your friend, and the object of your protection.

However, a widespread and lasting rapprochement between Catholics and Protestants was impossible in the eighteenth century. This stark fact contradicts the standard version of Irish history. That version's current political myth, selectively drawn from history for present purposes (as we'll see, the myth has changed greatly over the years), says that Catholics and Protestants came together in the years before 1798 and joined in a battle to free Ireland from England, its ancient enemy. The great insurrection was yet another glorious rising of the Irish nation against the 800-year occupation. The Ninety-Eight became part of the romantic rebel ethos of blood sacrifice for Mother Ireland and a further celebration of the exploits of the boys—except that, this time, Protestants were part of it.

Protestant participation in the fight for Irish freedom in the 1780s and 1790s, relatively limited though it was, has been used for two present-day political purposes. First, to support the benign argument against the unionists of Northern Ireland ("unionism" is the constitutional unity of Britain and Ireland) that Protestants and Catholics have joined together before in the cause of a united Ireland and that, therefore, there is no reason why they should fear to do so again. The year 1798 is a precedent for cooperation and power-sharing between the two communities; the extremist Prod preacher Ian Paisley need not fear governing together with the ex-IRA gunman Gerry Adams. The second lesson of the insurrection is to prove that there is no such thing in Ireland as a separate Protestant people—British and not Irish—as the northern unionists claim. The Protestants of the North should just accept that they're "really" Irish and a minority part of the whole country. They "became" Irish in 1798 and can do so again. Only their own pigheadedness and wrong-headedness—and England's continuing and unwelcome intrusion into Irish affairs—prevents them from acknowledging that. They have to give up their separate little statelet, or entity, or whatever it is.

Unless, of course, you're a hard-line Catholic Irish nationalist, for whom the northern Prods are, indeed, British. In which case, you would offer them the less kindly advice: Get off the land you stole four hundred years ago and get out of the country.

The original, and simple, premise of the arguments to support the lessons of 1798—widespread and wholehearted sectarian cooperation and amity—is simply not correct. One of the historical "mysteries" of the Insurrection of 1798 was the fact that, when it was over, it seemed that the Protestants, who had been radical nationalists, became instant conservative unionists. The explanation is the simple one that the great majority of Protestants were never radicals to begin with. Even most Presbyterians—the ones outside Belfast and the radical towns of Counties Antrim and Down—remained staunch believers in the Protestant Ascendancy and in keeping Catholics in their place. The records of the Synod of Ulster, the Presbyterians' governing body, damn the insurrection and the egalitarian republican principles that made it happen.

The events of 1798 and the two decades leading up to it gave the nationalists and the republicans their few moments of opportunity and fame. But it's possible to view these years as an anomalous period in Irish history and as more of a local phase of an international turning point than as an emblematic Irish event. Afterwards, things returned to normal—sectarian politics, the Orange Order and Catholic Ribbonmen (the successors to the Defenders) fighting it out in the traditional way, and moderate Catholics struggling for emancipation. Ireland was still divided and complicated and, with the 1801 *Act of Union* joining the two countries—the response to the insurrection—more under English control than ever. There were obviously some exceptions: William for one. He never changed his mind about the rightness of the great cause and its prosecution. But he was part of that very small minority of Protestants who would continue to keep the faith of Irish republican nationalism and who would, in fact, contribute many of the movement's most powerful leaders for the next hundred years.

William's views on Catholics were representative of those of the minority liberal "New Light" tendency in Presbyterianism. In fact, his opinions were really a more radical version of those views—few, even among the New Lights, supported William's call for immediate and complete Catholic emancipation. Most favoured a "gentle, gradual" relaxation of restrictions—a position that William would later demolish with his usual sardonic wit. However, the majority "Old Light" viewpoint was one of unchanged hostility. As an example, the County Cavan minister John Rogers preached a sermon to four units of Volunteers (they were a favoured audience for these essentially political speeches) in June 1780. He told the men-in-arms that, in spite of the claims of so-called enlightened Protestants, it was his right to warn against popery's enduring threat, and he was happy to do so. There was very good reason to continue to designate the Pope as the Antichrist; Catholics had always persecuted Protestants as heretics and gone back on oaths with Protestants, said Rogers. In other words, nothing had altered in Ireland. There remained that irreducible fact of Catholic hostility and religious error. Protestants could never believe them or the stated intentions of their leaders, including their ultimate head, the Pope. This conclusion was the real fact on the ground, especially in Ulster, with its mixed-up pattern of settlement; there was no true safety for the Protestants, no room for them to make a mistake, such as trusting the Taigs. They simply couldn't afford to take the chance. The memory of risings and of their terror was still an indelible part of the Protestant mind: "Remember the steel of Sir Phelim O'Neill / Who slaughtered our fathers in Catholic zeal."

We get the sense throughout the period of the Volunteers, and right up to the Insurrection of 1798 itself, of a small number of Ascendancy reformers and New Light Presbyterians who were fighting a battle for toleration and religious unity they couldn't win. They were public men who wrote and talked a lot, and superficial history rewards such people with its undivided attention. Therefore, their politics and ideas were given a disproportionate amount of attention in the historical record. In reality, that record was not equipped to take note of the unexpressed views of the silent, unmovable, overwhelming majority. In retrospect, the enlightened tolerance of the reformers has the air of a brief interruption in the normal scheme of things—almost like a conceit in the face of the entrenched sectarian hostility of the mass of Protestants and Catholics. When the bulk of the people got involved, the old fear and hatred would overwhelm these optimistic and, one has to say, naive reformers (arming Catholics wholesale during that period might well, in fact, have triggered sectarian warfare and massacres). They were struggling to push back the great weight of the Irish past, and that simply couldn't be done. For the great majority of Protestants, William and his comrades were merely Lundys before their time.

The Dublin-based Protestant reform movement inspired by the American rebellion and backed up by the armed Volunteers appeared to achieve remarkable things. Its chief leaders were Henry Grattan, a Dublin lawyer; Henry Flood, the son of a former chief justice; and the Earl of Charlemont, whose ancestor had come to Ireland with the Earl of Essex during the Enterprise of Ulster, one English settler hardy enough to stay. The Patriots won economic and political victories. The British government was caught between the debacle in America and the implied threat of force represented by the Volunteers. Once again, we see the intimate connection between successful political action in Ireland and the presence of armed men in the background. The Volunteers paraded through Dublin with a cannon bearing a placard whose blunt, unequivocal message read "Free trade or this!" Flood was one of their colonels; Charlemont became their commander-in-chief. In 1779, Britain removed its restrictions on Irish trade, but too late and too grudgingly to gain any gratitude. By that time, everyone in Ireland thought the move was long overdue and, in any case, regulation had been unjust from the beginning.

The British commander in the Thirten Colonies, Lord Cornwallis, surrendered at Saratoga in the autumn of 1781 to an American army and a French fleet. It was a low moment for England. The capitulation demonstrated that the British Empire was "degenerating into a state of political dotage, prophetical of its final dissolution," said the Ulster Presbyterian William Drennan, the future chief architect of the United Irishman.

In England's loss of confidence and resolve, the Irish smelled opportunity. Representatives of the Volunteer units of Ulster held a convention in a parish church at Dungannon, County Tyrone, in February 1782 and passed resolutions demanding legislative independence for Ireland. The English Tory government that had prosecuted the war in America had fallen and a new anti-war Whig government, which favoured Irish concessions, was in power.* Whig legislation abolished restrictions on the Irish Parliament to the point that the only English power remaining was the right to veto bills. Ireland suddenly found itself—at least on paper—an independent kingdom sharing a monarch with Britain. For once, optimism and satisfaction, instead of war or famine, broke out in the country. The mundane but essential apparatus of sovereignty began to assemble itself: a separate post office, the Bank of Ireland, the Custom House, and the Four Courts. Irish judges could only be removed by the Irish Parliament, an essential condition for homegrown jurisprudence. The great canals linking Dublin to the Shannon River in the west were built, as were some of Dublin's elegant squares—Rutland and Merrion (the latter, where Yeats would later live). The Irish capital began to look like one, more so than the cramped, ad hoc aspect of London itself. The penal laws dealing with land ownership were repealed in 1782, but Catholics did not get political power in any form or disguise, nor could they join the legal profession—hard restrictions for a growing middle class.

The treatment of Catholics demonstrated the provisional nature of the new sovereign kingdom: only the Irish Ascendancy Protestants had won legislative independence. A stable nation could not be built on such a discriminatory foundation. Furthermore, the Protestant reformers themselves soon found out that their independence looked good in theory, but in practice was English control by other means. The Lord Lieutenant was English and appointed by the English government. He chose and controlled the Irish executive, which in turn controlled patronage and effectively influenced how members of parliament voted on anything. Two-hundred-and-thirty-four of the three hundred members were elected from "close"

---

* Ironically, the names of the two English political parties, the forerunners of the Conservatives and the Liberals, had origins in Celtic banditry: "Whig" from the Scots *whiggamer*, who were seventeenth-century rebels; "Tory" from the Irish *toraidhe*, "raider" or "outlaw," another kind of kern.

boroughs in which one wealthy, aristocratic patron decided who sat. The rest were elected on a narrow franchise based on property.

In reality, Ireland could not govern itself in its own interests with such a Parliament. The underlying result was the creation of the preconditions for radical politics: the majority Catholics were excluded, while the expectations of the Protestant reformers were first raised and then drained away in the realization that not much had changed.

A second Volunteer convention gathered in Dublin in November 1783. It demanded parliamentary reform. The Ascendancy Parliament rejected it and dared the Volunteers to use their arms to enforce change if they wanted it so badly. The respectable, middle-class Volunteers, officered by Ascendancy men, backed down. A subsequent convention the following year failed. The reformers had run into the entrenched privilege of the Irish Ascendancy government and its tame legislature, both of which simply refused to refurbish themselves. The standard Irish story is wrong again—its simple version of Irish against English for Ireland's freedom. In fact, Irish Protestants in power stood as much in the way of real Irish independence as did the English. One historian has described the Irish Parliament as "little more than a gigantic relief scheme for the nobility and their relatives." The lessons were clear: first, to effect change, Irish reformers needed more radical politics and a more ruthless use of armed men; second, if it came to a fight, it would be as much civil war as a war against England. But all that lay in the future. In the meantime, the impetus for reform lost momentum and public support, and the country languished again.

If political myths, or standard received versions of history, depend not only on selective remembering but also on selective forgetting, any past events that inconveniently contradict the mythology must be eliminated from memory. In creating their stories of themselves, both Catholic Irish and Ulster Protestants have found it necessary to forget that the idea of an Irish republic, as free from England as economic, strategic, and political realities would allow—supposedly the great Catholic, Gaelic ideology—began among the Presbyterians of Ulster. That's been mostly forgotten in modern Ireland, both north and south. The popular idea has been that the French Revolution was the inspiration for the Irish desire for an independent republic. But we've noted how the American War and the raising of the Volunteers helped prepare the ground some time before the French stormed the Bastille in 1789. And so did the nature of Presbyterianism, too. After his release from prison, as we've seen, William became the minister at Second Keady, so-called because it was the dissenting portion of the dissenting congregation of the small town. The Presbyterian Church was about as democratic as an organized religion could be. And its idea of religious freedom—the freedom to practise its religion, which it sought for so long—was inevitably tied up with the idea of political action. To get the former, it seemed that you had to engage in the latter.

Presbyterians, as well as other Irish Protestants, believed that the Volunteer movement embodied one of the notions of the Greek and Roman city-states: the armed citizen as the guarantor of individual liberty in the face of the great and arbitrary power of the state. The American Minutemen were another example to emulate. Two years before revolution in France, the Lord Lieutenant of Ireland lamented that "the Province of Ulster is filled with dissenters, who are in general very factious—great levellers and republicans."

Nevertheless, the French Revolution electrified all the discontented Irish. America had been one thing: a minority group of physical-force malcontents in a collection of undeveloped colonies upset over a matter of unfair taxation and rebelling against the imperial power five thousand kilometres away. They had been better off than most Irishmen to begin with, and two-thirds of them had stayed neutral or loyal to Britain. France was completely different. The people of an ancient civilization, and one with no Glorious Revolution in its past as a constitutional precedent, rose against its own absolutist government. The whole structure of the three Estates, the monarchy, and the casual exercise of arbitrary power untrammelled by the rule of law collapsed in a matter of months. Admittedly, many of the principles espoused by the French revolutionaries had been entrenched in British and Irish political life for a century. In France, however, they were being used not to reform a monarchy and create a working parliament but to examine every state and government institution and to remake them from scratch. It was a new start, the creation of a new world on the old ground of

Europe. If such a thing could happen in France, anything was possible in Ireland—or around the world for that matter.

The revolution had a particular significance for Protestants. It had been carried out by Catholics in a profoundly Catholic country. The revolutionaries had disestablished the church and abolished tithes—one of the greatest of irritants for non-Anglicans in Ireland and almost always a motivation for the violence of the agrarian secret societies. If French Catholics could do all that and regard themselves as citizens first, before any religious affiliation, there seemed to be no reason why Irish Catholics could not do so, too. For Protestant reformers and New Light Presbyterians, this model seemed to make an alliance with Irish Catholics a plausible idea. In the second of three sermons subsequently published under the title *Scripture Politics,* one preached to his Portaferry congregation on Christmas Day, 1792, William exclaimed the general sentiment of the Irish reformers: "One great and enlightened nation has burst the chains of prejudice and slavery, disclaimed the idea of conquest for dominion, opened the temple of liberty for all religious denominations at home, and sent forth her arms, *not to destroy,* but *restore* the liberty of the world, and extend her blessings to all who dare, and by daring, deserve to be free."

13

"UNITED" IRISHMEN

WILLIAM WAS NOT AMONG the founders of the Society of United Irishmen in Belfast in October 1791. One can't help but think that his absence was just a matter of geography—he lived in rural isolation, far from the centre of things in the city—and of circumstance.

His sermons about scripture politics and arming Catholics were making him well known—and infamous—to many in Ulster. But his private life went on, too. He and the unknown and enigmatic Isabella had their first child, Jane, in 1775, the year the American Revolution began. By then they had been married for four years, a long time to be childless in those days. Perhaps Isabella had earlier pregnancies or the children died; we have only the Ballyhalbert baptismal register to go on, and it does not record infant mortality. Perhaps there were other factors: incompatibility or reticence. The use of a form of birth control other than abstinence seems unthinkable for someone like William. Still, he was radical in his politics, so why not in sexual matters, too?

It's interesting that William's sudden awakening into vigorous politics and the conception of his first child both took place in the same year of the American rebellion. The delay was not because of any fertility or potency problems. Once they got going, William and Isabella turned out six children in ten years. Their second child, David McMinn (the tradition of giving the mother's birth name to the first son supports the view that Isabella had been a McMinn and not a Gamble), was born in 1776, Mary Charlotte the next year, followed by John Echlin in 1780, Henry William in 1782, and William Galaway in 1785. David became the young navy surgeon whose pay helped keep the family going until he died of unknown causes, probably of disease, in service in 1798.

William must have been a busy man. He had a living to make: running his farm—although his growing labour force of children must have been a help with that—teaching the boys at his income-supplementing private school, tending his congregation's needs for comfort and advice, composing his carefully wrought sermons each week with their mix of God-praise and politics, being a husband and father.

In 1780, the congregation of Portaferry called William to be its minister. The town was a pleasant place about twenty-five kilometres south of Ballyhalbert, at the end of the Ards Peninsula beside the narrow entrance to Strangford Lough. As the town's name suggests, a ferry crosses the fast tidal run of the water ("Strangford" is a Viking name meaning "violent fjord") to the other side, eliminating the need to drive, or ride, close to eighty kilometres around the long, narrow inlet. William and his tired horse would have taken the ferry to get to his portable parish duties in Saintfield and Ballee and to the soothing waters of Ballynahinch—and his arrest there—all of which are on the other side of the water from his home.

The record of William's activities during the 1780s is sparse. He won academic honours in 1784, when he was awarded a Doctor of Divinity degree from his alma mater in Glasgow. Presumably the university had heard and read a great deal it liked about its alumnus's prowess as a preacher and about his political opinions, which accorded admirably with the views of the Scottish Enlightenment. From then on, everything that William wrote or said had the authority of Doctor Dickson behind it—not a small thing among the Presbyterians of Ulster, with their Scottish respect for education.

There are conflicting accounts of whether William attended the Volunteer conventions at Dungannon in 1782 and 1783, but he probably did not. However, according to one historian, William "threw himself into the Volunteer movement with all the ardour of his enthusiastic nature." He certainly became involved in local County Down politics. He campaigned in the general election of 1783 for

Robert Stewart, the son of his old patron, Alexander Stewart. William brought forty freeholders in to vote for his man, but Stewart lost anyway against the entrenched power of the Ascendancy land-lords. In the election of 1790, William worked even harder for the Stewarts, this time for the previous candidate's son, also named Robert. This Stewart won, although it took sixty-nine days of voting and cost him the astonishing expenditure for the time of £60,000— buying votes wasn't cheap. William spent three months travelling the county for his candidate. He wrote that he was on horseback nearly every day and seldom spent a night in his own house. "I canvassed far and wide, regardless of interest, influence and connexions."

He regretted it all later, "in the bitterness of [his] heart." The country would have been better off if Stewart had lost. Once the young reformer, he became Viscount Castlereagh (later, Lord Londonderry) and chief secretary of the Ascendancy government. In that position, he was the heart of the English overlordship of Ireland, and he played his part without hesitation or pity in the dirty business of putting down the rebels of 1798. Castlereagh sanctioned William's arrest in May 1798. "From his popularity in the year 90," said his lordship, "I know he would be a very dangerous person to leave at liberty now." William, trusting and loyal to three genera-tions of Stewarts, never got over the terrible sting of betrayal and ingratitude. Of course, that was the very essence of civil war—the breaking of old ties of family and friendship, the bitterest battles of all between men who were once so close.

The standard received version of Irish history says that the Protestant Dublin lawyer Theobald Wolfe Tone was the founder of the United Irishmen. He forged the society and brought in the Catholics; he went to France and convinced the revolutionary gov-ernment to send a fleet and an invasion force to Ireland. Then he called out the rebellion. He was arrested, tried, and sentenced to death—to be hanged and quartered. "A fig for the quartering if you hang me first," he told the judge. He cut his own throat before the English could execute him. He is the face of stylish revolution and the father of republican physical-force nationalism in Ireland. The revolu-tionary Fenians of 1867, the men of the Easter Rising of 1916, and the Irish Republican Army, including the Provisional IRA of our time, all took their inspiration from the witty, eloquent, doomed rebel.

Most of this account is true. But Tone did not become the quintessential republican until Patrick Pearse so proclaimed him before
the Rising of 1916. (In William's time, "republicanism" described
non-monarchical government and had none of its later mystic aura.)
And Tone did not conceive the idea of the United Irishmen.
William Drennan, a medical doctor from Belfast, the son of a New
Light Presbyterian minister, a Volunteer veteran living in Dublin in
1791, a graduate (like William) of a Scottish Enlightenment university—in his case, Edinburgh—began it all with a letter to his
brother-in-law, Samuel McTier of Belfast. They should form a
secret society, he proposed, "the Brotherhood its name—the rights
of man and the greatest happiness of the greatest number its end—
its general end real independence to Ireland, and republicanism its
particular purpose." McTier happened to be a member of a secret
committee of Volunteers in Belfast composed of eleven radical
dissenters, including Samuel Neilson, a linen merchant and also the
son of a Presbyterian minister—these radicals had learnt well at
their fathers' knees the Dissenter catechism of rebellion and democracy. They couldn't agree more with his suggestion, McTier wrote
back to Drennan.

That's where Wolfe Tone comes in. In September 1791, he
authored a pamphlet called *An Argument on Behalf of the Catholics of
Ireland*. Its argument was that England was the root cause of
Ireland's endless problems; English influence was "the radical vice
of our government." That was his "great discovery," said Tone, and
he had found it in the works of the Ascendancy radicals Jonathan
Swift and William Molyneux. The only solution for Irishmen was a
union of Catholics and Protestants to overthrow the Ascendancy
and, therefore, English domination. Catholics must be given the
vote. No reform would be "honourable, practicable, or efficacious"
without that. The aim, wrote Tone (in his most quoted passage)
must be "to unite the whole people of Ireland, to abolish the memory of all past dissensions, and to substitute the common name of
Irishman in the place of the denominations of Protestant, Catholic,
and Dissenter."

Most of the Belfast radicals weren't exactly eager to welcome
Catholics into the fold, but Tone's arguments—together with the
example of the French Revolution—persuaded them that the enemy

of their enemy might, at least, become their friend. Drennan and Neilson invited Tone to Belfast, and in October they, the secret committee and others—thirty-six in all—formed the Society of United Irishmen. The next month, Tone and Drennan set up a branch in Dublin. At the beginning, there was no talk of revolution or armed resistance. For now, the society was a polite, genteel, middle-class political movement. Its initial resolutions proposed a "cordial union among all the people of Ireland" to counter English influence in the government, a "complete and radical reform" of Parliament, and, following Tone's lead, the inclusion of Irishmen of every religion.

Another man was present at the beginnings of the United Irishmen, although only in spirit: the American Revolution's pamphleteer and theoretician Thomas Paine. The Englishman's *Common Sense* had laid the foundations for the Declaration of Independence. Back in England, Paine published the first part of the *Rights of Man* as a rebuttal of the Ascendancy apologist Edmund Burke's attack on the French Revolution and his praise for the French monarchy. A hereditary monarch was about as sensible as a hereditary mathematician, Paine scoffed. The philosophically ubiquitous John Locke, as well as Jean-Jacques Rousseau, were his sources: sovereignty lay with the people of the nation, and each citizen was subject only to the laws he himself made. Furthermore, the people had a right to overthrow any government that failed to guarantee the rights and sovereignty of the nation. No wonder Paine didn't think much of the Irish Parliament or of the English institution, with its "filth of rotten boroughs." The English government returned the contempt: it indicted Paine for treason, and he had to escape to France.

Paine became famous. His pamphlet may have sold as many as a million copies, perhaps an unprecedented distribution for any piece of writing in English (except the King James Bible). By the time Wolfe Tone travelled to Belfast to help found the United Irishmen, the *Rights of Man* was everywhere. It was a major part of the ferment of avid discussion in the city. Tone called it the "Koran of Belfast"—in a phrase that may suggest much more to us today than Tone intended. Paine's work did not originate the ideas and principles of the Society of United Irishmen, but it was certainly one of the things the new society used to promulgate its program of reform.

Less than two months after the organization's founding meeting, William made the fifty kilometre ride to Belfast and joined up.

From the moment of United Irish inception, the possibility of Catholics and Protestants coming together alarmed both the Ascendancy executive and the English government. They were very attached to the present situation of sectarian division, which allowed a de facto policy of divide and rule. Two days after the Belfast society announced itself, the English home secretary wrote to the Lord Lieutenant in Dublin: "I may be a false prophet, but there is no evil that I should not prophesy if that union [Protestant and Catholic] takes place."

The Englishman seems prescient now. And he had reason to fear his future. We can empathize with him in our time—the sense of inchoate and perhaps catastrophic threat building around us; the feeling of a greasy slide down to dirty war, disorder, and chaos. In Ireland near the end of the eighteenth century, there were many malignant signs: the growing size and daring of the boys—Steel, Peep o' Day, Orange, Defenders; the aggressive, restless Dissenters in the north; the frustrated Dublin Patriots; the Volunteers, reduced in numbers, but still mustering thousands of armed men; the loss of America; the revolution in France and its lesson that all the old orders might be in jeopardy; the Catholic Irish with their two-pronged campaign—the well off agitating for emancipation through the rejuvenated Catholic Committee, and the peasants with their ineradicable hostility to the English and the Protestants (including the Dissenters), calling all by the same term: *sassenagh*. Now there was this new society to reckon with, and its promise of joining together the disparate sects and classes of Ireland. For an English imperial minister, the only bright spot was the lack of recent precedent: the Irish hadn't risen in actual, full-scale rebellion for almost a hundred years.

In July 1792, the *Northern Star,* the United Irishmen's newspaper, reported on the great celebrations in Belfast on the third anniversary of the storming of the Bastille. The impetuous and furious rush of things in Paris on that day still resonated in Ireland. Five thousand armed Volunteers paraded in Belfast, and thirty thousand people watched (the population of the city was only twenty thousand). By then, the French *sans culottes* were fighting off the professional armies of Austria and Prussia that had attacked France without cause, other than fear for their own *anciens régimes*. Irish nationalists could support the French Revolution wholeheartedly because the National Assembly had not yet executed the King, and the Jacobin Terror was more than a year away.

The United Irishmen demonstrated the early limited nature of their aims, although hinting, perhaps unconsciously, at later, more extreme demands. They cheered on what they saw as their French compatriots and exemplars: "We trust that you will never submite the liberties of France to any other guarantees than God, and the right hand of the People." They hailed "that imperishable spirit of Freedom alone, which always exists in the hearts of man." But the people of Ireland did not have to do what the French had done; they had merely to "remove with a temperate and a steady resolution the abuses which . . . the great body of the people . . . have suffered to overgrow and to deform that beautiful system of government, so admirably suited to our situation, our habits and our wishes. We have not to innovate but to restore. The just prerogatives of our monarch we respect and will maintain." What they wanted was simple, and it was their right: "Our due weight and influence in that estate, *which is our property*, the REPRESENTATION OF THE PEOPLE IN PARLIAMENT."

Enthusiasm overcame them, and they added that this demand applied to "all sects and denominations of Irishmen. . . . We should be ashamed at the moment when we are seeking for liberty ourselves, to acquiesce in any system founded on the slavery of others."

But wait a minute, said Henry Joy. These fine words implied the immediate emancipation of Catholics, and they weren't yet ready for it. Someday, yes, so why not insert "gradual" before "emancipation"? A debate ensued, reports the *Northern Star*, of "very considerable length." Would the old prejudices override from the beginning the pretensions of the United Irishmen? Would they feel they had to keep the Taigs at arm's length in spite of Wolfe Tone and their own fine words?

The matter was decided only when "the Reverend Doctor Dickson" intervened with a speech made "with such strong sense and keen irony, as renders [us] unable to give our readers an adequate conception of it." In his *Narrative*, William protests modestly that he "only hung a few rags of ridicule on the stepladder of 'gradual emancipation.'" In fact, he seems to have swept them all away with his wit and passion, his "ease and good humour." There's no direct record of his speech, just the *Northern Star*'s paraphrase. What on earth did "gradual emancipation" mean?

> In this generation? Or is it to be postponed to the future and by intermarrying with capable Protestants, and particularly with us Presbyterians, they may mend the breed and produce a race of beings who will inherit a capacity from us. . . . It is not up to this assembly to dictate anything to Catholics. Perhaps we should hope that the men of religion will be gradually emancipated from the slavery of prejudice and bigotry and, their reason and their conscience having fair play, they may become as enlightened as they seem to think it necessary their brethren should be.

The assembly then unanimously supported the original wording, and it was off to the Donegall Arms for many toasts—assuredly these Presbyterians were not yet given over to temperance: "The Rights of Man!" "Confusion to the Enemies of French Liberty!" "The Abolition of the Slave Trade!" and the philosophical compliments: "Mr. Paine!" "The Memory of John Locke!"

It's a long way from making witty and ironic speeches to lively, celebratory crowds in the heady springtime of a new political movement to the grim subterfuge and conspiracy of life as a general in a hunted, armed secret society bent on imminent insurrection. It must have been an even less likely transformation for a man of God like William, although the militancy of the dissenting church, with its tradition of prickly independence and long memory of persecution, may have made it easier. If we think Reverend Ian Paisley or Wahhabi mullah rather than stuffy country vicar, we're nearer to the state of things for William and his New Light radicalism. Nevertheless, a lot had to happen in Ireland, and particularly in Ulster, between the lighthearted Belfast celebrations of 1792 and the great rising of 1798 to undo the innate constitutional moderation of a United Irishmen like William and turn him into a radical. As usual, the governments in Dublin and London obliged.

In theory, nothing was inevitable. The Dublin government could have acceded wholesale to the measured proposals of the Dungannon convention, which asked only for fair representation in Parliament of adult, Protestant, propertied males and, soon after, the same category of Catholics. These were big changes, to be sure, but they could all be accommodated within the framework of monarch, Parliament, and ultimate English control. The concessions could have been enough to satisfy the United Irish moderates and undermine the radicals. Reform was palpably necessary in England, too; its government knew that. And England had long urged the repeal of the penal laws against Catholics. With the war joined against France, it was arguably more urgent than ever to head off the usual Catholic sympathy and connivance with England's enemies. The British government at first did force the issue, pressuring Dublin to pass the *Relief Act,* which allowed Catholics to practise law, and in 1793 the British Cabinet forced Dublin to accept the enfranchisement of Catholic "40 shilling freeholders."

After that, neither the government in Dublin nor its English handlers was prepared to give any more ground. Both acknowledged a series of propositions: the Ascendancy's power was based on British arms; British authority in Ireland depended on the Ascendancy; therefore, to hold Ireland in difficult times, Britain had better support the Ascendancy. Further reform would be dangerous. Now, the governments acted with the instinctive reflexes of the corrupt-in-power and the challenged imperial overlord.

The standard received version of Irish history blames it all on the English because it's necessary for the later ideological scheme of things to recall the Irish as united against a foreign occupier and repressor. Modern republican ideology blames the late twentieth-century Troubles on the British presence in Northern Ireland. It's inconvenient to acknowledge that the northern Protestants don't want to have anything to do with the rest of Catholic Ireland and that they, not the British, are the problem. Therefore, it's equally inconvenient to admit the precedent, that it was Irish Protestants, not the British, who were the real problem in 1798, too. The truth is that the Irish Ascendancy Parliament was the main actor. It began a campaign of reaction and repression that, together with English military measures, grew heavier and more brutal year by year, provoking, in turn, more radical action by the United Irishmen, which then demanded more government crackdowns. The Ascendancy Parliament may well deserve one historian's accusation that it, rather than any English government, was "the bloodiest repressive institution in modern Irish history." The vicious, inevitable cycle ending in civil war could not be stopped.

The government passed the *Convention Act,* which prohibited any representative assembly in Ireland, apart from Parliament. It was an invitation to clandestine meetings and organization—no more intense, yet open and amiable, conventions at Dungannon. The Lord Lieutenant proclaimed all Volunteer assemblies unlawful. The units went underground and began to meet in resentful secrecy.

In March 1793, the government sent troop reinforcements to Belfast, a regiment of dragoons—mounted infantry. The *Belfast News-Letter* reported that soon after their arrival in the city, the troops "rushed from their quarters and drove furiously through most of the principal streets with their sabres drawn, wounding and maiming some of the unoffending inhabitants and attacking houses." Getting cut down in his own street or home by rioting *sassenagh* soldiers tended to radicalize a man. In Belfast, the dragoons helped along the coming confrontation: they scared the moderates and angered the radicals.

Looking back, two things surprise: the government's determination and willingness to confront the United Irishmen in 1793 and 1794—it may have been corrupt and reactionary, but it wasn't timid—and the ease with which the radicals buckled. The society had many members, but they were not that committed to its principles. It was no big thing for them to back down when the government got tough. And the middle-class membership of the United Irishmen was a problem, too. These men had a lot to lose, and if reform meant risking their property, maybe even their lives, they weren't desperate enough for that. Not yet.

The radicals became more and more isolated from the mainstream United Irish, and the government was able to cut them down one by one. "Their great aim is to get rid of us by prosecution, persecution, or the terror of it," Drennan wrote to McTier. Drennan was tried for addressing an illegal Volunteer meeting in 1794. He

was acquitted but scared enough by it all to make an effective withdrawal from radical politics.

The final suppression of the open society of United Irishmen—
the Dublin chapter was the last—was made easy for the government
when it caught some of the members discussing with the French
enemy the possibility of rebellion in Ireland. It was the end of the
United Irishmen as peaceful reformers. But, of course, the government's very success in ending the society's middle-class moderate
phase simply guaranteed that the agitation would assume another
form as a radical, underground, physical-force, plebeian revolutionary movement which sought a separate republic. No more talk of
moderate constitutional reform; the society now tapped into the old
tradition of the violent agrarian secret societies, the ready-made
model for armed rebellion. The new underground United Irish, in
effect, revived "Whiteboyism"; they became a new version of wood
kern. They swore oaths in the form of catechisms: "What have you
got in your hand? A green bough. Where did it first grow? In
America. Where did it bud? In France. Where are you going to
plant it? In the crown of Great Britain."

Just when we most need William to tell us his state of mind, he
equivocates in his *Narrative* or falls silent. He could show us how a
man dedicated to peaceful reform by constitutional means becomes
a revolutionary. His conversion might illuminate how anyone in any
time or place crosses the line from political agitation—lobbying,
meeting, or shouting in the streets—to ambushing government
troops or putting bombs on civilian trains and airplanes.

It could have been big things: the recall of the sympathetic Lord
Lieutenant, Earl Fitzwilliam, in 1795 because he favoured imme-
diate Catholic emancipation and fired a handful of Ascendancy
bigwigs; or the raising in 1796 of the tough sectarian (mostly
Protestant) auxiliaries, the yeomanry, many of whose members were
Orangemen (although most were also ex-Volunteers), to counter
United Irish mobilization; or the effective military occupation of
Ulster and the harsh imposition there of martial law during 1797.
The government saw the "dragooning of Ulster" as necessary
because the province had become almost ungovernable, with ram-
pant robberies, arms raids, assassinations, and the traditional night

assemblies. Troops and yeomanry reverted to English form in Ireland, responding with atrocity and terror—the tactics William and his dinner-mates discussed that night at M'Neown's farm, a few days before his arrest. They hanged and half-hanged men, flogged and "pitch-capped" them, burnt houses and "free-quartered" (billeted troops with suspected rebels). "Fathers and sons were murdered," wrote the moderate reformer William Campbell, "or torn from their families, put to torture, or sent into banishment, without even the form of a trial." Worst of all for the United Irishmen's organization, government militia destroyed the office of the *Northern Star* in Belfast. Gerard Lake, the English general who oversaw the Ulster operation, went on to conduct a similar campaign of terror around Dublin in early 1798. After the insurrection broke out, he ordered his commanders to take no prisoners, and they seldom did.

We know William now, his passionate, impetuous, and uncompromising nature. We can imagine the effect on him of martial law and the military's outrages. It's easy to conclude that this dissident preacher was unable to resist the impulse to fight back, that his rage overwhelmed him. And he must have remembered how easy it would have been after the Dungannon convention for the government to have made a few concessions and to have avoided this terrible slide into chaos and war. Perhaps something small finally tipped the balance for William. In the seventeenth century, the Gaelic lord of Inishowen, Sir Cahir O'Doherty, had stayed loyal to the English Crown through egregious provocation. Finally an Englishman struck him. Only then did he attack and burn Derry and kill its people. Maybe something like that happened to William, or the combined effect of many such personal insults pushed him over the line. Perhaps he got manhandled by soldiers once too often. He accepted his fate and became a rebel general. There were more than enough good reasons in the late 1790s in Ulster to convince even a doctor of divinity, ex-moderator of the Presbyterian Church, rural preacher, farmer, husband and father (although a former armed Volunteer, too) to decide to go "on his own keeping"—one of the old phrases (the Gaelic syntax and phraseology tumbling into English) to describe a man on the run and committed to revolution in Ireland.

In his *Narrative,* William writes: "A series of acts of parliament, which followed each other, with hasty pace, and voice terrific, extinguished hope, revived alarm, and excited a mixed feeling of sorrow, indignation, and horror." He deplores the proclamation of "the Northern counties, out of the king's peace, without cause, or provocation." The Battle of the Diamond between Orange boys and Defenders and the formation of the Orange Order took place in 1795, and William records the growing sectarian tensions in his own neighbourhood: the Presbyterians one night and the Catholics the next "running from house to house, under the alarm that a massacre was to take place on the succeeding night, and that their neighbours, with whom they had lived in peace and friendship, were to be the perpetrators."

The Gaelic habit of unreliable allegiances readily exchanged had persisted into the 1790s; the informer had long been a national conspiratorial stereotype (and remains so today—British "supergrasses" within paramilitary organizations). The government's spies and moles riddled the new, supposedly secret United Irish society. William's enemies thought they knew what he was up to during these years. With his open style of dissent, he was an easy man to keep track of. For example, an anonymous letter addressed to an Ascendancy administrator refers alliteratively to the "Presbyterian Parson of Portaferry who hath long been notorious for preaching sedition and who hath published inflammatory sermons."

During the winter of 1796 and the spring of 1797, the government rounded up most of the northern United Irish leaders. It also arrested the entire Leinster directory; an informer had fingered them all. These were the sweeps that caught up two of William's brother ministers and half-a-dozen members of his congregation and occasioned his travel to Dublin to try to free them. That was when Lord Londonderry advocated William's detention as a "suspicious personage." The government promised to pay one of William's congregants, a poor weaver called Carr, £1,000 (a fortune then) if he provided information that would convict William—some distorted sense of due process was apparently still operating. Carr was unable to come up with enough; but neither was he willing to lie, and the government eventually jailed him instead. However, they continued to follow William's trail. A Colonel Savage wrote to Lord Downshire that the Devil, "Dickson's true friend," might leave him in the lurch. "I'm sure he must trip some time or other."

He never did. They never pinned anything on him. We return to where we began his story: late in 1797 and early in 1798, he was laid low with bilious attacks and fevers. Then he travelled to Scotland to sort out the affairs of Isabella's uncle, and when he got back to Portaferry, the suspicious yeomanry nearly broke open his rusty tobacco box looking for secret incriminatory documents. The insurrection began in the south. William rode around to Ballee and Saintfield, and to Belfast, to find a horse. He visited various United Irishmen and had dinner with M'Neown and others, one of whom was a government informer. Then he rode to Ballynahinch to drink in peace the soothing waters. Finally, his immunity ended. They arrested him, although they still had no proof of his revolutionary generalship. Two days later, the United Irishmen of Ulster rose in belated rebellion, and the Year of Liberty, the Year of the French, began its last gasp.

14

THE NINETY-EIGHT

WHAT IF? That's the nifty, boy's-own parlour game of amateur (and, sometimes, professional) historians with too much time on their hands. The Insurrection of 1798 is a natural for this exercise. What if the government had not been so resolute and brutal in its military countermeasures during 1797? Or if the United Irishmen had risen in 1797 before the government had weakened them? If the Leinster directory and the Ulster leaders (including William) had not been penetrated by spies and arrested before the rising? If the insurrection had been carefully coordinated and planned so that the United Irishmen of the four green fields rose on the same day, instead of here and there over a period of weeks? The society claimed in 1798 that it had 280,000 men armed and ready for battle out of a membership of half a million. What if they had risen all at once, instead of the fraction of that number who did? Who could have stopped them? What if a large French expeditionary force had actually landed on the south coast in coordination with the rising (instead of the raiding party that did so after the rising was effectively broken), its thousands of regulars stiffening the Irish amateur enthusiasts and undisciplined kerns?

One view is that the insurrection would have succeeded, and Ireland would have become a united secular independent republic. There would have been no 1801 *Act of Union* joining Ireland to England in one political structure; no need for the Fenians, the home rule campaign, and Ulster Protestant resistance; no Easter

Rising or war of independence; no terrible, scarring civil war, no repression of the Catholic minority in the north, and no thirty years of Troubles at the end of the twentieth century, all with their many thousands of dead and wounded. The Irish problem would have been solved.

It's all nonsense. To suggest that success of this sort was feasible depends on accepting the distortions of the standard received version of Irish history: that 1798 was a case of "us Irish" against "them English," of plucky Ireland against its *sassenagh* occupier. The insurrection was certainly a rising against English domination of Irish affairs, and of English military occupation, but it was also a civil war. The yeomanry and militia that fought the rebels, alongside British regulars, were all Irishmen. The government that directed them was the Irish Protestant Ascendancy government in Dublin. Its top executive officials were Englishmen to be sure, but everyone else was Irish. The government won against the rebels because it had the support of many Irishmen—at least, of the politically minded Irish.

The other face of civil war in 1798 was the same old story of division between Protestant and Catholic. Military and revolutionary cooperation between Protestant and Dissenter radicals and the Catholic Defenders was shaky all along; it deteriorated and collapsed fast once the fighting got under way. The sectarian divisions showed up everywhere: for example, at Ballynahinch, with the desertion of the Defenders, who suspected the Presbyterian rebels of wanting them only for cannon fodder. Sectarian bitterness reached its apogee with several documented atrocities: Catholic Defenders burnt to death two hundred Protestant prisoners, including women and children, in a barn at Scullabogue; they massacred others at Wexford bridge and murdered ninety-three Protestants in Wexford town.

These killings or, more particularly, the usual exaggerated accounts of them, reactivated the dormant but always present memories of 1641 and 1688. In the Protestants' view, it never failed: whenever the Taigs had an opportunity, they killed Prods. The Defender outrages alienated even committed Presbyterian radicals and were another reason for the Protestants' fast coalescence into sectarian solidarity and their support of unionism after the rebellion failed. The massacres were not extensive enough to constitute a sectarian peasant rising, as some historians have claimed, but they showed how fragile was the unity of the United Irishmen.

Soon after its formation in 1791, the Dublin society had circulated a letter that denounced the tenacity of Irish memory. "In thus associating, we have thought little about our ancestors—much of our posterity. Are we forever to walk like beasts of prey over fields which these ancestors stained with blood? In looking back, we see nothing on the one part but savage force succeeded by savage policy; on the other, an unfortunate nation." They would look to the future, "to brighter prospects . . . to a posterity established on civil, political, and religious liberty." Seven years later, the reality was that most Irishmen continued to think much about their ancestors and could not stop themselves from staining more fields with blood. The United Irishmen could not wish a united secular republic into existence against the profound power of the ancestral voices.

Furthermore, the radical Presbyterians of Ulster (like William) expected quite different things from their campaign than did the radical Catholics represented by the Defenders. The society of United Irishmen was the creation of middle-class city boys, Presbyterian lawyers, linen weavers, merchants, publicans, and scripture-politics ministers. They wanted to reform a Parliament they saw as made up of a sorry collection of renegades who had been corrupted and bought off by English power and patronage. But it was one group of Irishmen trying to convince another group of Irishmen to mend their ways and to return to the constitutional contract between rulers and ruled promised by the Glorious Revolution of 1688–89. The bulk of Protestants wanted to end bad government, but not at the cost of the perquisites and privileges of the Ascendancy.

To the poor rural Catholics who formed the backbone of the Defenders, the Ascendancy was unreformable. It was the abhorrent creature of conquerors and settlers and must be overthrown. The Dublin Parliament and government, the Prods who formed it—and the Dissenters of the north, too—were all the same: Englishmen, or English-backed squatters on Irish land. The only solution was to sweep them away, back to Scotland or England, into the sea, into the ground—What did it matter? The Catholics wanted what they had always wanted: to undo the conquest. Even William advocated nothing remotely like that. Wolfe Tone saw clearly the contrast between north and south: the nationalism of the Dissenters was based on "reason and reflection"; that of the Catholics on "hatred to the English name." These irreconcilable assumptions and aims fettered the two groups when they tried to join together in republican conspiracy and in battle.

The United Irishmen were hamstrung by two other contradictions. First, the radicals had reconstituted themselves as a secret society after the initial reform movement failed. But it was a secret, oath-bound organization that still sought mass membership and mass mobilization. Those may have been admirable strategies, but they were hard to reconcile, and that was the reason the government found it so easy to infiltrate and spy. When the administration began to "dragoon" Ulster, for example, it found many United Irishmen who had taken the oath casually or in a fit of enthusiasm and who were easy to turn into informers. If intelligence (as in "military intelligence") is crucial to fighting rebels, then the Ascendancy government and the English army always had the advantage. They always knew, for example, where William was, if not exactly what he was up to.

Second, the United Irishmen needed French help. But in order to convince France to send troops across the Celtic Sea, they were obliged to conform to French expectations and demands: the United Irishmen had to be radical republicans, and this stipulation continued to alienate the moderate reformers. The radicals lost their flexibility—they had to wait around for the French to get organized and to send an invasion force. Wolfe Tone had to spend almost all his time from 1795 (when he had agreed to go into exile) until 1798 in France trying to persuade the French that helping the Irish was a good bet for them. In fact, he had astonishing success: a Dublin lawyer with no official standing convinced a foreign government with the most powerful military force in Europe, which was already fighting against numerous continental enemies, to commit itself to the aid of an Irish underground revolutionary army. Of course, France always saw Ireland as the means to get at England. And Tone had the old Wild Geese connections and traditions to smooth his way. The French army still had its brigades filled with men called O'Neill, Lynch, Kelly, although they spoke French now, not Gaelic, and guzzled wine, not poteen.

If all the "what ifs" had come to pass, the Insurrection of 1798 might have succeeded in the sense that the rebels defeated the English army and the government's auxiliaries. The country would have been free of British soldiers for the first time in six-hundred years.

But then what? Can we envisage mass moderation suddenly breaking out? The yeomanry and the militia surrendering, too? Disbanding and going quietly home? Giving up their arms? As always, Ulster was the crucial place. Could the Prods and Taigs in the patchwork Plantation areas and borderlands quietly accept the new order, forget their fear? What about the Defenders and the other secret societies, with their simple world view: Prod equals conqueror? And would the Orangemen respond all of a sudden with reason and restraint? Could Catholic Defenders, Belfast Presbyterians, and Dublin Ascendancy men cooperate in some form of government?

And what about France? In the "what if" scenario, it would have troops on the ground in Ireland. How could the French fail to take advantage of this opening on England's doorstep? They were still at war and would not be able to resist the opportunity. Perhaps Bonaparte would have become interested in Ireland instead of Egypt as a means of attacking the English—although he would still have had the infernal Admiral Nelson and his navy to deal with. For its own security, England could never allow the French that foothold. A revived and strengthened English army would invade Ireland again—their irreducible national interests would demand it; it would be an iron necessity.

In fact, a "successful" insurrection would have resulted in chaos, civil war, international war, reinvasion, sectarian massacre, political paralysis, years of killing and suffering on a scale that would, indeed, have made Ireland the most distressful country. It was far better for the Irish that the rebellion failed. That avoided all-out Hobbesian war and instituted instead a century of peace, more or less, and the chance for the Irish, particularly the Catholics, to carry out political action and to create the political culture and institutions they needed for successful independence. The violent interludes that did occur in 1803, 1848, and 1867 were brief "cabbage-patch" rebellions, with a few dead, and a few executed, jailed, or exiled. It's difficult to see that anything the English did to Ireland between 1798 and the Easter Rising of 1916 was remotely as bad as the Irish would have done to themselves if the Ninety-Eight had been a "success."

Even so, like the siege of Derry, the insurrection became an occasion for remembering, forgetting, and commemoration—and, of course, for myth-making. It was a real military challenge to English rule. It also became a potent symbol, succeeding as a form of that other enduring element of aspiring Irish nationhood: the blood-sacrifice. The men of the Ninety-Eight didn't intend to martyr themselves for the *Shan Van Vocht*—they wanted to succeed—but that was the effect of their failed action. The meaning of 1798, like that of the siege of Derry, would evolve, wobble, and morph, but it would never be less than epochal.

The Derry siege mythology evolved into a straightforward representation of Protestant solidarity, endurance, and resistance to Catholic aggression. And it was one people's property. Protestants imbued it with its profound runic meaning for themselves, but, for Catholics, the siege had significance only as one lost opportunity among many to turn back the *sassenaghs*. The Ninety-Eight was different. Its commemoration remains a varied and ambiguous matter. Even now, the parties and paramilitaries of both sides in Northern Ireland use 1798 for their current political purposes.

This equivocal response provides an illustration of that infamous Irish inability to allow the past to become mundane history. The Irish appear to be preoccupied with the past and unable to accept time for what many others take it to be—an amnesiac healer. In reality, however, 1798 is still a matter of contentious interpretation because the ancient issues of power, faith, and land that caused the rebellion are still unresolved in Northern Ireland. Even in the Republic of Ireland, the bicentenary of the rising was an important political matter because of its continuing significance for the six partitioned counties of Ulster. Without that concern, the commemoration of 1798 in the Republic would have been part of the usual theme-park celebration of "Oirishness," on the same level as Bloomsday, the

Irish roots and heritage industry, *Angela's Ashes,* the blarney stone, and the drink.

At first, everyone in Ireland did try to forget 1798. It was the traumatized amnesia of shock. For years, the insurrection was an occasion for denial and silence. Presbyterians in Down and Antrim who had lost a United Irishman marked gravestones "1797" or "1799," any year that was not the fateful one. At least thirty thousand people died in the few months of the insurrection—there's no record of the number of wounded; many thousands more were killed, transported, executed, or jailed before and after the rebellion. William got off lightly, but even he served hard time and didn't get back home until 1802. In those regions of the country where rebellion had broken out—Antrim, Down, parts of Connacht, and especially Wexford—hardly a family escaped its sorrows. The United Irishmen had hoped to establish a "brotherhood of affection between Protestant, Catholic, and Dissenter," but this naïveté had an opposite and destructive effect. After the rebellion, the Prods and Taigs were more divided than ever, more organized into their armed societies—the Orangemen, the Defenders (soon to become the Ribbonmen)—even more used now than ever to the idea, and the actual bloody process, of killing. The Wexford massacres had been small in scale but enough to remind Protestants in Plantation Ulster bandit country of their daily danger. The promise of amity or alliance between Presbyterians and Catholics was done for.

Revisionist history began right away. In 1801, Sir Richard Musgrave, an Ascendancy parliamentarian who had once personally flogged a convicted Whiteboy, published *Memoirs of the Different Rebellions in Ireland.* It was a partisan polemic that became the standard loyalist Protestant interpretation for generations. The rising was a priest-led conspiracy in the tradition of 1641 and the reign of James II. Thus, the atrocities against Protestants at Scullabogue and Wexford were the same old Taig story. The Ulster rising was a matter of misguided Presbyterians led astray by traitorous rabble-rousers. And there never was any United Irish unity among Protestant, Dissenter, and Catholic. If a hard-line Prod in Belfast today gives a thought to 1798, it may still be in these terms.

The people who suffered through that other terrible event in Irish history, the Great Famine, denied and forgot it as well. Only successive generations could bear to contemplate and recall the trauma of the Great Hunger. It was the same with 1798. Eventually, memory returned, and it became possible—and convenient—for some Irish to remember. The standard story of Irish history appropriated 1798. The famous and notorious ballad of 1842, "The Memory of the Dead," was one of the means of recovering the insurrection's "living blaze."

> Who fears to speak of Ninety-Eight?
> Who blushes at the name?
> When cowards mock the patriots' fate,
> Who hangs his head for shame?

By the middle of the nineteenth century, the Insurrection had assumed its role as the inspiration for physical-force republican nationalism through the rising of 1848, the Fenians, the IRA of the war of independence, and the Provisional IRA of the Troubles.

The Ascendancy bigot Richard Musgrave wrote the insurrection's Protestant propaganda; the Franciscan priest Father Patrick Kavanagh contributed the equivalent Catholic version. In 1870, he published *A Popular History of the Insurrection of 1798*. It certainly was popular, going through nine editions before 1928. The Wexford rising, the only aspect of the whole rebellion worthy of the name, he wrote, was the reflexive reaction of "morally pure" Catholic peasants led by heroic priests provoked beyond endurance by the torment of brutal and vicious Protestants. "When Wexford stood at bay, the United Irishmen were not to be found," wrote Kavanagh. Protestants were sectarian killers and nothing more. For generations, this "faith and fatherland" story was the Catholic standard received version of 1798. A Catholic in Belfast today who recalls the Ninety-Eight might do so in these terms.

We see with vivid clarity the oddly similar elements in the contrasting visions of Musgrave and Kavanagh: the denial of complexity, the resort to simplicity. In both cases, their people's present needs dictated each man's selective appropriation of the past, the political myth he chose to create. Both Musgrave's and Kavanagh's "histories" were historical nonsense. But they served their purpose of reflecting and augmenting the sectarian divide: Musgrave, by branding Catholics as reflexive murderous ruffians whom Protestants could never trust; Kavanagh, by branding Protestants as reflexive murderous ruffians who should be excluded from Irish history.

In the standard story of that history, the insurrection's supposed mastermind and purported United Irish founder, Wolfe Tone, was the quintessential Irish revolutionary, the rebel *beau-idéal,* as Sean O'Faolain called him. Tone became the prototype for the romantic rebel who fails, but whose sacrifice, whether it's known or anonymous, bears witness to the Irish nation. He is the first self-conscious modern martyr for the *Shan Van Vocht.* "There was only one thing at which the rebel wished to be a success and that was at rebelling," wrote O'Faolain. "Death did not mean failure so long as the Spirit of Revolt lived." But O'Faolain underestimates the degree to which Tone desired and expected the actual success of the United Irish insurrection. Tone, one historian writes, became both the St. Paul and the St. Augustine of the Irish revolution. Patrick Pearse referred to "our Fenian dead" during his peroration at O'Donovan Rossa's funeral in 1915: "While Ireland holds these graves, Ireland unfree shall never be at peace." He could just as well have said "our United Irish dead." Tone's grave at Bodenstown, County Kildare, became a place of pilgrimage and a political prop. Pearse called it "the holiest spot in Ireland." Even now, the *taoiseach* ("*tee*-shuck," prime minister) of the Republic of Ireland travels to Tone's tomb to make an annual state-of-the-nation address.

In the remembering and the commemoration of 1798 began the tradition of the rebel martyr which would reach its apotheosis in the Rising of 1916 and, even in our own time, in the ten republican paramilitary hunger strikers fasting to death in Belfast in 1981. As he slid into his dire death coma, the gunman Bobby Sands dreamt of Wolfe Tone.

15

PREACHERS

ONE COLD, SUNNY, SUNDAY MORNING at the end of November 2003, I walked from my apartment in Belfast near Queen's University to go to a church service. It was a half-hour walk in the city which, by chance, happened to go through the territory of my childhood in Northern Ireland. It was filled with its memories, and with the ache of remembering.

I crossed the Malone Road and took the shortcut through the Botanic Gardens, where I had run and caught balls as a little boy, and walked past the Ulster Museum and the Greenhouse. There, one day when I was fourteen, my father, Alexander, and I had sat on a bench. He put his arm around me—he never did that—and told me how much he had hated this poor, grimy, violent place and had wanted to get out, and he had, and now, on a visit back to it, a well-to-do Canadian immigrant, he was so proud of what he had done, and the opportunities he had created for me. I didn't know what to say; I felt intensely uncomfortable and couldn't wait for the strange moment to end. Now, I long for the touch of my father's arm around my shoulders.

I left the gardens and walked past Botanic School, where Alexander had been a pupil. I almost went there myself. After we had been in Canada for a year, the only work he had found paid a starvation wage; the country was in a recession. We were poorer than we had been in England and out of time with our sponsoring relatives, who were sick of us; there was no government help for immigrants

205

then. We booked a sea-passage back to Belfast—steerage in reverse—and the little house on the border of the Holy Land, and I thought it might be all right to go to the same school as my father had. I had been excited to emigrate to Canada, but we had settled close to a city in a village where it was cheap to live. The place hadn't seen an immigrant with a funny accent in three generations. I was picked on, beaten up; the school principal, and then the police, got involved. I was battle-weary and longed for what I thought of as the close, cosy confines of my childhood-summer streets. Then an Irish friend in another town convinced my father to try one more time. He was desperate and went for broke: he invented a resumé, lied through the interview, got the job, and we stayed in Canada. But we came that close to being in Northern Ireland for the Troubles.

I went on down Agincourt Avenue, which had only a few abandoned, derelict, or burnt-out buildings. Queen's University students live in many of the houses now. The old families had gone: they had moved out or had been burnt out or intimidated away to safer Prod territory. The students are all Catholic—the Protestant ones live up near the Stranmillis, Lisburn, and Malone roads. As I walked, I realized that something was missing from the past; I couldn't identify what it was. Then I caught a whiff of smoke from a coal fire. Everyone had one going when I had been here as a boy and a young man. Even in summer, people needed a fire in this cold, damp north. The brief Proustian smell of coal burning completed my memory.

I walked past the streets of the Holy Land—Carmel, Palestine, Jerusalem, Damascus, Cairo—past Collingwood Avenue, then Curzon, and turned into Cadogan Street, which was only fifty paces long, past number seven, the little worker's house three generations of us had lived in, two born there. It, too, was now a student home. How strange and sad not to be able to go in, but just to walk by its green door and front-parlour window, past the whole narrow house in four strides.

I crossed the small wasteland I had played in when we travelled from England to stay with my grandmother. There used to be a bombed-out ruin there; once, I climbed up into it and couldn't get down again. Bernard Ferguson had to get my father to rescue me. Bernard was the Catholic boy on the street, the one who later joined the Provos and was killed. I went on up the Ormeau Embankment beside the fence I used to climb over, in defiance of every adult's command, to get to the bank of the fast, muddy Lagan and plop stones into the brown liquid. I crossed the Ormeau Bridge and entered the Ormeau Park, almost across from where I had watched a man shot in a store thirty years earlier. I walked on through the park where I had run and gone on the swings and played French cricket, skirted the small golf course to the Ravenhill Road, and turned left. I saw a grafitto on a house wall: "Short Strand Taigs Off Our Streets. Use at Own Risk." The church was a little way down. It is called the Martyrs Memorial Free Presbyterian Church, and its minister is the Reverend Ian Paisley.

Paisley may be the loud, ranting, public, rosy-red face of Prod intransigence and bigotry, the man people outside Northern Ireland think of when they think at all of its bizarre, endless, vicious little war. He seems to be the persona of the province's incomprehensible religious bigotry. An outsider who sees Paisley, the "Big Man," shouting politics in his preacher's cadences may not understand any more about why the Prods and Taigs are still at it, but will immediately recognize the emotion in his bombast: rage, outrage, fear, paranoia. Listening to Paisley speak is like listening to symptoms. You can't tell whether he's giving a crazy political speech or a seventeenth-century fundamentalist sermon. In either case, it's out of time; it seems to be from another world.

He's old now, but he has been at the heart of hatred and violence in Northern Ireland since the start of the Troubles. Indeed, some may consider him to have been one of the instigators. The common view is that the Troubles began with the first Catholic civil rights marches in mid and late 1968. Certainly, they were under way by early January 1969, when, over a period of several days, Protestants made running attacks on a Catholic "People's Democracy" march from Belfast to Derry. Loyalist gunmen escalated the sectarian violence when they carried out several bombings a few months later. Paisley ended a speech that year with the following words, and they provide an idea of his rhetorical style:

> Oh God, save Ulster from popery!
> Oh God, save Ulster from apostasy!
> Oh God, save Ulster from going into an Irish Republic!

> Save Ulster from being sold down the river!
> Oh God, give us a great deliverance!

The last phrase repeats Thomas Macaulay's description of the successful defence of Derry in 1689.

However, Paisley had been busy long before that. It's feasible to date the real beginning of the Troubles to his protest against a republican tricolour displayed in the office window of Sinn Féin during the 1964 Westminster election. The flag was illegal under the *Flags and Emblems Act,* but the Royal Ulster Constabulary (RUC)—the Protestant police force, which looked like an army with its machine guns and armoured cars—ignored the Irish flag. It was in the Catholic territory of Divis Street, and they knew what would happen if they tried to enforce the (quintessentially Northern Irish) law. Paisley threatened that if they didn't, he would. The RUC took the flag by force and set off days of riots, the worst since 1935—which, in turn, had been the worst riots since the Civil War.

The next year, the Protestant paramilitary Ulster Volunteer Force (UVF), a revived version—although immeasurably debased in ability and diminished in numbers—of the 100,000-strong army of 1912 that had been formed to fight home rule and to keep Ulster British, "went on the kill." They "stiffed Taigs," murdering several Catholics picked at random—the first of the Troubles' most brutal terror tactics—and set off bombs. In June 1966, a Paisley march ended in rioting, and he was jailed for three months. Paisley's short jail time made him very popular, as imprisonment did for all Irish leaders. That year was an especially emotional one in Ireland: it was the fiftieth anniversary of the blood-sacrifice of the 1916 Easter Rising, and northern Catholics celebrated it with what seemed to the galled Protestants like provocative glee. For Prods, the Rising was still the act of cowards who had used Britain's difficulty in the Great War to rebel and, in the faulty Protestant memory of it, to murder Protestants.

Paisley objected specifically in 1966 to the fact that the Northern Irish prime minister, Terence O'Neill, had had actual conversations with Sean Lemass, the Republic's *taoiseach*. In that year of Catholics celebrating their own perfidy, all the old Protestant fears of treachery and betrayal welled up. O'Neill was a Lundy, said Paisley, who has often used the denigrative, slanderous word.

While in jail, Paisley wrote *An Exposition of the Epistle to the Romans* of St. Paul. Paisley identified with the saint who had also done time in an imperial prison; Paul's ambivalent relationship with the Romans seemed similar to Paisley's with the British. Paisley wrote: "The church needs to return to preaching, old-fashioned, heaven-blessed, soul-stirring, sin-slaying preaching. The greatest need of the hour is a band of prophets with flaming message to set the land on fire." It wasn't only his message that did it, but the land burned for more than thirty years.

Paisley founded the Free Presbyterian Church (more dissenting Dissenters) in 1951. But he was a politician as well as a preacher. He established the Democratic Unionist Party (DUP) in 1971, and it has always been one of the most extreme of the several unionist parties. Its policies, like those of any political party, have swung here and there over the years, but they have been consistent on the basics of Ulster Protestant political fundamentalism: smash IRA/Sinn Féin; stop the "sellout" to the Republic and cross-border collaboration with it; bring back a Northern Irish government, if possible, but not if Sinn Féin is part of it. In 1979, Paisley was elected as the member for Northern Ireland in the European Parliament in Strasbourg, receiving more votes than any other member elected. It was sad and embarrassing, but appropriate, that the representative of Northern Ireland in Europe should be a noisy, bigoted, fundamentalist whose political views were formed by a mythology of terror that depended on remembering 1641, 1688, and 1916, but on forgetting the tantalizing moments of his co-religionists' sectarian amity in 1788 and 1798.

Paisley followed the old tradition of successful politics in Ireland: he had an ambiguous kinship with the hard men. On the one hand, he condemned outright the Protestant paramilitaries—their tit-for-tat assassinations were crimes "just as heinous and hellish as those of the IRA." On the other hand, the gunmen were useful to him; their ever-present threat of atrocity, and even of all-out civil war, suited him. He could condemn them, knowing that he was the politician they felt closest to; they would vote for him and intimidate others into doing so as well. And if he decried their "cowboy" killings, he made it clear that they might be necessary to defend the Protestant

people from extermination if the Catholics rose up, as they had
before, and the British Army couldn't control things—or no longer
had the stomach to do so. The Ulster Defence Association, the
Ulster Freedom Fighters, the Ulster Volunteer Force, and yes, the
Red Hand Commandos, would come in handy if 1641 happened
again, or Scullabogue Barn. In any event, Paisley's inflammatory
sermons and speeches, his venomous anti-Catholicism, and his
refusal to negotiate with Sinn Féin or the Republic put him on the
same side as the paramilitaries. They all knew it; he might condemn
them, and they might distrust him, but if the worst happened, they
would stand together. They were loyalists joined by a link of fealty,
the same one that, in 1912, an earlier loyalist leader had said "will
neither break nor bend before the King's enemies. We are King's
men. We will be with you to the end."

The DUP was the little party that grew, and eventually it won.
In the elections for the Northern Ireland Assembly (set up as part of
the 1998 Good Friday Agreement) held in November 2003, Paisley's
DUP got the most seats. Sinn Féin was second and became the dominant Catholic party (beating the moderates decisively). These
results were augmented in the 2005 Westminster election. The DUP
and Sinn Féin represented the spectrum-ends of Protestant and
Catholic politics in the province; the extremists had won. The moderate Official Unionist Party had lost out to Paisley, although "moderate" in the context of Northern Ireland is a misnomer anywhere
else. After the 2003 election, Paisley described Sinn Féin—his putative partners in a government—as "a bunch of renegade rebels."

The Sunday I went to Paisley's Martyrs Memorial Church was the
day after his 2003 election win. (Each side has its remembered martyrs; just down the road, the Catholic area of the Short Strand—
whose Taigs the grafitto warned off Prod streets—is famous for its
Martyrs Memorial Flute Band.) Paisley was in his pulpit: he is the
old lion, white-maned but still tall, powerful, his voice strong. You
can see the shadow of that robust, big-bodied sexuality that drew
women to his church and his cause. He thanked God for "a miracle"
in answer to prayer—the triumph of the DUP. From the audience:
many "Amens," a single "Halleluja!" He joked with the press in the
visitors' gallery. He was eloquent, funny, and likable. His son, Kyle

Paisley, who is also a Free Presbyterian minister, gave the sermon, which was based on Jeremiah 31 and 33. His other son, Ian Junior, is a DUP member—his progeny has all the old man's bases covered. Kyle is a young, studious-looking, brown-haired man, much shorter and slighter than his overbearing father, and without the older man's great voice and strident delivery. Kyle's sermon was logical, low-key, earnest. I had the impression the congregation was listening politely because of their love for the old man, but they didn't care much for the son's rational expressions of faith. They had got used to that old-time demagoguery, and the boy was wimpy and unsatisfying. In fact, his restrained and earnest eloquence reminded me more than anything else (and unexpectedly) of William's sermons.

People round about smiled at me, the stranger; they said hello and shook my hand with warmth during the congregation's greeting. The church service brochure said: "The Kirk Session and members join in congratulating our minister, Dr. Paisley, on his election victory." Paisley has an honorary doctorate from the Christian fundamentalist Bob Jones University in Greenville, South Carolina, awarded after his release from prison in 1966. (In a coincidence, one of William's grandsons and his family emigrated to Greenville in the 1840s, and there are many descendant Dicksons there; perhaps they're now Prod fundamentalists themselves.) The brochure also said that all readings of the Word of God would be taken from the "Authorized Version," meaning the King James Bible. "No modern perversions used in this church."

Paisley stood to give a long prayer based on Jeremiah 32 (he and Kyle had coordinated their message). The chapter describes how the Jews, whom God led out of Egypt into Israel, the land of milk and honey, have turned their backs on Him and disobeyed His commands for piety and modesty. Therefore, God has allowed the Babylonian king Nebuchadrezzar to take Jerusalem "by the sword, and by the famine, and by the pestilence." But afterwards, God says, He would gather together the people of Israel again and make an everlasting covenant with them. "I will rejoice over them to do them good," He promised. "I will plant them in this land assuredly with my whole heart and with my whole soul." The land will be theirs forever.

The message is a reiteration of Paisley's mantra in innumerable speeches and sermons. Like the Jews, the Protestant people of

Ulster, or, at least, the "born-again" among them (and there are many), are a chosen people. "God has a people in this province," he said in a 1985 sermon at Martyrs Memorial, and they have had "the peculiar preservation of divine Providence." Just read the history of Ulster, and you'll see that, time and again when the province faced disaster beyond rescue—the siege of Derry, for example—God intervened. Why? Because "God has a purpose for this province, and this plant of Protestantism sown here in the northeastern part of this island. The enemy has tried to root it out, but it still grows today." Strange—and divinely diminishing—as it may seem, God is on the side of Ian Paisley and the Free Presbyterian Prods of Ulster. And the God Paisley claims for the Protestant tribe of Ulster is the ferocious tribal God of the Old Testament who favours and, sometimes advocates, implacable enmity, dispossession, annihilation, striking down by the edge of the sword. The Pentateuch, as one example, makes the Koran look moderate and merciful in comparison.

After the service, I walked back to my apartment over the same route. As I crossed the Ormeau Bridge towards Cadogan Street, the sun shone out between low sinister clouds. Bright shafts of light pierced the clear air. I had forgotten that, if you looked past the rows of little red houses and beyond them, past the church steeples and the office towers downtown, and farther away, past the two huge yellow cranes of the shipyard, you could see the green hills of Antrim and the green hills of Down. In the strange, variegated light of that winter day, they were beautiful, peaceful, and unchanged, the city an abrupt intrusion below them. I watched the hills for as long as I could, until they disappeared when I submerged once again into the petty, wounded streets of the divided city.

All the time I read about William, or read his own words, and came to like and admire him so much, I felt in the back of my mind a faint unease. William disturbed me in some way.

It wasn't his politics. Those still ring clear, true, and unchanged. The rule of law, the locus of power and authority in the citizens, the deference of the executive to the people's representatives: these all remain the crucial elements of enlightened political life. I understood his arguments in favour of organized armed citizens as a

defence against tyranny. As a good Canadian, I believe that this pre-
caution is an unlikely necessity in my own country, but I know
enough about Ireland and other places to believe that, sometimes,
there is no alternative to armed vigilance, even violence. I even see
how William might have found himself, much against his nature
and his will, in despair and anger, sliding down to desperate,
winner-take-all rebellion.

These were the secular elements of his character and experience,
and I felt comfortable with them. I was aware that part of my discomfort with William was his religious analysis, his profound belief
in God and prayer, and in the living example of the Bible's stories.
In his seminal sermon on the war in America, he argued that it was
God's punishment for the "national wickedness" of English and
Irish society: that was "the probable cause of our divided opinions,
and distracted counsels, and of that confusion, war, and blood-shed
which rage thro' our King's dominions." Repentence was the solution: "If we turn from our wicked ways, God will hear our prayers,
forgive our sins, and heal our land." William used the Bible and, in
particular, the Jewish civil war and the resurgence of the Philistines
following the death of Saul, as the reference for his assault on the
current war. The application of biblical precedents to contemporary
events was the beginning of his vision of scripture politics, which he
would articulate more fully in later sermons.

To me, all this was a useful warning against making too much of
a modern man of the eighteenth-century clergyman (although it's
arguable that a form of scripture politics is becoming a more distinct
force in American politics these days). I know the disastrous effect
that religious division has had in Irish history and in most other histories. The fundamentalist versions of any religion are even more
dismaying, with modern weapons and communication to make the
most the destruction and the killing. I know that William would
reject these brutal visions as vigorously as I do. But at the same time,
he's one of their antecedents. There's an antique air to William's
belief, a breath of fundamentalist religiosity in his linking of biblical
principles and prayer to the political process.

Then another sobering realization came to mind. It seems contrived, but it occurred to me only after my visit to Paisley's church.
In fact, the thought struck at the exact moment I was crossing the

Ormeau Bridge and lifting up my eyes to the hills: William often sounds like the Reverend Ian Paisley.

I believe that Paisley is a dangerous, sectarian bigot, and I found it difficult at first to accept any association between the two men. Yet Paisley's methodology is nothing less than a form of scripture politics. He engages in biblical exegesis as a template for the Protestant chosen people of Ulster to use in their fight against popery. His view of politics and theology is similar in form to William's open and tolerant vision, although it's a debased distortion of it. In one scholar's description, Paisley combines the seventeenth- and eighteenth-century Presbyterian idea of activist politics grounded in religious precedent with the new, twentieth-century fundamentalism of the United States and its emphasis on the New Testament, personal salvation through a personal ecstatic transformation, and the secular love of country. Paisley is an old-time Presbyterian radical in contemporary Bible-thumping form. He could step into an Old Light pulpit in Down or Antrim in 1790, and the congregation would have no idea he was from the twentieth century. William would have vehemently rejected Paisley's characterization of the Pope as the Antichrist or his view that Catholicism is evil. But the image of the man of God—as "terrorist" or "freedom-fighter," depending on your point of view—bulling full bore into politics, rousing the people to battle, damning either tyranny or compromise, fits both of these Dissenter preachers. Neither one hesitated to advocate the use of weapons to settle matters in Ireland. Each went to prison because he had the uncompromising idea that he possessed the truth. Each rests his political ideas on a foundation of Christian theology.

However, I take comfort in the much greater differences between the two men: William's sincere, goodhearted, ecumenical, scholarly patriotism against Paisley's simplistic, fundamentalist vision of good and evil, his antiquated fear of "popery," and his vicious sectarian exclusionism. The congregation at the Martyrs Memorial Church will never hear their minister denouncing, as William did, the historical treatment of Catholics: "with the twisted chains of mental darkness, and corporal incapacity, by a body of laws, which humanity views with horror, justice reprobates, and religion pronounces *accursed*." On the contrary, Paisley would see such measures as the just, necessary reactive restraints by God's chosen people beset by the papish Antichrist and his forces in Ireland. Paisley is not an intellectual descendant of William's, but he does represent a descent: the degeneration of the benign ideal of united Irishmen into the fearful, self-destructive dead-end of fundamentalist Prod intransigence.

16

A PAUPER'S GRAVE

AFTER HIS RELEASE AS A STATE PRISONER, William led a more or less quiet life at the plain little church in Keady, County Armagh—although it might be considered quiet only in contrast to his previous public activity. After everything he had gone through and all his family's suffering, it must have been soothing to be home again, reunited with Isabella and their remaining children, even in their poverty and dislocation. We can imagine that the simple things he took for granted before—a meal, conversation, sunset, the privacy of a house and garden—were sweet and intensely satisfying.

However, we can assume that he could not have avoided anger, too, at all the ramifications of his unjust imprisonment and impoverishment, and sorrow at the bloody shambles the United Irish insurrection became. He must have seen all the malign consequences of the failure of rebellion: the new tight grip of England through the *Act of Union,* the independence of Ireland further away than it had ever been; the reassertion of the real face of sectarian relationships in Ulster in the Ribbonmen and the Orange Order; the tense animosities in County Armagh with its Plantation mosaic of vulnerable Prods and Taigs. The kerns were still out there, and the settlers, after two centuries, were still uneasy in the land. Bittersweet to come home to all that.

His sermons in Keady were mostly about God and man, not politics. But, sometimes, he alludes to his suffering. He begins one sermon: "Arduous undertakings are ever attended with danger; and those who engage in them, exposed to difficulty, persecution and distress." He goes on to argue that the introduction of Christianity holds first place in this category of undertakings. But he must also have been referring to his own time as a rebel and to the failed visionary promise of the Ninety-Eight.

The government kept its eye on him. It knew where he travelled and when. Officials in Armagh wrote to the Dublin Castle authorities to tell them William had settled in Keady: they didn't think they could lay any charges against him at the moment for "corrupting and influencing the minds of the people," but they would keep the government informed.

It seems that William paid a visit to Dublin in 1803, just a few weeks before Robert Emmet's abortive rising. The Protestant Emmet and some other United Irish veterans of 1798 hadn't quit. They got another rebellion together, solicited French aid once again, and stockpiled weapons. Things were ill planned; only three hundred men turned out to seize parts of Dublin. Fifty were killed, and Emmet and twenty-one others were executed. This was the real end of the United Irish revolutionary movement. Emmet made a speech from the dock that became famous as a piece of nationalist polemic. He was a poor strategist and planner but very good at dying the martyr's death. He became the romantic hero of the republican tradition of physical force and blood-sacrifice, until the men of 1916, planning their own martyrdom, included Wolfe Tone as well as Emmet in their inspiration.

William doesn't mention what on earth he was doing in Dublin so soon after his release and the shaky assumption of his new job. Government spies report him visiting a Presbyterian minister near Dublin and collecting money from Catholics. For what possible purpose? But it didn't look good when Emmet attacked Dublin. A rumour circulated in County Down later that summer that William was in the Mountains of Mourne awaiting the arrival of thirty thousand armed men from France. The informer adds that he longs "to see Dickson's neck stretched." The report was ridiculous, but it indicates the tension of the time: the government's continuing fear of rebellion and its view that William, the aging country preacher and revolutionary general that no one would turn in, was still a dangerous man. Lord Annesley in Dublin ordered William's arrest in

August 1803, two weeks after Emmet's execution. But for some reason the order wasn't carried out, or someone else higher up countermanded it. William stayed free.

Even though he was sequestered in the backwoods of Armagh, William worked during the 1805 election in his former bailiwick of County Down. He supported the man running against his old nemesis, Lord Castlereagh, the former Robert Stewart. The peer's supporters obviously feared the great influence of the old United Irishmen on his own turf. In an election pamphlet, they denounced him as "one who led some of your own brethren to the rope" and the parish to the edge of perdition. It discusses with relish his fate had he not been lucky enough to have been arrested before the battle of Ballynahinch, and it notes that he was lucky to have got out of Dublin just three days before Emmet's insurrection. It seemed that William was a man always around just when the pikes and muskets were coming out. William's candidate won in spite of, or perhaps because of, all these supposedly damning references to the rebellious past. Castlereagh's defeat must have been a bitter satisfaction to William, betrayed and deeply wounded by him.

Friends warned William that his life might be in danger from the vengeful Castlereagh, and he thought about emigrating to America. But he could never leave under those circumstances. He had to demonstrate that the Ascendancy blackguard had no power over him. Besides, he wrote in his *Narrative:* "I would have proclaimed myself to the world, as a *villain,* if I had acted otherwise, let the consequence be what it might." He would fight on in Ireland.

William had one more battle. His own church had punished him from the moment the Insurrection of 1798 failed. It sanctioned him for mere suspicion of sedition and rebellion—not a whiff of proof, except the reports of spies and informers. In 1799, the Synod condemned "with grief and indignation" the conduct of "some members . . . who have been lately implicated in seditious and treasonable practices." The minutes noted, with relief, that only a relatively small number of its ministers and probationers had been engaged in insurrection. Of those, two had been executed, some had "expressed their sincere contrition," others had withdrawn from the Synod, many had "either voluntarily, or by permission of Government, removed from the kingdom"—a euphemism for

permanent exile in Australia or America—and two were still in
confinement. One of those was the minister of Portaferry and now,
the Synod ruled, he could consider himself the ex-minister.

When William was released from prison, he found the Synod
under the control of the Reverend Robert Black, who was also a
close friend and political ally of Viscount Castlereagh. Nevertheless,
even Black could not prevent William's readmission to the Synod
after the brave parishioners of Keady gave him a job. He laid low
for a while and tended his flock. Life there was hard for the
Dicksons—the state grant, the *regium donum,* was never restored to
him. An undated letter from Isabella (the only instance of her voice,
her only written proof of existence) to a daughter-in-law's brother
shows their desperation. She makes a humble and pathetic plea for
a place to stay for the winter. Where they are "it is hardly possible
to exist." She concludes: "If the liberty I have taken offends you,
I beg you will good-naturedly forget that I have used it in consideration of my present unsettled uncomfortable position." Her
daughter-in-law's brother turned her down. Perhaps some of
William's family disapproved, or were ashamed, of his violent,
rebelly past. Or they had suffered because of their connection with
a man of the Ninety-Eight and a state prisoner, and they were fed
up with all of it.

In spite of these personal hardships, William couldn't let go of the
Synod's condemnation; its hypocrisy continued to rankle. In 1810, he
was sixty-six years old but far from done for. He asked for access to
documents he needed for his last great effort at vindication, his
Narrative. The Synod's clerk, an ally and brother-in-law of the
implacable Robert Black, refused. William argued to the full Synod,
which, perhaps mellower than before, granted his request.

He even got back into politics again and addressed Catholic
political meetings in Dublin and Armagh, probably the first Irish
Presbyterian minister to speak to wholly Catholic gatherings. On his
way back home from the Armagh meeting, William, the old pastor,
was assaulted and nearly killed by unknown assailants, although
they were probably Orangemen. There was an inquiry, but nothing
came of it. He was lucky they hadn't killed him, and he knew it.
Prison, poverty, ostracism, his near-murder, none of it made any
impression on him; he hadn't changed his mind about anything. He

told the Catholics that the great majority of Presbyterians in Ulster were friends of the Catholic cause and that reports to the contrary were malicious rumours (he was wrong, of course).

William's defensive, self-justifying, defiant *Narrative,* published in 1812, raised hell at the Synod meeting that year. We've got a sense already of its curious selective, evasive quality. But alone among the radical Presbyterian ministers who had been United Irishmen and who had survived, William did not go into exile, leave the Synod, or express contrition and remorse. His *Narrative* is a fighting document. Robert Black responded in kind—the two old men still fighting the bitter, ruinous civil war. Theirs must have been a pattern repeated often all over Ireland: men who had fought on one side or the other never able to come to terms with each other. It was the same after the twentieth-century civil war; no one wanted to speak of it or, if they did, the words were always rancorous. Civil wars end only when the men who fought them finally die, and, even then, they devise a bitter bequest. That's what it was like with William and Robert Black. They had always been personal rivals, but in the normal sense; the insurrection, with its terrible memories of conflict and killing, had made them irreconcilable enemies.

Black challenged William: "Stand up in this place and declare that you were not concerned in originating, fomenting or fostering the rebellion of 1798." William replied: "I am astonished at such a proposal, what end could such a declaration serve? Even Dr. Black has not said that he would believe it. I will make no such declaration. If any man has a doubt of my innocence, let him prove me guilty."

The Synod belonged to Black. It ordered William to retract the "gross misstatements and misrepresentations" in the *Narrative.* He refused. The Synod gave him until next year's meeting, or it would suspend him. William replied with *Retractions,* a facetious title because the book did everything but retract anything he had said. Mostly it demolished Black's position and, by implication, that of the Synod. I read the *Retractions* as if they were one of William's speeches on Catholic emancipation in 1792, reported with such admiration in the *Northern Star,* but without the lighthearted wit. Here, he is scathing, harsh, sarcastic, bitter, bleak; his analysis is precise, implacable, devastating, unanswerable. He will not back down an inch. Let any man who can prove him guilty. The government could not; the Synod of Ulster cannot. In that case, let them stand down and admit their fault. At the end, he writes: "Hence, instead of retracting, I avow every sentence in my Narrative."

The Synod could not resist William's barrage of learned argument. The next year, it knuckled under. The phrase in its 1799 minutes, "'implicated in treasonable or seditious practices,' as applied to two of its members then in confinement [a probationer called Smith was held with William], was inaccurately used, inasmuch as it appears to be liable to an unfavourable construction respecting them."

The Synod also moved that it disassociate itself from Black's charges against William. Black's influence within the Synod declined from that point. Four years later, he killed himself by jumping off the Derry Bridge into the River Foyle. In a strange, grisly congruence, William's other old enemy, Robert Stewart— Viscount Castlereagh—later killed himself, too, by slitting his own throat. William became the last man standing.

But now the endgame. William was old, sick, tired. In 1815, he gave up his church in Keady. He and Isabella retired to Belfast in extreme poverty. They lived in a cottage provided by a Presbyterian supporter and survived on a subscription raised by his friends, old United Irishmen, or their sons. While they lived, the network was still there. William did manage to publish his last collection of sermons, fifteen of them, in 1817. In one of them, he wrote: "The vast extent of the works of God—their magnificence, beauty, and order—their mutual dependence, harmonious operation, and combined tendency to diffuse happiness, wide as the capacity of enjoyment, impress the mind of the intelligent observer, with an irresistible conviction of his boundless understanding, unerring wisdom, almighty power, and kind intention."

Isabella, who had been an invalid since William's release, died in 1819. Her small annuity stopped, and William was even poorer. He died two days after his eightieth birthday and was buried in an unmarked pauper's grave in the Clifton Street Cemetery in Belfast, a short walk from the city centre. Only eight or nine people attended his funeral service.

But William did not die out of history. Irish nationalists remembered him. In 1909, when the home rule campaign was approaching its climax, an Ulster Protestant nationalist, Francis Biggar (obviously a Lundy), raised money to put headstones on the unmarked graves of old United Irish rebels. William's was one of them. It was crowned with a Gaelic cross, and on it were chiselled his name, dates of birth and death, then the words "Patriot, Preacher, Historian," and an inscription in Irish—a little of the Gaelic for an Ulster Prod.

When I visited his grave in 2003, I saw that at some time during the Troubles, someone, most likely Protestants from their nearby territory of the Shankill, had scaled the high, razor-wired cemetery wall. For some reason, they had left the Irish cross intact, but they had hacked off the abhorrent Gaelic phrase, leaving an ugly, rough gash. Nevertheless, I knew what the words had been: *Do cum onora na h-Eireann*—"For the honour of Ireland."

PART THREE

Billy

17

ALL THE SONS OF ULSTER

AT SEVEN-THIRTY in the morning on July 1, 1916, the Protestant men of Ulster entered into their agony and martyrdom.

The soldiers of the 36th (Ulster) Division of X Corps, Fourth Army of the British Expeditionary Force in France, were ready for battle. Most were Orangemen and wore the Order's orange sash over their khakis and field equipment. They prayed and sang hymns. It was a holy day to go to war because the date was the same as that of the great battle on the River Boyne 226 years earlier, when William defeated James.* In the Protestants' story of themselves, the Boyne was still a vivid and live chapter. Now they were about to fight on the banks of other rivers, the Ancre on their left flank, the Somme to the right. The Somme *was* the Boyne, the Lagan, the Bann, the Foyle. On these French fields the Ulster Protestants would prove their loyalty to the King and to Great Britain in the only way this Great War allowed: they would die for a few hundred yards of useless, busted-up sod and dust.

When the creeping artillery barrage lifted, bugles (not Lambeg drums) sounded the "Advance." The soldiers rose up out of their trenches and holes and from leafy Thiepval Wood and went out into

---

* The Battle of the Boyne was fought on July 1 under the old-style Julian calendar, which became July 11 under the new-style Gregorian calendar, adopted in Britain and Ireland in 1752. The Orange Order decided to celebrate the battle on July 12 because it seems to have misunderstood the calendar reform.

no man's land. Some of the Ulstermen, against the prescribed attack regulations, had slithered up behind the cataclysmic fall of the big guns' shells to within a hundred metres of the enemy's line. They weren't professional soldiers and didn't give a damn about the regs. It just made sense to use the cover of more than fourteen hundred big cannon and hundreds of trench mortars blasting away. There was a sunken road running across no man's land, and they also made use of that as a forward assembly position. When the barrage lifted, they didn't wait to form up into the usual waves of fighting and mopping-up platoons but, instead, charged helter-skelter across the half-kilometre of open ground uphill towards the first line of enemy trenches. The shocked, numbed Germans were slow to climb up out of their deep dugouts. Paddies and Huns fought a brief, vicious melée along the whole length of the line—hand to hand with the sword-like bayonets and rifle butts, close-in firing—and then, just like that, the Ulstermen had captured their first objective. Their speed in doing so was remarkable. And they had suffered few casualties, which was astonishing. It wouldn't last.

Their second objective was the Schwaben Redoubt, four hundred metres ahead, and their third the German second-line trenches another kilometre farther on. As its name suggests, the redoubt was a formidable strongpoint, uphill from the first trenchline and composed of a web of machine-gun positions and firing points that allowed for cross and enfilading fire against attackers. The Ulstermen's dash and intelligent tactics had got them far ahead of the more pedestrian units on their flanks, but they didn't wait for support. The attacking platoons pushed on towards the Schwaben. The succeeding waves of men began to leave their lines and the cover of Thiepval towards the German trenches. The quick advance had created a salient for the 36th Division, always a dangerous and exposed shape in battle. Now the Ulstermen would begin to die.

The bullets from German machine guns—their rate of fire, six hundred a minute—sliced across no man's land from the side, from the village of Thiepval and a nearby ruined château. Enemy artillery opened up. The advancing soldiers fell in windrows like scythed barley. Some men wavered in the shock and storm of bullets and shells. A company commander of the West Belfasts took off his Orange sash, held it high over his head, and roared: "Come on, boys!

No surrender!" They all took up the old battle cry of Derry's siege and pressed on. The Schwaben defenders had had time to climb up out of their well-prepared deep dugouts, and they were ready. The fighting was elemental, a swirl of savage combats. It could have been Greeks before Troy, Spartans at Thermopylae, Romans at Cannae, any battle that dissolves into its most basic form of man to man, kill or be killed. A private of the Belfast Young Citizens watched his sergeant-major take a rifle from a wounded German sniper and obliterate his face with it. A private in the Tyrone Volunteers heard a loud explosion almost on top of him, and part of a man's torso landed right in front of his Lewis gun. A private in the Derry Volunteers dropped trench mortar bombs down ventilator shafts into a dugout and heard the frantic screams of agony and terror from the shattered Germans inside. A Belfast man with terrible head and leg wounds begged a comrade to kill him, but his companion couldn't do it. As there always is in battle, a moment of compassion: a Belfast lance-corporal fell over a badly wounded German who was obviously mad with thirst. The Ulsterman gave him water from his own canteen, even though it was against orders.

It took two hours for the men of the 36th Division to capture the Schwaben Redoubt. Those who were left, just a few hundred who were able, began to push on to the second line of German trenches. They got close, but then their own artillery, following a prearranged schedule, began to fire on the German line. Many shells fell short and killed the attacking Ulstermen—the generals hadn't expected them to get so far so fast. A few men reached the trenches anyway. Along the entire thirty-kilometre battle front, and of the sixty thousand first-wave attackers (not a conscript among them), they were the only major unit of British Army troops to reach the German second lines. But they couldn't hold their position against their own "friendly fire" and enemy machine guns, rifles, and cannon. Under fire, they fell back to the Schwaben, and there, still under fire, waited for the counterattack. The remnants of the Ulstermen, in their unsupported forward position and almost surrounded, were— grim irony—virtually under siege.

They couldn't hold the redoubt, of course. It was impossible to get reinforcements to them. They endured throughout the afternoon and into the evening under constant fire and bombardment, and fought off several infantry counterattacks. But they began to run out of ammunition and, worse, water. It had been a hot July day, and their exertions were strenuous. The thirst was almost worse than the fire. Even these tough, devout Prods were reaching the end of their endurance. Some men were shell-shocked; some tried to run; others broke down, crying, chuckling, gaping with the universal soldier's thousand-yard stare. Each man discovered where his limit lay.

By evening, almost every officer who had attacked was dead or wounded. Finally, a major gave the order to withdraw, and the Ulstermen began to leave the Schwaben and to head back to the former German front-line trenches for a last stand. After fourteen hours of fighting, they had gained a section of enemy front lines 800 metres long. Out of approximately 10,000 attacking troops from the 36th Division, over half—5,104—were casualties, of whom more than 2,000 were killed. Nine Victoria Crosses were awarded on the single day of July 1, 1916, and four of them went to Ulstermen of the 36th Division, even though they made up only about eighteen percent of the total British attacking force. Over the course of the war, the Ulster Division would suffer 30,000 casualties, virtually its entire initial strength. Long before the end, the division ran out of Ulstermen and took in Englishmen and Scotsmen to maintain its complement.

The fierce and terrible fight all through the first day of the Battle of the Somme, like all such days, changed every man there. And like many such days, somehow it changed the whole people these men came from. Vimy Ridge did the same thing for Canada; Gallipoli for Australia. Perhaps in America it was Gettysburg, because of Lincoln's three-minute address, whose odd modernity was derided at the time but preserved it forever. Somehow, the expenditure of soldiers' blood—if the soldiers are merely the men of the nation in uniform—seals something, confirms and consecrates a profound unity among the men themselves and, through them, the people. That's what that first day of July 1916 did for the Protestants of Ulster. And it demonstrated that they, too, were prepared to carry out the old Irish tradition of blood-sacrifice for a cause. Assuredly not for the *Shan Van Vocht,* but for Ulster and Protestantism and their way of life in Ireland, more than three centuries old. After the Somme, surely no one could refuse to take their claims and their separate, irascible existence seriously. Surely no one could force these loyal, decimated Protestant men into a Catholic Ireland against their will.

My grandfather William Lundy—Billy—was a soldier of the 36th Division. Until just a few months before writing these words, I had assumed he had been in France and at the Somme. I knew he wasn't one of the men who attacked the Schwaben Redoubt because he hadn't been an infantryman. Instead, he drove a horse-drawn wagon in the divisional train of the Army Service Corps—there was little motorized transport in that war. I had envisioned him, reins in hand, bullying horses on rough, shell-pocked, dusty or muddy roads with loads of ammunition or food for the attacking platoons. Not martial, but necessary, and it would have had its own dangers from enemy artillery, especially if he had been engaged in supplying right up to the front lines.

Then, my uncle—Billy's other son, my father, Alexander's, brother—told me about Billy and the war. I had never talked to my father about it, as with too many other things. Billy didn't get to France, said my uncle. He had an accident before the 36th Division shipped out, and he spent the war working in the Belfast shipyards. Sometime before the division was sent to England in July 1915, Billy was walking back to the Victoria Barracks after a visit home. He was in uniform, and because he was a teamster, his uniform included spurs on his boots. On Grosvenor Street at that time, there was a section with steps down to a lower level. Billy caught a spur on one of the steps and went ass over mug, injuring his head and face. It was enough of a debility to get him discharged. The army wanted its young men to be completely fit before it sent them to be slaughtered—a kind of anti-Darwinism: destruction of the fittest. Billy could have slogged across no man's land and got himself wiped out by a German machine gun just as well as a flawless athlete. But there it was: back into his shipyard job as a riveter, which was, in any event, necessary work for the war effort. No wonder there were no bullet holes in his army helmet.

Missing the main event was getting to be a family theme: Robert was kicked out of Derry before the actual siege began; William was

arrested before the Insurrection of 1798 broke out in the north; and
now I discovered that Billy missed the Somme, missed the whole
war. Still, given the Ulster Division's casualties, the latter may well
have been a precondition for my own existence. I had assumed
Billy was there because of the helmet I had played with and also
because of a little New Testament, which has passed down to me
from him through my father. This and his juvenile Orange sash
are the only things I have of Billy's. The book was issued to all soldiers of the Protestant private army, the Ulster Volunteer Force,
when they formed up into the 36th Division after the war began.
It is a pocket-sized edition, with a cheap, khaki, clothbound card-
board cover and very small print. Its only ornament is a small
Ulster flag on the front: white background, red cross, and, at its
centre, the bloody red hand.

On the fly page of his New Testament, Billy wrote: "Driver W.
Lundy, 254 Coy A.S.C., 36th (Ulster) Divisional Train," and he
added his number, "73/031155." On the facing page is printed a message to the Ulster Volunteers from Lord Roberts, the British
supreme commander at the time. The peer, who died in 1914, but
who, if he had lived, would have remained comfy, warm, well fed,
rested, louse free, and alive all through the war, wrote: "When in
any doubt, difficulty or anxiety, pray to God and read this little
book. God will strengthen you, He will uphold you, your path will
be made straight, and God will help you to see clearly what to do."
Not bad writing—strong, simple declarative sentences—but not
much good against machine guns or artillery fire.

If I had thought about it, I should have suspected Billy's role in
the war. The small, fungible book of the Word of God is still in good
shape, even after I have lugged it around with me for years, none too
gently. Surely it couldn't have survived the weather and permanent
funk and sweat of the Western Front! Billy didn't use it much anyway; it doesn't exactly look as if it's been well thumbed through. He
could be described as having been anticlerical. When the local
church minister came on his regular visits to the little house on the
border of the Holy Land, my grandmother, Maud, would pour tea
and chat while Billy would retire to the outdoor toilet in the tiny
yard, chill-cold in the wintertime, and read the newspaper—there
was always one there for other purposes—until the Holy Joe had

gone. Once the minister caught Billy in the act of heading out the back door and shouted (in the forthright style of Ulster men of God): "You can't run from the Lord God, William." Billy replied: "Whoever told you you were the lord bloody Jesus Christ?" and headed for the loo anyway. Being an Ulster Protestant (or Catholic) doesn't necessarily involve the slightest measure of actual religious belief. The old joke isn't really a joke: Q: Prod or Taig? A: I'm an atheist. Q: Aye, but are you a Protestant or a Catholic atheist?

Perhaps, if you're from Northern Ireland, it's a status you can never escape or be released from no matter how long you've been away, even if you've lost almost all your connection with the place. Whichever tribe you were born into, or belonged to at one time, it seems never to let you go. Once, I visited Belfast during the Troubles, not long after the imposition of internment without trial, and when the fighting was at its worst—open sectarian war and twenty thousand British soldiers in the province. My grandmother was still alive, and I stayed with her in the little house on Cadogan Street. It was a hundred strides from the Ormeau Road, which was then a borderland between the small Protestant enclave of the Holy Land and its adjacent streets and, on the other side, the Catholic territory of Hatfield Street. Now it would be called an "interface area": a volatile, perilous frontier along which Prods and Taigs are separated by a few metres.

One evening, after I'd been there a while, I needed to get out for a drink. There were three pubs nearby, two on the "no-go" Catholic side of the Ormeau Road and one on the Protestant side. It was too dangerous to cross the road to the nearer Catholic pub. It wasn't inconceivable to be shot on sight for doing so; my great-uncle Benjamin had been killed by a sniper a hundred metres away fifty years earlier. I walked farther along to the pub on the Protestant side. All of them were like fortresses: heavy wire mesh over windows, sandbags around the walls, a net stretching from the roof down to the ground to deflect thrown stones or grenades or bombs—in their armature, they didn't look much different from police stations. It would have been sensible to abandon them and drink somewhere farther back, behind these front lines. But that would have been a retreat, a loss; maybe it would allow the other side a toehold onto your ground, the tentative beginning of a larger invasion.

The taciturn man on the steel-reinforced door of the pub admitted me after a thorough frisking. As I came in, I saw twenty or so men—no women—drinking pints of beer or Guinness at old wooden tables; a decrepit bar, smoke and grime. Everyone turned towards the door to see who had come in, and it was like the scene from an old Western movie when the stranger walks through the saloon's swinging doors: all conversation stopped; no one moved; absolute silence, all eyes on me. A mass of blue eyes, too—I remember being struck by that, inconsequentially, in the static hot buzz of the moment. The Irish, Protestant and Catholic, are predominantly light-eyed (mostly blue); it's the only reliable "racial" characteristic you can hang on them. This room stared back at me in blue. The men did a variation of that Northern Irish stare, which always seeks out your religious affiliation: with my beard and "Fenian-lookin'" face, I might be a Catholic, but only a suicidal Taig would come in there. I had to be a Prod, then. But just who the hell was I?

I felt protected by my status as a Canadian visitor—I had my passport in my pocket because I had to wave it at soldiers and coppers pointing rifles and submachine guns at me every ten minutes on the street. And I was, after all, a Protestant in a Protestant pub. I walked to the bar between tables of silent, watchful men, feeling as if I was, in fact, in a movie. Some of them would be armed, I was sure of that, although no one, as far as I could see, was reaching for a weapon. I asked the bartender for a pint of Guinness. He didn't move but said, with that endearing Belfast directness—you always knew where you stood—"Who the fuck are you?" I said in a loud clear voice, emphasizing my Canadian accent, because I knew it was for the whole room, "I'm Maud Lundy's grandson on Cadogan Street, visiting from Canada."

It was if a wand had waved over the men, waking them from a fierce, rapt paralysis: an eruption of laughter, talk, fragments: Maudie's grandson? Och, away! Holy Land. Canada. Billy—at the gasworks? I knew he couldn't be no fuckin' Taig. The barman began the long, slow, Guinness pour. As I waited, a few men came up to me to say hello, shake hands, Where in Canada? I've family in Hamilton, Vancouver. How's Maudie? How's Alec? You can't be too careful these days, son. You've chosen a bloody fine time for a wee visit, son. Welcome back. Are you staying long? Welcome. Welcome home. Home.

I'd been in Belfast for a week or so, but I still felt out of place, already worn down by the tension. Armed men were everywhere, gunfire in the distance—and sometimes not far away at all—bombs going off in restaurants and, yes, in pubs, newspapers full of photographs of the dead and wounded, the cold rain, my cold, damp room, shitting outside in the cold yard toilet, the constant searches, English soldiers scoping me with their rifles from passing Saracens and shoving me around at roadblocks, the people's "cowled and haunted faces," the appraising gaze—Prod or Taig? It was as if I'd been dropped into a dangerous alien place. Even after a few days there, I was choking under the low sky, in the mean little streets, among the people twisted by the ancient hatred and fear. And underlying all was the sensation that things could go berserk in a flash: the troops might lose control; the armed mobs could overwhelm whole neighbourhoods; maybe the army of the Republic would intervene; perhaps a Protestant commando would sweep down to Dublin, the entire island going up, just like 1921 or '22. All of that seemed conceivable then. It was a genuine civil war that could bloom anytime into full-blown massacre and pogrom. Even as a Canadian, long in the Irish diaspora, although perhaps too well read in Irish history, I could wake up to a scatter of close-by gunshots at four in the morning with a sweaty recollection of 1641 and 1688 and Scullabogue and Wexford and all the communal killing in between and since. The little house on the border of the Holy Land would be indefensible if the kerns came calling again.

That evening in the Protestant pub on the Ormeau Road, I got drunk and never parted with a penny. Everyone wanted to buy me one. The alcohol and the words of the men were quieting, reassuring. For the first time since I'd been in Northern Ireland, I relaxed the way I would feel relaxed at home in Canada. Nothing could touch me there with these men around me; they would protect me; they would fight for me because I was a Prod, just like them. They would stand by me to the death against a Taig gunman or mob. Most of this warmth was the booze working its usual sentimental way, of course, but I felt that deep, primitive, tribal, comforting belonging, too. In the pub, these were my people and this was my place once again— home. That evening, the word meant the same thing to me as it had for my parents, who always referred to Ireland simply as "home."

The next day, I remembered my gush of tribal solidarity with a discomfort exacerbated by a very serious Guinness hangover. I was ashamed of my emotion and all the conversation about dirty Fenians and fuckin' Taigs I'd acquiesced in by my silence. For the rest of that time in Belfast, I never went back to the pub, and I avoided walking by it in case anyone I knew saw me. But I remember how easy it was to subside into that collective, yet compromised, reassurance, to forget the hard history and to be soothed by the old mythology. After a while, it didn't matter; I went back to Canada, my home now.

I have realized with surprise and sadness that I know as much about my ancestor William in the eighteenth century as I do about my grandfather Billy in the twentieth. Billy died when I was seven years old, but I don't remember him in person. It's odd, because we had made two or three of our summer visits to Belfast when I was old enough to have sure memories. I see Billy in a handful of old photographs. I try to recollect the sight and feel, the smell, of the actual man, but, for whatever reasons, I can't do it. I remember with clarity many other things about Ireland in those days, but not him, the most important thing.

In one of the photographs—it's in front of me now—my grandfather, Billy, wears a suit and tie with a sweater under the jacket and a flat hat. It looks like his Sunday-best outfit. He is a stocky man, square-faced, handsome. He's kneeling beside me and holding my arm; he looks at the camera smiling and saying something, pointing to the ground in front of us. I look as if I'm about four years old, a cute little boy in a knee-length coat with velvety collars, shorts you can't see under the coat, white ankle socks and scuffed brown shoes, a little pigeon-toed. I'm looking more or less at the camera; I appear to be on the edge of tears, or, at least, glum and recalcitrant. Billy is trying to get me to do something for the photographer (my father?), but I'm resisting, being bolshie, staging my personal juvenile Irish rebellion. All that can be seen in the background is grass and a tree-shadow. I imagine it's the Botanic Gardens, near the little house on the border of the Holy Land, through which I walked memory-bound towards Paisley's Martyrs Memorial Church fifty years later. In this photograph, Billy must be only a few years from his death. I see in his face the lineaments of my father's, but no live memory comes to me. The scene once took place; it left a literal trace of itself in the photograph, which remains an abstracted and bloodless memento, a mere record, or perhaps a symbol of the vanished past.

There are, however, some things I know about Billy: he was a bigot, signatory of Ulster's Solemn League and Covenant, a member of the Ulster Volunteer Force, a shipyard man, and then a gasworks labourer, inhaling all day long the sour, death-dealing stench. Other things, too, although only a few. My father could have told me so much about Billy—he had a precise and lucid memory—but I never asked him. I was Billy's first grandchild, and, my mother said, "He thought the sun rose and set on you." When we were leaving Ireland for England, Billy held me in his arms on the Irish Sea ferry and wouldn't let go. Then he refused to get off the boat. He cried, out in the open—that hard Ulsterman. Finally my parents got him to go ashore. We were Irish people, or British people in Ireland, but whatever we were, we were following the old emigrant path over the water and, in those days, even England seemed so far away.

Billy's job as a riveter at the shipyard had been a good one. He was considered a skilled tradesman, a good many notches above the other men in the neighbourhood, who were labourers, tram drivers, mailmen. He helped to build the *Titanic,* and the joke was that it was his fault the vessel sank: "If you hadn't buggered them rivets, Billy, the damn ship'd be doin' rightly the day." During the Depression, he lost his job, along with twenty thousand other "yard men," and didn't work for four years. He made a ship model of the sort of square-rigger his father and uncles had sailed on. I remember seeing it in the attic I slept in as a boy on our visits to Cadogan Street. It has long since disappeared, together with the family Bible—which went back to my great-grandfather Alexander Dickson, Maud's father—and Billy's war helmet, victims of the Troubles and my family's displacements. There were also various heirlooms—antique crystal goblets, for example, and Billy's gold watch that he got from his father—which Maud pawned in shame and secrecy to buy food in those hungry years.

Sometimes Billy looked for work; sometimes he got together with the other men from the streets on the waste land by the Lagan, where I played years later, to discuss the Depression and propose that, maybe, some kind of revolution was in order. What the hell was the point of Northern Ireland if Protestants were out of work just as much as the bloody Taigs? Later, he kept going at his gas-works job, returning to work every day still sick to his stomach from the day before, stinking of coal gas and half in a stupor, because there were thousands of men who would do it if he wouldn't or wasn't able. The job meant that the family could afford to buy meat again, and new clothes and go to church once more.

The pugnacious Irishman is, of course, a stereotype, and it seems completely out of place applied to the gentle, courteous people of the south of Ireland. But, as usual, Ulster is different. There, the precon-ception is more or less the truth, and Billy was an example of it. Once, when a tram missed his stop one rainy night, he punched the driver. When the tram made a belated halt, Billy hopped off and walked casually home. Nothing came of the incident; it wasn't unusual. He could have been the man in the quintessential Belfast interaction: he's standing in a bus queue and someone next to him catches his eye—momentarily, the way it happens, nothing in it, an innocent and quick contact. He responds: "What the fuck are you lookin' at?" And the fight's on. Billy's brother, my great-uncle Jack, once punched a milkman, laid him out cold with a quick sucker blow, because neither man would give way to the other when they passed on the sidewalk. Jack was striding along somewhere while the milkman was trying to put a pint bottle on a doorstep, and they collided. As I've heard the family stories, these sorts of things hap-pened all the time. It's the Ulster way of things.

On the Falls and Shankill roads on any Saturday night in so-called peacetime, before the Troubles began, police patrols were made up of four men in combat helmets with submachine guns, severe black tunics, and capes against the rain. Armoured cars and reinforcements lay in tactical proximity. This was just to handle the after-pub punch-ups among co-religionists, never mind what might happen if the boys from the two sides got at each other. The coppers' robust tactic was designed to head off that as well—it was always only a short walk to the Prod or Taig frontier.

This was Billy's world, and he inhabited it without self-consciousness. It was my father's, too, and although he presented himself as amiable and calm, that was a public conceit. In private, his melancholy felt threatening, and sometimes the dark Ulster fierceness broke through in sudden physical anger. He hit me too often and sometimes much too hard, and that made me afraid of him. That happens everywhere, of course, but in the context of Northern Ireland, it manifests itself as a natural intimate family extension of the vehement communal anger.

18

HOME RULE, ROME RULE

BILLY WAS BORN in 1890 in Carrickfergus on Belfast Lough in the town's Irish Quarter, which Louis MacNeice called "a slum for the blind and halt." Billy's father, John (not another William, for a change), was a seaman before the mast, and, as a member of that despised class of men—and a Presbyterian, too—he was a natural inhabitant of the old bog-Irish ghetto. MacNeice, the son of an Anglican clergyman, was born in the natty Scotch Quarter with its rows of fine houses and neat cottages. Billy's birthplace was twelve kilometres from Carnmoney, where William Steel Dickson was born, and five kilometres from Kilroot, where the young Jonathan Swift spent the first unhappy years of his Anglican ministry surrounded by the Dissenters he detested.

Billy's grandfather Robert (there's the name of the old traitor of Derry) also spent his life at sea—part of my family's long history of seagoing. He was one of the iron men who sailed wooden wind ships around the Horn and across the perilous and beautiful Southern Ocean. Billy's uncle, another William, was a seaman who got his mate's papers, but he is listed in the parish records as a "yachtsman." This makes him sound like a man of substance or an eccentric, but he was neither. Sir Thomas Lipton, the Ulster prince of tea, recruited William as one of the crew on his *Shamrocks*, the huge, expensive racing yachts he built to challenge for the America's Cup. William, the tough, deep-sea sailor, must have been able to keep the fine balance between deference and authority. He was one of the professional seamen aboard who knew what it took to get a vessel under sail across an ocean while making the rich men on the afterdeck look good.

Like every human being, Billy was a universe of singularity, but we might also think of him as an Ulster Protestant Everyman who lived through one of the great crises in Irish history: the country's stirring, final break for freedom and its sad and unavoidable partition. His year of birth was also one of those years in which a single event involving one man would change both politics and literature in Ireland. These have always kept close company there (as they do in repressed or occupied countries), but never more so than in the decades before the First World War—although Ulster is the notable exception once again. In 1890, Charles Stewart Parnell, the leader of the Irish Parliamentary Party, fell from power. It seemed to many in Ireland at the time that his fall began to shift an entire nation from one path to another. William Butler Yeats wrote: "All that stir of thought which prepared for the Anglo-Irish war, began when Parnell fell. . . . A disillusioned and embittered Ireland turned from parliamentary politics; an event was conceived; and the race began, as I think, to be troubled by that event's long gestation."

The "event" was the blood-sacrifice of the Easter Rising, the trigger of the war of independence. The "race" refers to the Irish, but in the myopic tradition of southerners it obviously does not include almost a million Ulster Protestants—they were assuredly not involved in conceiving any event other than staying out of an Ireland run by Catholics. Once again, we see the inexplicable ignorance, and ignoring, of the northern Prods, as if they were inconsequential. Instead, they were the pivot on which everything would turn. Even the perspicacious Protestant Yeats was blind to Ulster's special situation. And while he understood that Parnell's fall was a crucial moment, he overestimated its effect on parliamentary politics in Ireland. In fact, the Irish doggedly pursued peaceful, constitutional reform for sixteen years after they lost Parnell. The great majority of Catholics had turned from violent solutions to parliamentary politics and the gradual path to limited and, eventually, complete, independence. It took the old combination to flip them back again to the ancient, deep-rooted ways: martyrdom for the *Shan Van Vocht;* English brutality in response.

In the standard received story of Ireland, Parnell was the country's "uncrowned king." That's an accurate enough description. He led the Irish nation (although always with the unheeded exception and implicit exclusion of the Protestants of Ulster) by mostly peaceful constitutional means to the very edge of home rule—a quasi-independent status like Canada's or the other self-governing dominions of the empire. He cajoled and manipulated, and played the parliamentary game; and he did not deny the threat of that violence in Ireland which alone guaranteed in England a hearing for moderation. In other words, it's me or "Captain Moonlight"; deal with us, or perhaps the kerns will rise again.

Parnell was an Ascendancy Protestant, a quiet, handsome, cold, complicated man, the grandson of an Irish chancellor of the exchequer who had opposed the *Act of Union,* which was the English response to the Ninety-Eight. Since its inception in 1875, the home rule campaign had been led mostly by southern Irish Protestants, members of the Ascendancy. This was nothing new, of course; they had played the same part in the Irish Patriot Parliament a hundred years earlier. They continued to live an ambivalent existence in Ireland—as one writer says, poised on the hyphen between "Anglo" and "Irish"—but they were Irish, and human, enough to want more power and one degree or another of independence. Most Ascendancy Protestants may have possessed nothing more than "an insidious *bonhomie,* an obsolete bravado and a way with horses," in the words of Louis MacNeice. Nevertheless, some of them also managed to fulfill the usual role of all local elites dominated by foreign power: they resisted, and they led the people in resistance.

However, as we've seen, the north of Ireland was different, and Ulster Protestants were never part of the Ascendancy. Yeats saw this—expressed in his description of them as "a horrid lot"—who, he added, in a veiled suggestion of partition, "within our borders, would sour all our tempers." Everything that had happened in Ulster—the risings, the massacres, the Plantation, the siege, 1798, the sheer dense Scots and Presbyterian presence on the ground, the nineteenth-century industrialization that had taken place disproportionately in the north—had created a different people altogether.

For a while, Parnell led the Catholic Irish like a Gaelic O'Neill or MacDonnell: he was a chieftain to whom the nation bore love and swore fealty. He was the centre of a romantic personality cult of leader worship; Parnellism was like Bonapartism. Parnell became a great national hero, as another parliamentarian said, "with his superb silences, his historic name, his determination, his self-control, his aloofness." That status was confirmed when the authorities arrested him and put him in jail for seven months after agitation for land reform became too extreme. As always, nothing sealed an Irish patriotic reputation like being put in prison by the English. "Politically it is a fortunate thing for me that I have been arrested," he told his mistress, Kitty O'Shea, with prim certitude.

Although Parnell's political power had weakened over time, he fell abruptly because Kitty was a married woman whose long-cuckolded husband finally sought a divorce. The morality of those times meant that even Parnell could not brazen it through or slough it off. As many in Ireland saw things, the English government's hypocrites and their own priests brought down their king. Still, the behaviour of this Protestant scandalized devout Catholics, as it alienated Parnell's ally, William Gladstone, the conscience-stricken nonconformist English prime minister, who for a while had spent his spare time seeking out whores—although solely for the purpose of reforming them.

Parnell fought a bitter fight for power and for his reputation, but he died within a year, at the age of forty-five. The cause of his long-premature death could be nothing else than having been hounded out of his job and bullied in his personal life by bloody-minded little people: another Irish hero martyred, although this time not only by a beef-headed English government but by a faction of his own nation, too. What was a woman and her oafish husband against the "sight of the promised land" that home rule revealed to a yearning people?

To those Irish who were striving for the limited, reasonable, yet ever-denied emancipation of their country, his death seemed, for a while, to be the death of hope. But soon, Parnell's fall and dying became an archetypal Gaelic story: a hero who seems to have suffered defeat but is not defeated. In one of the great Irish myths, the Ulster hero Cúchulainn has suffered a mortal wound. He ties himself to a rock so that he will die standing, like a warrior. As his life flows out of him, he laughs at a raven that lands, slipping in the blood flowing from his wounds. In his standing and in his laughter, he triumphs over death.

Like Cúchulainn and the old Gaels, Parnell, too, had his poets—Yeats went to the Dublin docks to meet the ship carrying Parnell's body back to Ireland—and the gods: a meteor seemed to fall from the sky the day he was buried at Glasnevin. In "Parnell's Funeral," Yeats wrote that strangers had murdered the old Irish patriots—Robert Emmet, Wolfe Tone—while the Irish watched. But this time, to Parnell, they did it themselves:

> *Hysterica passio* dragged this quarry down.
> None shared our guilt; nor did we play a part
> Upon a painted stage when we devoured his heart.

Early on in *A Portrait of the Artist as a Young Man,* James Joyce describes Stephen as a young boy lying sick in his boarding-school infirmary. He has a vision or a dream. He sees his school's kindly Brother Michael on the deck of a ship entering harbour, where a multitude of people are gathered in the dark, moonless night:

> He saw him lift his hand towards the people and heard him
> say in a loud voice of sorrow over the waters:
> —He is dead. We saw him lying upon the catafalque.
> A wail of sorrow went up from the people.
> —Parnell! Parnell! He is dead!
> They fell upon their knees, moaning in sorrow.

The period of agitation for home rule lasted from about 1875 until the beginning of war in 1914. The movement got some of its beginning impetus from the Fenian rising of 1867 and the usual heavy-handed English reaction to it, and especially the execution of the three "Manchester Martyrs." The Fenian rebellion was meaningless in military or revolutionary terms—a mere gesture, a kind of dramatically violent street theatre. It nourished the old republican mythology of physical-force resistance to the 800-year occupation, but the Irish had been essentially quiescent since 1803, and they still had no stomach for rebellion. The Fenians did renew resistance, but in the form of the peaceful, political home rule campaign.

That campaign was a peculiar phase in the politics of Ireland: a brilliant, sustained endeavour which was, nevertheless, bound to fail. It combined agitation in the countryside for land reform—the "land war"—with a vigorous battle in the British Parliament for the hearts and minds of the mostly sympathetic Liberal Party led by Gladstone. In 1885, the pragmatic prime minister became a convert to the idea of home rule when the nationalist Irish Parliamentary Party won eighty-six seats at Westminster. He needed its votes, and he introduced the first home rule bill in Parliament the next year. Gladstone took the varied and ambiguous notions wrapped up in the Irish concept of home rule and made them limited and concrete. Using other parts of the empire—especially Canada—as models, he planned a two-chamber local assembly in charge of Irish internal matters. The English would keep for themselves a few items like imperial and foreign affairs, the armed forces, currency, security, and major taxation. With not much of importance left for the Irish to look after, home rule was a mandate for national adolescence. Nevertheless, the changes were real for both England and Ireland. The English proposed to loosen their grip, and not at the point of the gun or the pike. For the first time in hundreds of years, they would, voluntarily, cede a little real power to the wild and "most salvage Irishe."

It wasn't the first time that England had appeared to do so; the Irish Patriot Parliament had had similar powers in the 1780s and 1790s, but they were only on paper. As a practical matter, corruption, a severely limited franchise, the exclusion of Catholics and Dissenters, and a rogue executive had doomed the whole political enterprise. These were the conditions that had infuriated the Ulster Presbyterians in particular and had inspired William to berate the Ascendancy from the pulpit of his Portaferry church.

Home rule was different. In theory, it could have provided the Irish with at least an acceptable form of the independence they had sought for so long. There were precedents in other parts of the empire, although England would have had difficulty—it always did—in dropping its habit of treating Ireland with more offhand severity and prejudice than it treated its later acquisitions overseas. A century of union with England, as well as the legislative reforms wrung out of it by the land war—the "three Fs": free sale, fair rent, and fixity of tenure—had created the economic infrastructure of small farmer-owners and the political culture on which to base a feasible form of responsible self-government. The Anglican Church had been disestablished and Catholics effectively emancipated. The prosperous Catholic middle class was reasonably content and, with property and income to lose in uncertain or unstable times, was actively hostile to the revolutionaries. The English had tended to experiment with things in Ireland and, if they worked there, to adopt them at home later. Many new things did work out in this social laboratory, and Ireland in the 1880s and 1890s was more advanced than England: it had a better system of national education and a country-wide postal network (which Anthony Trollope had helped to establish after he had finished writing novels each day). The country also had an evolving idea of government based on the rights of the citizen—not the first time Irishmen had thought so, of course, as the history of 1798 and any of William's scripture-politics sermons attest.

Indeed, by the late 1800s, Ireland, like a good dependent subaltern, had absorbed its master's lessons. It had shed its language and culture, held the kerns mostly in check for a century, and abandoned its old, bad habits of refractory warfare. Rural violence continued, but in the "normal" ritualized manner of the secret societies or the limited actions of the "land war"—except, perhaps, in Ulster, where sectarian emotions made the conflicts more intense and unpredictable. Small numbers of fierce men can derail a peace process with dismaying ease, a few bombs or gun attacks destroying a high-strung consensus. Things often appeared to be bad in Ireland. For all but sixteen years during the whole of the nineteenth century, the country was subject to suspension of habeas corpus, or to a *Crimes and Outrages Act,* or to *Peace Preservation* or *Protection of Life* acts, or to some combination of them all. But the Irish en masse had shown they could ignore that sort of thing and carry on with their constitutional effort. It might have helped that they were used to a background hum of mayhem; it had long been a condition of life in the country and was nothing to get excited about. Most important, perhaps, Ireland had accepted that its future lay with Britain, not with some continental power that was hostile to England. The latter no longer had to view Ireland as the large hole in its security perimeter. Assuredly the country had proven itself worthy of home rule and responsible enough to carry it out. It took a while, but, eventually, with the passage of the third home rule bill in 1912, a sufficient number of the English agreed.

There was just one problem: home rule could never succeed, for the simple reason that it was based on a fundamental error. The home rulers suffered from a delusion that was almost pathological in its complete separation from reality: they acted as though they represented everyone in Ireland and all the Irish shared their vision; but—to use a line from the 1916 rebel, Patrick Pearse: "The fools! The fools! The fools!"—that was not true. The Irish nationalists had forgotten the Protestants of Ulster and their old fears, their history of passionate dissent, their unity and determination and their profound sectarian animosity. Or, if nationalists hadn't forgotten, they devalued the threat to home rule of northern Protestants as a numerous—900,000 strong—and mostly adverse group. As it had always been, Ulster was the problem. And the Protestants of Ulster were the nut of it (as they still are).

A little power or a lot; it didn't matter to the Protestants. They saw the way things were going—one thing would lead to another. They did not want home rule, whose doctrine and legislative form through three parliamentary bills made no particular mention at all of them and their undeniably special position in Ireland. They were a kind of "distinct society," and they thought that surely they needed protection after independence in a Catholic country with its precedents of rebellion, massacre, and expulsion. Home rule would be Rome rule by another name. The Prods more and more often made the claim that they weren't even Irish; they certainly wanted to maintain the union and to stay with Britain. Parnell might have been a fellow-Protestant, but he was one of the old, jumped-up southern Ascendancy types with his Big House and languid certainties. His exotic "Englishness" of character and demeanour might have created a kind of charisma that impressed Catholics, but it meant nothing to the Anglican, and especially the Presbyterian, small farmers and workers of the industrialized north. They didn't see that Parnell had much in common with themselves at all. He was just another bollocksey, Taig-loving, traitorous Protestant, a Lundy for his time.

The creation of real Ulster Protestant solidarity began in 1886, when the first home rule bill was introduced; it was complete by 1914, when the third bill was due to become law. That unity would stand rock hard for sixty years, adamant, cutting through the old lines of class or sect and uniting workers, landowners, and tycoons, Presbyterians and Anglicans. The Protestants followed the ancient human imperative: their internal amity increased in proportion to external enmity and threat. They forgot their old divisions, trifling now in the face of resurgent Catholics. Liberals became instant Conservatives. The Orange Order and the Apprentice Boys clubs were invigorated and gentrified as the landlords and other members of the middle class joined up.

Two other ominous elements of Protestant resistance surfaced. First, there was discussion of using armed force. The Orange Order was a ready-made scaffold of a private army, and advertisements appeared looking for weapons and army veterans to teach the necessary skills. The Belfast riots of 1886 protesting home rule were the worst the city had ever seen (which is saying something). They began almost inconsequentially in the shipyards, the story goes, when a Catholic worker told a Protestant that the days of the Prod ascendancy were numbered. But they spread to the point that civil war was barely avoided, and Unionist leaders saw the formation of a paramilitary army as a means of controlling and channelling mob violence as well as of threatening the government.

The second portent of things to come was talk of partition of Ireland. This idea wasn't new. The obvious and dramatic distinctness of Ulster from the south made partition an unsurprising suggestion. Thomas Macaulay, the instigator of the Derry siege myth, had recognized its logic as early as 1833. If the Irish needed a legislature in Dublin to deal with domestic problems, as the Catholic "Liberator," Daniel O'Connell, demanded, then the radically different north needed one in Derry for the Protestants just as much. In 1886, the complete rupture over home rule encouraged the same reasoning. Because of the differences in the north in "race, religion and politics," said the English unionist, Joseph Chamberlain, then surely "there could be conceded to Ulster a separate assembly."

It's not just historical hindsight to be astonished at the self-absorption of the home rulers, their easy, dismissive assumption that the Ulster Protestants would either acquiesce in the nationalist agenda or be intimidated into accepting it because of its near unanimous support by Catholics and a few southern Protestants. The home rulers really were obtuse or naive, or both. When they thought of Ulster Protestants at all, the nationalists believed that their own moderate concept of a sense of national identity that included both Irish nationalism and British patriotism would encompass the northerners enough to reassure them. The home rulers foresaw a new "union of hearts" that would reconcile both Ulster and Britain to the Irish nation. It was a nice idea, but it didn't account for the unalterable state of things on the ground in Ulster, the way that the two religions lived there, in their tense, jumbled Plantation laagers, with the heavy weight on them of violent sectarian history.

The home rulers' lack of understanding of the north also underscored again the very separateness they minimized or believed they could overcome. In the 1830s, when Daniel O'Connell had wanted to travel to the north—something he rarely did—to organize northern Catholics for his emancipation campaign, Orangemen mustered by the thousands to repel him and his party. They viewed O'Connell's visit as an incursion into their territory. The Protestants of the relatively prosperous, industrializing north feared that the Catholic parliament O'Connell wanted would threaten their wealth and, as always, that Catholic enablement could occur only through their own diminution. The border between Protestant "north" and Catholic "south" had a de facto existence that had been recognized as such since the Plantation, long before partition formalized it in the twentieth century.

That sense of separateness had only increased and consolidated itself since O'Connell's time. The moderate Irish constitutional nationalists never understood the extent of Ulster Protestant bloody-minded alienation because the Prods were anything but moderate. The physical-force revolutionary separatists—the Fenians and the men of the 1916 Rising—had a much clearer sense of things in the north. Protestant intransigence was comprehensible to them because both they and the unionists had decided to fight rather than to compromise to achieve the one thing they desired: independence or union. It's so often the case that the extremists on each side of a bitter battle comprehend each other—like calling to like—as if the ends of the spectrum they represent curl back and wind up side by side in murderous, yet fathomable, proximity. For the Protestants, there wasn't much to choose between the frivolous misconceptions of the Irish constitutionalists and the hostility of the separatists.

The constant whisper of violence was another thing that made northern Protestants suspicious of Parnell, the way he was often reluctant to quite dissociate himself from the boys and took advantage of their unruliness. If English attention to the Irish question faltered, the thrum of murder and maiming in the country coincidentally rose. The English refocused, and Parnell was able to do more business with them—at least for so long as the Irish Party held the balance of power in Westminster minority governments. Later, Parnell distanced himself more from the hard men, especially when savage crime went too far. He had no hesitation in denouncing the Phoenix Park murders. A Fenian fringe group calling itself the Invincibles assassinated the new chief secretary and undersecretary just arrived in Dublin from England, carving them up with surgical knives in a display of redundant barbarism. The murders emphasized that even a "peaceful" Ireland was not peaceful in the usual sense of the word; it was a relative term.

If the unionists in contemporary Northern Ireland refused to deal with the nationalist political party, Sinn Féin, it's because they saw IRA guns behind it. It was the same in Parnell's time and into the 1890s and the early 1900s. In the background of the so-called politics as usual of the Irish Parliamentary Party, Protestants saw the old beast: turbulent Taigs, many of whom in Ulster still believed that Prods were settlers on stolen land and that they had no right to remain there.

The Ulster Protestants needed some comfort, and they did one of the things that a people that perceives itself in jeopardy always does: they plunged back in time, into the chaos and multiplicity of history, to draw out the clear and simple things they required to help them in their present trouble. They needed a mythology for the moment. The "Glorious Twelfth" (the anniversary of the Battle of the Boyne) celebrations became much bigger and gaudier—aided by greatly increased membership in the Orange Lodge and, as with the Derry siege commemorations, the railway, which could ship in outsiders to augment local parades. "Remember 1690" became a wall grafitto whose real purpose was to remind Protestants of their contemporary jeopardy. Protestant memories of the Rising of 1641 were also resuscitated by their perception of new danger and by the attention paid to the seventeenth-century massacres in the widely read book *The English in Ireland* by the English historian J.A. Froude. His book did for 1641 what Macaulay's had for the siege of Derry.

And, above all, Protestants reached back for the siege myth itself, which was already close to fully formed, tried and true. It was their real symbol of cohesion and their hope of deliverance. They believed they had been in this hard place of abandonment and isolation before and, by their tenacious courage, had won through. That was the harsh yet hopeful lesson of 1689.

The centenary of the siege had included Catholics and had emphasized the constitutional victories of the Glorious Revolution. But there was no question of inviting any Catholics to join in the bicentenary celebrations of 1888 and 1889. The Bishop of Derry confirmed Protestant unity: "We must aim at the union of Presbyterians and Church-people [Anglicans] for our common preservation from a yoke [Catholicism] which we are at one in detesting." The relief of the city of Derry itself became less important than the celebration of this drawing together of the Protestant nation of Ulster. It was celebrated in Belfast, Larne, and Coleraine as fervently as in Derry.

The Protestants of Ulster needed something else to complete their seminal siege myth: the Traitor. Robert was drawn back into the scheme of memorial. "Lundy" had long meant compromiser or turncoat. During the home rule period, it acquired another more specific meaning as a term of abuse for Protestant home rulers. The annual burning of Robert's effigy was "a warning to nominal Protestants who would presume to trifle with the dearest interests of their fellow-men."

The mosaic of sectarian settlement that the Plantation of Ulster created had never changed. To survive in such uncertain and hostile conditions, the Protestants always had to be able to count on the loyalty of other Protestants. They had to test the mettle of everyone within the Plantation: of the Irish themselves to sniff out rebellion; but, more important, of their fellow Prods, to head off the insidious change that seemed to happen to everyone who settled in this odd country. It was the seductive process of hibernicization, of becoming like the Irish, and therefore untrustworthy. Ulster was never a place the Prods could relax in—not for a moment. The split between Presbyterians and Anglicans was an enormous complication in the Protestant quest for comfort, as was the presence of the Scots in large numbers. Only the overwhelming press of events in the nineteenth century—the mobilization of Catholic political power, Fenian violence, and, above all, the home rule movement—overcame these long-standing deterrents to the unity of the Protestant tribe.

19

FINN AGAIN AWAKE

NORTHERN PROTESTANTS felt even more estranged from the rest of the country when Ireland's old Gaelic culture made a reappearance. The so-called Gaelic Revival was not spontaneous, of course. It was a self-conscious attempt by nationalists to resuscitate a few of its parts for the revivalists' present needs, a sure sign that a displaced culture is essentially moribund. There was no chance of bringing back the whole apparatus of the "Gaelic way of life." It had been intractable but not indestructible, and its main components were long gone: the Brehon laws; the land system of *tuaths;* the quasi-feudal knot of fosterage, kinship, and fealty; taxation in kind rather than money; the ritualized warrior violence (although, arguably, the latter had only evolved into different forms). Most important, what had disappeared was the underlying idea of Gaelic life, its temporary contractual nature, its fluidity—which the English interpreted as anarchy—that allowed each generation to redefine the fundamental relationships of power and property. For example, a chief didn't necessarily inherit his land; rather, it was assigned through election by his extended family. These things were seen as temporary, flowing through the generations like streams, evanescent as life. All that was over with.

But the Irish nationalists of the late nineteenth and early twentieth centuries, with the scent of independence in their nostrils, naturally looked back to the last time Ireland was truly on its own, when *sinn féin*—"ourselves"—still applied. In attempting to revive the Gaelic past, the nationalists could try to salvage only some things—

the old games, the literature, the beautiful, dying language—none of which mattered to most of the Protestants of Ulster. In each case, culture quickly became radical politics.

The Gaelic Athletic Association was founded in 1884, when Parnell was in his heyday, with the goal of doing away with crooked (because they were associated with gambling), exclusivist, profane (because they were English) games like cricket and rugby and replacing them in the people's affections with Gaelic football and hurling (which resembles extremely violent field hockey). Fenians took over the association almost from the beginning. The hurley stick became a radical nationalist symbol, and carrying one was made a criminal offence. At Parnell's funeral, hundreds of young men marched in formation packing illegal sticks. The Fenians thought that Gaelic sports would foster among young Irishmen a sense of militant manhood and a willingness to fight the English. The old Irish games were an Everyman's symbol of the old Irish nation. They still are in Northern Ireland, where sports are one of the markers of who's who and whether you are, in fact, Irish, or something else: Gaelic football grounds on the Falls Road; cricket pitches in Bangor.

Sports were important, but language was much more so. The Gaelic League was founded in 1893 by Douglas Hyde. He was a southern Protestant, and so were many of the league's early members. They were well off and could indulge their antiquarian interests in the old language. Devout Protestants could use it to proselytize among Catholic peasants. Most of all, however, speaking Gaelic was a way for southern Protestants to claim they were Irish without the necessity of being Catholic; perhaps they could circumvent the main criterion for membership in the Irish nation and substitute something else. In the long run, this scheme wouldn't work. The league was supposed to be a nonpolitical organization, and it remained so for some of its members disillusioned by the sordid collapse of Parnell's politics. Its general aim was the "Irishing of Ireland," the cultural purification of the country through "de-Anglicization." Above all, that meant reviving the old language, now disappearing faster than ever, even in its last bastions in the west of Ireland.

The attempt at a cultural revolution in Ireland attracted what Lenin said of all revolutions: so many adolescent minds. Some odd suggestions were made: that Irish was really a Catholic language and that English was Protestant—or worse, maybe not even Christian at all. Therefore English literature itself, said the more extreme self-appointed cultural commissars, was non-Catholic, even anti-Catholic. Anglo-Irish culture and tradition is a "mongrel upstart," said the *Catholic Bulletin*. "The Irish nation is de facto a Catholic nation," wrote the influential journalist D.P. Moran. Speaking English has "diseased" the "public mind," he said, and Anglicization has "enfeebled" the "national body." He described the revered Wolfe Tone as a Frenchman (because of his French revolutionary ideas) born in Ireland of English parents (they were Irish Protestants). If the father of Irish nationalism wasn't really Irish, what chance did an Ulster Protestant unionist have?

In part, these examples of cultural revivalism are the usual fear of the modern that all traditionalists display. But they are also the foreshadowings of the later puritanism and fundamentalism of the Republic of Ireland, with its strict Catholicism, long-lived laws against contraception and divorce, its index of banned books—one of the longest in the world along with those of the Bolshevik Soviet Union and the People's Republic of China—all enforced, as one scholar put it, by the "mullahs of the triumphalist church."

However, all emerging European nations of the time had to decide what constituted their own nationality, and the Irish needed to define Irishness, its ethnic and national characteristics. In other words, they had to create a mythology that would give purpose and direction to their political campaign. How the Catholic Irish chose to define themselves would be completely distinct from and, in fact, antithetical to the myth that the Protestants of Ulster were building simultaneously. The two peoples contended on the ground of Ireland, but also in their evolving ideas of who and what they were. Independent Ireland became a conservative Gaelic and Catholic state that was oblivious to the irony of its adamant territorial claim to jurisdiction over a million non-Catholic, non-Gaelic people in Ulster. This policy would confirm the worst fears of the Ulster Protestants and further estrange the south and the north. Neither side's political myth was prone to compromise.

The Gaelic-speaking area—the *Gaeltacht*—had mostly contracted to the west of Ireland, so the Gaelic League's urban, middle-class members idealized and sanitized it as "the West;" they ignored its mean poverty and overlooked the desire of many of its inhabitants to get out through immigration as soon as they could. Instead, the West became a "cultural homeland" where the old virtuous Gaelic life persisted. One of the league's typically dour, earnest members was Patrick Pearse, the future funeral orator and sacrificial rebel, for whom a trip west was like a pilgrimage to the racially pure remnant of the old Irish nation.

All of which was fuel for the mythological fire, but nonsense. The Irish, like virtually everyone else in Europe, had long ago lost any claims to racial purity. In fact, the country's long, turbulent history of invasion, settlement, immigration, and forced population movement had mongrelized it more than most. Assimilation had been the pattern, rather than extermination, separation, or expulsion—the sectarian apartheid of Plantation Ulster the exception once again. Becoming "more Irish than the Irish" implied mixing up the genetic pool. And the supposedly pure West of Ireland was as "racially" complicated as Dublin or Armagh. There was no such thing as a "Celtic race" or a "Gaelic race." It is a "hackneyed myth," said George Bernard Shaw. "We are a parcel of mongrels: Spanish, Scottish, Welsh, English, and even a Jew or two." But Ireland's assimilative capacity was prodigious. It lay in its very air, which, Shaw said—with his mandatory passive-aggressive dig at England—the English should be compelled to breathe "just to make their minds flexible."

The supposedly quintessential part of the West was the remote Aran Islands off the mouth of Galway Bay. Yet studies of blood group ratios (in pre-DNA times) show that their inhabitants owe a good part of their genetic inheritance to the worst possible polluting source: soldiers of Cromwell's hated army who had been recruited from the English fenlands. Some of these veterans fought on the isolated, but strategically important, islands (they dominate the entrance to Galway Bay) and settled there after the war. They were absorbed completely, but old Gaels they were not. Scots-descended Presbyterians of William's Portaferry or of the Antrim coast near Billy's Carrickfergus may well be less "adulterated" than the Irish of Aran.

The West became a literary trope, too. Yeats and the playwright J.M. Synge, for example, found inspiration for a new literature there, the poet appropriating the ancient Gaelic mystical traditions and beliefs for his occult spirituality; the playwright finding a new kind of language through the transliteration into English of Gaelic syntax and idiom, and its sheer verbose eloquence. The burghers of Dublin rioted in outrage at Synge's idealized version of Irishness in *The Playboy of the Western World*. They had no objection in principle; they just thought that some of the play's lines were insults to their own idealized version of Irish womanhood. The trigger, as Lady Gregory noted in her telegram to Yeats ordering him back from Scotland, was one word: "shift," as in "it's Pegeen I'm seeking only, and what'd I care if you brought me a drift of chosen females, standing in their shifts itself maybe." We begin to understand why a divorce action ended Parnell's career. It was all hypocrisy, of course. A young doctor who was at the theatre during the riot told Synge that he could hardly restrain himself from standing up on a chair and pointing out all the rioters he had treated for venereal disease.

The riot was one highlight of a long campaign by purists and idealizing patriots to stop people from going to see "dirty" or English (which usually amounted to the same thing) plays and musicals. Synge, a self-confident writer, responded, with the traditional viciousness of public debate in Dublin—although it was gleeful, too, and full of the *craic*—that between Irish peasants and Irish men of genius, there always stood "an ungodly ruck of fat faced, sweaty headed swine."

If Synge found the new words he needed in the Aran Islands of the West, James Joyce might have received unexpected inspiration, if he had sought it, in the north. Ulster speech in English was, if anything, closer to the Gaelic in its admixture of words and syntax than the English spoken by the Irish elsewhere in the country. Perhaps its amalgam of Gael, Scot, and Planter had produced something just as authentic as the Aran Islands, but even richer and more resonant of the old language. Joyce could well have copied down something like this example from the 1930s and stuck it wholesale into *Ulysses* or even *Finnegans Wake:* "'Ere yesterday at dayligone he begood to the banterin' and starts junderin' our Jamie and him on his hunkers at the bing there, walin' a wheen o' clarty pritas" (Day before yesterday at dusk he began bantering and started pushing our James while he was squatting at the pit there, sorting a lot of muddy potatoes). No way of telling whether it was a Prod or a Taig speaking the words; both would sound the same. One thing it was not was English, in any sense related to the language of the Britain that the Ulster Protestants clung to in fear and hope.

The seductive, nostalgic image of the West persisted. Even the Carrickfergus Protestant Louis MacNeice, who suffered the dual alienation of his northern Irish origin and his intellectual nomadism, regretted his unrealizable sense of home and belonging in the West. MacNeice's parents had come from the West of Ireland, and they had impressed their son with their abhorrence of its neglect and decline after independence under the Free State government. It made the poet think about Ulster. If this was how Dublin treated the cradle of Irishness, what would it do in a suddenly united Ireland with a million alienated unionists whose very existence it treated as anathema? MacNeice always stood at a slight angle to Northern Ireland and to Belfast, "devout and profane and hard." But he has harsher judgments to call down on the new Catholic state, which is "a gallery of false tapestries."

The southern Ascendancy Protestants were trapped. They had almost nothing in common with their co-religionists in Ulster—that "horrid lot" again—but they were marginalized by the Catholics from whose own middle class they were barely distinguishable. Protestants in the south played a large, enthusiastic, and bitterly ironic part in the proceedings of the Gaelic Revival: enthusiastic, because they sought the belonging that speaking the old language might bring them; bitter, because none of it mattered to the increasingly chauvinistic Catholic revivalists. A Prod who might have fried his brain to learn Gaelic was still non-Irish. In a way, the Catholics were just giving the Ascendancy some payback for all its condescension towards the "priest-ridden" Irish in their bogs and coops. "Irish" meant Catholic; it was a sectarian definition. It wasn't a conscious plan, but once the Anglo-Irish Protestants had served their purpose, nationalists consigned them to political and confessional irrelevance in a puritanically Catholic Ireland. The event was prefigured in the Gaelic League: its first president was the nonviolent Protestant Hyde; his successor was the violent Catholic rebel, Pearse. Like the Athletic Association, the league eventually became another Fenian organization whose members were prominent in the Rising of 1916. The breaking down of the Protestant Ascendancy had, of course, been going on for some time. Yeats, for instance, was born in 1865 and, even by then, five of the twelve judges of the Irish Supreme Court were Catholic, as was half the top management of the banks and the entire administration of the three big Irish railway lines.

Yeats struggled all his life with the conundrum of the Anglo-Irish in Ireland.

> Out of Ireland have we come.
> Great hatred, little room,
> Maimed us at the start.
> I carry from my mother's womb
> A fanatic heart.

Yet his family had once been English and, most of all, there was the language and its writers: "I owe my soul to Shakespeare, to Spenser and to Blake, perhaps to William Morris, and to the English language in which I think, speak and write . . . everything I love has come to me through English; my hatred tortures me with love, my love with hate."

When Yeats was in England (he spent a good part of his life there), the English thought of him as Irish and nothing else—although some of them would later claim him as an English poet when he became Nobel Prize famous. However, he thought of himself as Irish and nothing else. He added his considerable heft to the nationalist movement, trying hard, perhaps, to compensate for his increasingly peripheral status as a Protestant. Yet he knew all along—with increasing emphasis after Ireland's more or less independence—that to many in Ireland he wasn't really Irish at all. The Free State government made Yeats and a few other Protestants senators in 1922. But they were token Prods, and their six-year terms were not renewed.

James Joyce resolved his anguished sense of disarray and displacement by leaving Ireland. Only in exile could he effect some sort of personal reconciliation, and, even then, only through an obsessive retelling of the story of the country and city he had fled; he could never stop. It began with *A Portrait of the Artist as a Young Man*. Stephen Dedalus, facing his director of studies, an Englishman, realizes with shocking force his colonial alienation, which is implicit once again in the form of words:

> The language we are speaking is his before it is mine. How different are the words *home, Christ, ale, master,* on his lips and on mine! I cannot speak or write these words without unrest of spirit. His language, so familiar and so foreign, will always be for me an acquired speech. I have not made or accepted its words. My voice holds them at bay. My soul frets in the shadow of his language.

Joyce wrote about Ireland in the most fundamental way. In a letter written later in his life, he said: "The problem of my race is so complicated that one needs to make use of all the means of an elastic art to delineate it." Thus *Finnegans Wake*—perhaps "Finn again awake"—Finn being the legendary Gaelic warrior-seer, Finn MacCool (in Gaelic, Fionn mac Cumhaill), hero of the Fenian Cycle, courageous and generous, the paragon of pagan Irish nobility. And *Ulysses* is the key text of Ireland's independence. One critic writes that the book redefines "the issues at stake in imagining an Irish identity" and "sense of nationhood."

However, Joyce understood the ambivalence of cultural purification. In *Stephen Hero,* he describes a professor who never stops trying to prove that Shakespeare was a Catholic. It's a comic scene but poignant, too. The obsessed academic has to try to reconcile the great English poet he loves with the imperatives of exorcising Ireland of Englishness and Protestantism.*

Samuel Beckett got out of Ireland, too. He was a Dublin County Protestant whose alienation from the country seemed complete. He

---

* Ironically, recent scholarship suggests that Shakespeare's mother, father, and daughter were secret Catholics—to be a priest was a capital offence in England when Will was a young man—and that the poet himself remained attached, at some level, to the old church. Perhaps the theatre was, for Shakespeare, in part a secular substitute for the ceremony and ritual that Protestantism abhorred— "Bare ruined choirs, where late the sweet birds sang."

left and tried to settle in England, but that was intolerable for him. The English treated him like a paddy, and he even hated buying a newspaper because the few required words made a mick out of him to the Englishman he was buying it from. He had no patience at all with Irish nationalism or the Gaelic revival. What did it mean to him, the Prod from Foxrock? The protagonist of some of his early stories says that home is "nowhere so far as I can see."

Beckett decided on France. He chose to write in French to free himself from the fatal Irish combination of wit and blarney; he wanted to purge himself of Irishness and, certainly, of "Oirishness." He may also have made the choice for esthetic reasons: to write "without style"—that is, the style of Milton, Coleridge or Keats. He could strip things down, pursue "lessness" although that might have taken a while: some critics have noted the "bawdy, exuberant" French of his early work. At first, he wrote in French like an Irishman. However, the new language also allowed him to use his Irish material but to avoid exploiting it, the eternal problem of Irish writers writing in English.

Later in Beckett's life, when he was asked the stock question—why the small country of Ireland had turned out so many writers—his response was angry as well as characteristically sardonic. "When you are in the last ditch, there is nothing left but to sing." The phrase "the last ditch" is first attributed to William of Orange; he vowed to fight to the death there. Beckett concluded: "It's the English Government and the Catholic Church—they have buggered us into existence."

Beckett was a lifelong friend of Ireland-obsessed Joyce. He kept his Irish passport and his accent. As an Irish Protestant, he had a head-start on estrangement and detachment; he was a natural out-sider. Was he Irish? No one could improve on Beckett's own jokey, ambiguous analysis. When an interviewer asked him: "Vous êtes anglais, Monsieur Beckett?" his famous reply was, "Au contraire."

As for Yeats, he could negotiate no truce in the war in his heart. He remained half in, half out of the enemy camp, an anguished Irish nationalist who, while loving English, hated what England had done. If literature and revolution can ever join together, they did so in Yeats's writing. In his 1902 play, *Cathleen ní Houlihan,* the with-ered old woman—another version of the *Shan Van Vocht*—will become a luminous queen only if young men come forward to kill for her and, more important, to die for her. The time is the Ninety-Eight, the Year of the French, for Yeats just a little over a hundred years earlier when, as it seemed to him, the Irish had come so close to becoming a nation once again. *Cathleen* was Ireland sovereign, free, and not English. To the rebels of 1916, the play was a sort of sacrament. When the Easter Rising took place and young men killed, and died, for Ireland, the play seemed more than ever to have been a prophecy.

Later, Yeats, self-dramatically, wonders: "Did that play of mine send out / Certain men the English shot?" The contemporary Irish poet Paul Muldoon reverses the question: "If Yeats had saved his pencil lead / Would certain men have stayed in bed?" Who knows? The speeches over Fenian graves by the hard man, Patrick Pearse, might have been more inspirational for rebels than anything written by the effete Anglo poet. But *Cathleen* certainly helped put them in a frame of mind that, among other things, made them willing to go out and be shot.

Yeats himself did not take to the streets with a rifle. He joined the Irish Republican Brotherhood only to try to please the radical Maud Gonne, whom he loved unrequitedly and to whom he proposed marriage. (She played the title role in *Cathleen ní Houlihan*.) But he could never become a revolutionary—he was incapable of discarding complexity and of embracing simplicity, "the purity of heart that is to hate one thing." That's what it takes to be a rebel under arms—or, depending on one's perspective, a terrorist. Or, perhaps, Yeats was simply never driven to that extreme—as William had been, the devout minister's faith in a beneficent God and the enlightened scholar's understanding of the intricacies of life overwhelmed by frustration and rage.

20

INTIMATE ENEMIES

THE IRISH NATIONALIST attempt to recover the Irish past, or parts of it, was an effort common to all nationalist movements, and a necessary one. If Ireland became a cultural nation once again—alive with the language, the old songs and poetry, the people's sense of themselves as Gaelic and Catholic and distinct from the Protestant English—then it could be, must be, a political nation, too. The recreation of the country in the imagination had to precede its actual recovery from its occupiers and colonists. In a sense, all nations are "imagined communities."

However, nationalists could only do so much. The Gaelic revivalists thought that getting back the old language was the most important thing. They were right, but they didn't understand that, even if they were successful, the recovery of Gaelic would not take them very far. The ancient language of a people, the speech that accompanied their shadowy beginning long in the past when the human brain and voice box evolved to allow speech to happen, is the expression of the people's essence. They see the world, name the things in it, and think about them through the language; its structure determines what world the people see and think they understand about it. Once a break is made with such a language—once the Irish gave up Gaelic—nothing could be the same again. Such a disruption is like a fall from grace, an expulsion from the garden; everything afterwards is different, diminished, compromised, tainted. And it is a permanent new condition.

It hardly matters that Irish nationalism was provincial and racist; all new nationalisms have been accused of that, and most were. But the ideology and rhetoric of a people looking to emancipate itself from a foreign dominating power must simplify the battle to a certain extent. The colonial power's relationship with its colony may be based largely on military strength and vigilance, but, more often, the connection is complicated and takes place on many interlocking levels, and these, rather than soldiers, are the basis for maintaining control. Achieving independence requires the colony to separate itself from what the Indian scholar Ashis Nandy calls "the intimate enemy." The problem was even more acute for Ireland because it was not a typical British colony—although theorists of colonialism and post-colonialism have lumped Ireland in with all the rest in a distorting Procrustean analysis. Colonies such as Kenya, India, and Egypt were each composed of a colonized people who may not have been homogeneous—there were tribal, linguistic, religious, or ethnic differences—but who were, nevertheless, clearly distinct from the colonizers, the British imperial overlords. The relationship was essentially an adverse one. For purposes of standing against the imperial rulers, there was no dispute in Egypt or India about just who was Egyptian or Indian.

Ireland was different: England's first overseas possession, close by, long held, and, above all, invaded and reinvaded, settled and resettled over and over again. Many of its inhabitants had come, long ago or recently, from the imperial centre. The Catholic Old English, the Protestant New English who became the Ascendancy, the Dissenter Protestants of Ulster, the Scots who saw the north of Ireland as a continuation of Scotland separated by a few kilometres of sea—all these people were in Ireland, and most of them had been for centuries. But were they, *could* they be, Irish in the same way that the "native" Catholic Irish were?

Anyway, the Irish, like those other Celts *manqués,* the Scots and the Welsh, began right away to participate in the British imperial enterprise. Some Irish might dismiss the empire, in Joyce's words, as "beer, beef, business, bibles, bulldogs, battleships, buggery and bishops," but they were complicit in its creation, even if their own country had been its first acquisition. It was difficult for an Indian or an African nationalist to identify with the Irish as fellow oppressed colonials when the man gunning down his demonstrating country-men, administering his imperial department, or lording it over dark skins with his Celtic pale skin was from Dublin or Kerry.

The small Caribbean island of Montserrat was the early demon-stration of the Irish as imperialists. Through the proverbial vagaries of history, it was the only part of the first British Empire (which ended with American independence) to have been settled and administered almost entirely by Irish people. The settlers arrived first in the early 1630s; they were direct migrants from Munster, refugees from other Caribbean island enterprises, and Catholics who had been kicked out of the Virginia colony by the fundamen-talist Protestants of the day. Throughout the seventeenth and eigh-teenth centuries, the Irish of Montserrat behaved just like their English (or French or Dutch) co-imperialists: they were swinish slave owners and enthusiastic advocates of Amerindian extermina-tion. They exhibited the same morbid symptoms of any people cor-rupted by the ludicrous and superficial idea that they are superior because of their skin colour and their temporary ascendance over others—the result of accident or bloody-mindedness, but certainly not greater ability or virtue. Today, the island's tourist industry has jumped on the Irish immigrant heritage bandwagon by exploiting Montserrat's Irish origins and by claiming that the Irish were "nice" slave owners—because they were Irish; and the Irish, treated like slaves at home, could only be nice to their slaves on Montserrat.

The English struggle to govern Ireland may never have been completed. One writer has called it "Britain's longest counterinsur-gency campaign." But it was a struggle in which Irishmen—or, rather, men born in Ireland and whose degree of Irishness was part of the problem—fought on both sides. It was not so much a matter of counterinsurgency as an 800-year-long civil war. After all, it began with Strongbow, the twelfth-century Englishman, or Norman, who was invited to Ireland by an Irish king to help him fight against another Irish king. The tradition of Irishmen fighting Irishmen was long established even then, and it has never fallen away. It carries on in Northern Ireland.

The questions arose again and again, and in Belfast or Armagh, they still do: Who is Irish? What is Irishness? In Joyce's *Ulysses*, Leopold Bloom haltingly defines "nation" to include the Irish at home but also the Irish nation worldwide, the diaspora of famine, want, and persecution: "A nation is the same people living in the same place . . . Or also living in different places," he says. But what is the "same people?" When the rabid nationalist "citizen," the ranter of the standard received version of Irish history, asks Bloom what is his nation, the bemused protagonist replies: "Ireland . . . I was born here. Ireland." The citizen says nothing, Joyce writes, only hawks the spit out of his gullet and gobs it.

Bloom speaks for Joyce, for whom the Gaelic revival was not the real world but "the land of faery" (admittedly a phrase—used by Chaucer to describe King Arthur's kingdom—he quoted in a university lecture when he was seventeen, but he never really changed his mind). However, neither spoke for the Fenians or the men of 1916; nor for the Catholic small farmers of Cork or Sligo recently empowered by the *Land Acts;* nor the slum-living workers or, more likely, the unemployed of north-side Dublin; nor for the government of the intolerant, repressive, insular, Catholic, nominally Gaelic Free State when it had formed itself. The Protestants of Ulster had been born in Ireland (what could be more Irish than Cúchulainn's Ulster?), but were they Irish? If the Protestants persisted in answering the question themselves, maintaining they were not Irish but were really British, who could blame them when, in the south, Catholic ideologues had come to the same conclusion? Catholics criticized Protestants for claiming the term "Ulster" for the six of the ancient province's nine counties they viewed as their territory. But nationalists had already appropriated "Ireland" and "Irish" for themselves, and to the exclusion of Protestants. The two peoples' mutual rejection had divided Ireland long before the border was drawn.

In the mid-1980s, the southern Irish novelist Colm Tóibín walked the border between the Republic and Northern Ireland when the killing and bombing of the Troubles was intense and scary. He wrote a fascinating account of the modern version of the centuries-old sectarian warfare in the borderlands. Neighbours were killing each other for politics or land or as another instalment of payback for the old grievances; Catholic and Protestant gunmen and the British Army were absorbed in their traditional three-way combat.

But then he writes this. He is staying in a bed-and-breakfast in the North in which the other guests are all Protestants. He is a charming, unbiased man, and he is able to have an amiable enough conversation with them except that, at the end of the evening, he mentions the Pope. This word is one of the many wrong things to say in the presence of Protestants in Northern Ireland during these times, but he can be forgiven for his southern amiable insouciance. Then, in the morning, he notices in the guest book that one of the Protestant couples he spoke to signed themselves in the "nationality" column as "British." He's aware that the Prods claim to be British rather than Irish, but he is amazed that they would state it so baldly and unequivocally. They are from Omagh in County Tyrone, the middle of Ireland; they speak with Omagh accents. How can they be British? He signs himself "Irish," he says. As a rebuke? How else would he identify himself? Later that day, he comes to a belated awareness: yes, this is Northern Ireland; these Protestant people are different, or they're convinced they are. He gives himself a mental kick, he says, for mentioning the Pope, and another—yet only of the same footish magnitude—for being surprised that the demonstrably Irish couple would sign themselves "British."

Nevertheless, Tóibín's reaction is a sign. His confusion would be understandable in a North American or a European, but in an Irishman from the south, it seems almost like a later version—although a kinder, more benevolent one—of the negligent disregard towards Ulster Protestants of Parnell and the home rulers or the Gaelic League zealots. One of the reasons the border is there in the first place, and the Northern Irish have been killing each other, is that most of the Prods deny they're Irish and claim to be British. The Northern Catholics know themselves to be Irish while agreeing with the Prods that they (the Prods) aren't really Irish and may well, indeed, be British—in which case, what the hell are they doing in Ireland? On the little island, Tóibín's own home a few hours' drive away from the border, and after sixteen years (by then) of slaughter and thousands of dead and wounded in the northern green field of his sorrowful, partitioned country, it's odd, and somehow depressing, that he can be puzzled—even for a few hours—by the word "British" in a B-and-B guest book.

Or maybe it doesn't matter. Tóibín's surprise may be just the reaction of a foreigner in Northern Ireland and more proof that Ireland is two countries and two peoples, not one, and has been for a long time. However, that conclusion immediately oversimplifies. If Northern Ireland could be considered a separate Protestant state, it is one with a large Catholic minority that doesn't want to belong to it and doesn't recognize the legitimacy of its existence. That is the notorious problem of the "double minority": of Catholics in the North, of Ulster Protestants in all Ireland. Each is disaffected from one of the two political entities, and each is willing to go to war for its cause. The similarity of the people on each side—same colour, the same mix of DNA by now—only makes their hatreds more intense. Freud calls this the "narcissism of small difference." Nationalism is most ferocious where the peoples involved most closely resemble each other—Omagh, Ulster, the Balkans, Cyprus, any civil war, anywhere brothers kill brothers.

Growing up a poor proddy boy in the Irish Quarter in Carrickfergus, my grandfather Billy must have known little, and cared less, about the recovery of Gaelic, the corrupt effects of cricket or football, the home rule campaign, the legacy of Parnell the king after his fall and death. When Billy was eight years old, snot-nosed, kicking around the back alleys of Carrick, his aristocratic southern co-religionists Yeats and Lady Augusta Gregory (among others) established the Abbey Theatre in Dublin, a landmark of the cultural revival. Four years later, Yeats's play *Cathleen ní Houlihan* would open there, perhaps adding its impetus to the men of 1916. But Billy's eighth year also coincided with one of the always important commemorations of violence in Ireland: the centennial of the Insurrection of 1798.

It occurred at a crucial moment—although in the fraught calendar of Irish history, perhaps it would have been the same in almost any year. The 1916 Rising may not have been inspired mainly, as Yeats proposed, by the fall and death of Parnell but by the 1798 centenary. A Sinn Féin member recalled in 1923 that the commemoration was what began "all our modern efforts towards an ideal of independence."

The 1898 celebration served several purposes for the Catholic nationalists (which is to say, all but a handful of Catholics). It helped reunite the home rule Irish Parliamentary Party, which had fallen into lassitude and division after the death of Parnell and the failure of the second home rule bill in 1893—it was passed in Parliament but rejected by the House of Lords. The party had at first been hostile to the commemoration—it was a constitutional political party, not a band of kerns—but was forced by popular support to join the parade.

The centennial also encouraged the Irish Republican Brotherhood—the Fenians. They had become partly an open recreational, social group—it was fashionable, in a radical-chic way, to call yourself a Fenian. Nevertheless, the brotherhood also retained its role as the vanguard of the physical-force nationalists in the real tradition of the Ninety-Eight. The Fenians were the conduit through which the mythology of the great Insurrection flowed to the leaders of the Easter Rising and the Irish Republican Army of the war of independence and on to the debased, and later thuggish, Provisional IRA of the Troubles. In the meantime, however, almost all the Irish continued to support reform by peaceful and constitutional means; the Fenian gunmen were forced to remain on the periphery of the nationalist campaign.

The theme of blood-sacrifice was renewed, too. At the laying of the foundation stone for the Wexford 98 monument, the by then renowned author of the Catholic mythological version of the rebellion, Father Patrick Kavanagh, said: "The men whose memory we honour today, died for a persecuted creed as well as an oppressed country. . . . Their blood was not poured forth in vain. It made the earth which drank it ever sacred to freedom." He made no mention of Presbyterians or United Irishmen; they had been written out. Kavanagh's fairy tale of noble peasants, heroic priests, and Protestant beasts was supreme. It was a further foreshadowing of how the Catholic nationalist movement would ignore and trivialize Protestants, particularly those in the North.

In Ulster, needless to say, things were different: the Protestants wrote themselves out of 1798. Presbyterians had mostly carried out the insurrection there, but it was celebrated only by Catholics, in counties where not much had happened. In William's home county of Down, where the United Irishmen had died by the thousands, there was only one small celebratory club and no commemoration. In fact, Presbyterians in Down destroyed a memorial to their co-religionist, Betsy Gray, a rebel heroine. If they chose to remember 1798 at all, it was as a fight for religious equality or the elimination of the tithe, or for lower rents. They and the Anglicans were almost all one united bloc now, and those limited aims had long been achieved. A Presbyterian minister speaking at Ballynahinch— the site of the healing waters, William's arrest, and the bloody battle—said that if an inhabitant of the town in 1798 could stand in it now, he would see great change, "signs of industry and prosperity all around; he could see the descendants of the United men in thousands praising God for the union and wearing Orange sashes." Billy would have agreed with that, but we can imagine William's mocking, ironic response.

When they looked south, however, Ulster Protestants saw the same old thing: Catholic Irish so-called parliamentarians basking in the centennial afterglow of violent rebellion. They couldn't have it both ways. Either you were a peaceful political party or you were a Fenian war party. You had to make a choice. A hundred years later, the Protestants of Northern Ireland (and many politicians and commentators in the Republic of Ireland, for that matter) say the same things about Sinn Féin: it's the only substantial political party in Ireland—in all of Europe—with its own private army, the Provisional IRA. Protestants did remember some things about 1798 a century afterwards. In the July 12 celebration of the Battle of the Boyne, one Belfast neighbourhood put up an Orange arch with the words: "Scullabogue Barn Is Ever Green."

The persistence of the bigoted myths coughed up by Kavanagh and his Protestant equivalent, Sir Richard Musgrave (1798 as priest-led Catholic treachery, no Protestants need apply), was one of the reasons Northern Ireland broke down into war in 1969. On Sandy Row and in the Fountain, on the Falls Road and in the Bogside, the people were still infected with the old sickness. A twentieth-century vigorous Catholic civil rights initiative triggered the Protestants' reflexive mythology—and maybe a shadow of the old seventeenth-century fear, too.

When it came time to mark the bicentenary of 1798, the people of Northern Ireland had had thirty years—an entire generation—of killing and terror behind them. They were exhausted and wounded, and they needed from the Ninety-Eight something Hippocratic which, if it was not a healing balm, should at least do no harm. In 1998, the peace process needed to be nurtured or, at a minimum, not to be squelched by emotional memorializing before it had a chance. Perhaps because of that, northern Catholics held only a few events. More important, they didn't do what they had done before: hold a big parade down the Falls Road. (In 1948, thirty thousand Catholics had rallied there in an event that was used as a protest against unionist repression.) Only a few new murals appeared on Catholic walls. Perhaps it was the restraint of a people who saw that the grafitto was right, that their time was, indeed, and finally, coming. Seventeen ninety-eight had been the historical moment when "Ulster joined Ireland"; for Northern Catholics, the uprising was a precedent that implied it could happen again.

Protestants didn't exactly celebrate the occasion, but they did mark it. The Orange Order got involved. It had a complex relationship with 1798 which reflected the insurrection's real character as an Irish civil war. Orangemen played a large part in putting down the insurrection through enlistment with the government's yeomanry, but many of the order's current Presbyterian members are descendants of United Irishmen and rebels. The Orange Order held an exhibition at Comber, County Down. That was where the famous terror-and-massacre letter had been found which made the people of Derry, or some of them, decide on resistance in 1688. Perhaps the Orangemen were sending another cautionary message with their choice of location or trying to soothe the fears of their more recalcitrant members. Or, maybe, choosing Comber was another sign of reconciliation. Throughout the year there were genteel exhibitions in libraries, and both Protestant and Catholic local councils approved marking the occasion. The Ulster Heritage Museum Committee (which had close links to the Orange Order) organized a re-enactment of the Battle of Antrim. (This was the same sort of thing that the Derry Apprentice Boys' chief, Billy, wanted to do with the siege.) It was the thin edge of theme-park kitsch in the North. But it was also a welcome sign of the calm of peacetime, and much preferable to the fierce, intense, exotic concentrations of civil strife and dormant war. When an event becomes kitsch, it means that its real meaning has been leached away, and since, in Northern

Ireland, "real" usually means malevolent or sectarian, that's not a bad thing. Hokey is better than holy.

The government of the Republic of Ireland reinterpreted the meaning of the Ninety-Eight, too. Or perhaps we should say it spun and twisted it, although with a benign purpose. It made its commemoration statement: "The United Irishmen . . . imaginatively created a vision of a nonsectarian, democratic and inclusive politics, which would attract and sustain all Irish people in all their inherited complexities. . . . Firstly, we must discard the now discredited sectarian version of '98, which was merely a polemical, post-rebellious falsification. Secondly, we must stress the modernity of the United Irish project, its forward looking democratic dimension, and abandon the outdated agrarian or peasant interpretation."

What a rich and revealing statement this is! First, it's an overt acknowledgment that Ireland's history can, indeed must, be used selectively for present Irish purposes. It proposes doing away with one version of the political myth of 1798 and cobbling together a new one that is more useful, less abrasive, more politically correct, a unifying rather than a divisive mythology. Fair enough, because that's what happens to history, and this instance is in a good cause: to diminish sectarian animosity and to head off renewed killing. To do that, however, the Irish government must throw a few inconvenient facts down the old Orwellian memory hole. The "sectarian version of '98" was not "merely a polemical, post-rebellious falsification," nor has it been "discredited." There was never more than a tenuous accommodation across the sectarian lines between Presbyterians and Defenders during the great rebellion. Sectarian massacres happened—Scullabogue Barn, Wexford Bridge, Wexford Town. There was a terrible bloody Irish civil war in 1798 that had nothing to do with "inclusive politics." True, even if it takes more than a hundred years to do so, it's a good thing to abandon Father Patrick Kavanagh's sectarian "agrarian or peasant interpretation." But the Irish government substituted a new false claim for the old one. It butchered the past yet again to clean up and sanitize the butchery of '98.

And a hypothetical sceptical, war-weary Ulster Protestant reading the Irish government's 1798 commemoration mission statement might ask: What in the name of God took you so long? "All Irish

people in all their inherited complexities"? After eighty years of an
independent country and a partitioned bastard province, is this the
recognition, at last, that Protestants are an "Irish people," part of the
Irish nation? What else have they been all that time? They were
mostly happy to call themselves Irish—although not in quite the
same way as the native Catholics or the Ascendancy Protestants—
until they were finally alienated by the home rule campaign, the
Easter Rising, and Catholic exclusivist ideology. But the independent Free State government never acknowledged the northern
Prods as fellow countrymen (who, to be sure, were never less than
rancorous in return). The new Republic specifically denied the
official existence of Northern Ireland, the Protestant heartland
and homeland. The Republic's 1937 founding constitution claimed
all the island of Ireland as under its jurisdiction. Southern Ireland
was a haven for the gunmen who attacked the Northern Irish
statelet; the Unionist government was certainly repressive, but
IRA attacks and atrocities were not the way to make it less so. There
was no reaching out, no attempt to assuage the demographic and
political fears of the northern Protestants. In fact, the assumption of
the new Irish state's identity as a Catholic Gaelic nation-state
excluded even the Protestants in the south, including those who
had fought for it. They lost their political existence in the new
country and became marginal men and women. "How long, after
all, does it take to belong somewhere, without apology?" asked the
southern Protestant Elizabeth Bowen. "Surely 300 years is enough?"
Apparently, it was not.

When the Troubles became widespread in 1969, our hypothetical
Ulster Protestant might further observe—although not with dis-
passion—the Republic became once again a refuge for nationalist
gunmen. Southern Cabinet ministers (one of whom later became
taioseach) ran guns for the IRA. There were marches in support of
the northern Catholics—and, later, of the H-Block prisoners—the
burning of the British Embassy in Dublin, a culture of condemnation of the Ulster Protestants. Then as the violence went on and on,
the Republic began to scorn all the brutal and primitive Prods of
Ulster (and the Taigs, too). Then came the weariness, the washing
of the hands, the collective smirk, the "set-your-watch-back-300-
years" jokes, the "quack-quack" jibes at Ulster accents, the plague-on-

both-their-houses dismissal, the abdication of feeling for and association with their supposed countrymen. The Republic especially damned the Protestants whose sectarian government and bizarre "loyalty" to Britain had caused the explosion in the first place. No sympathy or understanding for these people whom history had driven to see themselves as both chosen and beleaguered. Now, after thirty years of killing, when the peace process is under way, the Irish government decides it's time to recognize the existence of the Ulster Protestants as part of the Irish nation. Better late than never, but damned late! Or so our hypothetical Ulster Prod might conclude.

Here's what 1798 really means: hope and its grim denial. In Brian Friel's *Translations,* the schoolmaster Hugh remembers:

> A spring morning. 1798. Going into battle. Do you remember, James? . . . Everything seemed to find definition that spring—a congruence, a miraculous matching of hope and past and present and possibility. Striding across the fresh, green land. The rhythms of perception heightened. The whole enterprise of consciousness accelerated. We were gods that morning, James.

The insurrection of the United Irishmen ended in a battle on Vinegar Hill, a bitter name and a bitter end. It was "the fatal conclave," writes Seamus Heaney. "Terraced thousands died, shaking scythes at cannon. / The hillside blushed, soaked in our broken wave."

The year after the centenary of the insurrection, Billy turned nine and the Boer War broke out in South Africa. The war was a crucial event for both Protestants and Catholics in Ireland. Nationalists identified themselves with the Boers, another white Christian people fighting for independence from the overbearing British Empire. They formed two Irish "brigades" to help the Boer commandos. However, only four hundred or so Irishmen, mostly from the South African diaspora rather than from Ireland itself, were willing to join up; but 28,000 Irishmen fought against the Boers in English and Irish regiments of the British Army. Nevertheless, the anti-war campaign in Ireland, which included Yeats, invigorated the

nationalist movement in its despondency after Parnell's death and
the failure of the second home rule bill.

There was something for everyone in the war. The Ulster
Protestants were as affected by it as the Catholics were. It was an
occasion to shout their loyalty to the empire: "It is we who are being
attacked, and the object aimed at is to drive us out of South Africa,"
said the *Belfast News-Letter*. The editorial meant "we" and "us"
British. Orange lodges offered volunteer companies; there were
"Patriotic Days" and "War Funds." One of the main organizers of
Ulster unionism, and the first prime minister of Northern Ireland,
was James Craig. He was a Boer War veteran, as were several of his
unionist colleagues. The war bound them together into a brotherhood, as war always does, in their case, one committed to Britain
and completely opposed to home rule. There were ironies in the
Protestants' loyalism: they supported the empire, but it supported
home rule; and even though they couldn't see it, they were much
like their fellow-Protestant Boers in their stubborn, dour sense of
themselves. The walls of Derry and the circled wagons of the
Trekkers' laager had the same presumed purpose: to protect God's
people from savage adversaries in a hostile land. As for the British,
they won, using tactics that Irish kerns would have found familiar:
scorched earth, destruction of farms and crops, and, sometimes, no
prisoners. The British were also innovative, inventing the concentration camp. Twenty thousand Boer women and children died in
them of starvation and disease.

In 1902, Billy was twelve and left school to work at a linen mill.
The following year, or perhaps the year after that, he began as an
apprentice at the Harland and Wolff shipyard in Belfast. He had
been willing to break with the old family seagoing tradition,
although he was still absorbed in ships. His doomed younger
brother, Benjamin, would join the Royal Navy, and perhaps that satisfied the Lundy sons' filial obligations to follow the sea.

In that year, the British Parliament passed the *Irish Land Act*,
which completed the process—in fact, a revolutionary one—of
turning the Irish countryside over from big, often absentee
Ascendancy, landlords to native owner-farmers. They would
become the upholders of the Irish Free State's narrow, conservative,
and, above all, Catholic character. Distributing land to Irish owners

also kept them focused on constitutional politics and lessened the appeal of the physical-force Fenians.

By 1905, Billy was two years into his apprenticeship, learning lay-out on steel, how to cut the plate and move the heavy slabs by crane and lever, carrying rivets. He was one of five thousand dark-suited, duncher-capped men who might cluster on a new ship at one time like a pullulating mass of ants, the huge vessel growing under their hands day by day as if it were a metal life form.

In the same year, the radical, nationalist political party Sinn Féin was founded. It was the first Irish party with an Irish name, and its goal was the de facto independence of Ireland through Irish equal partnership in a dual monarchy. That seems an odd, even Quixotic, idea now, but the party's founder, Arthur Griffith, adopted the model of Hungary's recent successful campaign of independence from Austria—although he ignored the fact that there had been no Hungarian Ulster to complicate things. Sinn Féin advocated domestic economic growth and new Irish industry sheltered behind tariffs to gain economic independence. The jobs and demand created would end the flow of emigrants, the hemorrhage of Ireland's children that had shamed and hobbled the country for centuries. The party's methods were passive resistance, the withdrawal of MPs from Parliament, and the formation of a national assembly in Ireland. Irish people would refuse cooperation with government institutions such as the courts and adhere to new, parallel Irish ones.

Sinn Féin did not advocate violence, but it was a natural attractor of the boys in their fringe groups, such as the Fenians. To them, and to increasingly radical organizations like the Gaelic Athletic Association or the Gaelic League, Sinn Féin was a political party made in Ireland. It was unlike the Parliamentary Party, which was an imitation of the British originals, a collection of Irish babus and subaltern lickspittles, playing the corrupt English political game by its dubious rules. Sinn Féin promised a break with all that: an Irish government made by the Irish, rather than one granted by the supercilious conqueror, and, above all, resistance—passive for now, but that didn't matter. Any hard man knew how quickly the emotions of passive resistance could cross the line: a thrown stone, a single gunshot, a peaceful march gone awry could do it. And the Fenians knew they could depend on the English to make a bollocks of it. Their heavy-handedness and cruelty were unavoidable because they were simple extensions of their ingrained contempt for the Irish. Sooner or later, English soldiers or their Irish mercenaries, the police, would make a hash of things, and then the gunmen would have their day. When the 1916 Rising made all that happen, Sinn Féin, hitherto a small party marginalized by the constitutionalists, would be the natural political organization for a nation turned once again towards physical-force rebellion.

In the general election of January 1910, British Tories and Liberals won almost the same number of seats. The Irish Nationalists under John Redmond—no Parnell-like charismatic, but a stolid, solid leader—held the balance of power for the first time in fifteen years. As before, they were in the position of being able to force on the—mostly sympathetic—Liberals the Irish political program: it was home rule bill time again. Redmond proceeded with methodical calm. The second home rule bill had been vetoed by the House of Lords. There was no reason to think that the peers had changed their reactionary minds. To get home rule passed, therefore, it was first necessary to deal with the Lords. Redmond used his leverage to get the Liberal government to introduce the Parliament bill, which was passed in August 1911. It was a hard and bitter fight with the Conservative opposition and required a second general election in December 1910, which reinforced January's result. The bill took away the Lords' ancient power of veto over legislation coming from the House of Commons. The Conservatives' high dudgeon grew higher: a passel of rebelly bogtrotters had brought down the ancient prerogatives of the peers of the realm. Instead, the upper house could only delay implementation for three parliamentary circuits, or two years. Thus, the third home rule bill, which the government introduced to Parliament in April 1912, would take certain effect by May 1914 no matter what the Lords did.

The scheme of home rule was much like the limited concession of power contained in the two previous failed bills: a lower and upper house and an Irish cabinet that would deal with everyday matters. But the British Parliament had ultimate supremacy, and the real executive power still lay with an English-appointed lord lieutenant. As with the previous home rule bills, none of this mattered to unionists, almost all of whom were in Ulster, unionism's epicentre. They noted again the absence in the legislation of something to assuage their fears and to guarantee their rights under a Catholic regime. There had been one concession in the government's original proposal: provision for the Irish to continue to elect forty-two members of parliament to Westminster. This allowance was supposed to demonstrate that home rule did not imply separation and to emphasize that the two countries would continue to be joined at the constitutional hip. But Redmond rejected the idea right away. For the unionists, there was only one explanation for that: nationalists saw home rule as the beginning, not the conclusion, of a process; the endgame was full separation.

The standard received version of Irish history is the account of a tragedy that is held to be unique in its duration and intensity. In this view, Ireland is exceptional, its people's long-suffering and oppression unparalleled in any other country and comparable, perhaps, only to those of the Jews—a people without a country. The standard version is half right. The Irish are not unique; they didn't suffer more than many other peoples; there's been more than enough agony to go around. But Ireland's experience was that of a nation to which many cruel things were done—unlike England, for example, which tended to do the cruel things to others—and whose fate was cultural extinction, poverty, hunger, exclusion, denigration, the desperation of rebellion. When such a country—after centuries of armed resistance and political effort, and after shedding much of its old culture and painfully transforming itself into a rough clone of its occupier and oppressor—finally achieves even limited autonomy, that is a great victory, indeed. Especially if that autonomy has the clear potential for full independence.

The passage of the third home rule bill in 1912 should have been that kind of event for Ireland. But the tragedy continued, even intensified. The historical conditions of plantation, religious difference, and endemic sectarian conflict sucked the life out of the great moment. If the Protestants of Ulster couldn't be brought into the scheme of home rule, it would be an occasion for continued dispute and, very likely, for more killing. And, indeed, the nationalists were unable or unwilling to assuage the ancient Ulster Protestant fear of Catholics and the native Irish, and of their distaste for Catholicism.

The fault lay on both sides—and in the tortuous past. Perhaps a Parnell could have drawn in the northern unionists, if he had taken note of their disaffection and its importance. His austere, implacable Protestant presence might have reassured his quasi-countrymen, although it seems unlikely. Anyway, the king was dead, and Redmond was not the man even to try it.

Unionists also had more mundane economic objections to home rule. The relatively well-off industrialized north looked south to rural poverty and urban slums that were unparalleled in Europe. To many Protestants, it looked as if the southerners couldn't wait to get their hands into northerners' pockets. Calhoon, one of the tough Prods in George Birmingham's 1912 novel, *The Red Hand of Ulster*, says: "Belfast will be the milch cow of the Dublin Parliament. Money will be wanted to feed paupers and pay priests in the South and west. We're the only people who have any money. . . . it won't do in Belfast. We're businessmen."

In retrospect, it seems that nothing could alter the course of things after 1910—the confrontation, intransigence, the slide to violence and partition. Neither history nor each side's political myths were of much use in substituting discussion for force. Birmingham's urbane narrator observes: "Moderation has never been of the slightest use anywhere in Ireland." And in the north, compromise was the work of Lundys.

21

THE REVOLT OF ULSTER

IN 1912, BILLY WAS TWENTY-TWO YEARS OLD and working as a riveter. The shipyard had built the *Titanic* the previous year. Billy was political in the manner of many Ulster Protestants of the time, a loyal and typical young man of the tribe. He joined the Orange Order when he was small enough that his juvenile Orange sash fit him. He signed Ulster's Solemn League and Covenant pledging "the men of Ulster"—the phrase redolent of the seventeenth century—to use "all means which may be found necessary to defeat the present conspiracy to set up a Home Rule Parliament in Ireland." The meaning of "all means" was made clear with the formation, in 1913, of the paramilitary Ulster Volunteer Force (UVF). Billy joined up right away.

Three-quarters of all Protestant males over the age of sixteen in Ulster signed the Covenant, and close to half of the signers joined the volunteeers—an astonishing display of unanimity. The UVF ran guns into Larne and other harbours, the weapons with which it proposed to wage war on Britain for the right to remain part of it— "Ulster will fight and Ulster will be right!" They knew the details of their glorious history and they named their arms ship the *Mountjoy II*—after the original vessel that, they remembered inaccurately, was the first to relieve Derry in 1689. My family's stories have Billy helping to unload the 26,000 German rifles and three million rounds of ammunition. If he did that—the sources are not completely reliable—he was certainly a foot-soldier in the vanguard of the Ulster Protestant insurrection. He was one of the "King's rebels."

As he lugged around the cases of rifles or greased bullets—if he did—perhaps Billy had his own thoughts of his namesake and possible ancestor, Robert Lundy, and the mythic siege of Derry. Maybe possessing the name "Lundy" encouraged an Ulster Protestant like Billy to try harder, to show that, even though he had been stuck with the name of the great traitor, he was true blue and would never betray his people or compromise their cause. My father told me about the times during his boyhood and adolescence, when mobs and gunmen were out on the streets, that he thought it would be wise to be careful about saying his name. If a Prod hard man wanted an excuse to assault or kill someone, the word "Lundy" might do the trick. It must have been much worse for Billy in those home rule years. I doubt that he defused things through humour and amiability. More likely, he let them know he was no easy mark; they would have a fight on their hands. Perhaps that's where the Lundy pugnacity came from: Billy and his brother Jack matter of factly punching tram drivers and milkmen. It might have become a habit for men with a traitor's name among a suspicious people.

The UVF was a huge, illegal, Protestant private army, and an organization unparalleled in Ireland since the late eighteenth-century Volunteers. It was no secret society or band of kerns but eventually 100,000 strong, well-organized, officered and NCOd by numerous veterans who were the useful legacy of the old Irish tradition of serving in the empire's military. It drilled often and in the open. It appeared to be a thoroughgoing army with cavalry, a special strike force, dispatch riders and signallers, and an ambulance unit. It lacked only artillery and aircraft.

The UVF's aspect was deceptive, however. It was never as numerous, unified, or well armed as its leaders claimed. And a big part of its appeal was to cater to the recreational need of men to play with uniforms and guns, finding that easy joy in the brotherhood of arms which comes when the arms aren't being used. But the UVF had an effect well beyond its actual military potential. The British government could not get around the fact that it now had to deal with Ulster unionist politicians who had behind them many thousands of armed Irishmen who at least appeared to be willing to fight a civil war. History would not allow any British government to doubt the readiness of Irishmen in Ulster to use violence. But in this case, surely it was a bluff, the usual Irish method of using the threat of force to ensure a hearing for political demands. However, you could never be sure. The danger lay in the logic: if the mere existence of the Protestant army could not stop home rule, then it would have to go to war. "If its bark was not enough, then all it had left was its bite," as one historian put it.

The UVF was a coarse and brutal anomaly in the tradition of politics in Britain. In drafting and signing the seditious and menacing Covenant and in forming their private army, the Ulster Protestants confirmed for the average Englishman how completely different they were. It was unimaginable that any group of people or any region in England would do the same thing. They had in the past, but not for centuries. It could happen only in Ireland because the Irish were foreign, irrational, and prone to violence. And to the English, it made no difference whatsoever whether they were talking about a Kerry Catholic or an Antrim Presbyterian. Again, we're struck by the irony, poignant in its intensity: the Ulster Protestants had begun to think of themselves as British; they wanted to be British, yearned to be, but, in their threatened resort to violent remedies, proved themselves Irish to the core.

The ultimate goal of nationalists, whether they were constitutionalists or gunmen, has always been simple. The writer James Fintan Lalor prescribed it from prison after the rebellion of 1848: "Ireland her own—Ireland her own, and all therein, from the sod to the sky. The soil of Ireland for the people of Ireland, to have and hold from God alone who gave it—to have and hold to them and their heirs forever, without suit or service, faith or fealty, rent or render, to any power under heaven."

In contrast to this lyrical certainty, things for the Protestants were—and remain—so complicated. Where do they belong? Where is home? Can it be "nowhere as far as I can see," as Beckett wrote? Surely everyone belongs somewhere? Perhaps, but it may be that not everyone knows where that is. A character in Roy Bradford's novel *The Last Ditch* (King William's and Beckett's phrase again), says: "We Unionists are doomed. . . . We're a race of

Flying Dutchmen, condemned to roam the seas forever, seeking a spiritual and political home."

Some English politicians were sympathetic to the Protestants. The Conservative opposition in Parliament abhorred home rule and the crack it represented in the empire's facade. Ireland had been the first colony—of sorts. Would it become the first to break away? An empire that allows one of its possessions to get out, especially the first and closest, is asking for trouble. But more important for the Conservatives, home rule was the lever they could use to force another election and get back into power. They offered what looked like unlimited support for Ulster. At times, it seemed as if His Majesty's Loyal Opposition was anything but loyal. It seemed to envision the possibility of civil war in England, too. At the very least, there was no certainty that the government could even count on its own army to fight against Ulstermen, if it came to that. In the "Curragh incident," or mutiny, sixty British cavalry officers at the Curragh camp near Kildare resigned their commissions when their commander took the bizarre course of giving them that option rather than obeying orders to coerce Ulster unionists into accepting home rule. The war secretary made the inept admission that the army would not be used against the UVF. When there was no doubt that the government would have to use force against unionists, it could not rely on the army to apply it.

The bellicosity of the Conservatives was, in any event, rhetorical. They would never have endorsed armed conflict—unlike the unionists, many of whom would certainly have gone to war. The Ulster issue was merely the means to destroy the Liberal government. Nevertheless, the political rhetoric was intense and emotional. It recalled the Protestant past and, on one occasion, emphasized how entrenched the myth of the siege of Derry and its traitor had become. At a huge rally at Easter 1912, the Conservative Party leader, the Canadian-born Andrew Bonar Law, speechified (with the sort of eloquence that escapes politicians today):

Once again you hold the pass—the pass for the Empire. You are a besieged city. Does not the picture of the past, the glorious past with which you are so familiar, rise again before your eyes? The timid have left you; your Lundys have betrayed you; but you have closed your gates. The government have erected by their Parliament Act a boom against you to shut you off from the help of the British people. You will burst that boom. That help will come.

No one in the crowd of a hundred thousand needed help in decoding Law's esoteric metaphor.

The Protestants got the "Big Man" they needed to head their political campaign and their army: the Dublin barrister Edward Carson. As a southerner, he had the charisma of exoticism to Ulstermen, much like Parnell's Englishness to the Catholic Irish. If Parnell had been the uncrowned king of Ireland, Carson became the prince of Ulster. He was a brilliant lawyer, a barrister's barrister, able to reduce any set of complex legal issues to a few simple propositions that a judge could gratefully adopt in his reasons for judgment. Carson's capacity for lawyerly reductionism enabled him to comfortably ignore nuance and ambiguity in politics, too; he seized on the essential elements of the unionist position and seemed to follow them, without hesitation, to their logical end. If these were armed rebellion, civil war, and partition, then so be it. "The Volunteers are illegal," he said, "and the government know they are illegal, and the government dare not interfere with them. . . . Don't be afraid of illegalities." In fact, Carson was much more cautious than his words, but his words, and the enthusiasm of the UVF, put him at risk of having to use force if his threat of it wasn't sufficient.

Carson had been the remorseless destroyer of his fellow-Dubliner Oscar Wilde, when Wilde foolishly sued the Marquess of Queensberry for libel for calling him homosexual. Like Wilde, Carson was charming and theatrical. They were both examples of the alternative Irish stereotype: not Paddy "farting in his corduroys," but intelligent, eloquent, quicksilver, beguiling Paddy. Carson was also a hypochondriac, tightly wound, emotional. He was the colonial man at his most culturally ambivalent: a stage-Irishman when he needed to be, but masterful in the imperial centre, and a ferocious devotee of empire. After he had been presented to Queen Victoria, he stood behind a tree and wept, overcome by the Queen-Empress who seemed, he said, "to embody in her person and her [Indian] attendants the breadth and majesty of the British Empire."

He was tall, lean, angular, with the strong-chinned face that is naively associated with men of action and that belied his sentimentalism; he was Mussolini-esque, like the proto-fascist he was. Carson, said one contemporary historian, had a nature that "ought never to be allowed within the walls of a Parliament." Ulster hard men soon saw him as one of themselves. From Dublin, he had been sent to them as "the saviour of their tribe." It was easy to set him up as a popular and, in effect, marketable, symbol of Ulster toughness and determination. Indeed, there were soon Carson memorabilia for sale everywhere in the north: postcards, badges, busts. He was the star of the unionist propaganda campaign. Even children knew about the prince of Ulster:

> Edward Carson had a cat,
> He sat it by the fender,
> And every time it caught a mouse,
> It shouted, 'No Surrender!'

Carson led the signing of the Ulster Covenant. Its crucial phrase, "all means necessary" to defeat home rule, was a challenge to the constitutional order and the rule of law, and it obviously implied the use of arms against the British government. It was a public and treasonable declaration of rebellion that was indistinguishable in its threat from Patrick Pearse's Declaration of the Republic from the door of the Dublin General Post Office four years later, although, in its plainspoken, matter-of-fact intimation of war, the Covenant seems somehow typically Protestant—unadorned yet deadly—compared with Pearse's ornate, millennial rhetoric.

Indeed, Pearse and other Fenians watched the people of Ulster organize and arm themselves first with amazement, then with admiration. Carson and the unionists had made physical force a part of Irish politics once again. It was a paradox that the extreme Catholic advocates of independence in the south were inspired by the extreme rejectionist Protestants of the north. In Fenian eyes, it was the Prods who were doing what the Irish had always done and should be doing now: no wishy-washy compromise and delay, forever begging some limited concessions from the conqueror when the whole of Ireland should be completely free by right; the will to get on with the job of independence, and, if the *sassenaghs* object, to arm themselves and fight them. Carson the Prod was the only man in Ireland with bollocks; Redmond their fellow-Taig was a *moiley*, no horns at all.

Extremist nationalist approval of extremist unionists has persisted up to the present. I once visited Dublin during the Troubles in the 1980s to interview David O'Connell. He was then president of Sinn Féin but, during the 1970s, had been IRA chief of staff in the North. There, he had approved indiscriminate terror bombing, and some of the worst outrages against civilians had taken place at his command. To Catholics, he was a republican patriot fighting the good old fight; to Protestants, he was a bloody terrorist—that old problem of the relativity of the nomenclature of violence. The Sinn Féin office was on the second floor of a decrepit house in north Dublin. The party was still far away from its current status as the major nationalist party in the North. A bodyguard frisked me at the door, something I was used to—having just arrived from Belfast, where I was patted down a dozen times on an average day. O'Connell had followed the usual route of republican gunmen made good: from desperate killing in the streets and alleys of Belfast or in Armagh bandit-country to the safety, if not yet the respectability, of Sinn Féin's quiet offices. Gerry Adams and Martin McGuinness, the party's current leaders, followed the same path. During their successive tenures as IRA chiefs-of-staff in the late 1970s and early 1980s, they continued O'Connell's policies, as the IRA carried out many attacks against civilians; for instance, it bombed the La Mon House Hotel outside Belfast, burning to death twelve people, and Harrods in London, killing eight.

During our talk, O'Connell kept to the party line—which Adams repeats today, in spite of overwhelming evidence to the contrary—that the IRA and Sinn Féin are completely separate organizations and that it's wrong to talk about one as the military or political "wing" or "arm" of the other. O'Connell also told me several times how much he admired the most extreme loyalists, such as the Ulster Freedom Fighters, and the modern reincarnation of Carson's old UVF, the Ulster Volunteer Force. They were straightforward men who, at least, believed in something enough to put their lives on the line and fight for it, unlike the sleek, slimy, unionist politicians whose patrician backgrounds and discriminatory policies kept down poor Protestants just as much as Catholics.

After my meeting with O'Connell, I went back to Belfast, where I was staying with a widowed aunt. A few evenings later, she had a dozen friends over for a party. They were typical Protestant small businessmen and wage earners. At some point in the evening, when I'd had enough to drink so as not to be thinking clearly, I mentioned that I had talked to O'Connell. There was sudden and complete silence; everyone stared at me. They were trying to decide whether I was crazy, evil, or just a stupid Canadian who had been away long enough that he had forgotten the rules. Some of the people there had had friends and family slaughtered by IRA bombs or gunmen. I tried to explain: it was just an interview for a story I intended to write for a North American newspaper. I meant no harm; it didn't mean that I approved of O'Connell or agreed with his views. Conversation started again, but it was strained, and several of the guests never resumed their previous friendliness to me. I had spoken to the enemy, and that was a terrible transgression. I imagined their thinking: No damn wonder his name is Lundy. It was as if I had casually admitted to a group of conservative Americans after September 11 that I'd just had a nice chat with Osama bin Laden.

There was yet another irony in the events of 1912 to 1914: the northern Protestants were the first to put the theory of *sinn féin*—ourselves—into practice. Whatever its purpose, the UVF was an astounding display of power and an audacious defiance of Britain. Its effect on the government—hesitation and lack of response—was the old lesson for Irish nationalists: that only the threat of force and force itself made the English pay attention and, perhaps, back down. With the smug, chilling air of a poet-ideologue (or, perhaps, with Swiftian irony, although that seems unlikely), Pearse displayed a premonitory view of the sacrificial bloodshed he would help trigger: "I am glad that the Orangemen are armed, for it is a goodly thing to see arms in Irish hands."(Unlike most of his fellow nationalists, Pearse was at least tolerant enough to view Orangemen as Irishmen.) "We must accustom ourselves to the thought of arms, to the sight of arms, to the use of arms. We may make mistakes in the beginning and shoot the wrong people; but bloodshed is a sanctifying and a cleansing thing." (In so saying, Pearse didn't sound much different from any of a multitude of enthusiastic English advocates of purifying war in the years before August 1914.)

Pearse even suggested that the northern provisional government that the unionists had prepared for in the event of home rule could become a provisional government of Ireland. "Why not unite and get rid of the English," he said. "They are the real difficulty; their presence here the real incongruity." But this was wishful, if unprejudiced, thinking, and it is more evidence of the extent to which most southern Catholics did not understand Ulster Protestants—apart from their mutual resort to force—for whom cooperation with Fenians was abhorrent, unthinkable.

In late 1913, the Fenians and other physical-force nationalists in the south followed the Ulster example and formed the equivalent of the UVF. The Irish Volunteers were led by a Gaelic League member, Eoin MacNeill, who was also a professor of ancient Irish at University College Dublin—the Fenian leadership was heavy with professors and poets. The Volunteers' stated purpose was to defend home rule, just as the UVF had formed up to oppose it. Eventually, between 160,000 and 190,000 joined—as much as a fifth of all Catholic men in Ireland. But the gun-running efforts by the Irish Volunteers were meagre compared with those of the UVF; it managed to land only a few thousand antiquated German rifles. The British Army, which baulked at confronting Protestant gunrunners, tried to stop Catholics from doing the same thing, although without much success. While marching back to their barracks, the soldiers were baited by a derisive crowd on Bachelor's Walk beside the River Liffey in Dublin. They opened fire, killing three civilians and wounding thirty-eight. It was a mere ripple then in constitutionally minded Dublin, but, later, people would remember it.

A few months earlier, another private Catholic armed force had been set up: the Irish Citizen Army was a "socialist militia" to protect workers from the police during the violent Dublin trade-union lockout of August and September 1913. After the crisis was over, the Citizen Army stayed together and would have its historical moment as part of the Easter Rising.

At the beginning of 1914, Ireland was a country of five armies: the regular British version, the UVF, the Irish Volunteers, the Irish Citizen Army, and the Fenians of the venerable Irish Republican Brotherhood. Even Redmond the quietist was forced into a more radical position. Fenians had infiltrated the Irish Volunteers, whose numbers grew fast and, in early 1914, Redmond had to seize control of them. Politics had become thoroughly militarized.

By the middle of 1914, Ireland was skidding towards civil war. Recruitment for both the UVF and the Irish Volunteers had come disproportionately from the borderlands of Ulster, the traditionally unstable sectarian killing zone. Everyone expected a long and bloody fight. The Irish Volunteers had more men, but the UVF was a far superior force in every other way. Unionists wanted only to secure their place in the north, but perhaps, when the war began, the nationalists would have to worry about an attack on Dublin by a Protestant army. The UVF planned a *coup d'état* and what amounted to a declaration of independence for a partitioned unionist entity. It had detailed and precise plans for everything, down to civilian evacuation routes and the design of a currency. Unionists refused to submit to Catholic home rule but proposed to set up their own northern state along identical lines.

If Britain insisted on implementing home rule on Redmond's terms, then partition was the logical outcome of the unionist response. The question was, How many counties could be included in a northern political unit? Traditional Ulster was nine counties, but unionists decided to carve out for themselves the six in which Protestants were most numerous so as to ensure a significant unionist majority in an Ulster parliament. However, one-third of the population in the six counties was Catholic. Whatever form a northern statelet took, the old Plantation settlement patterns would plague it, making questionable its stability, even viability. Prods and Taigs would still be over the hill from each other, or within sight, or a street over. In any event, permanent partition was anathema to nationalists; they would not allow the fourth green field to slip away forever from the new Ireland. But as civil war looked more and more likely, Redmond offered a concession: he would accept the partition of six counties of Ulster, but only on a temporary basis. The implication was that the unionists were merely delaying the inevitable—a unified Ireland under home rule, with Protestants as a minority countrywide. When the Great War began in August 1914, one of its more obscure effects was to head off civil war in Ireland. But it was only a delay.

One historian calls the crisis of the years 1912 to 1914 Protestant Ulster's "foundation moment." The Ulster "identity" emerged during those years, and it has persisted to the present: loyal (of course), staunch (the word is never applied to Catholics), determined, ready to go to war if necessary to preserve its Protestant "way of life." The final version of the Derry siege myth—a people alone and beset yet defiant—had entrenched itself as part of this identity. Yeats wrote that after the Easter Rising, "all changed, changed utterly." He could have said the same thing about the two years before the Great War, when the Protestants of Ulster came together in a militant, almost exalted, unity. They believed that it would see them through the coming tumult. But underneath their bravado lay the fear that nothing could preserve them forever.

22

MARTYRS' BLOOD

ON THE RADIO, the old man's voice wavered and quivered, in a soft southern accent. He sounded ancient, and the effect was amplified by the recording, which had been made on old-fashioned equipment. He spoke about a time that seemed long over with, although the events he described had taken place in the twentieth century only sixty years before. The recording was part of an oral history project by some researchers in the Republic of Ireland, and the old man was recalling what had happened on the first day of the Easter Rising of 1916.

He had been a member of the unit of rebels led by "the Mexican," the young future president of the republic, Eamon de Valera. (Irish nationalists considered the American-born de Valera, who had an Irish mother and a Spanish father, to be Irish—whereas the status of a Protestant born in Ireland whose ancestors had been in the country for three hundred years was doubtful.) When the English executed the leaders of the rebellion, they spared only de Valera, because of his American citizenship. Before dawn on April 24, de Valera's armed men walked through the streets of Dublin towards Boland's Mill, which it was their job to occupy. Other parties of Irish Volunteers were moving towards the General Post Office and similar prominent, although indefensible, buildings in the city to seize and hold them. They also occupied St. Stephen's Green, where Pearse's men seized the low ground—tall buildings overlooked the trenches they dug in the soft grass. Their formal aim was to fight off the British Army until the people of Ireland, inspired by their example, rose in general insurrection and threw out the English. In reality, they were engaged in a blood-sacrifice with uncertain prospects.

Before the rebels reached the mill, they ran into a policeman, an Irishman like them, who stopped the band of silent men. Where did they think they were going? he inquired in the officious, truculent tone of the universal copper. Get on out of it, they told him. This is the beginning of the last fight against England for a free Ireland, and we have no quarrel with you. But the policeman persisted in his duty; he wouldn't stand aside. He was going to sound off and expose them before they could get set up in position. The old rebel paused in his account, then said: "So, Seamus Lundy stepped up and shoved his pistol into the peeler's chest to muffle the noise, and shot him. I think that this was the first killing of the Rising."

When I heard his story, I wondered whether this Seamus was related to me. I had never heard of any southern and Catholic relatives, but it wasn't impossible they existed. What a strange and terrible symmetry if Seamus had been one of my ancestors. I could have claimed two Lundys—Seamus and Billy—as having played small roles in each of the seminal Irish dramas of the twentieth century: the Easter Rising for the Catholics, and, if not the Battle of the Somme, at least the foundation moment of the Ulster Protestants.

Seamus Lundy's murder of the policeman preserved the element of surprise for the rebels. There were between 1,200 and 1,600 of them, and they held out for six days in isolated pockets like the General Post Office and Boland's Mill, which was the last position to surrender; I don't know whether Seamus survived. The British used artillery to batter down the insurgents and bombed out much of the centre of Dublin. As usual, uninvolved civilians suffered the most, approximately 250 of them being killed. Among the combatants, 132 soldiers and 64 rebels died—an interesting discrepancy that suggests British restraint or incompetence. But there were only 1,600 rebels at most. Obviously the Rising could not succeed; it was a military farce. What had happened to the 180,000 men of the Irish Volunteers?

The answer is that, in 1916, Redmond's men were falling before German guns in no man's land on the Western Front at about the same rate as Ulster Protestants and British soldiers generally. When the Great War broke out, Redmond, ever the constitutionalist, pledged the Volunteers for the defence of Ireland. With the home rule bill in his pocket, he was eager to prove that his country was loyal. Britain could take its garrison out of Ireland to use in the war, he said; the Volunteers would hold the country for the empire. This was a reasonable and uncontroversial position, but, a month later, Redmond went much further. He committed the Volunteers to the empire and its army in exactly the same way as Edward Carson handed over the UVF: they could be used anywhere the British needed them—which meant, of course, the terrible killing ground of France. Many of the Volunteers were formed into the British Army's 16th Division. It would suffer losses comparable to those of the 36th, although in various engagements over time rather than in anything like the Ulstermen's impetuous rush to the Schwaben Redoubt and beyond. The dead included Willie Redmond, John's brother. The soldiers of the 16th Division (and to an extent the Protestants of the 36th, too) were valued by the British as "shock troops." They were supposedly undisciplined, unruly, and wildly impulsive—qualities that made them ideal for mounting what the French called the "crucial attack." It was a purely colonial attitude. The British viewed Canadian and Australian troops in the same way, and they were put to the same decimating use.

The 16th Division, and all the Catholic-Irish soldiers of the British Army—at least 65,000 volunteered—the dead and survivors alike, would become forgotten men much more completely than veterans usually do. Times changed in Ireland: after the Rising and the war of independence, no one in the Irish Free State wanted to remember that so many of their compatriots had fought for the old enemy. Indeed, only recently have these men even been officially acknowledged in the Republic of Ireland, let alone remembered.

Only ten thousand Volunteers, many of whom were connected with the Irish Republican Brotherhood, rejected Redmond's commitment in 1914 and broke away, still under the leadership of the professor, Eoin MacNeill. They engaged in the time-honoured games of amateur soldiers: they dressed up in smart uniforms and marched about and seemed to be little threat to the authorities. No one could see that the future of Ireland lay with them, or, at least, with a small faction of IRB men within them led by Pearse and other extremists. Their small martyrdom in Dublin, rather than the huge blood-sacrifice of the Volunteers in France, would make all the difference in Ireland.

In retrospect, Redmond's decision was a turning point of Irish history. It split the Volunteers, creating a disaffected and concentrated radical faction. And the war's disgraceful slaughter of men month by month, year in and year out, became one of the things that disillusioned the Irish and began to turn them away from peaceful politics. The bloody progression of the war put Redmond in an impossible position. He had arguably committed the Volunteers to France to try to assuage unionist Ulster's suspicions. If the Catholic Irish died alongside the Ulstermen, then surely they could live together in a home rule Ireland. There would be no need for partition. But Redmond, like Pearse, underestimated the unionists' fully formed intransigence. Nothing would convince them to go into a united country. Redmond's gesture was useless in three ways: it guaranteed the deaths of thousands of Irishmen in the trenches; it could not change unionist minds; and it became one of the main preconditions for his own political obsolescence in the south.

The Rising "came like a thunderclap from a blue sky," wrote one scholar. The authorities had no idea that anything like it was in the works—which makes it an atypical piece of Irish secret-keeping. They viewed the rump of Fenian Volunteers, with their amateurish drilling, as chocolate soldiers. British documents released and used by historians for the first time in 1966 make it clear that the British government was absolutely committed to handing over the government of Ireland (at least twenty-six counties and excluding the six "Protestant" counties of Ulster) to the elected representatives of the Irish people. On the edge of achieving the long-sought goal of home rule, what Irishman would engage in armed rebellion? There was simply no need for it. Two weeks before the Rising, the director of British military intelligence described things as "thoroughly satisfactory"—demonstrating once again the chronic difficulty for intelligence services of foreseeing either catastrophic attacks or quixotic gestures by rebels or terrorists. However, at least one acute Englishman caught intimations of trouble ahead. The chief secretary of Ireland, Augustine Birrell, sent a report to the British prime minister in late

1915. He had been reading the newspapers, he wrote. "I notice an increasing *exaltation of spirit*." Given England's difficulties in the war, "I feel the *Irish* Situation one of actual menace." However, Birrell's disquiet was not what might be called "actionable intelligence."

The Rising was really a "conspiracy within a conspiracy." MacNeill didn't know about it until the last moment and then refused to take part. In fact, he tried to head it off, but Pearse and the other hard-liners went ahead anyway. Without the main body of MacNeill's Volunteers, and with the failure of a plan to land weapons from Germany, the rebellion was useless militarily. Instead, it became another—and certainly the most effective—of the sacrificial dramas of Irish history. Pearse and the poets, play-wrights, teachers, and actors who led the Rising probably had mixed and contradictory motives. It's possible that they held the paradoxi-cal, and vain, hope of sparking an actual and more general uprising leading to an ultimate military victory. More likely, they believed only that they were heroes in a mystical tragedy, the end of a long line of martyrs and warriors winding back to Art Mac Murrough, the fourteenth-century king who fought to a standstill the invading English under Richard II.

The Rising took place at Easter for the practical reason that the rebels hoped to use the annual Irish Volunteer manoeuvres as a cover and diversion, but MacNeill cancelled them when he heard about Pearse's plans. Easter provided another providential opportunity: the identification of the rebels with Christ; the Rising would emulate his sacrifice. In a farewell speech to his students a month earlier, Pearse had said: "As it took the blood of the Son of God to redeem the world, so it would take the blood of Irishmen to redeem Ireland."

MacNeill, although a radical in comparison with the constitu-tionalist Redmond and the great majority of the Volunteers (and the Irish people generally), deplored Pearse's apocalyptic sacrificial vision. In contrast to the poet-playwright's almost insane desire for apotheosis in a theatrical death, MacNeill remained a realist. He did not see Ireland as a poetical abstraction created by patriotic literature and the mythology of the past. There was no such person as *Cathleen ní Houlihan*, he wrote, nor *Róisín Dubh* ("Dark Rosaleen," another personification of Ireland), nor the *Shan Van Vocht* "who is calling us to serve her. What we call our country is the Irish nation which is a concrete and visible reality." With an acute psychological insight, MacNeill recognized in Pearse the extremist's fear of complexity, his rage at all his life's frustrations. But "no man has a right to seek relief of his feelings at the expense of his country."

The effect on the Irish of the Rising lay less in the six days of stubborn, even heroic, resistance by the rebels and more in the aftermath of the military action. It was a matter of the way in which the British executed Pearse and fourteen other leaders. The people were alarmed and then appalled by what seemed to be the languorous cruelty of the drawn-out ten days of killing. The revulsion of the Irish, who were supposed to revel in their state of endemic violence, made them seem gentle in comparison with the ferocious English. In fact, the process was slow because the English were trying to adhere to a legal form of trial and conviction, but they appeared mean and vengeful. George Bernard Shaw campaigned to have the leaders of the Rising treated as prisoners of war, not as traitors. The population of Dublin, which had jeered the rebels as they were marched to jail, began to protest.

The government reacted in the traditional heavy-handed manner. Irish secretary Augustine Birrell's easy-going civil government, with its appreciation of the subtleties of the situation, was replaced by an obtuse, rigid military governor, Lieutenant-General Sir John Maxwell. He imposed martial law and arrested more people than had actually taken part in the Rising. During the fighting, residents of North King Street had been indiscriminately massacred by soldiers. Afterwards, the army under Maxwell carried out other reprisals against obviously innocent noncombatants. The popular pacifist Francis Sheehy-Skeffington reportedly saw a British officer kill an unarmed boy. When he protested, he, too, was summarily shot. The soldier was later tried and found guilty but insane. The incident had a huge effect on public opinion. All these provocations of an occupying army in the streets—raids, house searches, press restrictions, arrest and detention without trial—worked to radicalize the Irish. When an army is reduced to these measures, it has already lost the people.

Britain's reaction to the Rising was, at least, comprehensible, if irrational. It saw itself and its empire in a struggle to the death with Germany. It was almost as if the government and its generals—like all the governments and generals of Europe—had fallen into a state of obsessive psychosis: they had come to believe that it was necessary to keep driving the empire's young men to slaughter, as though they were some subordinate species, to gain another few hundred yards of French ground stinking with the already dead. The government held the strong, although exaggerated, belief that the Germans had had a big role in the Rising. The prime minister, Herbert Asquith, called it "this most recent German campaign." Pearse's Proclamation of the Republic had, indeed, referred to "gallant allies in Europe." Sir Roger Casement, the Irishman who had served the empire for years as a distinguished diplomat, had committed treason by negotiating for arms and aid in Berlin. He was like Sir Cahir O'Doherty three hundred years earlier: England could never be sure even of these knighted Irishmen, tamed, trusted, honoured, and brought without prejudice into the imperial enterprise. The Rising was the ghost of the past: Irishmen joining with England's continental enemies, the ancient weakness in English homeland security. It seemed as if there would always be some in Ireland to the end of time who would strike at England when it was in preoccupied difficulty. In response to this apparently instinctive Irish behaviour, the English responded with their own. Both sides renewed the old cycle of rebellion and its harsh suppression.

Redmond and the Parliamentary Party waffled, trapped in their untenable position. His party's power depended on being able to speak to England on behalf of Ireland. With the elimination of British civil authority and the increasing hostility of the Irish people towards military rule, Redmond's strategy was no longer relevant. The Rising had become known as the Sinn Féin Rising, and the party made the most of it all. Such "stigmatization" was its "political kiss of life." In the 1918 election, Sinn Féin won seventy-three seats; the Unionists took twenty-six; the once dominant Parliamentary Party managed only six. In the men of 1916 and in Sinn Féin, the middle-class Catholics of Ireland, whose support was crucial for any independence movement, had found radical leaders who were, like themselves, Catholic and not Anglo-Irish. The latter began their submersion into irrelevance. Sinn Féin constituted itself as Dáil Éireann, an independent Irish parliament. It began to carry out its founder Arthur Griffith's original policy of passive resistance and the creation of separate government and legal institutions. When Britain showed no signs of acquiescing—and when the Versailles Peace Conference after the war, including the American president Woodrow Wilson, refused to consider the Irish case for self-determination—the Irish Republican Brotherhood prepared for savage and uncompromising guerrilla war against the empire.

"How deep in Irish hearts lies this passion for insurrection," said Augustine Birrell. The irony of the Rising is that the rebels' irrational and seemingly ill-timed strike, scorned at the time, quickly achieved its purpose. It was as if these poets and intellectuals, confused as they were by love and rage, had somehow intuited the unconscious mind of the Irish. The great world empire of Britain was against them; four in five of the people of Ireland consciously disapproved of their action or were neutral and puzzled by it. But—strange paradox—in reality, the rebels had Ireland. They pulled all the old triggers; the centuries fell away; time collapsed. In spite of what MacNeill thought, the call of the *Shan Van Vocht* could not be resisted. Even Pearse's association of the Rising with the passion of Christ resonated in Ireland. Soon afterwards, posters appeared in Dublin with the caption, "All Is Changed." They show a martyred Pearse, in the position of the *Pietà*, in the very arms of the *Shan Van Vocht*, Mother Erin, who is waving a tricolour.

Yeats never liked Pearse, whom he had long criticized as "half-cracked and wanting to be hanged—has Emmet delusions same as other lunatics think they are Napoleon or God." The Rising astonished Yeats as much as anyone. But even the great poet's cold eye could not resist the compelling imagery that Pearse and the other "lunatics" had created, especially after their executions and the other recurrent brutal themes of English occupation. In his poem "Easter 1916," which he wrote that summer but did not publish until 1920, when the war of independence was in full spate—perhaps a calculated career move—Yeats still had second thoughts about the rebels: "Was it needless death after all? . . . And what if excess of love / Bewildered them till they died?" They are almost like children led astray by emotions they could not understand or control—perhaps another instance of the patronizing stance of the Anglo-Irish aristocrat towards the mere Irish. But Yeats had seen the totemic power of their actions too. The rebels,

> Now and in time to be,
> Wherever green is worn,
> Are changed, changed utterly:
> A terrible beauty is born."

This is the Ur-poem of the new Irish state.

Myth, memory, and imagination could transfigure death and failure into triumph. Pearse and the others had created a kind of virtual Irish republic which would not go away. The long, peaceful, political campaigns for Catholic emancipation and home rule seemed more and more like futile, and perhaps shameful, diversions from the real and necessary agenda that England had always forced on Ireland, and had done so again: only physical force would work to achieve independence. A conversation between an Irish Sinn Féin sympathizer and an English journalist who was trying to get information about the Rising reads like a jokey catechism of Irish grievance, a demonstration of different conceptions of time and history, of mutual incomprehension:

> "Is there a rebellion?" asked Aitken.
> "There is," replied Healy.
> "When did it break out?"
> "When Strongbow invaded Ireland."
> "When will it end?"
> "When Cromwell gets out of Hell."

The Battle of the Somme began almost three months after the Rising. When the Protestant men of Ulster read their Bibles and prayed and sang "Oh God, Our Help in Ages Past" and put on their Orange sashes and, on the same date as their old battle on the green, grassy slopes of the Boyne, on the banks of another river, walked towards the German machine guns, they must also have had in mind the Rising in Dublin. To the Prods, it provided the most pungent of contrasts. The Taigs had demonstrated their treachery yet again. Even on the verge of getting everything they wanted in the form of home rule—to the detriment of Ulster—they still could not break their ancient habits of violence and rebellion. True, some

Catholics had volunteered—the Ulstermen must have known well the 16th Division—but surely they were the aberration. The rebels in Dublin reflected the real Catholic Irish attitudes. In contrast to their stab in the back, the Protestants of Ulster were here on the fields of France, their numerous presence the best possible proof of their loyalty. Their dying throughout that hot July day would confirm and consecrate it.

It's unlikely that any of the Ulstermen speculated about their own example in having egged on the rebels. In 1912, the UVF had pledged to go to war, and would have done so; Pearse and the other Fenians had simply taken things that little extra step—although that was as far as the similarity went. Their rising was like the old "cabbage-patch" rebellions: short on military acumen, long on rhetoric and useless gesture. Pearse's admiration of Ulster's armed defiance was not reciprocated. Protestants, like most Catholics immediately after the Rising, could not foresee its very failure as victory.

Redmond's attempt to reconcile the Protestants to constitutional nationalism was destroyed by the Rising and by the Somme. Ulster was more alienated than ever. The future lay with the physical-force tradition of Wolfe Tone, Robert Emmet, the Fenians—with William Steel Dickson, for that matter—all the rebels and martyrs. The standard received version of Irish history justifiably emphasizes the Rising as a crucial event but, typically, almost ignores its estranging effect on Ulster Protestants, as well as the impact on them of the radicalization of nationalists in the succeeding years. But it was the unionists, not the British, who were the real enemy of Redmond and Pearse, of constitutionalists and Fenians alike. From 1912 to 1914, the unionists were the problem, blocking home rule, which the British had conceded. The Rising, the military repression afterwards, and the atrocities and heroism of the war of independence temporarily substituted the British—the ancient *sassenagh* oppressor—for the unionists and made Britain the enemy. Dying simply and purely for the *Shan Van Vocht* was more attractive than dealing with the real and difficult problem of a million recalcitrant people sharing the same island. Eamon de Valera (foreign-born, half-Spanish) summed up Sinn Féin's attitude: the Ulster unionists were a "foreign garrison" and "not Irish people," he said in 1918.

Afterwards, when the inevitable time came to negotiate a settlement, nothing had changed in the north. The unionists were still
there and, needless to say, more convinced than ever that they
should have nothing to do with a Catholic state. Partition had been
the only and necessary solution in 1914; it remained so in 1921. And
it was a solution for both sides. Perhaps the new southern state felt
secret relief. It would have enough trouble dealing with its own
hard men, who rejected the half-measures of the treaty with Britain,
let alone the numerous, armed, and fierce northern Prods.

The men of the Somme, and unionists generally, thought that their
blood-sacrifice of July 1, 1916, was a terrible, yet luminous, moment
that contrasted vividly with the unnecessary and traitorous Rising.
They believed that the British would see that and acknowledge it, and
that they would never again even think of thrusting Protestants
against their will into Ireland among the Fenians. Unionists thought
that the contrast between the Somme and the Rising would seal the
identification of Ulster Protestants as British people within Britain,
and that the "mainland" British would see that, too.

The unionists were deluded, dead wrong. The British pursued
the partition of the six northern counties because it was the only conceivable solution (and, they hoped, a temporary measure) that did
not involve intense civil war and the continued need for large numbers of British troops in Ireland. And, in fact, nothing could change
the British view of Ulster Protestants as just another version of
fanatical Irishmen. The Somme made no difference. British soldiers
had died there, too, by their hundreds of thousands. Elsewhere,
Canadians, Anzacs, Indians, men from every part of the empire had
fallen on the Western Front. A few thousand Irishmen was a negli-
gible number amid the colossal slaughter.

As Britain became absorbed in the aftermath of the Rising and
with the war of independence, Ulster turned into a diminished,
regional issue, and Carson—who had played a big role in the War
Cabinet—and the other unionist leaders became a species of marginalized micks once again. They would get their own little statelet
with a form of home rule within the United Kingdom, but it would
be a diseased and febrile entity from the beginning. Shaw called
Northern Ireland at its inception "an autonomous political lunatic
asylum." As it collapsed fifty years later, one writer described it as

"the cadaver politic." The province was a political expediency to avoid more killing, or to reduce it as much as possible. Its creation had nothing to do with any sense of British solidarity with Ulster Prods or of gratitude towards them.

The Rising reiterated that the political mythology of Catholic nationalists includes the idea of individual suffering as part of the people's ultimate redemption. Terence MacSwiney, the lord mayor of Cork, died in 1920 on the seventy-fourth day of a hunger strike in an English jail. Before his death, he said: "It is not those who can inflict the most, but those who suffer the most who will conquer." The cult of martyrdom, its reflexive, perhaps pathological, quality, was also evident in the fasting to the death of the ten republican H-Block prisoners in 1981. The sacrifice didn't immediately get the men the political-prisoner status they had demanded (although it was essentially conceded a few months later), but there was immense sympathy for them in Ireland and the United States. Each funeral drew as many as 100,000 people. The modern version of Sinn Féin came into political prominence, and Gerry Adams, as well as Bobby Sands, the first to die, were elected to Westminster. (Another hunger striker won election to the Dáil before he died.)

The "Ten Men Dead" had the same effect on Catholics in the North as the executions after the Easter Rising had had throughout Ireland. The IRA could rebut its critics' charge that it had degenerated into a mafia; members of mafias don't starve themselves to death for an idea. But the young men who died emaciated, long-haired, and bearded—Christ-like—were indoctrinated victims, as well as practitioners, of the old tribal tradition of sacrifice. They are not quite the Irish equivalent of Islamist suicide bombers who aim to take as many infidels as possible with them—who, in killing others, seek to redeem themselves. The Irish martyrs killed themselves but no one else; in doing so, they sought to redeem their mythological country, the Ireland of their dreams.

The Ulster Protestant mythology, based on the ideas of siege and resistance, has been described by one historian as "an endless repetition of repelled assaults, without hope of absolute finality or of fundamental change." "No Surrender!" but no victory, either. The collapse of the sectarian state of Northern Ireland, and now the Good

Friday Agreement's putative power-sharing arrangements with Catholics, has emphasized as part of the hard-line Protestants' self-image the idea of ultimate defeat, too. They are being ground down by time, demographics, politics. Their resistance is a holding action in a struggle they cannot win and must eventually lose. Unless they can do something they've never done before: think and move later-ally. Perhaps there really isn't any more need for a struggle; maybe there's nothing to lose.

In the meantime, there remains the apparently sterile, limited, and unimaginative nature of Ulster Protestant nationalism. It is a creature of the rejection of unionists by both the Catholic Irish and the British, and it defines itself solely as not "the other," which means, not Irish. (Not so different, perhaps, from English-Canadian nationalism, which has mostly defined itself as "not-American.") Protestant nationalism is intensely ritualistic—exemplified by the thousands of annual parades with their fearful and defiant claim of territorial dominion. Ritual is a form of obsessive, repetitive behaviour that pur-ports to assuage anxiety in the face of the enemy—the Catholic nationalism of the island's majority—and the ever-present threat of physical force. When you're under siege, you can only man the walls and wait. You don't need a sophisticated or imaginative political phi-losophy; there's little time or inclination for culture. Pyper, the would-be sculptor in Frank McGuinness's play *Observe the Sons of Ulster Marching Towards the Somme*, smashes his work in despair, "for when I saw my hands working they were not mine but the hands of my ancestors, interfering, and I could not be rid of that interference. I could not create. I could only preserve. . . . I was contaminated."

A recent joke (or maybe it's a true anecdote): Orangeman of Sandy Row to British reporter: "Hey, mister, we're British, and that's something you British had better remember!" The Ulster Protestants' definition of themselves as British, so as to avoid admit-ting that they are Irish, is an existential subterfuge and, in their hearts, they know it. A writer about Northern Ireland during the Troubles observed the following scene aboard a train travelling from Belfast to the loyalist bastion of Larne. It is a parable.

Three young men were fooling around, throwing cans and bot-tles out of the window. "In the middle of the mayhem, one of the youths shouted breathlessly, 'No wonder they say the Irish are mad!'

There was a short but sudden silence. His two companions looked at him uneasily, and he almost blushed with embarrassment. It was as if a taboo had been broken, and in front of strangers. After a second or so, the biggest youth, obviously the leader of the group, shouted with bluff confidence and an aggressive voice, 'Hey, what d'ya mean? We're not Irish—we're British.' They laughed at each other, but rather self-consciously. It was obvious they were discomfited, unsettled, and they flung themselves with increased vigour into another round of furious and distracting activity."

Billy lived through it all, the Ulster Protestant Everyman in a time of tumult and dread. He signed a document that committed him to treason, and he joined an illegal private army. He fell over his spurs, missed the war, and had to read about the Somme in the newspapers. But he lived. His brother-in-law and a cousin were killed on the Western Front—perhaps some more distant relatives, too; some of his friends must also have died. Certainly a great many of his old comrades in the 36th Division didn't return.

He married moody, buxom, green-eyed Maud Dickson, the descendant of a rebel Presbyterian, and moved, matrilocally, into the little house on the border of the Holy Land where she had lived since she was four years old. He had two sons: my father, Alexander, and William—my uncle Bill—both of whom would grow up to be free of prejudice.

The first sectarian fighting in what would become the new Northern Irish statelet broke out in 1920 in Derry, which was no surprise. (Billy would have thumped anyone who called the city anything other than "Londonderry.") The city fulfilled its traditional role as the trigger of violence in Ulster. Fifteen hundred British troops put a lid on the place, although they had to shoot dead thirty people to do it. A few months later, loyalist workers—Billy was one of them—at the Harland and Wolff shipyard in Belfast violently expelled all 5,500 Catholics who worked there. The standard story of Irish history calls this event a "pogrom," but it wasn't. The action also affected 1,900 Protestants, most of whom were suspected of socialist—and a few, of nationalist—sympathies. Even then, the Prods were not a single bloc of believers but had some Lundys among themselves (there are always moderates, even within what appears to be the most comprehensive extremist consensus). The expulsion was supposedly in retaliation for the refusal of southern Irish rail workers to transport home the body of an Ulster-born police commissioner who had been assassinated in Cork by the IRA. Catholic crowds attacked Protestants in reprisal for the job expulsions. Gunfire broke out all over the city, and, in three days, eighteen people were killed; in the next three months, eighty-two.

Shipyard employees passed a series of resolutions, one of which said: "We . . . hereby declare that we will not work with disloyal workers . . . and until Sinn Féin ceases its foul murder." All future employees, they suggested, should be "loyal ex-service men and Protestant Unionists." In fact, seven hundred of the expelled Catholics were veterans, but that made no difference. John Redmond's hope that the Great War would unite Protestants and Catholics through the experience and memory of their common suffering on the Western Front had been stillborn; it was buried in the Belfast shipyards and in the crowded narrow streets round about, which became sectarian killing-grounds.

The people of Ulster were drawing the lines that would remain in place for fifty years. Nationalists saw a second Protestant Ascendancy establishing itself in Northern Ireland. It was beginning to look as if the forever bigoted and intransigent Prods were going to set themselves up once more as a ruling caste over the Irish on whose land they were still squatting. In the south, there was independence—of a sort. But in the North, the Unionist government was systematically reducing 450,000 Catholic Irish to the status of helots in their own country. The Bishop of Down and Connor sent an Orange songbook to Pope Pius XI, urging him to look through it. It would "give His Holiness an idea of the Orange spirit . . . some idea, though faint, of the spirit of these savages."

Unionists saw only the unregenerate IRA continuing to kill Protestants and members of the Crown's forces, northern Catholics refusing to accept partition, Sinn Féin fomenting sectarian disturbances, all of them trying to undermine the new province. The *Northern Whig* said there were "two peoples in Ireland, one industrious, law-abiding and God-fearing, and the other slothful, murderous and disloyal." In a speech at Westminster, Edward Carson said: "You will have no unity in Ireland until the people of the south and west give up their hatred and hostility to Great Britain. We feel that our interests are identical to those of Great Britain, and we will have no unity as long as this insane hatred is preached from the housetops in the South and the West of Ireland."

Around the time Billy's first son, Alexander, was born in 1921, some Black and Tans carried out an atrocity on my mother's family. The Tans were British ex-army officers—war's usual detritus of racked veterans who can't adjust to a quiet life—recruited into an auxiliary police force that became notorious for its indiscipline and murderousness. Billy didn't know his future daughter-in-law Mary Baird then, of course, but newspapers would have reported the event. The Greys were Mary's cousins and lived in the end-house of a posh row in the town of Newry in the Ulster borderlands. The father was a well-off coal merchant. Their son was involved in some sort of political or paramilitary activity—no one can remember what it was. One evening, he left a meeting and headed home. Some Black and Tans had marked him, and they followed him to find out where he lived. Later that night, they invaded the Greys' house and took the son, his two sisters, and their mother and father outside. The Tans lined the family up against the house end-wall and opened fire on them with rifles and pistols. Maybe the armed men were drunk— they often were. They killed the mother and the son, invalided the father for life, and wounded both daughters. None of the attackers was ever identified, and no charges were laid. It made no difference to the Tans that the Greys were Protestants and loyal to Britain and its King, and that their mutual co-religionists had suffered at the Somme. A paddy was a paddy.

When my mother was a little girl, her family would visit the surviving Greys, and that was when she was told the story. Of course, it frightened her. As she grew up in Belfast, this massacre was one of the things that made her cleave to her tribe's safe territory around the Woodvale Road. It seemed the only sure refuge for the timid, skinny girl when mobs rioted and gunmen fought in the streets.

Later—long after we had emigrated to Canada and during the Troubles—Mary visited Northern Ireland from time to time. She went mostly to see her sister, who lived on a pleasant middle-class street of semi-detached homes on a hill near the affluent Antrim

Road. The house had a long, beautiful view of Belfast Lough and the shores of the County Down side. One day, she looked out the front window, across the little garden, in which grew roses and annuals in flower, and over the low wall to see a British Army patrol. It was proceeding in the accustomed, disciplined manner: eight men, wide-spaced, the last man in a continuous, almost balletic, pivot, walking backwards most of the time, watching his brothers' backs. They were in full battledress and had smeared their faces with black camouflage cream, but in individual patterns, like warriors' war paint, each man's design a personal creation. Mary was at first startled to see them there on that quiet, well-to-do Protestant street (although it was only a few over from a dangerous Catholic territory). Then she felt fear, almost panic. Sixty years later, nothing had changed; British soldiers were still outside her family's door in Ireland. She thought: Dear God, will it never end?

Perhaps Billy participated in the frequent communal riots in Belfast during 1920 to 1922. The sectarian warfare in Ulster was as intense as the guerrilla war in Dublin, or the one in Munster between IRA flying columns and British troops. Billy may not have been a mere bystander; he joined the Protestant B Specials and might have roughed up a Taig or two. Maybe he did worse things than that. The Specials, essentially part-time paramilitary policemen, were notorious among Catholics for doing what ethnic or sectarian militias always do: intimidate, assault, torture, kill. They were the Ulster Protestant equivalent of the Black and Tans. The Specials were mostly war veterans of the 36th Division and were, in effect, a reconstitution of the Ulster Volunteer Force. It was, said one general, the "raising of Carson's army from the grave."

Billy was sufficiently tough, prejudiced, authoritarian, and habituated to violence—not war, but the everyday conflicts of life in Ulster—to have followed whatever orders he was given to do bad things to Catholics or, indeed, to do whatever he thought was necessary quite apart from any orders. Because he had missed the war, he may even have thought he had to be tougher than the ex-soldiers; they had nothing to prove, but maybe Billy thought he did. He got through the sectarian battles of 1920 to 1922 unscathed, although his brother, Benjamin, was killed. And the little house on the edge of the Holy Land, a few paces from the sectarian border of the Ormeau Road, must have felt, as it did during the recent Troubles, a precarious place.

Unionists were fearful about what might happen to them in a united Ireland. There were stories and rumours about atrocities committed against the outnumbered and dispersed Prods outside Ulster. Sinn Féin and the Dáil struggled to head off sectarian conflict, but, inevitably, attacks on Protestants took place in the south. Between January and April 1921, twenty of them were murdered. However, we're struck by how few Protestants were killed, or harmed in any way, even during the angriest and most anguished periods of the guerrilla war. There were certainly expropriations, expulsions, house-burnings, and shootings, but there were no massacres, no repeats of 1641 or 1688.

Nevertheless, the Protestant presence in the south was dramatically eroded. A Presbyterian Church report of 1922 noted the decline in its population: down 45 percent in the Cork presbytery, 44 percent in Munster, 36 percent in Connacht, 16 percent in County Dublin. Protestants were intermarrying with Catholics, begetting few children, and getting out, moving north or, more likely, to England or North America. In this sterility and drifting away from an Ireland growing more Catholic, alienating, and closed, Ulster Protestants thought they saw their own future if they did not resist incorporation into a Catholic republic.

In the south, the IRA was engaged in fighting the English; in Ulster, its goal seemed to be to kill as many Protestants as it could. In fact, the IRA never really let up. It carried on operations in the north until partition and afterwards. In February 1922, it killed twenty-seven Protestants in Belfast alone. After the formation of Northern Ireland, its gunmen attacked across the border. It occasionally assassinated policemen and government officials, including the minister of justice, in the Irish Free State, refusing, even after the end of the civil war, to acquiesce in the treaty that had fallen short of outright independence.

The Northern Irish government favoured Protestants and excluded Catholics; it kept the Special Constabulary mobilized, and it gerrymandered electoral districts so as to ensure a perpetual unionist majority. The prime minister, James Craig, now Viscount

Craigavon, claimed that any inequities in the North were the result of Catholic abstention, not Protestant discrimination. For example, Catholics had refused to fill their allotted one-third of the Royal Ulster Constabulary; the government had to fill their spots with Protestants, and that was why the RUC became a "sectarian" force. This was an exaggerated and tortuous argument, but it had some force: Catholics did refuse to participate in the business of Northern Ireland because they believed it was illegitimate. In fact, both the British province and the Irish Free State consolidated their power through coercion, the abuse of minority rights, religious and political discrimination, the suspension of habeas corpus, and restrictions on public assemblies. None of it looked much different from what the English had been doing for all those centuries. The Free State never did manage to suppress the IRA—although there was considerable ambivalence in the south about how hard the government should try—and, in the North, Unionist repression ensured Catholic alienation and eventual rebellion.

Northern Ireland had one sectarian, limited, and uninspiring *raison d'être*: to maintain Protestant dominance and keep down its disaffected Catholic minority. Like all such regimes, its days were numbered. It would inevitably collapse; the only question was how long that would take.

As for Billy: he built ships; he was unemployed for four years; and he endured the gasworks. He lived through the terrible 1935 sectarian riots in Belfast—which almost became civil war and triggered attacks on Protestant homes, shops, and churches in the Free State—and he punched a tram driver who richly deserved it. Just after the end of the Second World War, his only, and beloved, grandson was born and, a year later, was taken away from him to England. Billy became ill with some form of kidney disease, and in 1954 he died. He missed the ineffectual IRA border campaign of the late 1950s, but it wouldn't have surprised him to see Catholic gunmen attacking the North once again. They would never stop—the unending assaults to be repelled confirmed the rightness of the siege mythology. Even if he had been healthier, it's very unlikely he would have lived long enough to see the Catholic civil rights movement and the Troubles, although I'm sure he would have liked the warlike preacher Ian Paisley, just as he had revered Edward Carson, the last Protestant "Big Man." At least Billy didn't have to watch his home crack up and fall once more into a maelstrom of terror and sectarian killing. I'm sure he would not have been disconcerted by it; to him, Catholics were murdering, uppity Taigs who were always unfinished business.

My father met me one day when I came home from school to our second-floor flat in Cheltenham in the English West Country. I was seven years old. He was quiet and sad and home early, and I knew something terrible had happened. He sat down in an armchair, and I stood in front of him. I remember his words exactly. In his formal way, he said: "Derek, I have some bad news. Your Grandpa Lundy has died." He screwed his knuckles into his eyes and began to cry. He wept for several minutes. I stood in front of him and watched, but soon I turned away in embarrassment and looked out the window. I felt sad but astonished. It was the first time I had seen my father cry. I remember the gleaming tears that ran out of his pale, ice-blue eyes. His eyes were always startling under his dark-brown hair and Viking-blond brows. When he stopped and wiped his face and blew his nose with his handkerchief, I was relieved. I wanted things to get back to normal as fast as possible. I didn't cry, nor did I feel the need to. Billy was an old man, remote in Belfast, and had nothing much to do with me; I was a little English boy whose parents happened to speak with Irish accents. My father left the next day on the train to catch the Heysham ferry for the funeral. My mother and I stayed behind. She had to go to work; I went to school as usual.

Billy was buried in the Belfast City Cemetery, which is on the Falls Road. My grandmother used to make regular trips to his grave to keep it in good order—"Protestant lookin'"—and every so often she brought flowers for it. But after the Troubles began, it was difficult for Protestants to visit the cemetery because the Falls was Catholic territory. My grandmother never got to her husband's side alive again. She made it there only when she was buried next to Billy—they had long ago bought their plot. For years, her grave, too, was unavailable to her family because it lay in dangerous enemy ground.

For some reason, I had never visited my grandparents' graves. In 2003, I went to the cemetery office to try to find out where they were in the sprawling settlement of the dead. A young man who told me his name was Paddy ("Catholic," I reflexively said to myself) searched through the record books. They were handwritten, grubby, and tattered from much use, a line per person. For some reason, he couldn't find any notation of either Billy or Maud. He wasn't supposed to let me look through the books myself, he said, but "Ah g'won, take a look, just." I spent twenty minutes leafing through them as he courteously ignored the time. But there was nothing, and Paddy had no idea why. As far as he knew, all the records were there; his predecessors had kept them undamaged through all the years of the Troubles. That had sometimes been problematic; republican gunmen and British soldiers had fought firefights along the cemetery's shady roads and paths and through its pleasant wooded glades. The gravestones had provided good cover for the armed men.

EPILOGUE

IN 1921, when it came time for my grandmother Maud to give birth to my father, the Irish war of independence was under way in the south, Protestants and Catholics were killing each other in the north, and Belfast was under the taut control of the police and the army. They had the right to shoot anyone found on the streets after the evening curfew. My grandmother's labour began during the night, and Billy had to fetch the midwife. He took a bed sheet and went out from the little house on the edge of the Holy Land. The army was everywhere, and soldiers saw him almost right away. Billy waved his sheet like a massive white flag; he didn't want any misunderstandings about why he was out there. The soldiers were kind; they took Billy in their truck to the midwife's and then drove both of them back to Cadogan Street. My father, Alexander, was born the next day. As he entered the world, the people on the street could hear gunfire chattering away here and there in the mean, sundered city. By the time he was eighteen months old, almost six hundred people had been killed in Ulster.

Alexander and the province of Northern Ireland came into existence in the same year. Now they're both dead, although my father outlived the political entity by a good margin. He died of a mundane heart attack when he was seventy-four. He could have delayed his death for many years if he hadn't stubbornly refused treatment for the symptoms, even when they became alarming and persistent. He didn't want to die, but he didn't exactly want to keep living either. Northern Ireland was killed off as a self-governing entity after fifty-one years of violent, repressive life: the British dissolved the sectarian government in 1972 when widespread violence made the province unmanageable. The six-county statelet had had a Hobbesian life: nasty, brutish, and short.

Both Alexander and his province demonstrated morbid symptoms. If the unionist Northern Irish state had been a person, a diagnosis would have been comprehensive: deeply neurotic (anxious, obsessive behaviour), fundamentally sociopathic (lack of moral responsibility and social conscience), and episodically psychotic (loss of contact with external reality). Alexander was equally complicated, a solitary, melancholy man, hard to know or touch. Like all sons, I wanted my father to be as the Ulster poet John Hewitt describes his: "the greatest man of all the men I love." But Alexander and I could never make that bond. He became lost in his own sadness, absorbed in his fight to avoid a terrible and long-prefigured breakdown and depression. It effloresced when he was forty-four and could no longer stave it off, and it went on for years. Even a son beloved in a way could only loiter on the fringe of such an obsession with mere endurance.

Alexander left school when he was fourteen because his family needed the money he made as a butcher's delivery boy and then as a post office telegram messenger. In both jobs, he pedalled around Belfast, a wheeled *flâneur*, absorbing the city's sectarian geography, its crackles and murmurings of tension, anger, hatred. During the 1935 riots and near civil war, he stayed home. The messengers' uniforms with their British Crowns stood out, and the post office didn't want its boys to be run down by mobs or shot by nationalist gunmen. When the Second World War began, my father tried to run athwart family naval tradition and join the air force as a pilot. But in the war's early days, there were too many of the few, and he could become only a navigator. He accepted his fate and joined the navy.

That was the beginning of his departure from Northern Ireland. He came back for a few years to marry my mother, whom he had met just before the war began, and to have me. But there was nowhere for us to live in bombed-out Belfast, except with Billy and Maud in the little house on Cadogan Street. Alexander had spent years in the space and light of the open sea and in the tropics. Recuperating from malaria, blackwater, and dengue fevers, he had lived for a year on a farm in South Africa. When he was well enough, he herded cattle on horseback across the endless, rolling hills of Natal and rode to Zulu kraals to drink moonshine. He had mingled with men from everywhere in the empire, and it was impossible for him to subside again into the narrow ground of the sectarian Protestant province. In spite of his scant formal education, he got the second-highest marks in Northern Ireland in the Imperial Civil Service exams. He had the choice of Singapore or London; he chose London, and we went out of Ireland.

Alexander was an intelligent man who scored high in the genius category on IQ tests. Perhaps he was just too smart to absorb the old prejudices. Inherited hatred isn't just a matter of stupidity, but a good brain is one defence against it. And there's always the tantalizing possibility of William Steel Dickson's tolerant inheritance finding its way to Alexander through Maud, inoculating him against Billy's prejudice. My father's destiny, like William's, was to use his fierce and focused intellect to haul himself up and out of the Ulster Prod lower class. Both men hungered for history's truths and rejected the mingled fear and triumphalism of their people's mythology.

Alexander remained out of place and deracinated. He left Ireland and his origins behind, in the process losing intimacy, indeed almost all connection, with his family. But he was never able to clinch his upwardly mobile transition either. He couldn't break completely free of Belfast's residues of poverty and meanness. And the city always retained for him the subtle, nostalgic hold of the place of childhood and youth. He had emigrated and did not want to go back, but he felt like an exile nevertheless. The immigrant always carries an unavoidable burden: the web of memory and imagination that used to be "home." For the rest of his life, Alexander talked—Joyce-like—about the streets and characters of Belfast that he knew so well. In Canada, he was never able to assume without ambivalence his higher social and economic status. Behind his white shirt and tie, his regular schedule, his private office and desk, his clean un-sweaty work, the seductive, dismissive glee of rebellion and self-sabotage worked on him all his life.

Alexander became a socialist for a while before the war—he

certainly didn't stay one—going to rallies for the Belfast labour leader Harry Midgley and singing the "Internationale" instead of "The Sash My Father Wore." He read the young Karl Marx's *Economic and Philosophical Manuscripts*, and that must have provided perspective, of a sort, on communal hatred and violence. For a while, he thought in terms of the international proletariat rather than Prods and Taigs.

My father also rebelled against the vehement authoritarianism and certainties of his father. If Billy was a Prod hard man who had unloaded the UVF's rifles, joined the B Specials, and hated Catholics, then Alexander would do the opposite. He said to me: "I paid attention to my father for as long as I had to, and when it wasn't necessary any more, I ignored him." What was there to keep him in Belfast? He had to get out—of his family, the mind-prison of sectarian hatred, and the miserable, bombed-out city, the whole damned country. It could all go to hell. It's not quite true to say he was without prejudice: he disliked Northern Irish Protestants and Catholics equally—their closed little minds and mealy-mouthed hatreds. Even after we had emigrated to Canada, he could not abide the assumptions of brotherhood and shared prejudice that other immigrant Prods, with their Orangy Freemasonry, tried to hang on him. He brushed them away with the shudder of an arachnaphobe shaking off spiders. He was not stirred by the stories of Derry's walls or of the Ninety-Eight. No call of the *Shan Van Vocht* for him, either. He would have agreed with the poet of our day on that Old Woman:

> Folly, I'm saying, gets worse with every generation:
> Anything, every old cliché in the book, anything at all
> To get this old bitch to shut the fuck up.

Alexander's departure was Ireland's loss. Some good people go and some stay, but the bad bastards always stay. It's possible that there's no moral or lesson or particular reason for hope in Alexander's avoidance of the conditioned loathings of his Ulster tribe. It may be just chance that once in a while a man or a woman escapes it altogether, or is able to ameliorate its effect—all a matter of the random conjunctions of personality and experience. The people who run things are gunmen and fundamentalists, not peaceable, tolerant agnostics. Secret police, not poets, are the unacknowledged legislators of the world, said W.H. Auden. The fact is that in Northern Ireland, as in other violent and divided societies, most people can't avoid absorbing the ancient hatreds. The best one can hope for is that they will learn to stop killing each other because of them.

The first intimation of the Troubles, the foreshadowing shivers and tremors of alarm and suspicion, began with a "Lundy." From 1963 until 1969, the prime minister of Northern Ireland was Terence O'Neill, yet another of these perpetual O'Neills of Ulster, although this time a privileged Protestant—Lord O'Neill of the Maine—the descendant of some earlier apostate. He met with Sean Lemass, the *taoiseach* of the Republic of Ireland (who had fought at the General Post Office with Pearse during the Easter Rising). It was the first time any northern leader had come out from the walls of Northern Ireland to treat with the encircling Irish. O'Neill wanted to ameliorate the condition of Catholics in the North and to modernize the economy, but he had no thoughts of surrender in any sense. (He bitterly denied the later claim by Lemass's widow that they had talked about "Irish unity.") On the contrary, he was a good unionist who wanted to try to convince the southerner that Northern Ireland was a fact that the republic would have to accept. The article in the Republic's 1937 Constitution claiming jurisdiction over all of Ireland, including the six counties of Northern Ireland and its Protestant people, was a "grandiose and empty" claim. It was an unprecedented attempt by an Ulster Protestant at public relations. O'Neill tried to show that it wasn't the Prods who were aggressive, recalcitrant, and stubborn, and therefore standing in the way of decent neighbourly relations. On the contrary, the two parts of Ireland couldn't cooperate because of the vanity of the Republic's refusal to recognize the democratic will of the Protestants. Lemass was guardedly sympathetic to O'Neill's overture, and O'Neill argued that the meeting, which took place in the North, was a de facto recognition by the Republic that Northern Ireland was a separate entity.

O'Neill had joined the Royal Black Preceptory (the highest form of Orangeism) and the Apprentice Boys and had led the celebratory siege procession in Derry in 1964. None of it mattered to the Protestant hard-liners. He had joined late in life as a matter of obvious political expediency, rather than in his youth as an enthusiastic true-believer. And he had done something unforgivable: he had met the enemy; he had talked to a southern Taig. Is he "secretly selling us to the South?" asked Ian Paisley, the question summing up with admirable brevity all his (and Ulster Protestant) paranoia (unless we believe Lemass's widow) about conspiracy and betrayal. O'Neill had to be just another Lundy who was planning to open the gates of Ulster to the disloyal Catholics within and the Irish Republic outside.

The intense and prolonged phase of the Troubles broke out first in Derry. The city should not have been included in the province of Northern Ireland in 1921. It was predominantly Catholic, and it is situated on the West Bank, the Irish, Donegal, side of the River Foyle, which is a natural boundary. But the Ulster Protestants had been unwilling to let Derry, with its profound meaning and legacy, go into a Catholic Ireland. It seemed to be the destiny of the outpost on the Protestant frontier to trigger great and terrible things. The Battle of the Bogside took place on August 12, 1969, during the relief-of-the-siege celebrations by the Apprentice Boys. All the familiar elements of strife were present once again. Few, if anyone, in Northern Ireland would have predicted the ferocity and duration of what followed over the next thirty years. No one realized the depth of rage and fear still there.

The sectarian Protestant government of Northern Ireland ended in 1972 because of something else that happened in Derry. This time, it was one day, January 30, 1972: another Bloody Sunday.* It unfolded in the name's old tradition. British para-troopers killed fourteen unarmed civilians during a banned civil rights march in the city. The troopers sallied out from the Butcher Gate as if it was three hundred years earlier. They hunted down their targets through the crummy, narrow streets of the Bogside, killing Irishmen as if they were the wolves and kerns the

---

* The previously best-known Bloody Sunday in Ireland happened during the worst days of the war of independence, in November 1920. Twenty-eight IRA men, British Army officers, and Irish civilians died by assassination and murder, the civilians, twelve of them, when Black and Tans fired on the crowd at a football match.

seventeenth-century Thomas Blenerhasset had recommended slaughtering with such gusto in the early days of the Plantation. Once again, a few trigger-happy English soldiers engineered a mighty Irish reaction. Catholic rage was immense, overwhelming. This time, it swept away a government. Bloody Sunday triggered so much more blood in the streets that the little statelet of Northern Ireland came tumbling down. From then on, until the abortive power-sharing governments of the late 1990s, England ruled it directly with troops and proconsul as if it were a violent and refractory colony or, indeed, Ireland as it used to be.

The future of Northern Ireland is complicated by the increasing distance between the north and the south and by the persistence of the armed gangs of the boys. The IRA dislikes the increasingly commercial and consumerist nature of the Republic of Ireland as much as it abhorred the sectarian government of the North. The people of the Republic are less eager year by year to try to absorb the troubled province into a united Ireland. (Germany's recent difficulties in integrating the former East Germany may be a lesson.) Ulster has been separate and distinct for a long time. Perhaps the Republic would merely import south the northern sickness. The Protestant paramilitaries could be as much of a problem—as perennial guerrillas—for the government of a united Ireland as the IRA was for the Northern Irish regime and for the British.

The boys on both sides have a long history in Ireland. And they like the sensations that come from being armed and outside the law; it's hard for all men who have become acclimatized to that kind of power and excitement to return to tame domesticity. No man wants to give up weapons once he's become used to having them. Protestant paramilitaries and the IRA-run organized crime networks, and the more fractured Prods fight among themselves like mafia families. The gunmen on both sides still run their neighbourhoods through intimidation and terror (although perhaps that will change now the IRA has announced it will stand down and pursue peaceful solutions). When IRA men murdered the Catholic civilian Robert McCartney outside a bar in early 2005, none of the many witnesses (among whom were some members of Sinn Féin) felt safe enough to cooperate with the police and name the killers—who were well known. McCartney's sisters began a courageous public campaign for justice, and the IRA made them its ultimate offering: it would shoot in cold blood the men who had killed their brother. The family declined.

It's unlikely that Northern Ireland will surprise and horrify everyone again, as it did in 1969, and descend into an apocalypse of civil war and destruction. In the short run, the best we can reasonably hope for is that the IRA's cessation of violence will hold and the Protestant paramilitaries will reciprocate. We can also expect that the extremist Protestant politicians will eventually agree to talk to the extremist Catholic politicians, and share power with them in a government of a new, segregated, tenuously peaceful—or not at war—Northern Irish statelet.

In the long run . . .

Two men embody the choice for Protestants. My cousin Martin is a sixty-year-old Protestant who has driven a cab in Belfast for years. He worked during the Troubles, when taxi drivers were vulnerable; they were robbed, beaten up, kidnapped, tortured, shot. He was lucky and avoided all that, although he had to exercise his arcane knowledge of the sectarian streets: some were okay, some iffy, others suicide. He navigated the city like a ship's captain among intricate and deadly reefs. His father was an evangelical Protestant who, according to my family, hated Catholics. Martin denies that—his father would argue with priests and respect their point of view, he says—but his demurral has the air of filial loyalty. In spite of his father's influence and his own years-long jeopardy to attack by the IRA or freelance Catholic gunmen, Martin displays no prejudice at all. In that respect, he is like my father. Martin's tolerance is even more remarkable because he did not leave Northern Ireland as a young man, like Alexander, but stayed on through the decades of war and terror. To come through all that without hatred or rancour—and, even more compelling, with understanding and empathy for the other side—takes an astonishing and cheering purity of heart. "I could live in a united Ireland," he told me.

A few years after his wife died of cancer, when his grief had dulled, Martin started to go out with a Catholic woman. When he introduced her to his Protestant friends and told them her obviously Catholic name, they replied in rude disbelief, "You're jokin'!" They never thought a good Prod like Martin, even if he was soft on Taigs, would cross that line.

One evening Martin took me out to a pub in downtown Belfast to drink (he's an energetic drinker) and for the *craic*, and to listen to music. The group was Catholic, and some of the musicians played traditional Irish instruments—the *uillean* pipes, the *bodhran*—and sang nationalist and old Irish songs, and sometimes they sang in Gaelic. No "kick-the-Pope" or Orange sash music that night. There was the easy to and fro of jokes and banter between the players and the audience which happens in Ireland, even in the North. After a while, Martin turned to me and said it would have been too danger-ous for him to have come to a bar and listened to this music even a few years ago. And if he had chanced it, he could never have told any of his friends about it; they would have shunned him. He may even have been in jeopardy of punishment by Protestant paramilitaries. I nodded; it was a good sign that things were getting better. Then Martin the Ulster Prod turned back to me and said over the sound of the Gaelic song in the Catholic bar, with indignation, almost with anger: "And why shouldn't I listen to this? It's my music too. We're all Irish."

Then there's Billy, one of Martin's colleagues. He's getting close to middle age, but he has spent almost his whole life within the Troubles. He told me that he hated Taigs. He believed it was only a matter of time before the Brits caved in and allowed the Republic to absorb the North, and that would be the end of the Prods. In a united Ireland, unionists would have no say whatsoever in what went on. "They'll be nothin'," he said. "We might have to do what the IRA did—y'know, go to the gun again, keep shooting and bombing 'til we get our country back."

One day, I decided to knock on the door of the little house on the edge of the Holy Land instead of just walking by it. I had not been inside since my grandmother died almost thirty years earlier. After her death, my uncle and his family took over the house. But they soon emigrated to Canada, unstrung finally by intimidation and threats, broken car windows and flat tires, gunshots in the night. The Holy Land and its adjacent streets, hemmed in by the River Lagan, the blank middle-class unconcern of the university, and the surrounding Catholic territory, was one piece of Prod turf that couldn't be defended. Family by family, the Protestants moved out. For several years, the little house was listed in the Belfast City Directory as "vacant." Then Catholic names appear: Patrick Duffy and John Duffy.

During the Troubles, it was a very bad idea to knock on a door if the occupants didn't know you. However, I felt safe in these days of the peace treaty and paramilitary ceasefires. A university student, a young woman, opened the door. I explained who I was and that, if I had any claim to an ancestral home, this little house was mine. She was amiable and interested, but it wasn't convenient to come in now; tomorrow would be better.

The next day, the student, Leona, showed me around. I knew the place had been renovated, but it was a shock to see how much it had been altered—the gloomy scullery enlarged into a regular bright kitchen; the living room and formal, seldom-used front parlour collapsed into one airy room. There was an indoor toilet. Leona's bedroom was the attic, which had been converted into a loft-like, painted, carpeted haven. It was a comfortable place to live in, unlike the dingy, draughty, bare-walled slum I had slept in.

Leona was from Belleek in County Fermanagh, almost as far west as Northern Ireland protruded into the republic, a "skite down the road" from the border of Donegal, no more than ten kilometres from the Atlantic Ocean. By Irish standards, she was a long way from home. She was studying law and accountancy at Queen's University, but her goal was in the old tradition: she wanted to leave Ireland, in her case to work in England. The whole student area of the Holy Land and its adjacent streets was mostly filled with Catholic students. In the city's compressed geography, the Protestant students' area of the Stranmillis and Lisburn roads was only a kilometre or two away. I asked Leona why they kept themselves separated. She replied: it was just that Catholics didn't feel comfortable when they saw orange-painted kerbstones or Union Jacks or Protestant football flags. As far as I had seen, there were none of those sectarian markers along the relatively well-to-do Protestant roads. A little later, she said, without disjunction or irony: "Of course, it's the older people who still have the old prejudices and hatred; none of it means anything to us students and other young people."

I said it was strange to me that the Holy Land and the nearby streets were all Catholic now, because this used to be a Protestant area. Leona was surprised; she hadn't known anything about that. Now she looked at me a little differently, with that appraising Ulster gaze I knew so well; I had to be a Protestant myself, then. There was something else in her look: Leona was afraid of me. I had suddenly revealed myself as a Prod, whom she had casually admitted to her house, and who was standing in her room with his abrupt claim of ownership and, perhaps, of sectarian grievance. As for me, I felt the first few tremors of indignation and, yes, I had to admit, of anger, too.

It was only a flash through my mind, but it was there, surprising and clear—how sly and easy was anger's quick rise. Catholics had "ethnically cleansed" this street; I would not have felt this way if other Protestants lived here now. But, of course, they would have acquired the place through a normal commercial transaction, not by intimidation. This young woman stood there in "my" house in "my" neighbourhood, the bland and naive beneficiary of sectarian terror. All the families I had known—my own family—had been forced out by Catholic gunmen or gangs of young Catholics Leona's age. Of course, Protestants had done the same thing elsewhere, but here, it had been Catholics who had carried out the dirty business. Yet it had happened before she was born; she had no knowledge of the many small skirmishes fought along this sectarian line, the Prods eventually losing the battle to hold the Holy Land.

I wanted this meeting in this house to be a pleasant one; I was, after all, a self-invited guest. I felt the need to reassure Leona that I wasn't a returning Prod come to scare or harass her; that I was just a Canadian looking for my roots—the usual North American superficial fascination with the "old country." But that wasn't what I was, and that wasn't how I felt.

We talked about the Troubles. Leona said that the Protestant areas of North Belfast were very bad. The loyalist paramilitaries were fighting among themselves there, and elsewhere, carrying out punishments and shootings and intimidating people. She made no mention of Catholic West Belfast, which was as violent and fanatical as any Prod stronghold, or of the IRA and its equally vicious infighting and crime, or of the splinter Real IRA, which wasn't even on ceasefire but was continuing the old bombs-and-bullets campaign to kill Prods, kick out the Brits, and unite Ireland. Just as earlier, it seemed not to have occurred to her that Protestant students might feel as uncomfortable with Gaelic-language signs and tricolours as Catholics did with Union Jacks and painted curbs. In her own pleasant, new-generation way, Leona was beginning to seem to me as bigoted as any old-timer. She thought that Protestants were vicious and prejudiced (as many of them are), but that Catholics were nonsectarian normal people. Their violence throughout the Troubles was only a legitimate response to Protestant oppression. She seemed to have no sense that there might be culpability on both sides, or that Protestant grievances might be comprehensible, even credible.

I left the little house on the edge of the Holy Land for, I was sure, the last time. The real purpose of my visit had been to assuage nostalgia, but it hadn't worked. On the contrary, the renovations, Leona's odd and unexpected mindlessness, and my own surprising—if brief—anger had intensified my sense of estrangement. What a pair we were: the young, intelligent, and educated woman blind to her own prejudice; the sore man who had never even lived there. Instead of putting to rest the emotional artifacts of my half-remembered childhood and the things my father had told me about his city, I felt more than ever the strange longing for them, their pull and rasp, like thirst that couldn't be satisfied.

I walked over to the Ormeau Road. I could drink in any pub I wanted to these days. The two Catholic pubs on the other side of the street, while still seedy, were open and thriving. However, in a sign of their lost battle on this ground, the Protestants' pub I had gone into many years ago was a burnt-out derelict. As I walked towards the city centre in winter's early dusk, I came across a police checkpoint. One officer waved cars to slow down, peered inside, and then waved them on. Perhaps he was looking for someone in particular. A second policeman stood against a nearby house front, covering his partner with a submachine gun. Before the ceasefires, at a roadblock like this, there would have been half-a-dozen or more heavily armed policemen with a couple of armoured Land Rovers, perhaps backed up by a squad of British troopers with a Saracen standing by. They would have been on edge, paying very close attention to their surroundings, scoping passing vehicles. They would certainly have stopped and searched me, maybe pushed me around a little.

Now, I strolled by these bored coppers, and they didn't give me a glance. It was a kind of progress. In Northern Ireland, you take whatever you can get.

Robert Lundy lives on; his mythical persona is still vigorous. The Protestants think they still need their Traitor. In fact, there's no end of Lundys. As the Protestants become more beset, their position more tenuous, the more Lundys there are bound to be, the greater the need to name them and to expel them. It's getting harder to do in a time when some Protestants agree to share political power in Northern Ireland with Sinn Féin's ex-nationalist gunmen. That's a malign efflorescence of "Lundyism" that no one can scour out.

In his antique play *Ireland Preserv'd; or the Siege of Londonderry*, the soldier John Michelburne condemns Robert: "By private designs and villainy this treacherous governor and his friends are not contented to get this kingdom to themselves, but destroy us root and branch." The hard-line Protestants of Derry, and of all Ulster, believed that then and have believed it ever since. But the myth they created has been obsolete for a long time; it will no longer serve a purpose. Deep inside their fearful hearts, the Protestants of Northern Ireland know, although they will not, or cannot yet, acknowledge it, that the Lundys have been right all along. In the end, the Protestants don't have a choice. They will surrender, with caution and in unavoidable fear, to the idea that Ireland has contained them for four hundred years or more and that they belong there and nowhere else. They must compromise and agree to terms. The truth is that only a Lundy can save them.

AUTHOR'S NOTE

ON JULY 28, 2005, the Irish Republican Army announced it had ended its "armed campaign" in Northern Ireland. It ordered all units to "dump arms" and said it had instructed its "volunteers" to "assist the development of purely political and democratic programmes through exclusively peaceful means." The statement added: "Volunteers must not engage in any other activities whatsoever." However, the IRA statement also said: "We reiterate our view that the armed struggle was entirely legitimate." The organization was "conscious that many people suffered in the conflict," but it made no apology and expressed no regret for the hundreds of civilians it had killed. It did state it would verifiably put its arms beyond use in the presence of independent witnesses from both the Protestant and the Catholic churches.

In an immediate response, the British Army dismantled a number of its installations in south Armagh, Derry, and Belfast and announced it would reduce its troop levels in Northern Ireland by half—to approximately five thousand—over the next two years.

On September 26, 2005, the head of the Independent International Commission on Decommissioning, Canadian general John de Chastelain, announced that the IRA had put all its weapons beyond use.

I had completed *Men that God Made Mad* before the IRA made its statement and decommissioned its arms, although I was able to add a few sentences to take account of the putative end of the IRA's

The book is often pessimistic about long-term prospects for peace in Northern Ireland. I'm more optimistic now—but only a little. Time will tell what effect the IRA's stand-down will have. And many questions remain: Has the organization in fact destroyed all its arms? Will dissidents, unhappy with the cessation of war, break away and join the Real IRA or the Continuity IRA? Neither group has even declared a ceasefire. Will the republican paramilitaries be able to give up their criminal activities? They're long used to the power and money that crime brings in. Above all, how will the Protestants respond?

The IRA emphasizes that its goal remains a united Ireland and the end of "British rule," in spite of the clear desire of the Ulster Protestants to remain within the United Kingdom. One of this book's main themes is that the Protestants have always been the crucial actors in the affairs of the northern part of Ireland, and they remain so now. Will the Prods reciprocate the IRA's stand-down? Will the loyalist paramilitary groups disarm and give up their own criminal pursuits? Even Ian Paisley's radical Democratic Unionists (now the dominant Protestant political party) will eventually agree to participate in a government that includes Sinn Féin's ex-gunmen. But can the Protestants ever acquiesce in the absorption of Northern Ireland into a united Irish republic in which they will be a perpetual minority? Perhaps some Protestants will instead conclude: If the IRA believes it's time to stop the war because it can now rely on political means for achieving its long-held goals, then things look very bad for the Prods. Some of them may decide it's imperative to resist more than ever, and by whatever means, the end of Northern Ireland and their ancient connection with Great Britain and the Crown.

Nevertheless, there are also hopeful intimations of Northern Ireland's future: all those Protestants like my cousin Martin—tolerant pluralists who could move with ease and good humour into a united Ireland; and economic growth, which invigorates the secular and diminishes the sectarian. In Belfast, for example, work will soon begin on the "Titanic Quarter," a twenty-year, billion pound development of the city's defunct shipbuilding and docklands area. The project will result in 20,000 jobs; 2,000 homes; office and commercial space; and a huge *Titanic* visitors' centre and museum on the slipway where my grandfather Billy helped build the iconic vessel. In Derry, the municipal council will try to have the city centre registered as a World Heritage site. The council wants to promote for tourists the Bogside and its republican murals, the Fountain (in spite of its churlish Prods), the Apprentice Boys Memorial Hall, Saint Columb's Cathedral, and the Diamond. Above all, the council will tout Derry's well-preserved walls. Perhaps they will become more like picturesque remnants of the past—ordinary walls, which, once upon a time, withstood a siege—and less like the mythic totem of a fearful tribe.

Salt Spring Island, British Columbia
October 2005

ACKNOWLEDGMENTS

I GRATEFULLY ACKNOWLEDGE the help of the staff of the library of Queen's University in Belfast, and particularly Deirdre Wildy, Robert Hunter, and Gavin Carville of Special Collections. My thanks also to the staff of the Linenhall Library in Belfast, the Public Records Office of Northern Ireland, the Belfast City Cemetery, the Family Research Centre in London, the Robarts Library at the University of Toronto, and the McPherson Library at the University of Victoria, and to Dr. Brian Trainor and Dr. Jonathan Hamill at the Ulster Historical Foundation.

In Derry, my thanks to Paul Haslam for his generous hospitality and his friendship; to Richard Doherty for help with research; to Billy Moore for his invitation to the Apprentice Boys Memorial Hall; and to John Hume for a good quote. In Belfast, Mervyn and Pauline McMeekin and Martin Hawthorne put me up, took me out, and made me feel at home once again. I was welcomed into William Steel Dickson's last church by the Reverend Jonathan Curry, and into my family's house on the edge of the Holy Land by Leona McManus. Marilyn Ellis provided a sanctuary in England when the planes weren't flying. My warmest thanks to all of them.

In Canada, I'm grateful to William Lundy for his stories and memories and to Alan and Mark Lundy; to Eric Wredenhagen for his invaluable opinions on the book's first draft; to Walter Korinowsky, John Murray, and Christine Mauro for their perspectives; and to Harry Warner, who helped me with the Gaelic.

I thank the Canada Council for the Arts for its generous financial assistance during the writing of this book.

I'm most grateful to Dan Franklin and Alexandra Milner at Jonathan Cape, and to Jason Arthur at Vintage, for all their efforts in publishing the book in the United Kingdom and in Ireland. Thanks also to Michael Salu for the jacket and cover designs.

My warmest thanks to my agent, Anne McDermid, for everything; to Knopf Canada's publisher, Diane Martin, who provided, as always, her encouragement and advice; to John Eerkes-Medrano, who edited the manuscript with intelligence and insight; to Rosemary Shipton, who copy edited with precision and discernment; to Deirdre Molina and Angelika Glover, who performed, with cool and able collection, the myriad tasks necessary to get a book out there; and to Mark Veldhuizen for his splendid jacket design.

To my wife, Christine, and to my daughter, Sarah, my love and thanks once again.

TIMELINE

546	Saint Colum Cille founds Derry
795	Vikings begin to raid Ireland
1014	Battle of Clontarf: Brian Bóruma defeats a Viking-Leinster army
1170	Richard de Clare (Strongbow) lands in Ireland
1171	King Henry II lands in Ireland: beginning of the English occupation
1541	Act of the Irish Parliament declares Henry VIII King of Ireland
1561–67	Shane O'Neill's rebellion
1568–73	First Desmond rebellion
1573–76	Earl of Essex's Enterprise of Ulster
1579–83	Second Desmond rebellion
1585	Munster Plantation begins

1595–1603	Hugh O'Neill's rebellion, or the Nine Years War
1603	Conquest "complete"
1607	Flight of the Earls
1608	Sir Cahir O'Doherty of Inishowen attacks Derry
1608–10	Plans laid for Ulster Plantation
1610	Agreement with City of London for Plantation of Derry and surrounding area English and Scottish settlers begin to arrive
1641	Rising begins
1649–50	Cromwell reconquers Ireland; massacres in Drogheda and Wexford
1688	Derry shuts its gates Robert Lundy appointed military governor
1689	Robert Lundy expelled; Siege of Derry begins
1690	William III wins Battle of the Boyne
1691	William wins Battle of Aughrim War ends with Treaty of Limerick Presbyterian Synod of Ulster holds first recorded meeting
1695–1709	Popery Laws (or Penal Laws) against Catholics
1717	Robert Lundy dies in England
1718	Ulster Protestants begin large-scale emigration to American colonies

1744	William Steel Dickson born
1761	Whiteboy movement begins in Munster
1763	Oakboy agitation begins in Ulster
1769	Steelboy disturbances in Ulster
1775–83	American War of Independence
1778	Volunteer movement begins in Ireland
1782–83	Volunteer conventions at Dungannon advocate legislative reform
1784	Formation of Protestant Peep O' Day Boys and Catholic Defenders
1789	French Revolution; Bastille falls
1791	Formation of Society of United Irishmen
1795	Battle of the Diamond leads to formation of Orange Order
1797	"Dragooning of Ulster"
1798	Insurrection Arrest and detention of William Steel Dickson
1801	*Act of Union* between Great Britain and Ireland
1802	William Steel Dickson released
1803	Robert Emmet's rebellion
1808	Rise of the Catholic "Liberator," Daniel O'Connell

1814	Formation of Apprentice Boys Club
1824	William Steel Dickson dies
1845	Great Famine begins
1848	Young Ireland Rising
1857	Sectarian riots in Belfast
1858	Formation of Irish Republican Brotherhood (Fenians)
1864	Sectarian riots in Belfast
1867	Fenian Rising
1872	Sectarian riots in Belfast
1880	Charles Stewart Parnell elected chairman of Irish Parliamentary Party
1886	First home rule bill defeated in House of Commons
1890	William (Billy) Lundy born
1891	Parnell dies
1894	Second home rule bill defeated in House of Lords Sectarian riots in Belfast
1905	Formation of Sinn Féin
1912	Signing of Ulster's Solemn League and Covenant
1913	Formation of Ulster Volunteer Force Formation of Irish Volunteers

1914	Ulster Volunteer Force runs guns Third home rule bill passes; suspended after First World War begins
1916	Easter Rising; fifteen leaders executed
1919	Irish War of Independence begins Formation of Dáil Éireann; Eamon de Valera elected president Irish Volunteers become known as the Irish Republican Army
1920	Formation of Black and Tans Bloody Sunday Partition of Ireland through *Government of Ireland Act*
1921	Northern Ireland Parliament opens Anglo-Irish Treaty signed; formation of Irish Free State Alexander Lundy born
1922–23	Irish Civil War
1935	Sectarian riots in Belfast
1941	German air raids on Belfast
1948	Irish Free State declares itself a republic
1954	Billy Lundy dies
1956–62	IRA campaign in Northern Ireland
1964	Sectarian riots in Belfast
1965	*Taoiseach* Sean Lemass meets Northern Irish prime minister Lord O'Neill

1966	Celebration of fiftieth anniversary of Easter Rising
	Ulster Volunteer Force forms and kills Catholics

1968	First Catholic civil rights march
	Civil rights march and sectarian riots in Derry

1969	People's Democracy March ambushed by Protestants
	Bombings by Protestant paramilitaries
	Derry riots followed by introduction of British troops
	Sectarian riots in Belfast followed by arrival of British troops
	Beginning of widespread conflict throughout Northern Ireland

1970	IRA splits; formation of Provisional IRA
	Fighting begins between British Army and republicans
	B Specials disbanded

1971	Reintroduction of internment without trial

1972	Bloody Sunday in Derry
	Burning of British Embassy in Dublin
	Northern Irish Parliament and government suspended; British direct rule

1973	Act providing for power-sharing and Northern Ireland assembly
	Sunningdale Agreement on status of Northern Ireland and a Council of Ireland

1974	Ulster Workers' Council general strike
	Assembly prorogued; direct rule reimposed

1981	H-Block prisoners' hunger strike; ten die

1995	Alexander Lundy dies
1997	IRA ceasefire and beginning of all-party talks
1998	Good Friday Agreement
2003	Ian Paisley's Democratic Unionists become largest party
2004	Northern Bank robbery; IRA suspected
2005	Murder of Robert McCartney by IRA IRA announces end of armed campaign IRA "decommissions" its weapons

FURTHER READING

Bardon, Jonathan. *A History of Ulster*. London: Longman, 1992.

Boyce, D. George, and Alan O'Day, eds. *The Making of Modern Irish History: Revisionism and the Revisionist Controversy*. London: Routledge, 1996.

Brady, Ciaran, ed. *Interpreting Irish History: The Debate on Historical Revisionism*. Dublin: Irish Academic Press, 1994.

Foster, R.F. *Modern Ireland, 1600–1972*. London: Penguin, 1989.

Kiberd, Declan. *Inventing Ireland*. Cambridge, Mass.: Harvard University Press, 1995.

Lyons, F.S.L. *Culture and Anarchy in Ireland, 1890–1939*. Oxford: Oxford University Press, 1982.

MacDonagh, Oliver. *States of Mind: A Study of Anglo-Irish Conflict, 1780–1980*. London: George Allen and Unwin, 1983.

McBride, Ian, ed. *History and Memory in Modern Ireland*. Cambridge: Cambridge University Press, 2001.

Moody, T.W., and F.X. Martin, eds. *The Course of Irish History*. Cork: Mercier Press, 2001.

Stewart, A.T.Q. *The Narrow Ground: Aspects of Ulster, 1609–1969*. Belfast: Blackstaff Press, 1997.

Walker, Brian. *Past and Present: History, Identity and Politics in Ireland*. Belfast: Queen's University, 2000.

PERMISSIONS

The author has made every effort to locate and contact all the holders of copyright to material reproduced in this book, and expresses grateful acknowledgment for permission to reprint excerpts from the following previously published material:

Nuala Ní Dhomhnaill, "The Shan Van Vocht," translated by Ciaran Carson, in *Pharaoh's Daughter*, The Gallery Press, Oldcastle, County Meath, Ireland: 1990. Reprinted by permission of The Gallery Press.

Brian Friel, *Translations*, in *Selected Plays of Brian Friel*, Faber and Faber Ltd, London: 1984. Reprinted by permission of Faber and Faber Ltd.

Seamus Heaney, "Requiem for the Croppies" in *Opened Ground: Poems 1966–1996*, Faber and Faber Ltd, London: 1998. Reprinted by permission of Faber and Faber Ltd.

John Hewitt, "The Lonely Heart," part II of "Freehold," in *The Collected Poems of John Hewitt*, ed. Frank Ormsby, Blackstaff Press, Belfast: 1991. Reprinted by permission of Blackstaff Press.

Louis MacNeice, *The Collected Poems of Louis MacNeice*, Oxford University Press, 1967. Reprinted by permission of Faber and Faber Ltd. *Selected Poems of Louis MacNeice*, Faber and Faber Ltd, London: 1964. Reprinted by permission of David Higham Associates.

INDEX

Rebellion; the Oakboy agitation; risings; Robert Emmet's rebellion; Shane O'Neill's revolt; United Irish Rebellion
fear of, 61

the Red Hand (myth). *See* the Bloody Red Hand

Red Hand Commandos, 3, 155, 210

Redmond, John, 275–77, 284, 286–88, 298
volunteers his Volunteers to Briton, 290–92
in the wake of the Easter Rebellion, 295

Redmond, Willie, 291

redshanks, Earl of Antrim's, 43, 74–78, 81, 83, 91, 99

Reid, Robert Rollo, 129

the *Relief Act,* 190

religion. *See also* Anglican; Catholic; Dissenters; Presbyterian; Protestant
as a defining attribute in Ireland, 3–4, 49–50
unequal geographic distributions of, 51

religious affiliation, unsettling ambiguities concerning, 6–7, 49, 51–52

religious amity in Ireland, 100, 186

religious Puritanism and fundamentalism, 253

Renan, Ernest, 14

reprisals, 21, 23, 294, 303. *See also* revenge

the Republic of Ireland, 2, 8, 22, 108, 156, 201, 253, 268, 270, 289, 291, 314, 316

revenge, 66–68, 264
enduring desires for, 22–23, 66–67, 198, 201
fear of, 54–55, 68–69

revivalists. *See* Gaelic (culture), attempted revival of

the Ribbonmen, 102, 175, 216

Richards, Colonel Solomon, 89

Rightboys (protest movement), 150

Rights of Man (Paine's pamphlet), 186

riots, 2, 108, 147, 155, 208, 246, 255, 305, 307, 311, 330–32. *See also* sectarian riots

Rí Seamus vs. *Rí Liam,* 50, 83

risings. *See also* Easter Rising (1916); the Fenian Rising (1867); the Great Rising (1641); rebellions; the Young Ireland Rising (1848)

British savagery in suppression of, 20–21, 34, 51, 60–61, 125, 239, 242

river(s). *See specifics by name, e.g.* Foyle (river)

robberies, by paramilitary and related gangs, 6, 333

Robert Emmet's rebellion (1803), 106, 217, 329

Rogers, Rev. John, 176

Róisín Dubh (mythic woman symbolizing Ireland), 293

Rosen, Conrad de, 90

Rossa, O'Donovan, 20, 204

Rousseau, Jean-Jacques, 186

Royal Black Preceptory (Orange Order), 314

Royal Irish Constabulary (police prior to partition), 275, 290, 303. *See also* police

Royal Ulster Constabulary (Ulster police after partition), 3–4, 6, 8, 38, 110, 114–16, 208, 231, 236, 307, 310, 321. *See also* police Russell, Thomas, 129

Saint Columba, 15

Saint Columb's Cathedral, 115, 325

Saint Colum Cille, 60, 327

Saint Patrick, 15

Saint Patrick's Cathedral (Dublin), 142

Sands, Bobby, 155, 204, 300

schooling, Irish, 244

Scots' early settlement in Ulster, 59, 62–63

Scott, Sir Walter, 149

Sean-bhean Bhocht, 107

secret societies (Irish), characteristics of, 150–55

sectarian riots. *See also* riots; risings
Belfast, 330–32
Derry, 332

Sévigny, Madam de, 80

Shakespeare, William, Catholic ambivalence about, 258

Shamrock (racing yacht), 238

the *Shan Van Vocht,* 116, 149, 204, 239, 259–60, 293, 296, 298

Shane O'Neill's revolt, 16, 327

Shankill Road, 12

Shaw, David, 130

Shaw, George Bernard, 254, 294, 299

Sheehy-Skeffington, Francis, 294

BY DEREK LUNDY
ALSO AVAILABLE FROM VINTAGE

☐ **The Way of a Ship**   9780099286622   £7.99

FREE POST AND PACKING
Overseas customers allow £2.00 per paperback

BY PHONE: 01624 677237

BY POST: Random House Books
C/o Bookpost, PO Box 29, Douglas
Isle of Man, IM99 1BQ

BY FAX: 01624 670923

BY EMAIL: bookshop@enterprise.net

Cheques (payable to Bookpost) and credit cards accepted

Prices and availability subject to change without notice.
Allow 28 days for delivery.
When placing your order, please mention if you do not wish to receive
any additional information.

www.randomhouse.co.uk/vintage